The Islamic World in International Relations

STUDIES IN POLITICS, SECURITY AND SOCIETY

Edited by Stanisław Sulowski
Faculty of Political Science and International Studies
University of Warsaw

VOLUME 24

PETER LANG

Sylwester Gardocki / Rafał Ożarowski / Rafał Ulatowski
(eds.)

The Islamic World in International Relations

PETER LANG

Bibliographic Information published by the Deutsche Nationalbibliothek
The Deutsche Nationalbibliothek lists this publication in the Deutsche Nationalbibliografie; detailed bibliographic data is available in the internet at http://dnb.d-nb.de.

Library of Congress Cataloging-in-Publication Data
A CIP catalog record for this book has been applied for at the Library of Congress.

This publication was financially supported by the Faculty of Political Science and International Studies, University of Warsaw.

ISSN 2199-028X
ISBN 978-3-631-78566-9 (Print)
E-ISBN 978-3-631-78675-8 (E-PDF)
E-ISBN 978-3-631-78676-5 (EPUB)
E-ISBN 978-3-631-78677-2 (MOBI)
DOI 10.3726/b15483

Peter Lang – Berlin · Bern · Bruxelles · New York ·Oxford · Warszawa · Wien

This publication has been peer reviewed.

www.peterlang.com

Contents

Introduction

The Definition of Islamic World encompasses variable areas, basically inhabited by Muslims and represented by Muslims states. However, it also includes Muslims living in non-Muslim states considered religious minorities or refugees and even relates to processes and phenomena connected to Islamic World even if they are not a basic part of it. Thus the description 'Islamic World' is more complex and multidimensional and cannot be considered only in the terms of geographical area or Islam believers.

The presented book entitled *Islamic World in International Relations* edited by Sylwester Gardocki, Rafał Ożarowski, and Rafał Ulatowski is the effect of work of many scholars representing variable universities and research institutes. Thus, in the book, the perspective on Islamic World dilemmas is not homogenous but strongly diversified. It contributes a lot to understanding essence and specificity of analyzed problems and phenomena in the book.

The book has been divided into four parts which refer to the basic categories of research in international relations. First part consisting of two chapters relates to the international security; second is dedicated to the foreign policy issues and comprised of seven chapters and is the lengthiest part. The third part with four chapters refers to economy and energy policy, and the last one is devoted to the regional studies and consists of three chapters.

Chapters in the first part (1. Muzaffer Kural, *Geopolitical Rivalry between Saudi Arabia and Iran in the Middle East*; 2. Subtain Hussain Shah, *Comparative Study of Post 9/11 and Post Arab Spring Rise of Violent Religious Extremism in Pakistan*) refer to variable topics in the sphere of international security in the area of Islamic World, describing the issue of instability in the MENA region and reasons and consequences of geopolitical rivalry between Iran and Saudi Arabia, and finally the issue of religious extremism in Pakistan influenced by the events in the 'Arab World' named Arab Spring or 'Arab Revolutions'. Consequently, authors of these chapters make us aware of huge instability in the whole Islamic World and emphasize the issue of international security which is not restricted to the selected areas but considered globally.

Chapters contained in the second part of the book (1. Radosław Fiedler, *From Sanctions to War? Nothing New in the United States' Policy Towards Iran Since 1979*; 2. Rafał Ożarowski, *Re-Imposition of U.S. Sanctions*; 3. Hadi Ajili, Mohammed Oliaei, Javad Nori, *The Review of Stabilizing and Crisis Building of Iran and Saudi Arabia in the Middle East*; 4. Adam Szymański, *"Domestication" of the Middle Eastern Policy of Turkey*; 5. Sylwester Gardocki, *Russian Contemporary Policy Towards Syria*; 6. Hana, *EU Small States and Their Fight Against IS*; 7. Jiří Zákravský, *Sports Diplomacy of the State of Qatar and Its (Lack of) Success in the Czech Republic: Analysis of the Czech Nationwide Press in 2016*) regard a wide-range of topics. The biggest emphasis is put on the explanation of new era of sanctions imposed by the USA on Iran in 2018 (Fiedler, Ożarowski). However, the conflict in Syria take here also an important place in the terms of Russian Foreign Policy (Gardocki) or Turkish Foreign Policy (Szymański). The issue of "soft power" has been analyzed here in the case of Qatar (Zákravský) and the inadequately marginalized EU small states policy in relation to the Middle Eastern terrorist threat, what was equally explained (Hlaváčková).

Third part refers to economy and energy policy comprising of four chapters (1. Rafał Ulatowski, *The Paradox of the Shale Oil Market. The Middle East and the Global Oil Market*; 2. Fazli Doğan, Erdem Özlük, *Success of Integration Initiatives in the Islamic World: The Case of D-8*; 3. Iwona Sobol, Gabriela Mieczkowska, *Islamic Banking Development in GCC Region on the Examples of the Kingdom of Saudi Arabia and the United Arab Emirates*; 4. Martina Ponížilová, *China´s Risk-Averse Middle East Policy: Protecting Economic Interests while Staying Out of Conflicts*). Complex issues taken up in all chapters show how multileveled and diverse is the sphere of economic relations including energy policy in the Islamic World. Much emphasis has been put on the issue of oil shale market which is a quite new challenge for the energy sector worldwide (Ulatowski).

The last part consists of three chapters (1. Yuriy Skorohod, *"Consociational Democracy": The Model of the Democratization of Deeply Divided Arab Societies?* 2. Vladimír Naxera, *"Islamophobia Without Muslims": Anti-Muslim and anti-Arab Attitudes in Czech Society (Introductory Remarks)*; 3. Magdalena Ickiewicz-Sawicka, *Balkan Muslims – Origin, Structure, Identity*) devoted to regional studies in the context of Islamic issues – division of Arab society, Islamophobia, and the specificity of Muslims in the Balkan region particularly.

Editors would like to thank all contributors for the publication and all people engaged in work on this edition.

Part I – International Security

Muzaffer Kural

Geopolitical Rivalry between Saudi Arabia and Iran in the Middle East

Abstract: Iran and Saudi Arabia undoubtedly are two regional players in the Middle East. Both states have a long history of experience for competing. The geopolitical rivalry runs through the way of creating political, ideological, and economic influence in the region. Both sides have similar and different approaches. While geopolitically, Iran enlarges her sphere of influence over the demographic structure of region via Shia minorities mainly in Iraq, Lebanon, Yemen, and Saudi Arabia. By contrast, Saudi Arabia confronts via Sunni minorities in the region. Although, the rivalry between the two states dates back to the 1930s, this chapter aims to point out the effect of Islamic Revolution of Iran, Ousting Saddam Hussein in Iraq, and Arab uprisings to the rivalry between the two states.

Keywords: Geopolitics, ideology, sectarianism, sphere of influence, proxy wars

Introduction

Until the 1979 Iranian Islamic Revolution as a consequence of "twin pillar policy" of the USA, both countries were in harmony in the Middle East. Yet, with the collapse of Shah's regime, which closed the era of twin pillar policy, due to Iran's desires in the region leaded the rivalry, which runs multi-fronts, between Saudi Arabia and Iran. According to Islamic regime of Iran, protecting Iran requires to export regime of Islamic Revolution of Iran.

Exporting regime policy plays a significant role over the geopolitical rivalry. Iran's desires for exporting regime provides Saudi Arabia a leading role in the region by bringing Gulf countries together under the umbrella of Saudi Arabia due to fears stemming from Iranian policy of exporting regime. Both countries confront via their regional allies. On this context, both internal and external policy of regional countries are affected from the rivalry between Saudi Arabia and Iran. Both Saudi Arabia and Iran compete for regional influence through dynamics, mainly ideology, of region. Both countries attempted to use ideology as a tool on their foreign policy. Presence of both Saudi Arabia and Iran in the region is pragmatic rather than ideologic. On this context, it is necessary to answer certain questions such as: What are the challenges for both states on the rivalry? Which regional factors facilitate competition for the rivalry? What kind of role do regional states play on the rivalry between Saudi Arabia and Iran?

Is the presence of both states in the region, particularly in Iraq, ideological or pragmatical?

The aims of this work are to explain three turning points that have changed the course of the rivalry between both states. The first one is Islamic Revolution of Iran, which sharply changed the foreign policy of Iran. When the Mollas gained power on administration of Iran, not only Saudi Arabia, but also other Sunni Arab states in the Middle East perceived threats of exporting Shia regime. Therefore, Saudi Arabia as a leading country got support from other Sunni Arab states, by establishing Gulf Cooperation Council in the framework of the rivalry. The second point is collapsing Saddam's administration, which opened a new chapter for countries. It would not be wrong to state that Iraq became a battleground between both states while Saudi Arabia efforted to bring an anti-Iranian government to power, Iran extended her influence in Iraq via Shia population by forming pro-Iranian Shia government in Baghdad. Even though Iran had more influence in Iraq, Saudi Arabia kept her support for Sunni Groups so as to destabilize Iranian presence. The main reason for both countries to gain superiority in Iraq derives from importance of Gulf where Iraq plays a significant role due to her location. The third point is Arab uprising, which reshaped rivalry between both countries. With the following of Arab uprisings, the area for rivalry between both states has been expanded. In comparison to Iran, Saudi Arabia is able to keep her anti-Iranian administrations such as Egypt and Bahrain on power thanks to her Western allies. By contrast, Iran despite her influence on Shia, Hezbullah, Houthis, etc., needs to effort much more to keep her ally such as Syria on power.

Understanding the Case: Historical Background of Rivalry

To understand the current rivalry between the two states, it is necessary to look at the historical background of both Saudi Arabia and Iran. According to Axworthy, borders of Persia were extended from the eastern coast of Greece to the banks of Indus during the empires of Cyrus and Darius.[1] 1100 years after the Cyrus, Arabs came to Persia together with Islam and converted many to Sunnism. Later on, in the early 16th century, Shah Ismail changed the religion of Persia from Sunnism to Shia.[2] Throughout the Middle Ages, Shia clergymen did

---

1 Michale Axworthy, *Iran, Empire of the Mind: A History from Zoroaster to the present day* (Penguin, London: 2008), p. 12.

2 Simon Mabon, *Saudi Arabia, Iran and the Changing Geopolitics of the Middle East:* 21. Dec. 2017, http://eprints.lancs.ac.uk/76745/2/Saudi_Arabi1_1_.pdf.

not develop any consistent state theory. Shias refused caliphs by recognizing 12 Imams as a successor of Prophet. According to Shias, the Imam Ali, cousin and son-in-law of Prophet, was never assigned as a caliph after Prophet. The third Imam Hussein, son of Imam Ali, was martyred by Yazid in Karbala. This process ended with the 12th Imam Mahdi known as hidden Imam. During the Shah Mohammad Reza Pahlavi's secular administration, Islamic opposition movement gradually emerged. Under the leading of Khomeini it was empowered and toppled the Shah Reza Pahlavi. Khomeini transformed Iran from secularism to Shia's Welayeti Faqih. According to Welayeti Faqih, which currently leads Iran since 1979 Revolution of the Islamic Republic of Iran, Supreme leader rules country temporarily as representative of 12th Imam Mahdi, during his absence. Once he appears, at a time that has the highest level of chaos, supreme leader will transfer all authority to the Mahdi and he will rule the whole world.

On the other hand, Saudi Arabia, which was established based on Wahhabism, has a different background. According to Wahhabism, those who do not follow Wahhabi principles are infidels and their lives and properties are legitimate to be looted. The first destructive effect of Abdulwahhab's ideas occurred in Uyeyne, thanks to Ameer Othman bin Haddad. All yards, cemeteries, caves, and holy trees were leveled with the ground. But, Ahsa's Ameer Suleiman expatriated Abdulwahhab from Uneyne in 1774 through menacing Hamad. Upon this, as Taştekin points out, Mohammad bin Saud became aware of Abdulwahhab's ideological power. Abdulwahhab needed a sword and Saud needed an ideology. Thanks to this alliance many tribes in the region were taken under the control. The alliance of sword and ideology created Saudi Arabia.[3] Wahhabis, even though, undertook a leading role in the establishment of Saudi dominance, due to becoming a troublemaker for Saudis during the process of being a state, were liquidated in 1929. Following the liquidation, Wahhabis left their military wing aside and institutionalized within the state. Furthermore, When Saudi Arabia gained independence, the alliance of Abdulwahab and Saud was reflected on the flag.[4] On this context, historical heritage has an ideological influence on the policy of both states.

While the internal policy of both Saudi Arabia and Iran is based on religious values, their foreign policy has pragmatic approaches. Saudi Arabia's relation with the USA and Great Britain mainly through arms deals reveals her pragmatic

---

3 Fehim Taştekin, *Karanlık Çöktüğünde; IŞİD: Din adına şiddetin dünü ve bugünü* (İstanbul. 2016), p. 31.

4 Taştekin, *Karanlık Çöktüğünde; IŞİD*, p. 35.

approach to the foreign policy. Recent signing of "typhoon jet deal" in March 2018 can be assessed within this context.[5]

Nevertheless, as Osiewicz points out, "Across the societies of the Arabian Peninsula, tribalism remains one of the strongest forces, and its consequences for the region's foreign relations should not be overlooked. Tribal identity is deeply rooted in the region's heritage and history and is often manipulated by the regional leaders for purposes of political legitimacy."[6]

Similar to Saudi Arabia, Iran also displays the same approaches. For instance, it is a well-known fact that on the Nagorno-Karabakh issue between Azerbaijan and Armenia, Iran prefers to take place on Armenian side rather than Azerbaijan which is Shia.

Furthermore, although, Iran and Syria have different languages, culture, ethnicity, and sectarian structure, they have formed one of the strongest alliances in the Middle East.[7] Thanks to this alliance, during the Iran-Iraq war in 1980–1988, on the contrary to other Sunni Arab countries, Syria backed Iran. Likewise, Iran supported Hezbollah in Lebanon and Hamas in Palestine against Israel through Syria.

Yoel Guzansky emphasizes the fact that "relations between Saudi Arabia and Iran are characterized by religious-ideological antagonism and competition for regional influence. One of the results of the current turmoil in the Middle East is that the hostility between the two states and their struggle over the character of the region has sharpened and intensified."[8] In the same way, Sewag expresses, the war of geopolitical supremacy between Saudi Arabia and Iran creates an undeniable influence on the region's countries, particularly Iraq, Syria, Lebanon, Bahrain, Yemen, Egypt, Pakistan, and Afghanistan.[9]

---

5 George Allison, UK Defence Journal, Saudi Arabia and UK sign Memorandum of Intent for purchase of 48 more Typhoon jets: 07 Apr. 2018 https://ukdefencejournal.org.uk/saudi-arabia-uk-sign-memorandum-intent-purchase-48-typhoon-jets/.

6 Przemyslaw Osiewicz, *Ideological Determinants of the Current Saudi-Iranian Rivalry in the Middle East,* "Przegląd Politologiczny" No. 2, (2016), p. 117–118.

7 Atefeh Baghishadbad, *The Impact of the Syria's Crisis On the Rivalry Between Iran and the Saudi Arabia in the Region; Iran's Point of View,* "JAIRO", March 2016, p. 130–131, 22 Oct. 2017 https://doors.doshisha.ac.jp/duar/repository/ir/22933/049000060008.pdf

8 Yoel Guzansky, *The Arab Gulf States and Reform in the Middle East: Between Iran and the "Arab Spring"* (Palgrave Macmillan, New York 2015), p. 42.

9 Zulqarnian Sewag, *Sectarian Rise in Pakistan: Role of Saudi Arabia and Iran,* "South Asia Journal of Multidisciplinary Studies", Vol. 1, No. 3, February (2015), p. 2.

Geopolitical Factors in Iran-Saudi Arabia Rivalry after 1979 Iranian Islamic Revolution

With the following withdrawing British army from Persian Gulf, the USA, as a new gendarme of the Gulf, filled the power vacuum in the region. Both Saudi Arabia and Iran had become two pillars of the twin pillar policy of the USA.

Until the Iran's Islamic Revolution in 1979, both states had strong relations with West, and the USA was supporting both sides, relations between Saudi Arabia and Iran were based on mutual cooperation despite geopolitical rivalry.[10] Yet, Islamic revolution of Iran in 1979 has changed the power balance in the Middle East, particularly in the Persian Gulf. Ousting Shah Reza Pahlavi affected not the only policy of regional countries but also the policy of superpowers namely the USA and Russia. As Arikan states, ideological dimension was added to the geopolitical rivalry between Iran and Saudi Arabia.[11] As a result of Khomeini's declaration both the USA and Soviet Russia as an enemy by describing the USA is big satan and Russia is small satan, the "twin pillar" policy of the USA ended.

According to Terril, Persian Gulf traditionally has been the most important arena of conflict between Saudi Arabia and Iran. Saudi Arabia has had a higher level of influence on local states than Iran in the struggle for Gulf. On this context, Saudi Arabia established strong ties with Gulf monarchies and with Yemen to keep regional stability.[12] The Saudi-Iranian rivalry on regional security clarifies itself over the naming of Gulf as well. Iran insists to call as the Persian Gulf with the references of historical appellation and dominance in the past. By contrast, Saudi Arabia calls as an Arabian Gulf since the1960s with reference of pan-Arabism and Arab nationalism. This controversy has become a symbol of rivalry for dominance in the region between two states.[13]

---

10 Atefeh Baghishadbad, *The Impact of the Syria's Crisis on the Rivalry Between Iran and the Saudi Arabia in the Region; Iran's Point of View*, "JAIRO", March 2016, p.121: 22 Nov. 2017 https://doors.doshisha.ac.jp/duar/repository/ir/22933/049000060008.pdf.

11 Pınar Arıkan, *Iran-Saudi Arabia Tension between Conflict of National Interests and Sectarian Polarization,* "ORSAM Review of Regional Affairs", No. 38, January (2016), p. 3.

12 W. Andrew Terril, *The Saudi-Iranian Rıvalry And The Future Of Middle East Security,* "SSI" December 2011, p.14: 21 Mar. 2018 https://www.files.ethz.ch/isn/142831/pub1094.pdf.

13 Shahrbanou Tadjbakhsh, *The Persian Gulf and Afghanistan: Iran and Saudi Arabia's Rivalry Projected,* "PRIO" March 2013: 21 Mar. 2018, p.17. https://www.prio.org/utility/DownloadFile.ashx?id=368&type=publicationfile.

Iran accuses Saudi Arabia through three points that are perceived hostility. The first is about an Iranian nuclear scientist who was abducted by the CIA with the cooperation of Saudis. The second is Saudi Arabia cooperates with Israel on coordination that is against Iran's nuclear program.[14] The third is about that Jundullah, recognized by Iran as a terrorist, is supported by Saudi Arabia ideologically and financially.

On the other hand, three important developments caused Saudi Arabia to run her foreign policy based on rivalry. The first one that during the Israel-Lebanon war in 2006, Tehran supported Hezbollah and Hamas. What is more, Ahmadi Nejad tried to provoke Shias living in the Arab monarchies. The second is clashes between Hamas and Al-Fatih in Palestine. The third is the confrontation of Shia-Sunni-al-Qaida in Iraq.[15] On this context, both Saudi Arabia and Iran compete for regional influence through dynamics, mainly ideology, of the region. Both countries attempted to use ideology as a tool in their foreign policy.

For instance, discovering petroleum in 1938 had facilitated Saudi Arabia's spreading Wahhabi ideology as an instrument in foreign policy and creating influence in the Islamic world. During the Ibn Saud era, "Representative Office for Invitation" was established. First Madrasah was opened in Jakarta.[16] Also Community of Hadith and Ensar'u Sunni al-Muhammadiyah Group in India, Izale Community in Nigeria, and Subbanu Movement in Mali and Muceydiri School in Mauritania were empowered through Saudi's financial assistance.[17] In the same way, Saudi Arabia attempted to spread her ideology in Egypt via Ensarus Sunni which represents Wahhabism. After the Islamic revolution in Iran in 1979, Saudi Arabia's animosity towards Shias deepened hostility among Islamists. Saudi's embassy in Cairo was struggling to prevent publications against Saudi Arabia and provoking hostility toward Iran.[18]

Another destination for Saudi Arabia's spreading ideology is Afghanistan. While Iran has a closer historical, geographic, and cultural affinity with Afghanistan, Saudi Arabia has not stood idle. Both Saudi Arabia and Iran compete to shape Afghanistan's internal politics in various ways. For instance, using

---

14 Richard Javad Heydarian, *Iran-Saudi Relations: Rising Tensions and Growing Rivalry,* "FPIF", 6 August 2010: 12 Mar. 2018 http://fpif.org/iran-saudi_relations_rising_tensions_and_growing_rivalry/.

15 Özden Zeynep Oktav, *Basra Körfezi'nin Değişen Dinamikleri: İran-ABD-Suudi Arabistan İlişkileri* (Beta: İstanbul. 2011), p. 120–121.

16 Taştekin, *Karanlık Çöktüğünde; IŞİD,* p. 36.

17 Mehmet Ali Büyükkara, *Çağdaş İslami Akımlar* (İstanbul, 2015), p. 62.

18 Salih Elverdani, *Mısır'da İslami Akımlar* (İstanbul, 2011), p. 277–298.

their connections with religious and ethnic groups through propagating religious doctrines, attempting to create influence on potential insurgent groups, increasing economic ties, etc.[19] The main goal of Saudi Arabia's sending jihadists to Afghanistan was preventing Iranian exporting regime towards the Gulf Countries, which contains undeniable Shia population. On this way, the attention of those who were questioning the legitimacy of regimes in the Islamic world was turning to Afghanistan. Additionally, Saudi Arabia, describing herself as protector of two holy cities, was gaining popularity among Muslims, by providing the highest support to jihad in Afghanistan, and leading the Islamic world. Right after Taliban's coming to power in Afghanistan, the life of people was turned to hell by serial prohibitions such as burka obligatory for women, shutting down schools for female students, etc. Not surprisingly, Shias were declared as an enemy and Shia Hazaras, conditioned to converting Sunni, were massacred.

Afghanistan was on the radar of Iran as well for exporting ideology of Shia regime as a tool of geopolitical rivalry. According to Barzegar, geopolitical reality and its ideology has always affected Iran's regional policy. The current ongoing Shia-Sunni rivalry is a power-sharing conflict rather than ideological rivalry. Iran's presence in the Middle East has more pragmatic approach than ideologic.[20] Since the Arab uprisings, sectarianism has been used as a mean of framing conflicts in different ways within broader geopolitical narratives. For instance, in Bahrain non-sectarian protests was motivated as sectarian. On this way, the al-Khalifa secured the loyalty of Sunnis who had taken the streets in the past by inciting fears for Iranian influence in the region.[21]

A conversation sometime before 9/11, between Prince Bandar bin Sultan, head of Saudi intelligence, and Richard Dearlove, head of the British Secret Intelligence Service, MI6, clarifies the sectarian reality. As Cockburn pointed out in *The Independent* Prince Bandar told Richard Dearlove that "The time is not far off in the Middle East, Richard, when it will be literally 'God help the Shia'. More than a billion Sunnis have simply had enough of them."[22]

---

19 Shahrbanou Tadjbakhsh, *The Persian Gulf and Afghanistan: Iran and Saudi Arabia's Rivalry Projected,* "PRIO" March2013, p.viii: 21 Mar. 2018, https://www.prio.org/utility/DownloadFile.ashx?id=368&type=publicationfile.

20 Kayhan Barzegar, *Iran and the Shiite Crescent: Myths and Realities,* "The Brown Journal of World Affairs", Winter (2008), Vol. 15, No. 1, p. 97.

21 Simon Mabon, *Saudi Arabia, Iran and the Changing Geopolitics of the Middle East:* 21. Nov. 2017 http://eprints.lancs.ac.uk/76745/2/Saudi_Arabi1_1_.pdf.

22 Patrick Cockburn, *Iraq crisis: How Saudi Arabia helped Isis take over the north of the country.* "THE INDEPENDENT", 13 July 2014: 28 Mar. 2018 https://www.independent.

US Military Intervention to Iraq

Iraq is the epicenter of geopolitical rivalry between Saudi Arabia and Iran due to her geographic location and demographic structure. First off all, Iraq is the biggest power on the Persian Gulf after Iran and Saudi Arabia. Although, Shi'a population constitutes 65 % of Iraq, throughout the Saddam Hussein era Iraq was ruled by Sunnis which constitutes 20 % of Iraq's population. Right after the Iran's Islamic Revolution, Sunni regimes of Middle East began to fear that Iran may export her ideology of revolution to enlarge the sphere of influence over the Shia population in Arab countries mainly Iraq, Saudi Arabia, Bahrain, and Yemen.

As a matter of fact, in the view of Khomeini exporting ideology of revolution was an obligation. According to him so as to bring the Islamic countries together and protect them against external threats, Iranian revolution has to be exported to other Islamic countries.[23] Based on fears of exporting ideology of Iranian Islamic Revolution, Saddam Hussein declared war on Iran. Saudi Arabia, Kuwait, and Bahrain (due to Iran's claim that Bahrain is historically a province of Iran) supported Iraq. It was also the time when Gulf Cooperation Council was established under the leading of Saudi Arabia against Iran's geopolitical desires. However, both Saudi Arabia and Iran perceived Iraq as a threat due to Saddam's idea of being a leader of the Arab world. It is a well-known fact that Saddam was affected by Nasser's ideas during his time in Egypt. Nevertheless, both Saudi Arabia and Iran had concerns regarding US military intervention to Iraq. Iran's concern was US military presence in her western border is second threat as well as the same presence in her eastern border (Afghanistan). On this way, Iran would be surrounded by biggest military power from the east and from the west. However, in comparison to Saudi Arabia, Iran has more advantages thanks to Shi'a factors. For instance, despite US presence, Iran currently has more influence in Afghanistan than before 2001 US military intervention. Likewise, ousting a Sunni leader from power in Iraq is a nightmare for Riyadh due to Shia reality that with high possibility will establish a pro-Iranian administration.

The US military intervention to Iraq in 2003 has opened a new chapter in the regional affairs shifting power balance regarding geopolitical rivalry between Riyadh and Tehran. To open up it can be assessed that relations between Riyadh

co.uk/voices/comment/iraq-crisis-how-saudi-arabia-helped-isis-take-over-the-north-of-the-country-9602312.html.

23 Barış Adıbelli, *Pax Persica: İran Jeopolitiği*, IQ Kültür Sanat Yayıncılık: İstanbul 2017. p. 83.

and Tehran have been characterized by the religious ideological antagonism, political and geostrategic interest in the Middle East.[24]

As Czulda points out, Iraq is a vital bridge for Iran in the geopolitical rivalry. It provides a possibility to Iran to extend her geopolitical power from Iran to Palestine through Syria and Lebanon where Hezbollah, Iran's main ally, can threat Israel in case of necessary prevention toward the USA. Furthermore, a strong presence in Iraq empowers Iran to control Kurdish issue.[25] For instance, after the independence referendum of KRG (Kurdistan Regional Government), when Iraqi army attacked to Kirkuk and other disputed areas by Hasdi Shabi forces, which Iran has the undeniable influence on, Iran played a decisive role on withdrawing peshmergas from Kirkuk.

Iraq's election in 2005, which led to establishing pro-Iranian Shia government, was the most important event that affected Saudi Iranian relations in the Middle East. Without a doubt, losing Iraq and giving it to a rival was not acceptable by Saudi Arabia. Iran gained a Shia friend government without any effort and as a result gained more regional power in competition with Saudi Arabia.[26] From the geopolitical point of view, once Iran already controls Iraq, gets power through Houthis in Yemen means encirclements of Saudi Arabia. Therefore, since 2003, Saudi Arabia has got worries regarding empowerment of Shia in the region and emergence of a new Hezbollah in the region.[27]

After Mosul was occupied by ISIS and holy shrines of Shias were blown up, Patrick Cockburn described the situation as "Simply to be identified as Shia or a related sect, such as the Alawites, in Sunni rebel-held parts of Iraq and Syria today, has become as dangerous as being a Jew was in Nazi-controlled parts of Europe in 1940."[28] When ISIS turned her route toward Southern Iraq after Mosul, Iranian President Hassan Rouhani officially warned that in case of need to protect

---

24 Abhınav Sharma, *Severed Ties between Iran and Saudi Arabia: A Cold War or A Proxy War of Narratives, Influence and Power,* "CAPS IN FOCUS", 5 January 2016: 28 Mar. 2018 http://capsindia.org/files/documents/CAPS_Infocus_ANS_01.pdf.

25 Robert Czulda, *The Struggle of Iran and Saudi Arabia over Iraq,* [in:] Peter Bátor, Róbert Ondrejcsák (ed.), *Panorama of Global Security Environment 2015–2016,* (Bratislava 2016), p. 346.

26 Atefeh Baghishadbad, *The Impact of the Syria's Crisis On the Rivalry Between Iran and the Saudi Arabia in the Region; Iran's Point of View,* "JAIRO", March 2016, p.123: 22 Nov. 2017 https://doors.doshisha.ac.jp/duar/repository/ir/22933/049000060008.pdf.

27 Damla Kocatepe, *Suudi Arabistan-İran Rekabeti: Mezhep Görünümlü Çıkar Çatışması,* "ANKASAM; Bölgesel Araştırmalar Dergisi", (Iran Special Issue), Vol. 1, No. 2, p. 82.

28 Patrick Cockburn, *Iraq crisis: How Saudi Arabia helped Isis take over the north of the country.* "THE INDEPENDENT", 13 July 2014: 28 Mar. 2018 https://www.independent.

holy Shia shrines in Najaf, Karbala, Samarra, and Baghdad, Iran is ready for a direct military intervention.[29] Even though, Mosul and many other cities were liberated from ISIS, the current situation in Iraq is not in favor of Saudi Arabia since Iraq is weak to resist against Iranian influence. Once Iran gains permanent control over Iraq, Iran will be able to increase her military and political pressure on Saudi Arabia. Likewise, gaining control over Iraq creates opportunity for Saudi Arabia to increase pressure to collapse pro-Iranian al-Assad regime. In this way, Syria could be pulled out from Iran's sphere of influence, which certainly serves the interest of Riyadh.[30] Iran has cooperated not only with religious Shias, but also secular Iraqis to show that Iran has no tendencies to establish a religious state in Iraq. While Iran has strong relationships with Shia religious and secular Shia groups, it has strong connections with Patriotic Union of Kurdistan.[31]

The Arab Uprisings

On 17th December 2010, Mohamed Bouazizi, who is an engineer, was working as a vendor on Tunisian rural was banned for selling fruits and his workbench was taken by police. While he resisted to keeping his workbench, he was slapped. Upon this, since his honor was offended, he set himself on fire. Bouazizi's reaction was a symptom that people had enough of their authoritarian regime famous for oppression, corruption, and lack of individual liberty, human rights, and democracy. Number of people took place on the squares rapidly increase in Tunisia. In the beginning, decision makers of the Middle Eastern regime were confused. Yet, after Ben Ali fled from country and wave of protesters spread to other Middle Eastern countries such as Bahrain, Egypt, Libya and Syria, both Saudi Arabia and Iran became aware of the seriousness of the process. The uprisings contain both opportunities and setbacks together for Saudi Arabia and Iran.

In the beginning of uprisings, both Saudi Arabia and Iran had a different reaction. For instance, both countries did not take serious consideration towards

---

co.uk/voices/comment/iraq-crisis-how-saudi-arabia-helped-isis-take-over-the-north-of-the-country-9602312.html.

29 Gulf News, Iran vows to protect Iraqi shrines: Rouhani, 18 June 2014: 28 Mar. 2018, https://gulfnews.com/world/mena/iran-vows-to-protect-iraqi-shrines-1.1348782.

30 Robert Czulda, *The Struggle of Iran and Saudi Arabia over Iraq,* [in:] Peter Bátor, Róbert Ondrejcsák (ed.), *Panorama of Global Security Environment 2015–2016,* (Bratislava 2016), p. 347.

31 Mahjoob Zweiri, *Arab-Iranian Relations: New Realities?,* [in:] Anoushiravan Ehteshami, Mahjoob Zweiri (ed.), *Iran's Foreign Policy From Khatemi to Ahmadinejad* (Ithaca: Berkshire 2008), p. 118.

the uprising in Tunisia. However, once it spread to Cairo, both Riyadh and Tehran took different positions. While Saudi Arabia backed Hosni Mubarek, who had played a significant role against the expansion of Iranian influence in the Middle East by working against Hamas, which is Iran's main ally in Palestine, Iran supported protesters as describing Islamic awakening.

Once Hosni Mubarak was toppled, Saudi Arabia watched with horror. What is more, before Mubarak was toppled, during the protests, Saudi King Abdullah had revealed his seriousness to Obama by saying "King cannot let his friend to be humiliated."[32] By contrast, Iranian supreme leader made an enthusiastic statement and portrayed an event in Egypt as an Iranian-style revolution likely to lead an Egyptian Islamic republic.[33]

On the other hand, Houthis had attended protests toppled Saleh in Yemen. After Houthis took Sa'da city of Northern Yemen under control together with Ansarullah militia, they gradually moved toward southern and captured Yemen's capital Sana. Upon this, President Hadi stepped down from power in January. Prime Minister Baha resigned as well right after the president. On 6 February 2015, Houthis abolished parliament and captured administration. This progress of Houthis was evaluated by remarkable words by Iranian politicians. For instance, Tehran deputy, also known by having close ties with Supreme leader Hamaney, stated that 'of having taken Sana under control by Houths is the fourth Arabian capital that joins to Iranian Revolution.' Hamaney's advisor Ali Akbar Velayeti similarly stated that 'I hope Ensarullah in Yemen will assume a role that Hezbollah has assumed in Lebanon'.[34]

What is more, the geopolitical rivalry between Saudi Arabia and Iran had increased to the highest level when uprising spread to Syria. The conflict began with political demands between oppositions and Assad's regime. Even though, Assad committed for vital reforms such as individual liberty, human rights, etc. No such step was taken. Therefore, oppositions intensified their protests and Syria became an international battleground. While Saudi Arabia supported opposition groups mainly Sunnis logistically and financially, Iran strongly supported Assad's

---

32 *Suudi Kralı'ndan Obama'ya Mübarek Fırçası,* "Hürriyet", 10.02.2011: 13 Mar. 2018 http://www.hurriyet.com.tr/gundem/suudi-kralindan-obamaya-mubarek-fircasi-16988333.

33 W. Andrew Terril, *The Saudi-Iranian Rivalry and the Future Of Middle East Security,* "SSI" December 2011, p.11–12: 21 Mar. 2018, https://www.files.ethz.ch/isn/142831/pub1094.pdf.

34 Kemal İnat, Veysel Kurt, Abdullah Yegin, Recep Tayyip Gürler, Ömer Behram Özdemir, Ayşe Selcan Özdemirci, İsmaıl Akdoğan, *İran-Suudi Arabistan Rekabetinin Bölgesel Yansımaları,* "Analiz", No. 148, January 2016, p. 21.

regime. The question is why has not Assad been toppled during the last seven years, while presidents were toppled in Sana, Cairo, and Trypolis. Undoubtedly, Syria is a vital geostrategic location for both Russia and Iran. Iran delivers assistance to her ally Hezbollah in Lebanon and Hamas in Palestine via Syria. Losing Syria for Iran means paralyzing Baghdad-Damascus-Beirut route. In the same way, from Russia's side also losing Syria means putting Tartus base at risk. On this context, it is a fact that both Russia and Iran would do more than their best to keep Assad in power.

Furthermore, the Syrian uprising that started in March 2011 and turned to sectarian civil war and conflict in Yemen in 2015 confirmed that Saudi Arabia and Iran were indifferent sides. After that the Proxy war was mentioned between two states in multi-front such as Syria and Yemen. Simultaneously Saudi Arabia tried to isolate Iran through her influence on regional countries. For instance, after Saudi Arabia asked Iranian diplomats to leave from the country and cut diplomatic relations. Sudan, Bahrain, and Djibouti cut their relations with Iran as well. UAE downgraded its relations to the level of chargé d'affaires. Qatar and Kuwait withdrew their ambassadors from Iran.[35] Saudi Arabia and Iran have been actively supported opposite proxy groups in Syria. For instance, while Iran supports Lebanese Hezbollah and sends her Revolutionary Guards Corps to Syria, Saudi Arabia backs Salafi jihadist militias by sending arms and ammunition to rebel groups there.[36]

The main reason of Saudi Arabia's insistence on Syria is to prevent Iran's influence in the region. Because Damascus means great significances for Iran. Security of Shia population in Iraq under control of Iran, Iran's increasing influence in Iraq, and uninterrupted communication with Hezbollah is vital for Iran. In other words, the security of "Baghdad-Damascus-Beirut route" requires a strongly pro-Iranian government in Damascus since Iraq provides a path to Syria which allows Iran to send weaponry and supplies to Lebanon.[37]

With the following assassination of Hariri in 2005, Lebanon's domestic politics provided an opportunity for both Saudi Arabia and Iran to test each other's goals

---

35 Pınar Arıkan, *Iran-Saudi Arabia Tension between Conflict of national Interests and Sectarian Polarization,* "ORSAM Review of Regional Affairs", No. 38, January 2016. p. 6–7.

36 Helia Ighani, *Managing the Saudi-Iran Rivalry,* "Council on Foreign Relations", 25 October 2016: 28 Mar. 2018, https://www.cfr.org/sites/default/files/pdf/2016/10/Workshop_Report_CPA_Saudi_Iran_Rivalry_OR.pdf.

37 Usjid U. Hameed, *Saudi-Iranian Rivalry: A Foreign Policy Analyses Approach,* "Towson University Journal of International Affairs", Vol. L, No. 2, p. 27.

and intentions in Lebanon. While Saudi Arabia supported "March 14 Alliance," Iran and Syria supported the "March 8 Alliance" that includes Hezbollah.[38]

Saudi Arabia and Iran are neither natural enemies nor natural allies, but natural rivals.[39] Until the Iranian Islamic revolution in 1979 the rivalry was controlled by the USA due to twin pillar policy. Yet, after Shah Reza Pahlavi was toppled Khomenei did not hesitate to reveal the rivalry.

The previous decade has proved that neither Saudi Arabia nor Iran could resist an opportunity to strengthen herself and weaken the other. Therefore, the rivalry between both states intensified with the opportunities emerged starting from Arab uprisings.[40] The relations and identities of both states in modern era indicate the fact of geopolitical rivalry between Saudi Arabia and Iran.

Conclusion

Saudi Arabia and Iran, despite sharing the same religion, have sectarian and ideological differences. The main reason of geopolitical rivalry between both Saudi Arabia and Iran in the Middle East stems from perception of security threats. Therefore, both states endeavor to enlarge their sphere of influence to keep such security threats away from their borders. Upon this, the geopolitical rivalry between two states creates influence on regional states' internal and external policy. Particularly, due to fears of Iran's exporting regime policy, some of the Arab countries, such as Bahrain, voluntarily come together under the leading of Saudi Arabia. For instance, Gulf Cooperation Council can be assessed within this context.

On the other hand, historical heritage has influence on the foreign policy of both states. On this context, sectarianism as an ideology plays a key role in the rivalry between two states. Saudi Arabia nominates Sunni groups in various Middle Eastern countries, whereas Iran invests on Shia groups. Furthermore, such ideological groups wage direct military conflicts in the region to curtail influence of each other.

---

38 Frederic Wehrey, Theodore W. Karasik, Alireza Nader, Jeremy Ghez, Lydia Hansell, Robert A. Guffey, *Saudi-Iranian Relations since the Fall of Saddam; Rivalry, Cooperation, and Implications for U.S. Policy,* Rand: Santa Monica, Arlington, Pittsburgh 2009, p. 79.

39 Mohsen M. Milani, *Iran and Saudi Arabia Square Off: The Growing Rivalry Between Tehran and Riyadh,* "Foreign Affairs", 11 October 2011: 02 Mar. 2018, https://www.foreignaffairs.com/articles/middle-east/2011-10-11/iran-and-saudi-arabia-square

40 Simon Mabon, *Saudi Arabia, Iran and the Changing Geopolitics of the Middle East*: 21 Nov. 2017, http://eprints.lancs.ac.uk/76745/2/Saudi_Arabi1_1_.pdf.

The current rivalry between Saudi Arabia and Iran is driven by geopolitics rather than religious dogmas. Therefore, the geopolitical rivalry between both states is based on pragmatic competition for power and influence across the Middle East. In this context, Saudi Arabia wants to keep all potential threats away from her border, whereas, Iran's interest requires to push them back toward Saudi border. The foreign policy of USA affects the geopolitical rivalry between both Saudi Arabia and Iran. Therefore, it can also be predicted that the rivalry between Saudi Arabia and Iran will deepen in the coming years as it is almost impossible for Iran to abandon Syria, while Saudi Arabia will keep her effort to curtail Iran's influence in the region, particularly in Syria and Yemen to keep threats away.

Bibliography

1. Adıbelli, Barış. Pax Persica: İran Jeopolitiği, IQ Kültür Sanat Yayıncılık: İstanbul 2017.
2. Arıkan, Pınar. "Iran-Saudi Arabia Tension between Conflict of National Interests and Sectarian Polarization", "*ORSAM Review of Regional Affairs*", Vol. 1, No. 38, January 2016. pp. 1–13.
3. Axworthy, Michale. *Iran, Empire of the Mind: A History from Zoroaster to the Present Day*, Penguin, London. 2008.
4. Barzegar, Kayhan. "Iran and the Shiite Crescent: Myths and Realities", "*The Brown Journal of World Affairs*", Winter 2008, Vol. 15, No. 1, pp. 87–99.
5. Büyükkara, Mehmet Ali. *Çağdaş İslami Akımlar*, İstanbul. 2015.
6. Czulda, Robert. "The Struggle of Iran and Saudi Arabia over Iraq", In: *Panorama of Global Security Environment*, ed. Peter Bátor, Róbert Ondrejcsák, STRATPOL, 2015–2016, Bratislava 2016, pp. 343–352.
7. Elverdani, Salih. *Mısır'da İslami Akımlar*, İstanbul. 2011.
8. Guzansky, Yoel. *The Arab Gulf States and Reform in the Middle East: Between Iran and the "Arab Spring"*, Palgrave Macmillan, New York. 2015.
9. İnat, Kemal, Kurt, Veysel, Yegin, Abdullah, Gürler, Recep Tayyip, Özdemir, Ömer Behram, Özdemirci, Ayşe Selcan, Akdoğan, İsmaıl. "İran-Suudi Arabistan Rekabetinin Bölgesel Yansımaları", "*Analiz*", No. 148, January 2016, pp. 1–28.
10. Kocatepe, Damla. „Suudi Arabistan-İran Rekabeti: Mezhep Görünümlü Çıkar Çatışmas", "*ANKASAM; Bölgesel Araştırmalar Dergisi*", (Iran Special Issue), Vol. 1, No. 2, October 2017, pp. 67-101.
11. Oktav, Özden Zeynep. *Basra Körfezi'nin Değişen Dinamikleri: İran-ABD-Suudi Arabistan İlişkileri*, Beta, İstanbul. 2011.

12. Osiewicz, Przemyslaw. "Ideological Determinants of the Current Saudi-Iranian Rivalry in the Middle East", "*Przegląd Politologiczny*" Vol. 2, No. 2, 2016, p. 115–125.
13. Sewag, Zulqarnian. "Sectarian Rise in Pakistan: Role of Saudi Arabia and Iran", "*South Asia Journal of Multidisciplinary Studies*", Vol. 1, No. 3, February 2015, pp. 2–19.
14. Taştekin, Fehim. *Karanlık Çöktüğünde; IŞİD: Din adına şiddetin dünü ve bugünü*, İstanbul. 2016.
15. Zweiri, Mahjoob. "Arab-Iranian Relations: New Realities?", In: *Iran's Foreign Policy from Khatemi to Ahmadinejad*, ed. Anoushiravan Ehteshami, Mahjoob Zweiri, Berkshire: Ithaca 2008, pp. 115–128.
16. Hameed, U. Usjid. „Saudi-Iranian Rivalry:A Foreign Policy Analyses Approach", "TOWSON UNIVERSITY; Journal of International Affairs", Vol. L, No. 2, pp. 16–34.

Internet sources

1. Gulf News, Iran vows to protect Iraqi shrines: Rouhani, 18 June 2014: 28 Mar. 2018, https://gulfnews.com/world/mena/iran-vows-to-protect-iraqi-shrines-1.1348782.
2. Allison, George.; UK Defence Journal, "Saudi Arabia and UK sign Memorandum of Intent for Purchase of 48 More Typhoon Jets", https://ukdefencejournal.org.uk/saudi-arabia-uk-sign-memorandum-intent-purchase-48-typhoon-jets/ (07 Apr. 2018).
3. Baghishadbad, Atefeh. *The Impact of the Syria's Crisis on the Rivalry between Iran and the Saudi Arabia in the Region; Iran's Point of View*, "JAIRO", March 2016, p. 130–131, https://doors.doshisha.ac.jp/duar/repository/ir/22933/049000060008.pdf (22 Oct. 2017).
4. Cockburn, Patrick. *Iraq Crisis: How Saudi Arabia Helped Isis Take Over the North of the Country*. "The Independent", 13 July 2014, https://www.independent.co.uk/voices/comment/iraq-crisis-how-saudi-arabia-helped-isis-take-over-the-north-of-the-country-9602312.html (28 Mar. 2018).
5. Heydarian, Richard Javad. *Iran-Saudi Relations: Rising Tensions and Growing Rivalry*, "FPIF", 6 August 2010, http://fpif.org/iran-saudi_relations_rising_tensions_and_growing_rivalry/ (12 Mar. 2018).
6. Ighani, Helia. *Managing the Saudi-Iran Rivalry*, "Council on Foreign Relations", 25 October. 2016. https://www.cfr.org/sites/default/files/pdf/2016/10/Workshop_Report_CPA_Saudi_Iran_Rivalry_OR.pdf (28 Mar. 2018).

7. Mabon, Simon *Saudi Arabia, Iran and the Changing Geopolitics of the Middle East*, http://eprints.lancs.ac.uk/76745/2/Saudi_Arabi1_1_.pdf (21 Nov. 2017).
8. Milani, Mohsen M. *Iran and Saudi Arabia Square Off: The Growing Rivalry between Tehran and Riyadh*, "Foreign Affairs" (11 October. 2011). https://www.foreignaffairs.com/articles/middle-east/2011-10-11/iran-and-saudi-arabia-square (02 Mar. 2018).
9. Sharma, Abhınav. "Severed Ties between Iran and Saudi Arabia: A Cold War or a Proxy War of Narratives, Influence and Power", "CAPS IN FOCUS", (5 January 2016), http://capsindia.org/files/documents/CAPS_Infocus_ANS_01.pdf (28 Mar. 2018).
10. *Suudi Kralı'ndan Obama'ya Mübarek Fırçası*, "Hürriyet", 10 February 2011. http://www.hurriyet.com.tr/gundem/suudi-kralindan-obamaya-mubarek-fircasi-16988333 (13 Mar. 2018).
11. Tadjbakhsh, Shahrbanou. *The Persian Gulf and Afghanistan: Iran and Saudi Arabia's Rivalry Projected*, "PRIO" March 2013, p. 17. https://www.prio.org/utility/DownloadFile.ashx?id=368&type=publicationfile (21 Mar. 2018).
12. Terril, W. Andrew. *The Saudi-Iranıan Rivalry and the Future of Middle East Security*, "SSI" December 2011, p. 32.https://www.files.ethz.ch/isn/142831/pub1094.pdf (21 Mar. 2018).
13. Wehrey, Frederic, Karasik, Theodore W, Nader, Alireza, Ghez, Jeremy, Hansell, Lydia, Guffey, Robert A. *Saudi-Iranian Relations Since the Fall of Saddam; Rivalry, Cooperation, and Implications for U.S. Policy*, Rand: Santa Monica, Arlington, Pittsburgh 2009. https://www.rand.org/content/dam/rand/pubs/monographs/2009/RAND_MG840.pdf (21 Mar. 2018).

Syed Subtain Hussain Shah

Comparative Study of Post-9/11 and Post-Arab Spring Rise of Violent Religious Extremism in Pakistan

Abstract: This chapter covers comparative study on extent of violent religious extremism in the periods of post-9/11 and post-Arab Spring in Pakistan. The religious extremism in Pakistan mostly erupted in the late 1970s because of controversial Islamization of the country by the then military dictator General Zia ul Haque, Islamic jihad through Afghanistan's war, and Iran's Revolution and Arab's reaction on it as well as the Pakistan's sponsored war in Indian Held Kashmir (IHK).

The two post–Cold War eras, post-9/11 and post-Arab Spring, in Pakistan became more crucial in the context of religious extremism, the core motivating potency behind the terrorism. Islamabad's assistance in war on terror resulted in more violence in Pakistan and such trend increased in post-Arab Spring. Dissimilation in post-9/11 and post-Arab Spring is that in the post-Arab Spring era, local extremists established their links with the foreign groups like Islamic State (IS) having supranational identity while earlier, these groups were inspired by or affiliated with Al Qaeda and Afghan's Taliban. On other hand, more strict and hard actions of the state of Pakistan were observed in order to counter terrorism in both of the periods.

Keywords: Extremism, violence, injustice, national security and militancy

Introduction

The followers of different religions and diverse Muslim sects exist in Pakistan since its independence as a separate state in 1947. At that time, the situation regarding religious extremism was not much worse as it is today. In Pakistan, the severe religious extremism or violence based on the religion began after enforcement of Islamization by then the military dictator General Zia ul Haque, Afghanistan war, and Iran's Revolution and Arab's reaction to it in the 1970s and 1980s. At the same time, Pakistan sponsored a war in the Indian Held Kashmir. It was admitted by a former senior officer of Pakistan army that Zia's period was crucial in the context of so-called Islamization of the country, Afghan jihad, fighting in Kashmir, etc.[1]

---

1 Shahid Aziz, *How Long Will You Remain Silent? A Soldier's Saga of Love and Passion* (Islamabad: Seven Springs Publisher, 2012), p. 240.

The violent extremism continued in the post–Cold War era. Specially, Islamabad's assistance in war on terror resulted in more violence in Pakistan in post-9/11 era. Pakistan became further a victim of extremism and such trend increased in post-Arab Spring era. The country faced similar problems in both periods of post-9/11 and post-Arab Spring at domestic level while facing various external threats. Besides the other aspects of the national security of Pakistan, the country's economy was also badly damaged.[2]

The local difficulties which contributed to fuel the issue were political uncertainty, social and economic inequality, poverty, illiteracy, joblessness, lack of health facilities, and unsatisfactory education system. These altogether contributed to the violence including religion-based hate and hostility in the society. The issues also damaged the identity and image of the country, affected national economy, and even caused continuation of the brain drain. Existence of the problems shows irresponsibility of the state or lack of good governance.[3]

It was further crucial in post-Arab Spring era as the local extremists established their links with foreign groups like "Islamic State" (IS) having supranational and suprastate identity while earlier, these groups were inspired by or affiliated with Al Qaeda and Afghan Taliban.[4] Pakistan's military establishment, the most powerful state's entity of the country, also understood that the post-Arab Spring homegrown militancy under the garb of the religion has been a "biggest threat" to the national security of the country.[5]

Problematic Statement

Before appearance of "Islamic State" (IS) as one of most of the violent extremist groups of world, the terrorists groups in Pakistan had their own local links or had a strong affiliation with Afghan Taliban and Al Qaeda fighting in Afghanistan. The

---

2 Aqeel Yousafszai, *The Incomplete Operation* (Lahore: Nigarshat Publishers, 2009), p.120–121.

3 Manzar Zaidi, *Insights on Insecurity in Pakistan* (Lahore: Shirkat Printing Press, 2012), p. 98.

4 Farhan Zahid, "The Islamic State in Pakistan: Growing the Network," *Fikra Forum, Generating Dialogue, Impact Policy*, (2017): 17 Dec. 2017, https://www.washingtoninstitute.org/fikraforum/view/the-islamic-state-in-pakistan-growing-the-network.

5 "New doctrine: Army identifies 'homegrown militancy' as biggest threat," *Express Tribune*, (03 Jan. 2013): 02 Mar. 2017, https://tribune.com.pk/story/488362/new-doctrine-army-identifies-homegrown-militancy-as-biggest-threat/.

situation became more threatening in Pakistan, when IS's branch of "Khurrasan" was established in Pakistan and Afghanistan in 2015.[6]

"Islamic State" (IS) originated *as Jama'at al-Tawhid wal-Jihad* in 1999, which had pledged allegiance to Al Qaeda and participated in the Iraqi insurgency following the 2003's invasion of Iraq. The group proclaimed itself a worldwide caliphate in 2013 and began referring to itself as "Islamic State in Iraq and Syria" (ISIS), but in 2014, it adopted the name of "Islamic State". Soon after the creation of "Islamic State", many of the extremist groups and individuals in Pakistan started to pledge their support to this group and not only launched their activities in the name of "IS" in Pakistan but also sent fighters to Syria and Iraq for its support. Pakistan with a population of above 200 million, poor economy and unemployment, and a rapid rising of violent religious extremism was an attractive place for "IS".[7]

The religious radicalism or religious extremism can be triggered under excuse of many glitches in the society of Pakistan as it has already many related issues. For instance, differences among various religions, clash between Muslims and non-Muslims, divisions among the diverse Islamic sectarian division, etc. Unfairness and economic needs and many other issues can also be reasons which further fuel the violent extremism in the country. The religious extremism can also be exploited as an instrument by some of the political circles for their particular aims as well. The post-Arab Spring era can be more crucial as Pakistan's military, the most powerful entity in the country, changed its doctrine and declared "home-ground militancy" as the biggest challenge for the state's national security.

It was the post-Arab Spring era, when the groups affiliated with "IS" increased their terrorist activities in Pakistan, and these violent activities were included an attack on an international airport in Karachi, the largest commercial city of Pakistan in June 2014 and brutal massacre of 140 school children in an attack on Army Public School in Peshawar bordering Afghanistan the same year. Such happenings created seriousness among the ranks of state machinery, and they started huge operations in the country specially border areas near Afghanistan.[8]

---

6 Tariq Parvez, "The Islamic State in Pakistan, Peace Brief," *United States Institute of Peace,* (2016): 19 Dec. 2017, https://www.usip.org/sites/default/files/PB213-The-Islamic-State-In-Pakistan.pdf.

7 Farhan Zahid, "The Islamic State in Pakistan: Growing the Network," *Fikra Forum, Generating Dialogue, Impact Policy,* (2017): 17 Dec. 2017, https://www.washingtoninstitute.org/fikraforum/view/the-islamic-state-in-pakistan-growing-the-network.

8 Tariq Parvez, "The Islamic State in Pakistan," *Peace Brief, United States Institute of Peace.* (2016): 19 Dec. 2017 https://www.usip.org/sites/default/files/PB213-The-Islamic-State-In-Pakistan.pdf.

It was the time, when "IS" links with the local militant groups became stronger which caused more violent terrorism such as target killings and suicide bombings in different areas of the country. It was the period when a strong affiliation of "IS" in Pakistan posed a major threat to its national security. Specially, presence of the militant group, which believes in expansion under the pretext of a so-called international Islamic Caliphate, challenged the identity and national security of Pakistan.

The main intention of the study is to obtain inside information into the developments related to the violent religious extremism in order to comparatively analyze the situation in post-9/11 and post-Arab Spring eras in Pakistan.

The post-9/11 terrorist activities of the extremist groups were mostly in response to Pakistan's participation in War on Terror. In post-Arab Spring era, connection between local radical groups and foreign religious militant organizations having suprastate and supranational identity caused a more serious challenge for Pakistan. It has to analyze the distinguished situation in religious extremism in post-9/11 and post-Arab Spring era in Pakistan. What were the factors and what was the impact of extremism in both eras? The issue has to be explored from its diverse political, social, economic, and religious aspects. The opinions, analyses, and study of the various events with productive research should be used to develop a necessary solution to the problem. Review of the existing literature should also be conducted for better understanding of the gap in the study.

Literature Review

There are a number of books, e-books, articles, and research papers already existing on the topic of religious extremism in post-9/11 era, but less literature is available on post-Arab Spring violent religious extremism. Raising the issue of terrorist attacks in post-9/11 era, a Pakistani writer explained the gravity of the issue as writing, "Attack on Pakistan's Military Headquarters (GHQ) in Rawalpindi in October 2009 was a significant test case for military establishment, the most powerful entity of the country".[9]

Another writer who is a former foreign secretary of Pakistan's ministry of foreign affairs wrote that Pakistan's action against Al Qaeda and Pakistan's alliance with America in War on Terror increased the terrorist activities in Pakistan.[10] Another expert compared the situations in post-9/11 and pre-9/11 eras pointing out that

---

9 Yousafzai, *The Incomplete Operation*, p.120–121.

10 Riaz Mohammad Khan, *Afghanistan and Pakistan: Conflict, Extremism, and Resistance to Modernity* (Karachi: Oxford University Press, 2012), p.223.

it changed in law and order situation when Taliban and Al Qaeda infiltrated into Pakistan in the post-9/11 era.[11] Two authors of a research article were also of the view that terrorism emerged after 9/11 was the most serious threat. "Pakistan has its role as the frontline state in the war against terrorism".[12] It showed that most literature highlighted the serious situation in Pakistan but no one has evidently conducted a comparative study of both the period of post-9/11 and post-Arab Spring era.

Theories of Constructivism and Neorealism

In the context of religious extremism, the social constructivism stressed on the socially constructed character of the actors and their exclusive identities and particular interests. It is about the identity, nature, interests, and behavior of important actors and the structure of world politics.[13] The radical violence or violent religious extremism can be studied on the constructivist lines which is based primarily on socially constructed nature of the actors, their identities and interests. Such justification also emphasizes on the international character of the different religion in the society.[14] Such as separate characters of radical Islamist groups as their constructed political, social, and economic interests are more significant while shaping this identity in post-Arab Spring era. Religious extremism in post-9/11 was mostly connected with the Afghan war, but the radical movements in Pakistan became further borderless and suprastate as the extremist and sectarian groups in Pakistan established their links with foreign groups who believe in their own "Islamic rule" in the world.

Secondly, the religious extremism can be understood according to some aspects of the theory of neorealism which is also concerning survival of the states looking for more influence for their survival. The states want maximum power by execution of their ideologies at internal level and undermining other states at external

11 Umbreen Javaid, *Pakistan Fights Extremism and Terrorism* (Lahore: Vanguard Books Pvt, Ltd, 2013), p.191.

12 Razia Musarrat and Sumaira Khan, "Terrorism and Politico-Religious Extremism in Pakistan Post 9/11," *Journal of Public Administration and Governance*, Vol. 4, No. 1, (2014), p.170.

13 Matthew J. Hoffmann, "Norms and Social Constructivism in International Relations," *International Studies Association and Oxford Universiy Press*, (2017): 24 Jan. 2018 http://internationalstudies.oxfordre.com/view/10.1093/acrefore/9780190846626.001.0001/acrefore-9780190846626-e-60?rskey=NmcJ7D&result=4.

14 Dina Al Raffie, 'Social Identity Theory for Investigating Islamic Extremism in the Diaspora', *Journal of Strategic Security (JSS)*, Vol. 6, No. 4, (2013), p.76: 26 Dec. 2017 https://pdfs.semanticscholar.org/e85a/45123bbc73b199a4443b29c0e36ede079442.pdf.

level.[15] In a substitution tussle between Iran and Saudi Arabia, both back their favorite proxy groups in Pakistan in order to maximize their power in the region. Pakistan and India also exploit similar devices for protecting their interests in area.

Violent Religious Extremism in Post-9/11

Pakistan was a front line state in the American-led War on Terror in the post-9/11 scenario. This was the period, when Pakistan changed its policy towards Afghanistan and Taliban's regime was ousted from Kabul.[16] In the post-American-led attack on Afghanistan, various groups led by Northern Alliance, the largest opposition took power in the Afghan's capital. Many of the extremist groups associated with Taliban were attacked during US-led operations in Afghanistan which resulted in these groups escaping to Pakistan, where jihadi literature was also flooded into the country after 9/11.[17] Pakistan was already a witness of religious extremism and specially sectarian violence. Pakistan provided its military bases and logistic support to US forces against Taliban and Al Qaeda in Afghanistan. Its reaction was strong in Pakistan, even people of the country were divided on the issue. Violence increased after 9/11, as different violent groups started to commit terrorist activities inside Pakistan, specially its tribal areas bordering Afghanistan became victims of the brutal attacks. Suicide attacks were added to the terrorist activities in different cities of Pakistan. The religious places like mosques and churches were not safe. The terrorist groups also committed assaults on Pakistan's military installations and other state's departments. About consequences of US military actions in Afghanistan and Pakistan's assistance in these actions, an author argued that Pakistan will remain in a difficult position for a long time.[18] Pakistan not only faced several terrorist attacks resulting in death of thousands of people but its society was also affected by the extremism in the post-9/11 era.

Terrorist Incidents in Pakistan in Post-9/11 Era

Pakistan was already facing religious extremism and sectarian violence but it increased after 9/11 as Islamabad became an important ally to the USA in War on

15 Autorzy S. Thomas, *The Global Resurgence of Religion and the Transformation of International Relation* (New York: Palgrave Macmillan, 2005), p. 65–66.

16 Aziz, *How Long Will You Remain Silent?,* p. 240.

17 Ahmed Rashid, *Descent into Chaos,* (London: Penguin Group, 2008), p. 227.

18 As'ad AbuKhalil, *Bin Laden, Islam and American's New "War on Terrorism"* (New York: Open Media Seven Stories Press, 2002), p. 80–81.

Terror. The terrorism-based incidents resulted in deaths of thousands of people including civilians and security forces. It also damaged Pakistan's economy. Some of the major terrorist incidents in Pakistan were assassination of Danial Pearl, the then correspondent of Wall Street Journal in 2002, two attacks on the then President General Musharraf in 2004 and 2007, suicide attacks on Shia community in Quetta city since 2004, bomb blasts outside residence of American Consul General and US Culture Centre in Karachi in 2004, attack on convoy of a senior Pakistani military commander in Karachi in 2004, killing of 50 people in an attack on a religious gathering at the Nishtar Park Karachi in 2006, death of 13 policemen in an attack in Peshawar in 2007, assassination of a three-star general of Pakistan's army medical core in suicide attack in Rawalpindi in 2007, killing of 23 soldiers in a suicide attack on an army's convoy in 2007, death of 49 people including policemen in Swat in 2007, assassination of former Prime Minister of Pakistan Benazir Bhutto in a suicide attack in Rawalpindi in 2007, killing of 24 officers of a Pakistani intelligence agency at its headquarters in Lahore on March 11, 2008, death of six people in an attack on Danish Embassy in red security zone of Islamabad, death of 57 people in a suicide attack on Marriott hotel Islamabad, killing of 70 people in an attack on a military weapons factory in Wah area near Islamabad, and a ruthless attack on Pakistan's Army headquarter in Rawalpindi in 2009.

Fatalities in Terrorist Violence in Pakistan 2003–2010

	Civilians	Security Force Personnel	Terrorists/ Insurgents	Total
2000	45	0	0	45
2001	29	9	0	38
2002	88	7	44	139
2003	140	24	25	189
2004	435	184	244	863
2005	430	81	137	648
2006	608	325	538	1471
2007	1522	597	1479	3598
2008	2155	654	3906	6715
2009	2324	991	8389	11704
2010	1796	469	5170	7435
Total*	**9572**	**3341**	**19712**	**32845**

Source: South Asia Terrorism Portal, Institute of Conflict Management. Retrieved from: http://www.satp.org/satporgtp/countries/pakistan/database/casualties.htm

Talibanization in Pakistan in Post-9/11 Era

The term “Talibanization” was being used with rise of Taliban’s movement in Afghanistan as the group imitated the strict practices of the religion in that country. Oxford dictionary described it as an action or process of making something similar to the Taliban or its regime, specially through the imposition of an ideology based on a fundamentalist interpretation of Islam.[19] Another dictionary explains it as the process of converting something, specially a government or culture, into something based on the fundamentalist Islamic teachings of the Taliban group.[20]

It was the post-9/11 period that waves of violent religious extremism were started from the north-west borders of Pakistan and it spread into the city of Islamabad, the capital of the country. Pakistan became witness of growing Talibanization. Unexpectedly, a pro-religious political alliance known as *Mutahid-e-Majlis-e-Amal* (MMA) won elections in the Khyber Pakhtunkhwa and Balochistan provinces in 2002. It was the anti-American political alliance, and they raised the slogan against the US-led War on Terror in Afghanistan. Another episode of such trends was an agitation of management of a mosque known as “Lal Masjid” (Red mosque) against the state. Office bearers of this mosque and students of its affiliated religious schools wanted imposition of Islamic law according to their desire in 2007. “Red mosque was a feeding ideologically into the anarchic order of Talibanization in the Khyber Pakhtunkhwa and the tribal territories (FATA)”.[21] Then government launched an operation against the management of the red mosque and a number of people were killed in this clash. This operation also had a strong reaction by the extremist groups throughout Pakistan.

Government’s Responses against Terrorism

Government of Pakistan launched a number of operations against the violent extremism and terrorism in different areas specially tribal areas of Pakistan bordering Afghanistan in post-9/11 era. A short information about some of these actions are being presented here:

---

19 “Talibanization”, *Oxford English Dictionary*. 02 Mar. 2018 https://en.oxforddictionaries.com/definition/talibanization.

20 “Talibanization”, *Your Dictionary*. 02 Jan. 2018 http://www.yourdictionary.com/talibanization.

21 Khaled Ahmed, “How Pakistan built a terrorist haven named Lal Masjid and then tried to dismantle it,” *Scroll.in*, (2016): 13 Jan. 2018 https://scroll.in/article/813211/how-pakistan-built-a-terrorist-haven-named-lal-masjid-and-then-tried-to-dismantle-it.

- **Waziristan's Operation**
  In 2004, it was for the first time when Pakistani army launched a military operation in South Waziristan. It was against Afghan Taliban and Pakistani Taliban as a number of their militants escaped from Afghanistan and took refuge in this area.[22]
- **Bajaur's Operation**
  Bajaur area bordering Afghanistan was one of the strongholds of the militants in the tribal belt of Pakistan. This was a successful operation after Waziristan operation of 2003. Pakistani Army used tanks and air fighters in the operation. It was a critical test for Pakistan's military as this tough area was a hideout of Taliban and Al Qaeda in the region.[23]
- **Swat's Operation:**
  It was a large-scale operation in 2009 when the militants had taken control of Swat area in the Khyber Pakhtunkhwa province. It was the time when the militants had declared a war against the Pakistani government. During the operation, hundreds of thousands of local people were shifted from Swat to other areas. This was the operation that forced Pakistani state to declare War on Terror as its own war, not only American-led international war.[24]
- **US Drone Attacks in Pakistan**
  The drone's operation in Pakistani tribal areas was also launched in post-9/11 era. Though the Government of Pakistan had publicly deplored the American drone attacks, it was fact that initially, the attacks were operated from Pakistan's Shamsi Airfield in Baluchistan province. The drone targeted a number of the militants affiliated with Afghan's Taliban, Pakistani Taliban, and Al Qaeda since 2004.[25]

---

22 Suba Chandran, "Military Operations in South Waziristan: Issues and Implications," *IPCS ISSUE BRIEF*, (2004): 5 Jan. 2018 https://www.files.ethz.ch/isn/138028/IB17-SubaChandran-MilitaryOperationsInSouthWaziristan.pdf.

23 Ismail Khan and Carlotta Gall, "Battle of Bajaur: A Critical Test for Pakistan's Daunted Military," *New York Times*, (22 Sep. 2008): 02 Feb. 2018 http://www.nytimes.com/2008/09/23/world/asia/23assess.html.

24 Declan Walsh and Sana ul Haq, "Swat residents flee as army declares full-scale offensive against Taliban," *The Guardian*, (08 May 2009): 05 Feb 2018 https://www.theguardian.com/world/2009/may/08/pakistan-offensive-swat-valley.

25 "Pakistan: Reported US Strikes," Bureau of Investigative Journalism, (2017): 10 Dec. 2017 https://www.thebureauinvestigates.com/drone-war/data/pakistan-covert-us-reported-actions-2017.

- **Negotiation with Taliban**
  Once it was Pakistani government policy to negotiate with some allied groups of Taliban. The process was started in post-9/11 era. There was a mixed reaction on the initiative from the different Taliban groups. It did not impact on Afghan's Taliban as they continued their brutal activities in Afghanistan, but it brought some of the Pakistani Taliban groups closer to government of Pakistan. According to some of the experts, the government was trapped by the extremists in the context of dialogue with Pakistani Taliban.

Exploration of a Changing Scenario in Post-Arab Spring Era

It was in the post-Arab Spring era, that the Islamic State (IS) or *Daesh* set up its *Khurasan* branch of Pakistan and Afghanistan. Initially, government of Pakistan was denying the presence of *Daesh* in the country, but later on some of the officials accepted the existence of this group in Pakistan. First, there was a large recruitment by *Daesh* for its activities in Pakistan and a number of Pakistan religious volunteers traveled to Middle East in order to join this group in Syria and Iraq. Furthermore, a number of small groups or individual supporters of IS were exposed in different areas of Pakistan. Groups like Lashkar e Jhangvi also pledged their support to IS in Pakistan as the fatal ideology of this group attracted a number of individuals and groups. Second, *Daesh* mostly targeted government installations, Shia's communities, non-Muslim minorities, and religious shrines in different areas of Pakistan. Mortalities between 2011 and 2017 (in Post-Arab Spring Era) can be judged through the following chart:

Fatalities in Terrorist Violence in Pakistan 2011–2017

	Civilians	Security Force Personnel	Terrorists/ Insurgents	Total
2011	2738	765	2800	6303
2012	3007	732	2472	6211
2013	3001	676	1702	5379
2014	1781	533	3182	5496
2015	940	339	2403	3682
2016	612	293	898	1803
2017	540	208	512	1260
Total*	**12669**	**3013**	**13669**	**63086**

Source: South Asia Terrorism Portal, Institute of Conflict Management. Retrieved from: http://www.satp.org/satporgtp/countries/pakistan/database/casualties.htm

Pakistan's Responses to Terrorism in Post-Arab Spring Era

Operation 2014 known as "*Zarbe Azb*" was a crucial turn in the context of government of Pakistan's stronger action against the terrorists. This military operation cleared out safe havens of the militants in tribal areas of Pakistan specially North Waziristan. As the result of the operation, many of the terrorists were killed or many of them including militants of *Daesh* and Pakistani Taliban escaped to Afghanistan. The second phase of the operation by Pakistani military started with new title of "*Radul Fisad*" with a greater involvement of the local police in rest of Pakistan in February 2017.[26]

Though Pakistan's military changed its doctrine in post-Arab Spring era and launched wide-ranging operations against the homegrown militancy, the counterterrorism strategy was not included a soft combat against ideology of the extremism which was always used as tool for terrorism. The groups like *Daesh* easily exploited such ideology of a large circle of the masses. The governments at federal and provincial levels has so far not focused on developing of a national narrative of tolerance, pluralism, and rule of law in order to counter the spread of the religious extremist ideology.

Conclusion

There are many reasons behind the Islamic religious extremism in Pakistan, but it is a fact that the religion-based violent radicalism has badly damaged the national security of Pakistan in the last two decades, either it was the period of post-9/11 or post-Arab Spring. The issue can be addressed through understanding the situation in both phases of post-9/11 and post-Arab Spring. The misunderstanding of the masses and misinterpretation of Islamic rules by the radical groups prolonged the evil agenda of the fanatic groups which peruse their political objectives under the garb of extremism. The undemocratic rules, illiteracy, injustice, joblessness, and poor economy and absence of proper health care in the country further motivate the sparking radicalism. Intolerance towards other religions takes place due to the ignorance and lack of knowledge and modern education. The religious extremism also increases in the milieu of hatred, mistrust, and aggression. It is also reality that the religious extremism is not encouraged, preached, or motivated by any religion in its real sensible shape.

---

26 "Pakistan Army on Wednesday launched 'Operation Radd-ul-Fasaad' across the country," *Dawn*, (22 Feb. 2017): 15 Feb 2018 https://www.dawn.com/news/1316332/pakistan-army-launches-operation-radd-ul-fasaad-across-the-country.

Bibliography

1. Abu Khalil, As'ad. *Bin Laden, Islam and American's New "War on Terrorism"*. New York: Open Media Seven Stories Press, 2002.
2. Aziz, Shahid. *How Long Will You Remain Silent? A Soldier's Saga of Love and Passion*. Islamabad: Seven Springs Publisher, 2012.
3. Javaid, Umbreen. *Pakistan Fights Extremism and Terrorism*. Lahore: Vanguard Books Pvt, Ltd, 2013.
4. Khan, Riaz Mohammad. *Afghanistan and Pakistan: Conflict, Extremism, and Resistance to Modernity*. Karachi: Oxford University Press, 2012.
5. Musarrat, Razia and Khan, Sumaira. "Terrorism and Politico-Religious Extremism in Pakistan Post 9/11", *Journal of Public Administration and Governance*. Vol. 4, No. 1, (2014): p. 170.
6. Rashid, Ahmed. *Descent into Chaos*. London: Penguin Group, 2008.
7. Thomas, Autorzy S. *The Global Resurgence of Religion and the Transformation of International Relation*. New York: Palgrave Macmillan, 2005.
8. Yousafzai, Aqeel. *The Incomplete Operation*. Lahore: Nigarshat Publishers, 2009.
9. Zaidi, Manzar. *Insights on Insecurity in Pakistan*. Lahore: Shirkat Printing Press, 2012.

Internet Sources

1. "New Doctrine: Army Identifies 'Homegrown Militancy' as Biggest Threat." Express Tribune, 3 Jan. 2013. https://tribune.com.pk/story/488362/new-doctrine-army-identifies-homegrown-militancy-as-biggest-threat/ (02 Mar. 2017).
2. "Pakistan Army on Wednesday Launched 'Operation Radd-ul-Fasaad' across the Country." Dawn, 22 Feb. 2017. https://www.dawn.com/news/1316332/pakistan-army-launches-operation-radd-ul-fasaad-across-the-country (15 Feb. 2018).
3. "Pakistan: Reported US Strikes." Bureau of Investigative Journalism, 2017. https://www.thebureauinvestigates.com/drone-war/data/pakistan-covert-us-reported-actions-2017 (10 Dec. 2017).
4. "Talibanization." Oxford English Dictionary. https://en.oxforddictionaries.com/definition/talibanization (02 Mar. 2018).
5. "Talibanization." Your Dictionary. http://www.yourdictionary.com/talibanization (Accessed on 02 Jan. 2018).

6. Ahmed, Khaled. "How Pakistan Built a Terrorist Haven Named Lal Masjid and Then Tried to Dismantle It." Scroll.in. 2016. https://scroll.in/article/813211/how-pakistan-built-a-terrorist-haven-named-lal-masjid-and-then-tried-to-dismantle-it (13 Jan. 2018).
7. Chandran, Suba. "Military Operations in South Waziristan: Issues and Implications." IPCS ISSUE BRIEF. 2004. https://www.files.ethz.ch/isn/138028/IB17-SubaChandran-MilitaryOperationsInSouthWaziristan.pdf (5 Jan. 2018).
8. Hoffmann, Matthew J. "Norms and Social Constructivism in International Relations." International Studies Association. Oxford University Press. 2017. http://internationalstudies.oxfordre.com/view/10.1093/acrefore/9780190846626.001.0001/acrefore-9780190846626-e-60?rskey=NmcJ7D&result=4 (24 Jan. 2018).
9. Khan, Ismail and Gall, Carlotta. "Battle of Bajaur: A Critical Test for Pakistan's Daunted Military." New York Times, 22 September, 2008. http://www.nytimes.com/2008/09/23/world/asia/23assess.html (02 Feb. 2018).
10. Parvez, Tariq. "The Islamic State in Pakistan." Peace Brief, United States Institute of Peace, 2016. https://www.usip.org/sites/default/files/PB213-The-Islamic-State-In-Pakistan.pdf (19 Dec. 2017).
11. Raffie, Dina Al. "Social Identity Theory for Investigating Islamic Extremism in the Diaspora." Journal of Strategic Security (JSS), Vol. 6, No. 4, 2013: p. 76. https://pdfs.semanticscholar.org/e85a/45123bbc73b199a4443b29c0e36ede079442.pdf (26 Dec. 2017).
12. Walsh, Declan and Haq, Sana ul. "Swat Residents Flee as Army Declares Full-Scale Offensive against Taliban." The Guardian, 08 May 2009. https://www.theguardian.com/world/2009/may/08/pakistan-offensive-swat-valley (05 Feb. 2018).
13. Zahid, Farhan. "The Islamic State in Pakistan: Growing the Network." Fikra Forum, Generating Dialogue, Impact Policy, 2017. https://www.washingtoninstitute.org/fikraforum/view/the-islamic-state-in-pakistan-growing-the-network (17 Dec. 2017).

Part II – Foreign Policy

Radosław Fiedler

From Sanctions to War? Nothing New in the US' Policy towards Iran since 1979*

Abstract: The chapter encompasses various instruments in American policy towards Iran. Since 1979, Washington has imposed many different sanctions on Tehran, and at the same time tried to seek a kind of modus vivendi. For years, waging a war against Iran even for its proponents was perceived as an unrealistic plan more as a war game. Though, the nuclear deal was achieved in 2015, three years later Trump administration has returned to stick policy on Iran with revived military plans. Reimposing sanctions clearly express President Trump's expectations focused on the final demise of Iranian regime.

Keywords: Sanctions, military intervention, diplomacy, nuclear deal, USA, Iran

From Strategic Ally to Enemy State

In the 19th century, American-Iranian relations were modest and not well developed. The first manifestation of US activity in Iran was the presence of American missionaries who founded schools and hospitals. In 1856, the two governments signed a Treaty of Friendship and Commerce. As an indication of how distant the relations then were, it was negotiated and signed not in Iran or America but in the then capital of the Ottoman Empire, Constantinople.[1] Before the Second World War, American activity in Iran was basically nongovernmental. Unlike their Britain equivalents, American oil companies were not owned or controlled by the government. Nevertheless, they were powerful influences on the American government. In 1920, Standard Oil began negotiations with the Iranian government for a concession for oil exploration but, due to British opposition, these attempts failed. During the Second World War, Iran became more important strategic ally for Washington as a land connection with the Soviet Union within the lend-lease program. Until 1953, Iran was under British political influence.

Prime Minister Muhammad Mossadegh's decision to nationalize the Anglo-Iranian Oil Company was not recognized by London. The British also convinced the Americans that Mossadegh was cooperating with the communists and Iran

---

* The paper is developed under the project financed by the Narodowa Agencja Wymiany Akademickiej PPN/BEK/2018/1/00323

1 William R. Polk, *Understanding Iran everything you need to know, from Persia to the Islamic Republic from Cyrus to Ahmadinejad*, (Palgrave – Macmillan, New York 2008), p. 169.

would imminently become part of the sphere of influence of the Soviet Union. With the 1953 decision by the Eisenhower administration to participate in a British and Central Intelligence Agency (CIA) coup to topple the democratically elected government of Prime Minister Muhammad Mossadegh, the US involvement in Iranian politics became more visible.[2]

Iranians had often complained that the USA has denied Iran its sovereign rights and manipulated its internal affairs to its own advantage. In 1963, Washington obtained an exemption from Iranian law for its personnel, thereby humiliating Iran with the assumption that its justice was barbaric. Moreover, anti-Americanism in Iran was fueled by uncritical US support for the repressive regime of Mohammed Reza Shah Pahlavi in Iran in the 1970s, who established the repression apparatus SAVAK.[3]

In the late 1970s, Carter's administration did not notice that the Shah regime was on the brink of collapse. Just weeks before the revolution on November 9, 1978, US Ambassador William Sullivan sent a cable entitled *Thinking the Unthinkable* from Tehran to Washington, warning that the Shah's days were perhaps numbered. He pointed out that: "Iran's stability depended on mutual accommodation between two key institutions: religious hierarchy and the army."[4]

The Iranian revolution was met with surprise in Washington. Carter's administration initially sought to make contact with the new authorities, and especially with Ayatollah Khomeini. 'Business as usual' cooperation was proposed.[5] Iran was too strategic a partner for cooperation to end, even if the new authorities used anti-Americanism for political purposes.[6]

The occupation of the US embassy brutally dispelled any illusions regarding the intentions of Khomeini and his followers towards the USA. As noted by Mohammad Ayatollahi Tabaar: "the immediate fruits of the occupation of the

---

2 Abbas Milani, "U.S. foreign policy and the future of democracy in Iran", *The Washington Quarterly*, 28(3), (2005), pp. 41–56.

3 Ehsan Bakhshandeh, "How mainstream Iranian newspapers portray the West: the influence of anti-Westernism and anti-Americanism", *Journal of International Communication*, 20(2), (2014), pp. 184–199.

4 A quotation from: William Sullivan, *Mission to Iran* (New York: Norton, 1981), p. 201.

5 Barry Rubin, *Paved with Good Intentions: The American Experience in Iran* (New York: Penguin, 1981), p. 303.

6 As a confidence-building measure, US officials gradually began sharing intelligence with Iran. In October 1979 – a year before Iraq invaded Iran on September 22, 1980 – the CIA informed Tehran of Saddam Hussein's intentions and offered further intelligence collaboration against Baghdad; Mark Gasiorowski,"US Intelligence Assistance to Iran, May–October 1979", *Middle East Journal* 66, no. 4 (Autumn 2012), pp. 613–627.

embassy were greater than Khomeini could have expected (...). The Islamists could shape the elected and appointed bodies and thus effectively institutionalize Velayat-e Faqih (the clerical Rule of the Jurist) in those critical days of debating the constitution in the assembly. The Islamists labeled dissidents and opponents of Velayat-e Faqih as American spies. They silenced and intimidated their opponents, including the nationalists and the dissident moderate clerics, in the run up to the first presidential and Majles elections."[7]

In response to the hostage crisis, the Carter administration considered various options, from military action to sanctions and crisis diplomacy. The latter solution was chosen, in the hope that Khomeini would decide to end the occupation of the embassy due to rising costs resulting from sanctions. The sanctions and restrictions imposed on Iran were to show that Washington was ready to bring about its economic ruin, although there was little encouragement to be found in the example of Cuba, in which sanctions did not lead to the fall of Castro, but resulted in cooperation between Havana and Moscow.

As a consequence of the prolonged hostage crisis, Washington ended its military assistance to Iran and, on November 14, 1979, froze Iranian assets. The US Attorney General took action against 50,000 Iranian students and 80,000 other Iranian citizens who were in the USA on visas. Finally on April 7, 1980, the US cut off diplomatic relations with Iran.

Although President Carter was criticized for the prolonged hostage crisis and the unsuccessful 'Eagle Claw' operation, he began greater US military engagement in the security of the Persian Gulf. The hostage crisis accelerated America's strategic pivot towards the Persian Gulf. Brzezinski recommended a dramatic increase in America's military capabilities and offshore presence in the Persian Gulf region. This new security framework was based upon a close consultative security relationship with Egypt, Saudi Arabia, and Jordan, which, alongside Israel, would form an informal "inner cooperative core" as a counterbalance to unpredictable Iran.[8]

Sanctions and Timid Attempts to Repair Relations

For decades, sanctions had been imposing on Iran, intended to restrain the ability of the Islamic Republic to harm the interests of the US and its allies in the

7 Quotation from: Mohammad Ayatollahi Tabaar, "Causes of the US Hostage Crisis in Iran: The Untold Account of the Communist Threat", *Security Studies,* 26(4), (2017), p. 690.

8 Milani, "U.S. foreign policy and the future of democracy in Iran", pp. 41–56.

Middle East. In 1984, Iran was included on the list of states supporting terrorism by the US Department of State. Since 1992, a diverse range of sanctions have been imposed, some of which have had negative consequences for Europeans interested in doing business in Iran. The sanctions have all been focused on weakening the Iranian regime as much as possible, in the hope that it will be overthrown by Iranians frustrated with worsening economic conditions and inflation.

Under the sanctions imposed by the USA, Iran was also subject to the containment strategy. The USA decided to isolate Iraq and Iran after victorious operations such as Operation Desert Storm, and the intense military involvement of the superpower in the Persian Gulf since 1991 in general. The Arab monarchies of the Gulf Cooperation Council and Israel supported this policy towards Iran, which these states also regarded as a troublemaker. The Dual Containment strategy consisted of the following preventive actions against the Islamic Republic of Iran: sanctions, embargoes, and limits on the transfer of sensitive technologies to Iran and Iraq.[9] The harshest sanctions were directed at the oil and gas industry in Iran. The most spectacular example was when the US Congress prepared a bill that would impose sanctions on any foreign corporation that invested USD 40 million or more in the Iranian oil and gas industry (reduced to USD 20 million after one year). The bill was known as the Iran-Libya Sanction Act (ILSA), as Libya was later added by the Senate.[10]

The American approach to Iran is based on the fact that, on the one hand, under certain conditions an agreement can be reached with Tehran, and on the other, Washington has long awaited political change in Iran. As part of the containment strategy, in 1992 the USA adopted the Iran-Iraq Arms Non-Proliferation Act, the purpose of which was to restrict Iran's purchase of conventional weapons. The Act provided for sanctions against foreign companies selling components of weapons of mass destruction and advanced conventional weapons (tanks, fighters, submarines) to Iran.

In 2012, the joint US-EU round of energy and financial sanctions, implemented as a reaction to Iran's uranium enrichment program, had significant effects on key economic indicators.

9 Marin Indyk, Graham Fuller, Anthony Cordesman, "Symposium on Dual Containment: US. Policy Toward Iran and Iraq", *Middle East Policy*, Vol. *III*, No. 1 (1994), pp. 1–2.

10 Radosław Fiedler, "Hard power dismisses soft power – the United States' relations with the Iranian Islamic Republic in the shadow of the nuclear program", *Przegląd Politologiczny*, no. 3 (2013), pp. 27–38.

Tab. 1: Selected US sanctions imposed on Iran. Source: Kenneth Katzman, *Iran: Politics, Human Rights, and U.S. Policy,* (Congressional Research Service), March 26, 2018; https://www.refworld.org/pdfid/5a5f83524.pdf (June 25, 2018).

Type	Characteristic
Ban on US Trade with and Investment in Iran (May 6, 1995)	Bans almost all US trade with and investment in Iran, still in force
US Sanctions Against Foreign Firms Dealing With Iran's Energy Sector	The Iran Sanctions Act has been amended several times, and authorizes the imposition of 5 out of 12 sanctions on firms determined to have invested more than USD 20 million in the Iranian petroleum (oil and gas) sector; bought Iranian oil (unless the country has a sanctions exemption); sold more than USD 1 million worth of gasoline or equipment to import gasoline or refine oil into gasoline to Iran; sold USD 1 million or more worth of energy equipment to Iran; provided shipping services for the transport oil from Iran; engaged in a joint energy venture with Iran outside of Iran; or bought Iran's sovereign debt. Waived in accordance with the JCPOA.
Sanctions on Iran's Central Bank	Prevents foreign banks that do business with Iran's Central Bank from opening US accounts, unless the native country of the bank earns an exemption from the rule by "significantly reducing" its purchases of Iranian oil.
Terrorism List Designation Sanctions	Iran's designation by the Secretary of State as a "state sponsor of terrorism"
Sanctions Against Foreign Firms that Aid Iran's Weapons of Mass Destruction Programs	The Iran-Syria-North Korea Nonproliferation Act
Sanctions Against Foreign Firms that Sell Advanced Arms to Iran	The Iran-Iraq Arms Nonproliferation Act provides for US sanctions against foreign firms that sell Iran "destabilizing numbers and types of conventional weapons" or WMD technology. Remains in force.
Ban on Transactions with Foreign Entities that Support International Terrorism	Authorizes a ban on US transactions with entities determined to be supporting international terrorism. The order was not limited to Iran, but several Iranian entities have been designated. Remains in force.
Ban on Transactions with Foreign Entities that Support Proliferation	Provides for a ban on US transactions with entities determined to be supporting international proliferation. Numerous Iranian entities, including the IRGC itself, have been designated. Remains in force.

(*continued on next page*)

Tab. 1: (continued)

Type	Characteristic
Divestment	Authorizes and protects from lawsuits various investment managers who divest from shares of firms that conduct sanctionable business with Iran. Remains in force.
Sanctions Against Human Rights Abuses, Internet Monitoring, and Regional Activities	Various laws and Executive Orders impose sanctions on named Iranian human rights abusers, on firms that sell equipment which Iran can use to monitor the Internet usage of citizens or employ against demonstrators, and on Iranian persons or entities that suppress human rights in Syria or contribute to destabilizing Iraq. Remains in force.
Arms Transfer and Missile Sanctions in the Countering America's Adversaries through Sanctions Act (CAATSA)	The CAATSA law, signed on August 2, 2017, mandates sanctions on arms sales to Iran and on entities that "materially contribute" to Iran's ballistic missile program.
May 8, 2018 withdrawal from the Joint Comprehensive Plan of Action (JCPOA)	Two sets of sanctions. The first, coming into effect on August 7, 2018, includes restrictions on: Iran's purchase of US currency; Iran's trade in gold and other precious metals; and the sale to Iran of auto parts, commercial passenger aircraft, and related parts and services. Remains in force. The second set of sanctions, coming into effect on November 7, 2018, targeting Iranian energy sector

According to EIA (2018),[11] daily oil production in Iran dropped by almost 17 % in 2012 and by 9 % in 2013, resulting in the lowest oil prices since the end of the Iran-Iraq War in 1988. Furthermore, total exports of petroleum products showed a drop of 32 % in 2012 and a further decrease of 25 % in 2013.[12] However, estimates by local analytical staff and unofficial indicators show that, not only have trade relations been maintained, but they are continuing to operate at a high level. In 2012, Iran's turnover with international US entities ranged from 3 to 4 billion dollars. The largest share of this (about USD 2 billion) was constituted by trade in food and feed products. The largest US companies account for the remainder of the turnover, for example, Apple, HP, and Procter & Gamble. The

11 Mohammad Reza Farzanega & Bernd Hayo, "Sanctions and the shadow economy: empirical evidence from Iranian provinces", *Applied Economics Letters* (2018), pp. 1–5.

12 International Energy Statistics. Washington, DC: US Energy Information Administration.

vast majority of these transactions take place via third countries with the active participation of American companies interested in maintaining a presence on the Iranian market.[13]

American-Iranian relations would seem to be dominated by crises and subsequent US sanction regimes imposed on Iran. It turns out that there have been at least a few opportunities to repair relations between Washington and Tehran, but that these have been wasted.

A good example of the ambivalent policy of the USA to Iran was the Iran-Contra scandal. In return for arms sales, Iran facilitated the release of American citizens who had been held as hostages by Hezbollah and other Lebanese militias. Illegal arms deliveries violated the arms embargo on Iran imposed by Congress. Secret contacts between American and Iranian officials during the Reagan administration never developed into closer cooperation.[14]

Another attempt at repairing relations occurred in March 2000, when American Secretary of State Madeleine K. Albright acknowledged before the Conference on American-Iranian Relations that "the United States played a significant role in orchestrating the overthrow of Iran's popular Prime Minister, Mohammed Mossadegh." The coup on August 19, 1953 brought back Shah Mohammed Reza Pahlavi to power. "The coup was clearly a setback for Iran's political development," Albright admitted, referring to the Shah's regime, which "brutally repressed political dissent."[15] Unfortunately, no further attempt at thawing relations occurred from either side. However, Albright's statement remained an important gesture to Iran.

A further opportunity to improve relations occurred after September 11, 2001. Compassion expressed by the Iranians for the victims of the terrorist attacks on the USA contrasted with anti-American sentiments in the Arab World. In the case of Afghanistan, Tehran, unlike Russia and Pakistan, did not criticize the American military operation Enduring Freedom; instead, they offered concrete

---

13 Katarzyna Radwan, "Efektywność sankcji amerykańskich w Iranie", *Biuletyn Instytutu Zachodniego*, Nr 172/2014; https://www.rgib.org.pl/images/stories/dokumenty/grudzien2014/sankcje.pdf (accessed June 25, 2018).

14 Bartosz Bojarczyk, „Stosunki ze Stanami Zjednoczonymi jako determinant polityki zagranicznej Islamskiej Republiki Iranu" : Iran - 30 lat po rewolucji Seminarium Biura Bezpieczeństwa Narodowego 11 marca 2009 r. *Biblioteka „Bezpieczeństwa Narodowego", kwartalnika wydawanego przez Biuro Bezpieczeństwa Narodowego, tom 12,* pp. 60.

15 Remarks by Secretary of State Madeleine K. Albright on American–Iranian Relations, (17 Mar. 2000): 25 June 2018 http://www.parstimes.com/history/albright_speech.html.

help, especially in terms of intelligence cooperation with the USA.[16] Although there seemed to be quite significant progress in the difficult US-Iranian relations, unfortunately this failed to bring about a breakthrough. The return to more unfriendly rhetoric occurred with the incident with the ship *Karine A* in early January 2002, on which the Israeli services found an arsenal of weapons bound for the Palestinian Authority. As it turned out, the weapons came from Iran. President G. W. Bush incorporated Iran, alongside North Korea and Iraq, into the "axis of evil."[17]

After 2003, the US government additionally accused Iran of harming Iraq. One unintended consequence of the American intervention and the removal of Saddam Hussein was a significant improvement in the security of Iran in its immediate vicinity. In addition, Iran gained the opportunity to influence the internal situation in Iraq more than in the period prior to 2003. Possible American-Iranian cooperation on the stabilization of Iraq could have initiated negotiations on the atomic issue. During three rounds of bilateral consultations in May, June, and August 2007 on Iraq, besides mutual accusations between Iran and US representatives, no more constructive discussions could be held. The USA, Israel, and several European allies explicitly stated that they would not accept the possession of nuclear bombs by the Islamic fundamentalist regime ruling Iran.

Surprisingly, on December 3, 2007, the US released the National Intelligence Estimate (NIE) report entitled *Iran: Nuclear Intentions and Capabilities*. The NIE report made the surprising assessment that Iran had halted its nuclear weapons program in 2003. The report further added that Iran would not be close to acquiring nuclear weapons until late 2009, but would probably have the capability to develop nuclear weapons sometime between 2010 and 2015.[18] The report dismissed the Bush administration's claim that the military component of the Iranian nuclear program was very advanced. This could have opened the way to a diplomatic solution to the crisis surrounding the Iranian nuclear program. The possibility of negotiations was ignored both by the Bush administration and President Ahmadinejad.

---

16 Kenneth Pollack, *The Persian Puzzle: The Conflict between Iran and America* (Random House, 2005), p. 346.

17 Radosław Fiedler, *Iran a reżim nieproliferacji broni jądrowej. Dylematy i wyzwania* (Wydawnictwo Naukowe WNPiD), Poznan (2013), pp. 45–60.

18 Masoud Kazemzadeh, "U.S.–Iran Confrontation in the Post-NIE World: An Analysis of Alternative Policy Options", *Comparative Strategy*, (2009) 28:1, pp. 37–59.

Barack Obama was the first American president to declare his readiness to start direct talks with Tehran without the prior suspension of the Iranian nuclear program on March 21, 2009, the Persian New Year (*Norwuz*). In response to the US President's declaration, Iran launched the Safir-2 rocket (February 2009) that placed a satellite in orbit (dual-purpose technology). This evoked legitimate concerns in the Pentagon due to the evident progress in the production of long-range missiles.

President Obama, while continuing the policy of imposing sanctions on Iran, achieved more than previous administrations. US sanctions against the Iranian central bank had severely restricted access to international financial institutions and hampered Iran's ability to derive income from oil exports. Many corporations, including those from outside the West, withdrew from investing in Iran; Daimler, Toyota, Deutsche Bank, HSBC, Royal Dutch Shell, Reliance, and Lukoil to name but a few.

Additionally to the USA, uniteral sanctions on Iran were impsed by the EU. Based on statistics from the European Commission, Iran ranked 27th on the list of trading partners with the EU in 2010. The deterioration of political and economic relations between the EU and Tehran was also influenced by the Iranian nuclear program. The E-3 Group (France, Germany, and the United Kingdom) were involved in negotiations in Iran. The resumption of the program of enriching uranium by the Iranian authorities in 2005 and the rejection of subsequent offers from the E-3 group by Tehran led the EU to impose sanctions on Iran. The EU introduced additional sanctions in the same way as the US under UNSCR 1929. On November 21, 2011, the government of Canada and the United Kingdom together declared that they would not conduct transactions with Iranian financial institutions, including the central bank.[19]

In July 2015, intensive negotiations led to the final nuclear deal, known as the Joint Comprehensive Plan of Action (JCPOA). It aimed to eliminate the risk of exceeding the threshold beyond which the program could be militarized. The removal of this risk requires that, until 2030, Iran keeps its uranium enrichment activities below the rate of 3.67 % and maintains a total stock of uranium under 300 kg. The guarantee of the civilian nature of the nuclear program depends on Iran's commitment to reduce its total stock of enriched uranium by 98 %. Uranium enrichment activities are now limited to the Natanz facility only;

---

19 Ron Nixon, *Two Large Multinationals Pull Back from Iran,* "New York Times". (10 Mar 2010): 10 June 2018 http"//www.nytimes.com/2010/03/11/world/mieeast/11iran.html.

moreover, two-thirds of Natanz's centrifuges have been dismantled. Only 5,000 of the old IR-1 models are permitted for use until 2030. The 'breakout time' is defined as the amount of time it would take Iran to acquire enough fissile material for one nuclear weapon.[20] The JCPOA has considerably enhanced the chances of international inspectors detecting any Iranian noncompliance in good time. If Iran decides to abandon the provisions of the JCPOA, the international community would react immediately by reimposing all sanctions which were lifted in January 2016. Moreover, the JCPOA provides for the reconstruction of the heavy-water reactor at Arak, with a view to eliminating the production of plutonium for military purposes and devoting the plant exclusively to the production of medical radioisotopes. In short, the nuclear agreement contributes to the strengthening of the 1968 Nuclear Non-Proliferation Treaty.[21]

Despite these successful accomplishments, there are several weaknesses which may undermine the JCPOA's durability: (1) the agreement does not include the Iranian missile program and has not initiated more comprehensive dialogue with Tehran on its Middle East policy; (2) the nuclear deal has not changed Iran's behavior in regional politics, which threatens Saudi Arabia and Israel; (3) the agreement with the international community has not changed Iran's internal political situation and has not initiated political reforms to soften the autocratic regime; (4) the agreement is a disappointment for the Iranian authorities, as the increased scope for inspections and the significantly reduced enrichment of uranium has not led to the upholding of this agreement by the USA.[22]

Military Intervention as a Problematic and Recurring Possibility

In the global security structure, the security order designed by the USA is based on its military presence in the Persian Gulf. In recent years, the USA has deployed more than 100,000 troops in Iraq through the Iraq War and has maintained a certain amount of infantry and military bases in the Gulf Cooperation Council nations, through US military agreements with these nations. Usually, the USA

20 Oli Heinonen, "Iran's Nuclear Breakout Time: A Fact Sheet", *Policy Watch, Policy Analysis*, The Washington Institute, March 28,(2015).

21 Erik Jessen, "European Diplomacy in the Iran Nuclear Negotiations: What Impact Did It Have?" *Bruges Political Research Papers/Cahiers de recherche politique de Bruges* No 61, October (2017).

22 Adam Tarock, "The Iran nuclear deal: winning a little, losing a lot", *Third World Quarterly*, 37:8, (2016), pp. 1408–1424.

keeps about 7,000 troops in the GCC nations. Among these nations, Qatar is the location of the US Central Headquarters. There are 3,400 troops and an air force base in Qatar. There are also an additional 1,500 troops and the headquarters of the 5th Fleet in Bahrain.[23] Of course, the US military presence in the Persian Gulf region is completely unacceptable for Iran, perceived by Tehran as a direct menace and military imbalance which has been put in place to favor US allies – Saudi Arabia and Israel.

Military intervention in Iran has been considered several times in Washington's political and military decision-making structures. In the past, there have been examples of more direct American action against Iran. For example, during Iraqi war with Iran, the USA quickly began to supply Iraq with intelligence on the movements of Iranian forces. In 1983, the US State Department launched Operation Staunch to stop the flow of weapons to Iran. Washington and other Western allies strengthened economic ties with Baghdad and exported dual-use items and other materials that could be used for chemical weapons against Iranian troops. In the end, an accidental attack by the US Navy catalyzed the end of the conflict. On July 3, 1988, the USS *Vincennes* shot down a civilian Iranian airliner, killing all 290 of its passengers and crew. Iranian leaders claimed this was an intentional act and a warning signal by Washington that the USA was moving towards a direct confrontation. Two weeks later, Iran announced its willingness to accept United Nations Security Council Resolution 598 with no preconditions. Tehran sent foreign minister Ali Akbar Velayati to New York with the mission of returning with a ceasefire agreement. Tehran noticed that direct US military involvement on the Iraqi side had become a direct threat for the Islamic Republic.

For Washington, the greatest challenge is a nuclear-armed Iran, with the immunity that a nuclear deterrent provides, which would result in more open support for pro-Iranian Shiites and subversive activities aimed at Saudi Arabia and Israel – close allies of the USA.

A military solution, as the option of last resort, is very problematic and could ignite a regional conflict destabilizing the whole Persian Gulf area. In the report *Weighing Benefits and Costs of Military Action against Iran*, released in September 2012, the probable impacts of a military attack on nuclear facilities in Iran were presented. Bombing facilities in Isfahan and Tehran would also involve civilian casualties and damage to the neighborhood surrounding these nuclear sites. The

23 Bo Wang, "The Conflict between US and Iran in Designing the Persian Gulf Security Order", *Journal of Middle Eastern and Islamic Studies*, 3:2, (2009), pp. 39–48.

authors listed the following benefits resulting from a limited military strike on the Iranian nuclear facilities:[24]

- Destruction of nuclear infrastructure;
- Weakening of Iran's defense forces;
- Showing determination to halt proliferation in the region;
- A military operation would be welcomed by countries afraid of Iran's nuclear aspirations, and strengthen ties with regional allies such as Saudi Arabia and Israel.

The direct costs of such an operation include:

- Iranian rocket fire, aimed at US bases and installations in the region, could also hit installations in Saudi Arabia and Israel;
- Asymmetric and terrorist actions targeting Americans in the region and beyond, and the targeting of US allies in the Middle East, would be provoked;
- Mining the Strait of Hormuz would paralyze the oil flow there, which is equivalent to approximately 20 % of the world consumption.

For indirect costs:

- Serious costs to US interests would also be felt over the longer term, with problematic consequences for global and regional stability, including economic stability;
- Criticism of unilateral US activities without the authorization of the UN Security Council and disintegration of cooperation with China, Russia, and European partners regarding the Iranian program;
- Strengthening supporters of the 'hard' approach to the West in Iran, and driving up support for the acquisition of nuclear weapons and the direct arming of Iran's regional allies;
- Asymmetrical conflict between Israel and Hezbollah, Hamas and Islamic Jihad could be provoked;
- More direct Iranian assistance to the Yemeni Houthis could be provoked.

The direct and indirect costs of military intervention in Iran outweigh the possible benefits. In various 'war games,' possible retaliatory actions on the part of Iran are considered. It cannot be ruled out that Tehran would block the Strait of Hormuz and attack some targets with medium-range missiles, namely the US bases in Saudi Arabia and Israel. Other undesirable effects would include

---

24 *Weighing Benefits and Costs of Military Action Against Iran*: 25 June 2018 https://www.wilsoncenter.org/sites/default/files/IranReport_091112_FINAL.pdf.

the serious disruption of oil supplies, which would affect the condition of the global economy. It is unlikely that the attack on atomic facilities in Iran would lead to a change in the political regime, but would rather strengthen nationalist sentiments and encourage Iranians to rally around the leaders of the existing Islamic Republic. Undoubtedly, alongside many other negative results, Tehran would accelerate its development of a military nuclear program.

Analysts have also examined the bombing of Iranian nuclear facilities by Israel. Even a limited Israeli attack on Iran's nuclear facilities would have to be a complex and extremely difficult operation. While in the case of Iraq (1981) and Syria (2007), the destruction of one nuclear plant was all that was necessary, in the case of Iran there are many dispersed nuclear facilities, partly placed underground and located in hollow rocks or underground shelters. Meir Dagan, the former Israeli intelligence chief (Mossad), criticized these plans as adventuring which would only serve to undermine Israel's security.[25] To undertake limited air strikes, Israel needs Washington's support, not mere benign neutrality.

The old idea of military strikes on Iran, which had been rejected as unworkable in the past, has been revived by the Trump administration. After Obama's more conciliatory approach, the new administration has returned to a more hardline policy towards Iran. President Trump has criticized his predecessor's policy to Tehran as merely strengthening the unpredictable regime.

The Trump administration unilaterally withdrew the US from the JCPOA agreement. This has resulted in the following consequences:

- The weakening of, and even crisis in, relations between the US and EU[26];
- The undermining of cooperation with Russia and China on the Iranian question;
- The weakening of the nuclear agreement, which increases the risk of proliferation of nuclear weapons in the Middle East.

Once again, Iran can maintain that the USA is unable to comply with the agreements concluded. The current US administration has taken pride in the pro-Israel optics of its Middle Eastern policy. This is nothing new, but, compared to previous administrations, President Trump and his colleagues have ignored

25 Isabel Kershner, *Israeli Strike on Iran Would Be 'Stupid,' Ex-Spy Chief Says*: 23 June 2018 https://www.nytimes.com/2011/05/09/world/middleeast/09israel.html.

26 More on EU policy after JCPOA in Przemysław Osiewicz, "EU-Iran Relations in the Post-JCPOA Period: Selected Political Aspects", *Przegląd Politologiczny* (2018), nr 2, p. 153–163.

various problems and challenges. Unfortunately, decisions are also taken hastily, generating tensions and destabilizing the situation in the Middle East.

An example of the lack of realism in the approach towards Iran were the 12 'demands' put to Iran by the USA as a condition of the USA remaining as a signatory to the JCPOA. Secretary of State Michael Pompeo demanded various concessions from Iran, including the termination of Iran's ballistic missile development program, ending support for Hezbollah in Lebanon and Palestinian groups such as Hamas, allowing nuclear inspectors "unqualified access to all sites throughout the country," shutting down Iran's uranium enrichment program, ending involvement in Syria and Iraq and disarming Shi'ite militias.[27]

The lack of cooperation between Washington and allies on the Iranian issue, with the exception of Saudi Arabia and Israel, as well as hasty decision-making and a lack of consideration for the wider context of the Middle East region, unfortunately increases the risk of military intervention against Iran directly by the USA or Israel. If such an event were to occur, the expert opinions put forward in the past – that the costs of a war in Iran would far outweigh the benefits – are unlikely to be taken into consideration.

Conclusions

Before 1979, Iran was a strategic partner to the USA in the Persian Gulf. After the Islamic revolution, diplomatic relations between Washington and Tehran were broken off. This does not mean that all contacts were frozen. There are many examples of both sides acting pragmatically, such as by cooperating against the Taliban or Islamic State.

The core problem of US policy towards Iran is the lack of a coherent strategy. On the one hand, Washington would prefer a political change to precede any development of relations but, on the other hand, as in the case of the nuclear issue, sometimes *realpolitik* wins the day, such as the conducting of talks leading to the JCPOA. In US policy towards Iran, one can observe both extreme ideas and actions and much more practical ones, from sanctions to desire to bring about a political change in Iran.

In the case of the Iranian nuclear program, Washington's effectiveness in imposing sanctions on Iran was in ability to build a wide coalition to follow in

---

27 Manochehr Dorraj and Mahmood Monshipouri, *Trump's Iran Policy: From the Art of the Deal to the Mirage of Regime Change*, (14 June 2018): 26 June 2018 http://www.atlanticcouncil.org/blogs/iransource/trump-s-iran-policy-from-the-art-of-the-deal-to-the-mirage-of-regime-change.

this sanction policy. It took only a year of suffering the harmful effects resulting from these sanctions to bring Tehran back to the negotiating table, to cooperate more on the nuclear issue.

The military option, even limited to an air strike, may also have consequences that are difficult to imagine for global energy security. It also goes without saying that a land invasion would be fraught with difficulty, as Iran is a geographical fortress. Surrounded on three sides by mountains and on the fourth by the ocean, with a wasteland at its center, Iran is extremely difficult to conquer. Years ago, Saddam Hussein discovered this to his detriment during the Iraqi invasion; much Iranian land is swampy and easy to defend. Furthermore, not long after crossing into Iranian territory, any invading force would run into the Zagros Mountains.

The Trump administration has destroyed years of work and trust-building between the USA and Iran. Subsequent administrations may have to spend years rebuilding the credibility of the USA to a level at which it will be able to effectively cooperate with Iran on issues of regional security.

The costs of Washington ignoring Iran are too high. Iran plays a strategic role and one should look for a framework for cooperation and diplomatic solutions to crises, instead of contributing to new ones.

Bibliography

1. Bakhshandeh, Ehsan. "How Mainstream Iranian Newspapers Portray the West: The Influence of anti-Westernism and anti-Americanism", *Journal of International Communication*, 20:2, 2014, pp. 184–199.
2. Bajorczyk, Bartosz, „Stosunki ze Stanami Zjednoczonymi jako determinant polityki zagranicznej Islamskiej Republiki Iranu": Iran – 30 lat po rewolucji Seminarium Biura Bezpieczeństwa Narodowego 11 marca 2009 r. Biblioteka „Bezpieczeństwa Narodowego", quarterly published by Biuro Bezpieczeństwa Narodowego, 12, p. 60.
3. Rubin, Barry. *Paved with Good Intentions: The American Experience in Iran*, New York: Penguin, 1981.
4. Farzanega, Mohammad Reza, Hayo, Bernd. "Sanctions and the Shadow Economy: Empirical Evidence from Iranian Provinces", *Joint Discussion Paper Series in Economics*, 07-2018, pp. 1–5.
5. Fiedler, Radosław. "Hard Power Dismisses Soft Power – The United States' Relations with the Iranian Islamic Republic in the Shadow of the Nuclear Program", *Przegląd Politologiczny*, 3 2013, pp. 27–38.
6. Fiedler, Radosław. *Iran a reżim nieproliferacji broni jądrowej. Dylematy i wyzwania*, Poznan: Wydawnictwo Naukowe WNPiD, 2013.

7. Gasiorowski, Mark. "US Intelligence Assistance to Iran, May–October 1979", *Middle East Journal*, 66: 4, Autumn 2012, pp. 613–627.
8. Heinonen, Oli. "Iran's Nuclear Breakout Time: A Fact Sheet", *Policy Watch, Policy Analysis*, The Washington Institute, March 28, 2015.
9. Indyk, Marin, Fuller, Graham, Cordesman, Anthony. "Symposium on Dual Containment: US. Policy toward Iran and Iraq", *Middle East Policy*, Vol. *III*:1, 1994, pp. 1–2.
10. International Energy Statistics. Washington, DC: US Energy Information Administration. (14 June 2018) https://www.eia.gov/beta/international/country.php?iso=IRN
11. Jessen, Erik. "European Diplomacy in the Iran Nuclear Negotiations: What Impact Did It Have?" *Bruges Political Research Papers/Cahiers de recherche politique de Bruges*, 61, October 2017.
12. Kazemzadeh, Masoud. "U.S.–Iran Confrontation in the Post-NIE World: An Analysis of Alternative Policy Options", *Comparative Strategy*, 28:1, 2009, pp. 37–59.
13. Milani, Abbas. "U.S. Foreign Policy and the Future of Democracy in Iran", *The Washington Quarterly*, 28:3, 2005, pp. 41–56.
14. Osiewicz, Przemysław "EU-Iran Relations in the Post-JCPOA Period: Selected Political Aspects", *Przegląd Politologiczny*, 2018, 2, pp. 153–163.
15. Polk, William R. *Understanding Iran Everything You Need to Know, from Persia to the Islamic Republic from Cyrus to Ahmadinejad*, New York: Palgrave – Macmillan, 2008.
16. Pollack, Kenneth. *The Persian Puzzle: The Conflict between Iran and America*, New York: Random House, 2005.
17. Sullivan, William. *Mission to Iran*, New York: Norton, 1981.
18. Tabaar, Mohammad Ayatollahi. "Causes of the US Hostage Crisis in Iran: The Untold Account of the Communist Threat", *Security Studies*, 26:4, 2017, pp. 665–697.
19. Tarock, Adam. "The Iran Nuclear Deal: Winning a Little, Losing a Lot", *Third World Quarterly*, 37:8, 2016, pp. 1408–1424.
20. Wang, Bo. "The Conflict between US and Iran in Designing the Persian Gulf Security Order", *Journal of Middle Eastern and Islamic Studies*, 3:2, 2009, pp. 39–48.

Internet Sources

1. Dorraj, Manochehr, Monshipouri, Mahmood, *Trump's Iran Policy: From the Art of the Deal to the Mirage of Regime Change*, (14 June 2018), http://www.

atlanticcouncil.org/blogs/iransource/trump-s-iran-policy-from-the-art-of-the-deal-to-the-mirage-of-regime-change (26 June 2018).

2. Kershner, Isabel. *Israeli Strike on Iran Would Be 'Stupid,' Ex-Spy Chief Says*, https://www.nytimes.com/2011/05/09/world/middleeast/09israel.html (23 June 2018).
3. Nixon, Ron. *Two Large Multinationals Pull Back from Iran*, *"New York Times"*. March 10, 2010; http"//www.nytimes.com/2010/03/11/world/mieeast/11iran.html (10 June 2018).
4. Radwan, Katarzyna. "Efektywność sankcji amerykańskich w Iranie", Biuletyn Instytutu Zachodniego, Nr 172/2014; http://www.iz.poznan.pl/en/file,download,57,d187321db2ca961c4fd5f0503f8b9fd7/1075-sankcje.pdf (25 June 2018).
5. Remarks by Secretary of State Madeleine K. Albright on American–Iranian Relations, 17 March 2000, http://www.parstimes.com/history/albright_speech.html. (25 June 2018).
6. *Weighing Benefits and Costs of Military Action against Iran*, https://www.wilsoncenter.org/sites/default/files/IranReport_091112_FINAL.pdf (25 June 2018).

Rafał Ożarowski

What Is the Other Side of the Coin? Re-imposition of US Sanctions on Iran

Abstract: U.S. withdrawal from Joint Comprehensive Plan of Action (JCPOA) was defined as 'misguided' decision and implicated a lot of negative consequences. Flurry of condemnation hit President Trump and his administration and spread all over the U.S. and in the world. Close U.S. European allies felt deeply concerned about the step taken by Trump and then it was said about serious rift appeared in the relations between U.S. and Europe. Some states such as Israel or Saudi Arabia applauded greatly the President of U.S. for re-imposition sanctions on Iran what was particularly in their own interest.

Nevertheless, the decision over rejection of JCPOA had its justification, which is the title phrase – the other side of the coin. Sanctions are trusted method in U.S. policy to achieve different goals and U.S. is truly experienced with that. In particular, the most beneficial are smart sanctions which might be considered as coercive measures hitting the sanctioned state to a sufficient extent, simultaneously securing the global economy from decline or turmoil.

U.S. decided to restrict Iran's activity and expansion in the Middle East, what hardly collided with U.S. interests, at the expense of JCPOA which was regarded as 'worst deal ever negotiated'. Thus U.S. counts on Iran's economic decline followed by incapability of military and economic engagement in the Middle East.

Keywords: U.S. foreign policy, Iran, sanctions, Middle East, nuclear programme

When Donald Trump had become President of U.S, he decided to withdraw from Joint Comprehensive Plan of Action (JCPOA) named also a 'nuclear deal'. Actually he did what he exactly announced in his presidential campaign before the elections, calling the JCPOA as 'the worst deal ever negotiated'.

Although European signatories of JCPOA as France, Great Britain and Germany declared wide scepticism over rejection of the deal, Trump showed himself as strongly determined to put Iran against the wall. Thus Iran has been put in a political and economic deadlock. European Union did not tend to restrict mutual ties with Iran but under the U.S. pressure will not dare to support Iran at the expense of its own relations with U.S. China and Russia do not respect the U.S. decision but due to their own relations with U.S. and mutual inter-dependencies in different regions of the world, they cannot allow themselves to disregard Trump policy toward Iran. In that situation Iran is deprived of strong allies who would help him to survive under the sanctions without taking hard consequences. Facing the intensive economic decline Iran might be on the verge of internal disorder.

The aim of this chapter is to analyse the reasons of re-imposing the sanctions on Iran by U.S. and to explain motivations of American government in taking such decision. On the other side, comments and reactions in U.S. and throughout the world on Trump's decision are analysed.

The main thesis of the chapter is that U.S. has decided to take action against Iran in the way of imposing sanctions, determined by Iranian political expansion in the Middle East, e.g. in Syria, Lebanon, Yemen and Iraq what significantly collided with American interests in the region. In order to verify raised thesis two research questions have been put. First, how to explain beneficial dimension of sanctions in U.S. policy? Second, what were the main reasons of the U.S. government to impose sanctions again as a key method of fighting Iran's influences?

U.S. Sanctions on Iran: History and General Overview

U.S. sanctions on Iran has a long history. After the Shah's regime collapsed and Iran became Islamic republic, U.S. has taken an advantage of any occasion to restrict Iran in his political activity and aspirations. In the early 1980s on the strength of the Executive Order no.12170, all the Iranian property in U.S. was blocked, and Iran's assets rated at 12 billion USD was frozen in particular[1]. Outbreak of war between Iran and Iraq leaned U.S. government forward for more restricted sanctions, particularly referring to arms sales and spare parts for weapons of American origin still used by Iran's army. Partially because of Iran-Contra affair which emerged in public and revealed deals making with Iran under the authorization of CIA these measures did not restrict Iranian activity in the Middle East[2].

The U.S. sanctions policy toward Iran did not change even after ayatollah Ruhollah Khomeini's death in 1989 and the end of long-lasting and wasting war between Iran and Iraq. After the invasion of Kuwait by Saddam Hussein regime, the regional situation for Iran became more advantageous. However, U.S. administration still perceived Iran as a main enemy in the Middle East, and during the presidency of Ali Akbar Hashemi Rafsanjani even the sanctions were more strict than in the years of 1980. In 1992 U.S. Congress adopted Iran-Iraq Arms Non-Proliferation Act which opposed any transfer of goods or technology to both

---

1 See the full text of Executive Order No. 12170, Nov. 14, 1979, 44 F.R. 65729.

2 Ray Takeyh, Suzanne Maloney, "The self-limiting success of Iranian sanctions", *International Affairs*, 87:6, (2011), pp. 1297–1299.

states if it could contribute to Iran's or Iraq's acquisition of chemical, biological, nuclear or advanced conventional weapons[3].

In the 1990s President Bill Clinton tried also to induce reluctant European allies to respect sanctions on Iran. In its perception U.S. administration based on high level of economic cooperation with European States[4]. The efforts of President Clinton to drag European states into U.S. plan of sanctions were unsuccessful. Thus, Clinton issued two executive orders – Executive Order 12957 (March 1995), which banned U.S. investment in Iran's energy sector, and Executive Order 12959 (May 6, 1995), which banned U.S. trade with and investment in that country. Following these orders U.S. adopted Iran-Libya Sanctions Act in 1996 which obviously targeted at Iranian economy and was very harmful for all non-American companies which did not obey this regulation. Particularly, any company invested over 20 million USD in Iranian energy sector could have been sanctioned, what targeted Americans as same as non-U.S. companies[5].

In 1997 Mohammed Khatami became a president of Islamic Republic of Iran. His presidency envisaged more liberal approach in the foreign policy of Iran. Therefore sanctions became eased and U.S. had a little trust in Iran's attitude to changes in internal and external policy. It turned out quickly that named Khatami as a "liberal" was exaggerated and he was not able to implement himself any far-reaching changes. Thus, basing on the 11th of September 2001 al-Qaeda terrorist attacks on World Trade Center and Pentagon, President Gorge W. Bush announced the existence of "axis of evil" devoted to North Korea, Iraq and also Iran.

In the next years, Iran remained under U.S. sanctions and in 2006 under executive order of G.W. Bush when Libyan sanctions were lifted the sanction on Iran has been enacted as a "Iran Sanctions Act" firstly limited to five years. However, all existing sanction till 2010 had several drawbacks and U.S. was not able to fully enforce them. Yet, after new sanctions act accepted by Barack Obama the effectiveness of U.S. sanctions on Iran enhanced[6]. The Comprehensive Iran Sanctions, Accountability and Divestment Act (CISADA) strengthen U.S. sanctions on Iran

3 H.R. 5434 Iran-Iraq Arms Non-Proliferation Act of 1992, (1992): 17 Nov. 2018 https://www.congress.gov/bill/102nd-congress/house-bill/5434.

4 Takeyh, Maloney, "The self-limiting success of Iranian sanctions", p.1297–99

5 More about the ILSA provisions and its effectiveness see: Kenneth Katzman, The Iran-Libya Sanctions Act (ILSA) CRS Report for Congress, July 20, (2001): 18 Nov. 2018 https://www.globalsecurity.org/military/library/report/crs/rs20871.pdf.

6 Nikolay A. Kozhanov, "U.S. Economic Sanctions against Iran: Undermined by External Factors", *Middle East Policy*, vol. XVIII, no. 3, (2011), p. 146.

by limited access mainly to gasoline and petroleum products, petroleum-related investment, credit and financial services. What has also been noticed that Act authorised sanctions on any entity controlled another entities directly engaged in the activity related to business with Iran and also authorised US treasury Department to impose sanctions on foreign financial entities that engage in transactions with Iran. Thus the Act of 2010 had a great extraterritorial reach[7].

Consequently, United Nations Security Council adopted resolution No. 1984 (June 2011) that demanded ratifying Comprehensive Nuclear Test Ban Treaty (CTBT) by Iran and required also full cooperation with International Atomic Energy Agency (IAEA). The resolution extended the mandate of the Iran Sanctions Committee established in 2006 to control the implementation of UNSC resolutions (e.g. Resolution No. 1929). The resolution also banned foreign fiscal institutions to open branches and bank accounts in Iran what was in line with U.S. expectations. In the face of tightening sanctions European Union also took more active decisions and in 2012 imposed sanctions on Iran banning all Iranian oil export. Then U.S. froze assets of Central Bank of Iran in own state[8]. The action taken by EU was one of the most surprising. Oil was a core of Iranian export rated at 80 % what guaranteed government revenues at 50–60 %, and EU was one of Iran's largest customer (34 % of all Iranian oil export in 2010). Therefore, the sanctions imposed by EU increasingly affected Iranian economy.[9] In result of that, in 2013 sanctions reduced Iran's oil export to 1 million barrels per day comparing to the rate of 2,5 million barrels per day in 2011, and the oil revenues at that time decreased terribly, from 100 billion USD to 35 billion USD[10]. From that time on Iran's economy began to fall into a decline.

7 Carol J. Bilzi, Timothy J. Keeler, Simeon M. Kriesberg, "President Obama signs law imposing substantial new sanctions on business dealings with Iran", *Financial Regulation International*, July-August, Issue 13.6 (2010): 20 Nov. 2018, https://www.mayerbrown.com/files/Publication/cce75fd3-403b-4a9c-8dae-d449f767b095/Presentation/PublicationAttachment/5adc32cc-db42-4518-a86b-dbeb4057015f/Financial-Regulation-International-July-August-2010.pdf.

8 Farhad Rezaei, "Sanctions and Nuclear Rollback: The Case of Iran", *Middle East Policy*, No. 4, (2017), p. 80.

9 Matthew Kroenig, *A Time to Attack. The Looming Iranian Nuclear Threat* (New York, Palgrave Macmillan, 2014), pp. 73–74.

10 Rezaei, "Sanctions and Nuclear Rollback: The Case of Iran", p.10.

JCPOA and Its Conditions

When Hassan Rouhani was elected as President in 2013, he quickly started to lay ground for negotiations with U.S. and other states to get Iran out of sanctions deadlock. In October 2013 the Geneva meeting of P5+1 (UN Security Council permanent members plus Germany – biggest trade Iranian partner) and Iran was held. At the conference all parties reach an agreement known as interim accord which was a first step in the right direction to conclude more "comprehensive" pact. Iran promised to restrict its nuclear programme instead of sanctions relief[11].

After taking the first step, the next one was taken in March and April 2015 in Lausanne when Iran with P5+1 group along with EU reached compromise on key parameters of "nuclear deal"[12]. Finally, on 14 July 2015 after the meeting in Vienna, "Joint Comprehensive Plan of Action" (JCPOA) was announced.

According to provisions in JCPOA and five annexes, Iran was mainly obliged to: reduce number of centrifuges to around 6000 and dismantle advanced centrifuges with the exception of Natanz; keep 300 kg as maximum stockpile of 3,67 % enriched uranium and sell the rest of enriched uranium and store abroad; reduce possibility of nuclear research to one centre in Natanz; remove and disable the original core in Arak reactor and replace it with modernised reactor certified by Joint Commission; not to reprocess of spent nuclear fuel; dismantle heavy water reactors for 15 years and not to accumulate heavy water in Iran for the same period; to have approval of Joint Commission for purchasing all dual-use materials; to accept 25 years of supervision by Joint Commission consisted of P+1, EU and Iran with eight votes[13].

Consequently Iran accomplished initial requirements and JCPOA in February 2016 was implemented. Thus, U.S. and EU sanctions were gradually lifted. In case of U.S. it concerned mainly the sanctions against oil and banking system, removing designation of certain entities and individuals, allowing for licensed non-U.S. entities owned or controlled by U.S. individual to engage more openly

11 Matthew Kroenig, "Now for the Hard Part", *Foreign Policy*, November 24, (2013): 20 Nov. 2018 https://foreignpolicy.com/2013/11/24/now-for-the-hard-part/.

12 Eric Bradner, "What's in the Iran nuclear deal? 7 key points", CNN politics, April 2, (2015): 23 Nov. 2018 https://edition.cnn.com/2015/04/02/politics/iran-nuclear-deal-main-points-of-agreement/.

13 Joint Comprehensive Plan of Action, Vienna 14 July (2015): 25 Nov. 2018 full text: https://www.state.gov/e/eb/tfs/spi/iran/jcpoa/; Joint Comprehensive Plan of Action (JCPOA) at Glance, Arms Control Association, May (2018): 25 Nov. 2018https://www.armscontrol.org/factsheets/JCPOA-at-a-glance.

in activities with Iran; allowing for sale of commercial passenger aircraft to Iran. However, sanctions targeted human rights, terrorism, missile activities and nuclear-related issues remained in force. Simultaneously, UN also remained in force terminated sanctions on heavy arms for 5 years and ballistic missile for 8 years[14].

Initially, after the implementation of JCPOA, the international community praised the U.S. and all participants for signing "nuclear deal" and had a great conviction that the case of Iran was an example of peaceful resolution of conflict over the issue of proliferation of nuclear weapon. Delivering Iranian oil to EU has been restored which significantly increased mutual trade balance. U.S. companies declared interest in Iranian market including Boeing with presaging well prognosis. After sanctions relief, Iranian GDP growth in 2016 was rated at 13,6 % and nominal GDP of Iran notably boosted and in 2016 was estimated at 418,98 billion USD compared to 385,87 billion USD in the previous year[15].

U.S. Rejection of JCPOA: Comments and Reactions

President Donald Trump during his election campaign often reiterated pulling out of 'nuclear deal' with Iran. In his ferocious rhetoric Iran was depicted as a 'rough state' and the JCPOA negotiated during Barack Obama presidency named as 'worst deal ever negotiated' which was sort of a disgrace for America. Thus, election of Trump as a president seriously put 'nuclear deal' on a trembling ground. At the beginning of his presidency, Trump shared with Republicans in the Congress harsh objection to 'nuclear deal'. Likewise, even before the election campaign started, he had promised at the meeting with pro-Israeli lobby group to dismantle the disastrous deal with Iran[16].

At that time, many experts did not share Trump's decision about deal with Iran and warned of consequences. Suzanne Maloney – expert at Brookings Institution – pointed that the biggest winner would be Iranian clergy leader ayatollah Khamenei who would open the door for rejecting the 'nuclear deal' commitments and then shift the blame on the U.S. government. Zachary Goldman from the Center of Law and Security at New York University, quoted by

---

14 Joint Comprehensive Plan of Action (JCPOA) at Glance

15 Iran – Economic Indicators: 25 Nov. 2018 https://tradingeconomics.com/iran/indicators.

16 Yeganeh Torbati, "Trump election puts Iran nuclear deal in a shaky ground", December 9, (2016): 27 Nov. 2018 https://www.reuters.com/article/us-usa-election-trump-iran/trump-election-puts-iran-nuclear-deal-on-shaky-ground-idUSKBN13427E.

Y. Torbati, also underlined the negative implications of U.S. 'nuclear deal' rejection as the worst decision which would allow Iran to come back to its nuclear programme with the U.S. responsibility for this[17].

However, if one takes a closer look at the JCPOA arrangements, it was not a document free of flaws and vagueness. JCPOA somehow allowed Iran to carry on his research on nuclear weapon even abiding by the agreement. JCPOA also loosened sanctions on numerous issues in exchange just in one Iranian limitation even if it is a critical one. Additionally 'nuclear deal' proposed lifting the sanctions on nuclear restrictions, which was the crucial one, with definite time limit from 6 months to 13 years. It led to conclusion that JCPOA could have been saved by advocates or fixed by elimination of flaws by critics[18]. The problem was that Trump did not want to hear about fixing the deal and the rejection of JCPOA was the only option. Considering that, any attempts to modify 'nuclear deal', what would not be easy at all, could turn execution of the agreement into chaotic set of regulations. Such an action would also demonstrate the weakness and unreliability of the U.S. government which agreed for something what should have been reconsidered many times before that. From the other side, Trump's personality and his business experience showed his tendency to seeking compromises but under his conditions.

Finally, in May 2018 Trump announced U.S. withdrawal from JCPOA. International community expected such a decision for a long while, so it did not make any surprise. However, just after Trump's declaration analysts embarked on considering next steps after rejection of JCPOA. American experts like Suzanne Maloney, Natan Sachs or Bruce Riedel were deeply concerned about the future relations with allies and the position of U.S. in the international politics, especially that rejection of JCPOA was decided without any negotiations with key European partners who had signed 'nuclear deal' too. S. Maloney put an open question – how after Trump's announcement was the USA safer? In result, it was really hard to point out any advantages of refusing JCPOA but the benefits for Saudi Arabia as a harsh enemy of Iran, with one of the key ruler Mohammad bin Salman, heir apparent of Saudi dynasty and also Israel, one of the biggest critic of JCPOA[19].

---

17 Torbati, "Trump election puts Iran nuclear deal in a shaky ground".

18 Michael Singh, "Here's Where Advocates and Critics of the Iran Nuke Deal Can Agree", *Foreign Policy*, February 5, (2018): 27 Nov. 2018 https://foreignpolicy.com/2018/02/05/heres-where-advocates-and-critics-of-the-iran-nuke-deal-can-agree/.

19 Around the Halls: Brookings experts discuss the implications of President Trump's Iran nuclear deal announcement, May 8, (2018): 1 Dec. 2018, https://www.brookings.edu/blog/order-from-chaos/2018/05/08/

Lack of strategy among U.S. decision-makers became another key issue widely discussed by experts. Taking a crucial decision needs to have alternatives how to act in a further process. S. Maloney stated that rejecting of JCPOA was 'consequential decision of his [D. Trump] unconventional presidency' and 'dismantling of an agreement that was the product of more than a decade of intense diplomacy and economic pressure marks staggeringly counterproductive step'[20].

World political leaders were divided about Trump's announcement. Unrelenting enemies of Iran as Saudi Arabia, Israel or even United Arab Emirates mostly welcomed U.S. President's decision. Crucial NATO allies – France, Great Britain and Germany deeply regret that U.S. decided to leave JCPOA and called for maintaining conditions of 'nuclear deal' between three European signatories. Great dissatisfaction with the U.S. act was expressed by Frederica Mogherini, High Representative of the Union for Foreign Affairs and Security Policy who was an ardent advocate of preserving the deal[21].

Russia and China, states cooperating closely with Iran, certainly did not accept U.S move towards Iran and declared the deal was still in force. Obviously Iran was shocked, although leaders and the Iranian society were prepared for such predicament, and announced that all arrangements in the deal were maintained.

Flurry of critics was revealed also in the U.S. among former leading politicians. Barack Obama stated that withdrawal from the 'nuclear deal' was a 'misguided' decision and was equal with turning back on closest American allies[22]. Former Secretary of State John Kerry also issued a statement on U.S. walking away from the deal. He stated that decision over withdrawal implicated number of things but none of them was good. It weakened U.S. security, broke American word,

---

around-the-halls-brookings-experts-discuss-the-implications-of-president-trumps-iran-nuclear-deal-announcement/.

20 Suzanne Maloney, "After dumping the nuclear deal, Trump has no strategy for Iran", May 9, (2018): 1 Dec. 2018 https://www.brookings.edu/blog/order-from-chaos/2018/05/09/after-dumping-the-nuclear-deal-trump-has-no-strategy-for-iran/.

21 World leaders react to US withdrawal from Iranian nuclear deal, Al Jazeera, May 9, (2018): 1 Dec. 2018 https://www.aljazeera.com/news/2018/05/world-leaders-react-withdrawal-iranian-nuclear-deal-180508184130931.html.

22 Christal Hayes, "Obama: Trump withdrawing from Iran deal is 'serious mistake', turns our backs on U.S. allies", USA Today, May 8, (2018): 3 Dec. 2018 https://eu.usatoday.com/story/news/politics/2018/05/08/obama-trumps-iran-deal-decision-serious-mistake-risks-credibility-u-s/591974002/.

isolated U.S. from European allies, empowered Iran hardliners and devastated the U.S. ability of leading negotiations[23].

Is There the Other Side of the Coin? Reasons for Trump's Withdrawal from Nuclear Deal

It looked as if the decision taken by President Trump was not considered well and could be regarded as a consequence of declared words during presidential campaign. When Trump had become a president he was not willing to break promises made to his voters. Therefore, a lot of critics charged Trump and his Republican advocates with destructive activity lacking of any strategy what might have been connected just with satisfaction given to Trump's electoral ranks.

One can definitely agree that announcement of JCPOA withdrawal seemingly resembled impulsive decision taken by someone who was not conscious of its consequences. However, politics is an intentional activity and it is hard to believe in ill-considered decision taken by Trump. Thus, is there the other side of the coin?

First of all, sanctions are common measures used by the U.S. and they are still useful mean to achieve something as same as can be achieved by war but with no necessity to declare the war. That was the reason why sanctions became a permanent element of U.S strategy during the Cold War and after the collapse of bipolar system. Before the JCPOA was concluded sanctions on Iran created desired effect. Due to the declining economy Iran was put under heavy pressure and then Iranian leaders were forced to seek solution to get out of the predicament, thus they decided to negotiate a deal.

The U.S has a remarkable experience in using coercive measures, and they significantly developed the ways of having benefits as state-imposing sanctions. It is inevitably connected with two basic assets U.S. exclusively has. First is the global dominance of U.S. dollar, and the second is flexibility of U.S legal authorities which allows the Treasury Department to mind sanctions, update them or propose corrections if necessary. In this case U.S.' position is unique what enables to explain the effectiveness of U.S. sanctions on Iran in the past and these imposed on Russia when the conflict in Ukraine broke out.[24]. Additionally U.S. developed the skill of using sanctions very smartly. According to that, sanctions must be

23 Nik De Costa – Klipa, "Here's how John Kerry responded to Trump's decision to pull out of the Iran nuclear deal", May 8, (2018): 3 Dec. 2018 https://www.boston.com/news/politics/2018/05/08/john-kerry-iran-deal-trump-withdrawal.

24 Edward Fishman, "Ever Smarter Sanctions. How to Fight in the Era of Economic Warfare", *Foreign Affairs*, November/December, (2017), pp. 102–104.

precise and not shake the global economy as a side effect. Therefore sanctions on Russia targeted mainly state-business and were restricted to selected branches. That is the way of making sanctions most beneficial and simultaneously most harmful for the opponent[25].

In August 2018 first part of sanctions on Iran had been re-imposed which included restrictions on Iran's purchase of U.S. dollars, Iran's trade in gold and other precious metals and the sale to Iran of auto parts, commercial passenger aircraft and related parts and devices. In November 2018, second part of sanctions came into force, including restrictions of selling of oil and petrochemical products from Iran[26]. However, in accordance with the idea of smart sanctions, the restrictions hit precisely the most vulnerable sectors of Iranian economy but with preservation of global economic stability. Therefore Iran's oil sale is still reserved for its biggest customers (China, Japan, South Korea, India, Taiwan, Italy, Greece and Turkey) with the U.S consent for another 180 days. Having that waiver correlated with oil market stability was confirmed by President Trump saying that "I could get the Iran oil down to zero immediately but it would cause a shock to the market. I don't want to lift oil prices"[27].

As general overview on U.S withdrawal of JCPOA was talked over, it is noteworthy to explain the real reasons of Trump's decision over re-imposing the coercive measures on Iran.

First, the U.S. did not accept Iranian military and political engagement in the Middle East and hitting in this way American crucial interest in this region. Iranian expansion in Syria, Yemen or Lebanon was undermining U.S. policy and its allies such as Israel, Saudi Arabia or UAE. Re-imposed sanctions will bring about economic decline of Iran and then due to the lack of financial ability Iran will not be capable of maintaining its financial and military support in the Middle East. The U.S. is aware of power of sanctions as the only measure to achieve aims related to Iranian issue.

Second, President Trump and his administration must have calculated that staying with JCPOA, which obviously significantly restricted Iranian nuclear programme but did not make anything about Iranian military and political

---

25 Fishman, "Ever Smarter Sanctions. How to Fight in the Era of Economic Warfare", p. 104.

26 The Return of U.S. Sanctions on Iran: What to Know, Council on Foreign Relations, August 6, (2018): 3 Dec. 2018 https://www.cfr.org/article/return-us-sanctions-iran-what-know.

27 Trump allows Iran to continue selling oil to its 8 biggest customers, NBC News, November 5, (2018): 3 Dec. 2018 https://www.nbcnews.com/news/world/trump-allows-iran-continue-selling-oil-its-8-biggest-customers-n931891.

activity and expansion, was unprofitable. In this case, U.S. was considered as a state which deluded itself that the deal with Iran was of a great importance.

Third, re-imposing sanctions on Iran will hit his allies in the Middle East indirectly. Declining economically, Iran would become a weak link in the 'triangle' – Russia–Iran–Syria. For this reason Iran's ineffective activity in the Middle East would also diminish Russian influence capability. In the face of current U.S.–Russian rivalry, re-imposing sanctions on Iran has an extraordinary meaning.

Conclusion

After Trump had been elected as president, U.S. put more impact on particular interests at the expense of relations with allies or agreements signed in the past. Complying with the notion "America first", Trump considered JCPOA as a 'bad mistake' or deal which should not have been ever negotiated which directly hit American interests in the Middle East and in the relation with Iran. Therefore, decision over withdrawal from JCPOA was part of Trump's wider action of hitting the enemies (including Iran) and then trying to negotiate with them for agreements but under U.S. conditions.

Trump and his administration calculated that better option is to impose sanctions than stay with the 'nuclear deal'. In face of Iranian expansion in the Middle East, in Syria or Yemen in particular, U.S. being a part of JCPOA would have their hand tied and could do nothing effective in order to stop Iran's military and economic expansion. Therefore, re-imposition of sanctions probably will enable U.S. to restrict Iran's activity and its capability to use military and economic factor in the Middle East. Then U.S. will have a great opportunity to expand their control over Middle East.

Bibliography

1. Fishman, Edward, "Even Smarter Sanctions. How to Fight in the Era of Economic Warfare", *Foreign Affairs*, November/December, (2017), pp. 102–110.
2. Kozhanov, Nikolay A., "U.S. Economic Sanctions against Iran: Undermined by External Factors", *Middle East Policy*, vol. XVIII, No.3, (2011), pp. 144–160.
3. Kroenig, Matthew, *A Time to Attack. The Looming Iranian Nuclear Threat*, New York, Palgrave Macmillan, 2014.
4. Rezaei, Farhad, "Sanctions and Nuclear Rollback: The Case of Iran", *Middle East Policy*, vol. XXIV, No.4, (2017), pp. 74–90.
5. Takeyh, Ray, Maloney, Suzanne, "The Self-Limiting Success of Iranian Sanctions", *International Affairs*, vol. 87, No.6, (2011), pp. 1297–1312.

Internet Sources

1. Around the Halls: Brookings experts discuss the implications of President Trump's Iran nuclear deal announcement, May 8, 2018, https://www.brookings.edu/blog/order-from-chaos/2018/05/08/around-the-halls-brookings-experts-discuss-the-implications-of-president-trumps-iran-nuclear-deal-announcement/ (1 Dec. 2018).
2. Bilzi, Carol J., Keeler Timothy J., Kriesberg, Simeon M., "President Obama signs law imposing substantial new sanctions on business dealings with Iran", Financial Regulation International, July–August, Issue 13.6, 2010, https://www.mayerbrown.com/files/Publication/cce75fd3-403b-4a9c-8dae-d449f767b095/Presentation/PublicationAttachment/5adc32cc-db42-4518-a86b-dbeb4057015f/Financial-Regulation-International-July-August-2010.pdf. (20 Nov. 2018).
3. Bradner, Eric, "What's in the Iran nuclear deal? 7 key points", CNN politics, April 2, 2015. https://edition.cnn.com/2015/04/02/politics/iran-nuclear-deal-main-points-of-agreement/ (23 Nov. 2018).
4. De Costa – Klipa, Nik, "Here's how John Kerry responded to Trump's decision to pull out of the Iran nuclear deal", May 8, 2018, https://www.boston.com/news/politics/2018/05/08/john-kerry-iran-deal-trump-withdrawal (3 Dec. 2018).
5. Hayes, Christal, "Obama: Trump withdrawing from Iran deal is 'serious mistake', turns our backs on U.S. allies", USA Today, May 8, 2018, https://eu.usatoday.com/story/news/politics/2018/05/08/obama-trumps-iran-deal-decision-serious-mistake-risks-credibility-u-s/591974002/ (3 Dec. 2018).
6. H.R. 5434 Iran-Iraq Arms Non-Proliferation Act of 1992, https://www.congress.gov/bill/102nd-congress/house-bill/5434 (17 Nov. 2018).
7. Iran – Economic Indicators, https://tradingeconomics.com/iran/indicators (25 Nov. 2018).
8. Joint Comprehensive Plan of Action, Vienna July 14, 2015, https://www.state.gov/e/eb/tfs/spi/iran/jcpoa/ (25 Nov. 2018).
9. Joint Comprehensive Plan of Action (JCPOA) at Glance, Arms Control Association, May, 2018, https://www.armscontrol.org/factsheets/JCPOA-at-a-glance (25 Nov. 2018).
10. Katzman, Kenneth, The Iran-Libya Sanctions Act (ILSA) CRS Report for Congress, July 20, 2001, https://www.globalsecurity.org/military/library/report/crs/rs20871.pdf (18 Nov. 2018).
11. Kroenig, Matthew, "Now for the hard part", Foreign Policy, November 24, 2013. https://foreignpolicy.com/2013/11/24/now-for-the-hard-part/ (20 Nov. 2018).

12. Maloney, Suzanne, "After dumping the nuclear deal, Trump has no strategy for Iran", May 9, 2018, https://www.brookings.edu/blog/order-from-chaos/2018/05/09/after-dumping-the-nuclear-deal-trump-has-no-strategy-for-iran/ (1 Dec. 2018).
13. Singh, Michael, "Here's where advocates and critics of the Iran Nuke Deal can agree", Foreign Policy, February 5, 2018, https://foreignpolicy.com/2018/02/05/heres-where-advocates-and-critics-of-the-iran-nuke-deal-can-agree/ (27 Nov. 2018).
14. The Return of U.S. Sanctions on Iran: What to Know, Council on Foreign Relations, August 6, 2018, https://www.cfr.org/article/return-us-sanctions-iran-what-know (3 Dec. 2018).
15. Torbati, Yeganeh, "Trump election puts Iran nuclear deal in a shaky ground", December 9, 2016, https://www.reuters.com/article/us-usa-election-trump-iran/trump-election-puts-iran-nuclear-deal-on-shaky-ground-idUSKBN13427E (27 Nov. 2018).
16. Trump allows Iran to continue selling oil to its 8 biggest customers, NBC News, November 5, 2018, https://www.nbcnews.com/news/world/trump-allows-iran-continue-selling-oil-its-8-biggest-customers-n931891 (3 Dec. 2018).
17. World leaders react to US withdrawal from Iranian nuclear deal, Al Jazeera, May 9, 2018, https://www.aljazeera.com/news/2018/05/world-leaders-react-withdrawal-iranian-nuclear-deal-180508184130931.html (1 Dec. 2018).

Hadi Ajili, Mohammed Oliaei, and Javad Nori

The Review of Stabilizing and Crisis Building of Iran and Saudi Arabia in Middle East

Abstract: The regional conflict between Saudi Arabia and Iran has brought about so many misunderstandings. These misunderstandings sometimes interpret parties sometimes for stability and sometimes for crisis. By looking at the situation in countries such as Yemen, Syria, and Iraq, they are exposing both sides to various opposing positions. Saudi Arabia, with the support of terrorist groups, is trying to contain Iran's strategic depth and make itself a regional hub. This policy goes hand in hand with the support of the United States and some Western powers, and the Islamic Republic of Iran as a milestone in the fight against terrorist groups has been able to maintain the stability of the region. The hypothesis of this study is that the Islamic Republic of Iran as a crisis ceasing and stabilizing country in contrast with Saudi Arabia which is a tension making and an interfering country in regional security system. The methodology of research according to the subject is qualitative and is done in library research tool.

Keywords: Saudi Arabia, Iran, West Asia, intervention, crisis, stabilization

Introduction

From the point of view of international politics, the crisis is related to the incidents that governments have some interests. Although in the complex world of international relations, it is difficult to draw a line between domestic and international crises, as we are seeing, domestic crises are quickly becoming international and transnational issue and supranational actors become involved. For example, in the subject that we are discussing, Saudi Arabia involves in shaping many of the internal crises in the region. In sum, there is no comprehensive definition of the crisis, and each one of the researchers by taking into account some characteristics of an incident _ acuteness for instance _ called it a crisis. Some systemic thinkers consider the crisis to be a serious blow to the international system that removes it from balance. On the other hand, based on the decision method, there are three factors of threat, time, and surprise that determine the criticality of an event and its severity.[1]

1 Kazemi, A. *International crisis management* (Tehran: Political and International Studies Office, 1987), p. 77.

What is important is that according to any one of the above approaches, it is Saudi Arabia that is creating a crisis in the region. The Saudis made the foreign powers to meddle in the region and with their frequent and illegal interference in the affairs of the Arab and Islamic countries, as well as starting an illegitimate war in Yemen, caused a severe blow to the regional security system. In recent days, we witnessed a rare phenomenon that Saudi Arabia held arresting the Lebanese Prime Minister in Riyadh and forcing him to resign which was going to ignite a crisis in susceptible Lebanon.

The reasons for the deep divisions between Iran and Saudi Arabia are basically upon regional rivalries; from the Nixon-Kissinger two-column doctrine, which puts Saudi Arabia and Iran in charge of securing the region, especially the Persian Gulf, up to now that some signs of reconciliation between Iran and the United States was heard, Saudi Arabia was competing with Iran over regional influence. Saudi Arabia's concern over the Islamic Republic of Iran is strategic rather than tactical. There is plenty of evidences for this. For example, in the case of Iran's nuclear talks with the so-called "5 + 1" countries, we have repeatedly seen the Saudis were trying sabotage talks. In fact, the country tries to revive its leadership in the region and strongly opposes the rise of the Islamic Republic or the developments that lead to this. Now, by determination of the victorious side of the war in the Syrian crisis, Iran must be aware of the post-crisis era and should have a comprehensive plan for this critical period.

Turkey, Qatar, Saudi Arabia, the United Arab Emirates, Egypt, Israel, France, and the United States and Britain have almost similar look at Syria. They all called for the overthrow of Bashar al-Assad, but now, with the continuation of Iran's ally in Syria, all of these countries have been severely disputed multilaterally and bilaterally. Today, in addition to Iran and Saudi Arabia rivalry over regional influence, Saudi's see Turkey and Israel as rivals over its "hegemony power" ahead. Indeed, Saudi's regionalism focuses on supporting regional terrorism (groups like ISIL and al-Qaeda) and large and small countries in the Southwest Asia (Middle East) region. Saudi Arabia is in an all-out war with Yemen, and meddles in internal affairs of Lebanon, Iraq, and most importantly instigates the crisis in Syria; in these countries Saudi's see Iran as a bulk power that should be contained. Both countries use same geopolitical model to expand their influence in the region. Martyrdom of the Iranian diplomat in Yemen, the explosion of the Iranian embassy in Beirut, the domination of the ISIL group in north of Iraq, the various crises in Lebanon, Syria, etc, are the tip of the iceberg in Saudi interferences in the region under the pretext of Iran's influence in these areas. Many aspects of this complex conflict are unclear and require time to be revealed. Accordingly, in this chapter, we have tried to point out some of the important examples of Iranian-Saudi rivalries and the behavior that each of them has shown in these cases.

Reviewing the Positions of Iran and Saudi Arabia in the Crisis of Turkey

The coup began with the deployment of a Turkish army at the entrance to the Bosphorus Bridge in Istanbul and blockade of the road. Immediately, Turkish news became a top news story in world. Thereafter, there were the news of the shooting in Ankara and the flight of fighters were at low altitudes, but the Army forces were able to capture only limited hours of control of the state-owned TRT TV and Istanbul Ataturk Airport. Only a few hours later, Turkish authorities reported the failure of the coup, about 160 people were killed and 1,404 injured and 2839 others arrested.[2]

Saudi Arabia's Position

In this regard, various studies indicate that, in a cynical manner, the Saudi authorities played a direct role in the coup and coordinated with some Turkish citizens during the days before the coup.[3] The optimistic view is that the Saudis took a silent stand on this and did not support the government of Ankara. Qatar's former ambassador pointed out this issue.[4]

This is one of the most important evidence to prove the destabilizing policies of the Saudi kingdom in the region. Interestingly, the officials in the country pretend to have good relations with Turkey as well, but as mentioned at this critical moment, they acted against Erdogan. This policy also seems to be due to the widespread cooperation of Al Saud with the West and, in particular, the United States, which has made Saudi Arabia an agent for their interests in the Middle East.

2 Mehdi Shakibaei, "Did Saudi Arabia play a role in Turkey's coup?", Farda News Agency, 15 Jul. 2016. www.farda.fr/002HTG.

3 Mehdi Shakibaei, "Did Saudi Arabia play a role in Turkey's coup?", Farda News Agency, 15 Jul. 2016. www.farda.fr/002HTG.

4 Tom Finn, "Qatar says denounces military coup attempt in Turkey: state media", Reuters, Doha, 16 Jul. 2016. https://www.reuters.com/article/us-turkey-security-qatar-idUSKCN0ZV2Y6.

The Position of the Islamic Republic

Unlike the Saudi government, Iran took supportive stance for the legal government of Turkey in this internal crisis. The Iranian support was so generous that the Turkish officials praised and appreciated this position. In an interview with Sputnik, Farzad Ramezani Bonesh, an international and regional policy expert, said that if Iran did not support Turkey, the whole region, including Iran, would be affected. So it is clear that Tehran reacted well: "If we take a look at the relationship between Iran and Turkey over the past two years, we will see a significant improvement. Before the coup crisis it was a growing tension between these two countries but thereafter we witness significant positive change in their relations. In fact, we are now witnessing the mutual interests of these two countries.[5] It can be seen that Iran is considering regional stability and peace and security before considering regional competition, and this is the main difference between the policies of Iran and Saudi Arabia.

The Crisis between the Gulf States and Qatar

Saudi Government Measures

In case of Qatar blockade, Saudi and its allies are trying to destabilize this country to force Qatar to change its foreign policy agenda, and to achieve this purpose, they imposed massive terrestrial and aerial blockade. Rooting in the past; in the Arab Spring _the so-called Islamic Awakening _ the Saudis were deeply dissatisfied with Qataris positions, and eventually their force was one of the reasons of the Qatari Emir's resignation.[6] The new Emir emphasized on more independent foreign policy, and this led to a crisis with Saudi Arabia. About this crisis and Saudi's actions, the Emir of Qatar said to CBS channel "In this blocked, students were kicked out from those countries, Patients were kicked out from hospitals." "Our sovereignty is a red line. We don't accept anybody interfering

---

5 Marina Al-Shaalan, "Iran supported Turkey during coup", Sputnik news Agency, 16 Jul. 2017. https://ir.sputniknews.com/iran/201707162680858-%D8%AD%D9%85%D8%A7%DB%8C%D8%AA-%D8%A7%DB%8C%D8%B1%D8%A7%D9%86-%D8%AA%D8%B1%DA%A9%DB%8C%D9%87/.

6 Max Fisher, "How the Saudi-Qatar Rivalry, Now Combusting, Reshaped the Middle East" New York Times, 13 June 2017. https://www.nytimes.com/2017/06/13/world/middleeast/how-the-saudi-qatar-rivalry-now-combusting-reshaped-the-middle-east.html.

our sovereignty." He also added: "They don't like our independence, the way how we are thinking, our vision for the region," Qatari Minister of Foreign Affairs Mohammed bin Abdulrahman Al Thani told CNBC on October 2017 that Saudi Arabia is currently trying to destabilize the leadership of Qatar. "We see (Saudi) government officials talking about regime change. We see officials inciting the people to go and protest their government, so it is about regime change," he said. "We see a country that is bringing back the dark ages of tribes and putting them together in order to create a pressure on connected tribes in Qatar," the minister added.

Qatar's Minister of State for Foreign Affairs Sultan bin Saad al-Muraikhi during Arab Foreign Ministers meeting in September 2017 said: "Even the animals were not spared, you {Saudi and allies} sent them out savagely," referring to the thousands of camels left stranded on the border between Qatar and Saudi Arabia after borders were closed. He referred to Iran as an "honorable country" and said ties had warmed with its neighbor since the blockade. Many Western analysts warned Saudis that continuation of the crisis will maximize Iran's interests. [7]

Iran's Policy in Qatar's Crisis

In contrast, the Islamic Republic of Iran, aware of Qatar's aggressive actions in the region which was against its national interests, and in spite of rivalries in energy and extraction of oil and gas, supported the Qatari government. In Qatar crisis the Iranians have taken the diplomatic high ground, advocating cooperation in the region_ and offering food and airspace to the Qataris. Emir of Qatar said: "Iran from the very beginning of the blockade supported Qatar's stability and sovereignty." He also in an interview with CBS channel in the USA said: "More than 90 percent of our goods, food, medicine comes from this country." Iranian Foreign Ministry spokesman Bahram Qassemi, "calls on all the neighbors involved in the current disputes in the southern Persian Gulf region to learn lessons from the past bitter experiences of the region… show utmost restraint and move toward reducing tensions and returning to tranquility."

In August 2017, the Qatari government announced the expansion of its bilateral ties to the Islamic Republic of Iran in all areas and after a phone conversation between Qatar and Iran's foreign ministers, the Doha ambassador returned

7 Shahir Shahidsaless, "Saudi-led Blockade of Qatar Could Boost Iran". Atlantic Council, 10 Jul. 2017. http://www.atlanticcouncil.org/blogs//iransource/saudi-led-blockade-of-qatar-could-boost-iran-2.

to Tehran. This was a remarkable victory for Iran and a major advancement in its efforts to normalize relations with Gulf Cooperation Council countries. The normalization of relations between Iran and Qatar is likely to have significant consequences in resolving the Syrian crisis. Iran and Qatar had opposite positions in the Syrian crisis, but after the Gulf crisis, Qataris reduced its support to the opposition groups of Bashar al-Assad. What matters to the Iranian foreign policy ministry is that the development of its relations with Qatar coincides with the improvement of its relationship with Turkey. Saudi Arabia's sanctions against Qatar have also brought together the position of Iran and Turkey.

Terrorism and Takfir

By taking a look at the origins of the Takfiris in the region, we will always see the footprint of Saudi Arabia's Wahhabi doctrines. For example, in the memoirs of Ayman Dean, a former member of al-Qaeda, he repeatedly mentions that Wahhabi scholars and clergies are instigating people to join extremist groups, who are mostly from the Arabian Peninsula. He says he was deeply influenced by their speeches and ideas, and they were the ones who revived the Takfir flames (as he calls it Jihad) in his heart. There are lots of similar stories that can be added to Ayman Dean story.[8]

In recent years events in Islamic countries, especially in Iraq and Syria, we can clearly see the Saudi agents who are acting against the central governments of these countries. For example, in various wars against ISIL in these countries, there were Saudi weapons, money, equipment, and troops in terrorists' havens. In the days when the Iraqi people were eager to evict ISIL from the city of Mosul, Iraq's second-largest city, there were also documents of al-Saud's treachery in the region. Their covert support from this terrorist group, sought to prevent their early defeat in Iraq.[9] Senator Charles Schumer said at a US House of Representatives meeting to prohibit the sale of weapons to Saudi Arabia:

> "The human rights and humanitarian concerns have been well documented and are important: of equal concern to me is that the Saudi government continues to aid and

8 John-Paul Leonard, "ISIS IS US: The Shocking Truth: Behind the Army of Terror". (Progressive Press; 2016)

9 "150 Saudi intelligence officers joined Daesh in Mosul battle: Report", Press TV, 14 Jul. 2017. https://www.presstv.com/DetailFr/2017/07/14/528389/Saudi-intelligence-officers-Daesh-Takfiri-militants-assistance-Mosul-Iraqi-army-soldiers.

abet terrorism via its relationship with Wahhabism and the funding of schools that spread extremist propaganda throughout the world," Schumer said in a statement.[10]

The fact is that as studies show the Islamic Republic of Iran's actions are_ incomparable with the Saudi Arabia. Despite all the propaganda against Iran, no one can claim that this country has exported terrorism to the world, while this is true about Saudi Arabia. The performance of Iran has been completely unlike the Saudis. The Islamic Republic in different stages_ for example, the crisis in Afghanistan, the Syrian crisis, the Iraq crisis, etc._ helped the central governments and declared war against terrorists.

This is a very clear issue but many officials tend to ignore it. If they admit it, there will be no excuse to confront Iranian politics. Almost all regional and international actors in the region acknowledge that Iran is the best acting force against Takfiris.[11] Now, one has to ask which of the two countries, Iran or Saudi Arabia, is the cause of peace or instability in the region. "We know where the terrorists come from. We know the nationality of those who attacked the twin towers of the global trade, I can tell you that neither of them was Iranians." Foreign Minister Zarif said. From 2001, neither of those who carried out terrorist acts were Iranians, most of them were from the United States. I believe the ideology that is promoting extremism rooted in Saudi Arabia; they are creating such a dark screen that has no connection with true Islam. See Al-Nusra, see ISIS, see Al-Qaeda, none of them have a relationship with Islam, and they have nothing to do with Iran. Not only the ideology, but also the financial and arms support of these groups is provided by others who call themselves US allies."[12] We can also recall the controversial Tramp remarks against Saudi Arabia during the presidential campaign. Where he insisted on disclosing the report of the Committee of Inquiry on September 11, 2001, and insisted that the government of Saudi Arabia sponsors terrorism.

---

10 Arit John, "Bid to Stop Part of U.S.-Saudi Arabia Arms Sale Fails in Senate", Bloomberg, 13 Jun. 2017. https://www.bloomberg.com/news/articles/2017-06-13/bid-to-stop-part-of-u-s-saudi-arabia-arms-sale-fails-in-senate.

11 Asa Fitch, "Iran's Armed Forces Are Middle East's Best Defense Against ISIS, President Says", Wall Street Journal, 22 Sep. 2015. https://www.wsj.com/articles/irans-armed-forces-are-middle-easts-best-defense-president-says-1442924831.

12 Fareed Zakaria, "sits down with Iran's Foreign Minister", CNN: 25 Sep. 2017. http://edition.cnn.com/videos/tv/2017/09/25/exp-gps-0924-zarif-interview-iran.cnn.

Taliban in Afghanistan

Saudi Arabia has recently pretended to have different relations with the Taliban, but Saudi Arabia's position in the country's crisis is interesting: Saudis are on both sides of the field! Evidences suggest that, despite the official support of the Kingdom from the Afghan government, they have had behind-the-scenes ties with the Taliban and have provided support. (Gall, 2016). On the other hand, the Afghan government is aware of this issue, but it has supported Saudi invasion to Yemen because they need to maintain their relations with Al Saud, on hope of their financial assistance and their help in confronting Taliban.

But on the other hand, Iran has been trying to help the state-building process since the beginning of the new government in Afghanistan. Iran has committed itself to contribute in reconstruction of Afghanistan, and both countries recently agreed to work together to combat terrorism in that country. At the same time, Iran's efforts to rebuild Afghanistan and their security and educational cooperation, was not satisfactory, and this happened mostly because of the US interferences.

The Presence of the United States in the Region and the Purchase of Weapons

Iran and Saudi Arabia have opposite positions about the presence of foreign forces in the region. While Iran rejects any foreign presence in the region and seeks to establish a new security system in the Middle East, the Saudis welcome the presence of foreign agents in the region_in order to maintain the status quo_and have extensive cooperation with them in this regard.[13] As a result, Al Saud has equipped itself with advanced weapons which are bought from Western countries to contain Iran. Saudi Arabia is currently the largest buyer of US war weapons.[14] The value of their recent military contracts reached $ 460 billion, including an urgent provision for delivering nearly 110 billion arms, including a system of anti-missile, offshore platforms, ammunition, and smart bombs. The rest of the weapons which cost nearly $ 350 billion will be delivered over the next 10 years, and this is apart from Saudi Arabia's contracts and investments

---

13 Yoel Guzansky, "The Arab Gulf States and Reform in the Middle East: Between Iran and the Arab Spring", (London: Palgrave Macmillan, 2014).

14 Michael B. Sauter, "Countries Buying the Most Weapons From the US Government", Wall Street Journal, 24 Feb 2017. https://247wallst.com/special-report/2017/02/24/countries-buying-the-most-weapons-from-the-us-government/.

in US infrastructure. But the important thing about this massive purchase lies in the statements of a White House official who said: “the United States will remain committed to maintaining Israel’s military superiority in the Middle East. Though Tel Aviv is concerned about the massive transfer of military equipment to an Arab state, it is also argued that not only the US Army’s armament will keep Israeli’s superiority to Saudi Arabia and other Arabs, but also Western weapons sold to Saudi cannot be a threat to the Zionist regime. It is clear that US “Iran-o-phobia” policy will increase the profits of Western arm-selling companies. A report says that if the war between Iran and Saudi Arabia occurs, the United States will make the most advantage of it:

> “The biggest gainers will be the US franker’s,” says Matsopoulos. “With an extremely wide break-even range from $32 to $55 per barrel, an increase in the oil price to levels higher than $50 will make the overwhelming majority of them smile. The US will soon be able to finance its trading deficit and solidify even more its position as a major oil exporter. The longer a potential crisis in the Middle East lasts, the more the market share of the US companies will increase -- because apart from prices and commodities the political stability of the USA can act as a guarantee for a smooth supply of oil for many consumers.”[15]

On the contrary, Iran prefers a region free from the presence of foreign forces. This is not a cross-sectional policy; it has been repeatedly emphasized in the post-Islamic revolution years. Iran considers Westerners as the cause of most the crisis in the region, from interventions in the internal affairs of the countries of the region to the creation of a ruthless terrorist groups like ISIL.[16] In another example, the US-led so-called anti ISIL coalition not only was not decisive in fighting this terrorist group but also has provided them equipments and even moved its leaders from critical areas. A matter that the militias of Iraq have repeatedly stated and provided documents in this regard.[17] Mr Jurgen Todenhofer, an independent German politician and correspondent, has clearly described how the Arab and Western weapons are at the hands of the self-proclaimed Islamic

---

15 Panos Mourdoukoutas, “The Coming War Between Saudi Arabia And Iran Will Make American Frackers Very Rich”, Forbes, 25 Feb. 2017. https://www.forbes.com/sites/panosmourdoukoutas/2017/06/25/the-coming-war-between-saudi-arabia-and-iran-will-make-american-frackers-very-rich/#30e9033778da.

16 Hillary R. Clinton, “Hard Choices”, (Simon & Schuster Audio; Abridged edition, 2014).

17 Tony Cartalucci, “How the US Supports the Islamic State (ISIS): One « Accidental Airdrop » vs Billions in Covert Military Aid”, Mondialisation, 25 Jun. 2016. https://www.mondialisation.ca/how-the-us-supports-the-islamic-state-isis-one-accidental-airdrop-vs-billions-in-covert-military-aid/5409449.

state, during a visit to the ISIL-dominated areas in Iraq and Syria: Saudi Arabia, Qatar, the USA, France, Great Britain, and others tried to strengthen resistance to Assad with money and weapons. As well as by means of media campaigns_ primarily on Al-Jazeera and al-Arabiya_ that were reminiscent of the disinformation campaign in the 2003 Iraq War. While I was in Syria, I spent my evenings reading Western news reports on the Internet, and I often thought the Western media was writing about a completely different country from the one I was experiencing so intensely every day. The weapons that helped turn what had been initially peaceful demonstrations in Syria into ruthless civil war were delivered to Turkey with the USA's kind permission, either by ship in gigantic cargo containers or by air. From there, the weapons were transported to Syria and handed over to the rebels. Smaller smuggling routes led through Lebanon and later through Iraq. The deliveries were approved by CIA officers directly to Jabhat al-Nusra or other extremist groups _ though they had no control once the weapons passed into Syrian territory. They were aware that the weapons would eventually end up with terrorist groups _ as was anyone with even a passing knowledge of the military situation in Syria. The most militant rebel groups could always find the best weapons on the other side of the border. Often the groups considered to be more moderate simply sold the foreign weapons on to organizations with ties to al-Qaeda. A bloody and lucrative arms trade arose in Syria. Private donors and organizations from Saudi Arabia and Kuwait also contributed money, weapons, and fighters on a vast scale. Most of the money and weapons went to radical Islamic groups. This was forbidden under the laws of these countries, but that did little to deter them.[18]

Yemen Crisis

After 1000 days of Saudi invasion to Yemen, the Saudi government has begun an unjust and oppressive war against Yemenis. Their crimes were so intense and savage that even the closest western allies of the country have not been able to cover or reject it. Human Rights Watch has explicitly called Saudi attacks on Yemen a war crime.[19] Even though, according to its domestic

18 Jürgen Todenhöfer, "My Journey into the Heart of Terror: Ten Days in the Islamic State", (Vancouver: Greystone Books, 2017), p.13.

19 "Yemen: Coalition Airstrikes Deadly for Children", Human Right Watch: 12 Sep. 2017. https://www.hrw.org/news/2017/09/12/yemen-coalition-airstrikes-deadly-children.

law, it must stop selling arms to Saudi Arabia in the war against the Yemeni people.[20]

Yemen Crisis is going to be the deadliest humanitarian crisis of the millennium; Saudi's are supporting the resigned president of Yemen and claims that Houthi's and former president Ali Abdullah Saleh's took over a coup d'état. But the oppositions of Mansour Hadi argue that he was chosen as a president for a two-year transitional period on February 21, 2012, in an election in which he was the only candidate. In January 2014 his mandate was extended for another year. However, he remained in power after the expiration of his mandate and intentionally postponed the election. How a transitional president can block democracy and still be legitimate? How a president can get legitimacy from a sole candidate election?

As we can see, the legitimacy of Mansour Hadi is under a big question and it seems that "legitimacy" is defined by great powers' benefits not by law. Saudi Arabia-led military coalition against poorest Arab country goes beyond a destabilizing act to a flagrant war crime. Human Rights Watch, on September 2017, has accused the Saudi-led coalition fighting in Yemen of committing war crimes, saying "its air raids killed 39 civilians, including 26 children, just in past two months". "Such attacks carried out deliberately or recklessly are war crimes," HRW said.

The annual January, 2017 report by United Nation experts who monitor sanctions and the conflict in Yemen, a Saudi Arabia-led military coalition has carried out attacks in Yemen that "may amount to war crimes," U.N. sanctions monitors reported to the world body's Security Council, warning coalition allies including the United States, Britain, and France that they are obligated to respect international humanitarian law. "For all investigations, the panel considers it almost certain that the coalition did not meet international humanitarian law requirements of proportionality and precautions in attack," the report said. "The panel considers that some of the attacks may amount to war crimes."

Congressman Ro Khanna said on 17th November 2017 that: "Today, I believe that we are aiding Saudi Arabia in Saudi Arabia's committing war crimes." He also added, "by aiding the Saudis in airstrikes that kill civilians, we are creating a security vacuum that allows groups like ISIS to gain a foothold."[21]

---

20 Michael A. Newton, "An Assessment of the Legality of Arms Sales to the Kingdom of Saudi Arabia in the Context of the Conflict in Yemen", Vanderbilt Law Research Paper, No. 17 26. 19 May. 2017. https://papers.ssrn.com/sol3/papers.cfm?abstract_id=2971208.

21 "US aiding Saudi 'war crimes' in Yemen: Congressman" Al Jazeera News: 17 Nov. 2017. https://www.aljazeera.com/news/2017/11/aiding-saudi-war-crimes-yemen-congressman-171116150400085.html.

Mark Lowcock, the UN Emergency Relief Coordinator, told the media on 7th November 2017 that "It will be the largest famine the world has seen for many decades," "What kills people in famine is infections [...] because their bodies have consumed themselves, reducing totally the ability to fight off things which a healthy person can," added Mr. Lowcock.[22]

Iran rejects interference in Yemeni internal affairs and emphasizes on political intra-Yemeni solution for the crisis and rejects all accusations. In this way, Iran's foreign ministry spokesman Bahram Ghasemi said on 30th October 2017 "The Saudi foreign minister's claims that our country has been blocking peace efforts in Yemen are ridiculous and baseless." "Repeating such false accusations will not reduce the responsibility . . . of those who have committed heinous crimes, particularly murder, destruction of schools and hospitals and pushing an innocent population to famine," Ghasemi said.[23]

From the very beginning of invasion to Yemen Iran's foreign minister proposed a four-point plan to the UN to end the crisis 17 April 2015:

1. Ceasefire and immediate end to all military operations;
2. Unimpeded urgent humanitarian and medical assistance to the people of Yemen;
3. Resumption of Yemeni-led and Yemeni-owned national dialogue, with the participation of the representatives of all political parties and social groups;
4. Establishment of an inclusive national unity government.

These items are repeated in Mr. Zarif's recent letter to the UN in November 2017 and said: "I am confident that you will urgently use your good offices to help make the necessary arrangement for conducting consultation with all concerned parties and expeditiously initiate a genuine dialogue to explore a political solution to this tragic crisis." In advancing this objective, the Government of the Islamic Republic of Iran stands ready to continue to assist you and engage with you and all other relevant stakeholders in a meaningful dialogue so as to pursue and operationalize this peace plan. We also express our readiness to work with the United Nations in order to promptly dispatch the necessary humanitarian and medical assistance to the people in need in Yemen.

---

22 Giles Clarke, "Yemen facing largest famine the world has seen for decades, warns UN aid chief", UN News: 9 Nov. 2017. https://news.un.org/en/story/2017/11/570262-yemen-facing-largest-famine-world-has-seen-decades-warns-un-aid-chief.

23 "Iran rejects 'ridiculous' Saudi accusations on Yemen" Daily Mail: 30 Oct. 2017. https://www.dailymail.co.uk/wires/afp/article-5030915/Iran-rejects-ridiculous-Saudi-accusations-Yemen.html.

Lebanon Crisis

The most recent case of Saudi's destabilizing behavior is happening in Lebanon. In a master-slave manner, they urged the Lebanese Prime Minister, Saad Hariri, to go to Riyadh and then in an undiplomatic and rare phenomena he resigned in Riyadh and for nearly two weeks was held there mysteriously!

The country that has just been stabilizing has suddenly faced Saad-al-Hariri's forced resignation, his prime minister. He was taken to Riyadh, his mobile phone was taken and held in a respectable detention, and then read a text that included the resignation of the prime minister.[24] Lebanese Hezbollah secretary-general Sayyid Hassan Nasrallah called the Saudi government declaring war with Lebanon and insisted that Hariri should be released.[25]

Thamer al-Sabhan, the Saudi minister for Gulf affairs, said on Monday that Lebanon's government would "be dealt with as a government declaring war on Saudi Arabia" because of what he described as "acts of aggression" committed by Hezbollah. So it seems that Saudis are implementing the scenario of destabilizing Lebanon to contain and limit Iran's ally Hezbollah. To achieve this goal, they started with resignation of Hariri which was surprising and strange, and continued by accusing Iran and Hezbollah in an urgent Arab league meeting on 19 November 2017.

In this way, before Hariri's visit to Paris, Lebanon's President Michel Aoun in November 15, 2017 accused Saudi Arabia of having "detained" Prime Minister Saad Hariri. "Nothing justifies the failure of Prime Minister Saad Hariri to return for 12 days, therefore we consider him to be held and detained, contrary to the Vienna Convention," Aoun said.[26]

Lebanon's Foreign Minister Gebran Bassil in November 15, 2017 has also said "Any (Saudi) measures would not only be targeting Lebanon and its stability, this would be a punishment for the region because any instability in Lebanon would cause instability in the region."

---

24 Samia Nakhoul, "Exclusive - How Saudi Arabia turned on Lebanon's Hariri", Reuters: 11 Nov. 2017. https://uk.reuters.com/article/uk-lebanon-politics-hariri-exclusive/exclusive-how-saudi-arabia-turned-on-lebanons-hariri-idUKKBN1DB0QI.

25 "Saudi Arabia 'declares war' on Lebanon, Saad al-Hariri forced to resign: Hezbollah", ABC News: 11. Nov. 2017. http://www.abc.net.au/news/2017-11-11/hezbollah-says-saudi-arabia-has-declared-war-on-lebanon/9140498.

26 "Saad Hariri: Saudis detaining Lebanon PM says Michel Aoun", BBC News: 15 Nov. 2017. https://www.bbc.com/news/world-middle-east-41995939.

It seems that regional and international pressure forced Saudi regime to release Hariri. The European Union urged Saad al-Hariri to return to Lebanon, calling on all political forces inside the country to focus on the domestic agenda and warning Saudi Arabia against meddling. "We appeal first of all to the political forces to focus on Lebanon and what they can deliver to their citizens, Prime Minister Hariri to return to his country and the unity government . . . to focus on domestic achievements," the European Union top diplomat, Federica Mogherini, told reporters in November 14, 2017. She also added: "We expect no external interference in this national agenda. We believe it is essential to avoid importing Lebanon into regional conflicts."[27]

German Foreign Minister Sigmar Gabriel told reporters in November 18, 2017 that Europe "could not tolerate the adventurism that has spread there." For this remark, Saudi's had summoned the German ambassador in Riyadh and handed him "a protest memorandum over remarks made by the German Foreign Minister Sigmar Gabriel."[28]

Iran has repeatedly emphasized the stability and unity of Lebanon. Iran's foreign minister Javad Zarif wrote in twitter in November 10, 2017 that "A more experienced person might think doubling down on bad bets by stoking further crises would be unwise, and can only end in tears."

Conclusion

Iran and Saudi Arabia have shown that on issues like purchase of weapons to United States as well as the crises in Yemen, Turkey, Qatar, Syria, Iraq, and Lebanon, have different point of views.

The Islamic Republic of Iran has always tried to maintain regional stability and peaceful relations with its neighbors, but Saudi Arabia has tried its best to ruin and threaten the regional security system to change the balance of power against Iran. This conclusion can be seen clearly in countries like Qatar, Syria, and Lebanon. The style of Saudi's intervention changes from assisting a coup against Morsi's legitimate government to support terrorism to topple Assad's

27 Richard Balmforth, "EU says Hariri must return to Lebanon, warns against Saudi interference", Reuters: 13 Nov. 2017, https://www.reuters.com/article/us-lebanon-politics-france/eu-says-hariri-must-return-to-lebanon-warns-against-saudi-interference-idUSKBN1DD0YS.

28 Sami Aboudi, "Saudi Arabia recalls ambassador to Germany over Gabriel comments", Reuters: 18 Nov. 2017, https://www.reuters.com/article/us-saudi-germany-lebanon/saudi-arabia-recalls-ambassador-to-germany-over-gabriel-comments-idUSKBN1DI00V.

legal government, attacking Yemen and killing thousands of children and civilians, meddling in Iraqis' internal affairs, blockade of Qatar, and forcing the Lebanese prime minister to resign.

In spite of Saudi Arabia's destabilizing role and the propaganda of Middle East main stream media, Iran has tried to play a stabilizing role in Middle East uprising. Without Iran's intervention, which has done legally and with the request of legitimate governments of these countries, Syria and Iraq were at the verge of falling in hands of terrorist groups but Iran and its allies saved both countries and improved the stability and security of the Middle East and world. Iran is committed to the unification of Iraq and Syria.

All in all, Iran tries to behave in accordance to international law and help the legal governments of the region to maintain their stability and obstructing the spread of terrorism in the region. But Saudi Arabia, by funding terrorism and trying to topple legal governments, tries to destabilize the region and pave the way for foreign powers to meddle in the region.

Bibliography

1. Clinton, Hillary R. *Hard Choices*, New York: Simon & Schuster Audio, Abridged edition, 2014.
2. Guzansky, Yoel. *The Arab Gulf States and Reform in the Middle East: Between Iran and the Arab Spring*, London: Palgrave Macmillan, 2014.
3. Kazemi, Ali Asghar. *International Crisis Management Tehran*, Tehran: Political and International Studies Office, 1987.
4. Leonard, John-Paul. *ISIS IS US: The Shocking Truth: Behind the Army of Terror*; San Diego: Progressive Press, 2016.
5. Todenhöfer, Jürgen. *My Journey into the Heart of Terror: Ten Days in the Islamic State*, Vancouver: Greystone Books, 2017.

Internet Sources

1. Aboudi, Sami "Saudi Arabia recalls ambassador to Germany over Gabriel comments", Reuters. https://www.reuters.com/article/us-saudi-germany-lebanon/saudi-arabia-recalls-ambassador-to-germany-over-gabriel-comments-idUSKBN1DI00V (18 Nov. 2017).
2. Al-Shaalan, Marina "Iran supported Turkey during coup", Sputnik news Agency, https://ir.sputniknews.com/iran/201707162680858-%D8%AD%D9%85%D8%A7%DB%8C%D8%AA-%D8%A7%DB%8C%D8%B1%D8%A7%D9%86-%D8%AA%D8%B1%DA%A9%DB%8C%D9%87/ (16 Jul. 2017).

3. Balmforth, Richard "EU says Hariri must return to Lebanon, warns against Saudi interference", Reuters. https://www.reuters.com/article/us-lebanon-politics-france/eu-says-hariri-must-return-to-lebanon-warns-against-saudi-interference-idUSKBN1DD0YS (13 Nov. 2017).
4. Cartalucci, Tony "How the US supports the Islamic State (ISIS): one « accidental airdrop » vs billions in covert military aid", Mondialisation, 25 Jun. 2016. https://www.mondialisation.ca/how-the-us-supports-the-islamic-state-isis-one-accidental-airdrop-vs-billions-in-covert-military-aid/5409449 (25 Jun. 2016).
5. Clarke, Giles "Yemen facing largest famine the world has seen for decades, warns UN aid chief", UN News. https://news.un.org/en/story/2017/11/570262-yemen-facing-largest-famine-world-has-seen-decades-warns-un-aid-chief (9 Nov. 2017).
6. Finn, Tom "Qatar says denounces military coup attempt in Turkey: state media", Reuters, Doha, https://www.reuters.com/article/us-turkey-security-qatar-idUSKCN0ZV2Y6 (16 Jul. 2016).
7. Fisher, Max "How the Saudi-Qatar rivalry, now combusting, reshaped the Middle East" New York Times, https://www.nytimes.com/2017/06/13/world/middleeast/how-the-saudi-qatar-rivalry-now-combusting-reshaped-the-middle-east.html (13 Jun. 2017).
8. Fitch, Asa "Iran's Armed Forces are Middle East's best defense against ISIS, President says", Wall Street Journal, https://www.wsj.com/articles/irans-armed-forces-are-middle-easts-best-defense-president-says-1442924831 (22 Sep. 2015).
9. Irish, John "Lebanon's Hariri must return home from Saudi to prove he is free: foreign minister", Reuters. https://www.reuters.com/article/us-saudi-lebanon-france/lebanons-hariri-must-return-home-from-saudi-to-prove-he-is-free-foreign-minister-idUSKBN1DE29I?il=0 (14 Sep. 2017).
10. John, Arit "Bid to stop part of U.S.-Saudi Arabia arms sale fails in Senate", Bloomberg, https://www.bloomberg.com/news/articles/2017-06-13/bid-to-stop-part-of-u-s-saudi-arabia-arms-sale-fails-in-senate (13 Jun. 2017).
11. Mourdoukoutas, Panos "The coming war between Saudi Arabia and Iran will make American frackers very rich", Forbes, https://www.forbes.com/sites/panosmourdoukoutas/2017/06/25/the-coming-war-between-saudi-arabia-and-iran-will-make-american-frackers-very-rich/#30e9033778da (25 Feb. 2017).
12. Nakhoul, Samia "Exclusive - how Saudi Arabia turned on Lebanon's Hariri", Reuters. https://uk.reuters.com/article/uk-lebanon-politics-hariri-exclusive/exclusive-how-saudi-arabia-turned-on-lebanons-hariri-idUKKBN1DB0QI (11 Nov. 2017).

13. Newton, Michael A. "An assessment of the legality of arms sales to the Kingdom of Saudi Arabia in the context of the conflict in Yemen", Vanderbilt Law Research Paper, No. 17–26. https://papers.ssrn.com/sol3/papers.cfm?abstract_id=2971208 (19 May 2017).
14. Sauter, Michael B "Countries buying the most weapons from the US government", Wall Street Journal, https://247wallst.com/special-report/2017/02/24/countries-buying-the-most-weapons-from-the-us-government/ (24 Feb. 2017).
15. Shahidsaless, Shahir "Saudi-led blockade of Qatar could boost Iran". Atlantic Council. http://www.atlanticcouncil.org/blogs//iransource/saudi-led-blockade-of-qatar-could-boost-iran-2 (10 Jul. 2017).
16. Shakibaei, Mehdi, "Did Saudi Arabia play a role in Turkey's coup?", Farda News Agency. www.farda.fr/002HTG (15. Jul. 2016).
17. Zakaria, Fareed "Sits down with Iran's Foreign Minister", CNN. http://edition.cnn.com/videos/tv/2017/09/25/exp-gps-0924-zarif-interview-iran.cnn (25 Sep. 2017).

Adam Szymański

"Domestication" of the Middle Eastern Policy of Turkey

Abstract: The process of increasing the impact of the domestic factors on foreign policy has been observed in many countries in the current decade. This chapter is an analysis of the case of Turkey and its Middle Eastern Policy after the so-called Arab Spring. The author, using the foreign policy analysis (FPA), proves that the Post-Arab Spring Middle Eastern policy conducted by Turkey is to a large extent a function of the domestic factors - current and short-sighted domestic politics, ideology and personal factor. Their combination has a negative impact on the implementation of the key Turkish goal of becoming an influential and strong regional power.

Keywords: Turkey, Middle East, Arab Spring, foreign policy

Introduction

The explanation of the contemporary foreign policy of a state or another actor of international relations requires considering a set of external and domestic determinants.[1] While the analysis of the latter group of factors was often neglected in the past in the International Relations (IR) literature[2], it is a key aspect of studies on the foreign policy nowadays.[3] There are empirical works devoted solely to the domestic factors in the foreign policy of states.[4] Some theoretical approaches in IR have also as the basis the assumption about the significance of

---

1 See more, e.g. Ryszard Zięba, "Uwarunkowania polityki zagranicznej państwa," [Determinants of the Foreign Policy of a State] in: *Wstęp do teorii polityki zagranicznej państwa* [Introduction to the Theory of Foreign Policy of a State], ed. Ryszard Zięba (Toruń: Wyd. Adam Marszałek, 2007), pp. 17–36.

2 Helen Milner, "International Theories of Cooperation Among Nations, Strengths and Weaknesses," *World Politics*, Vol. 44, No.3 (1992), pp. 489–96.

3 Chris Alden and Amnon Aran, *Foreign Policy Analysis. New Approaches* (London, New York: Routledge, 2012), p. 7.

4 See, e.g. Hongyi Lai, *Domestic Sources of China's Foreign Policy* (Abingdon, New York: Routledge, 2010); James M. McCormick (ed.), *The domestic sources of American Foreign Policy. Insights and Evidences* Rowman & Littlefield Publishers, Lanham 2017).

the domestic politics. The best example is the democratic peace theory, which says that the democratic political regime generates more peaceful foreign policy.[5]

What is of a particular interest in this context is a dynamic approach and the analysis of the changing impact of the domestic determinants on the effective implementation of the foreign policy principles. This article is a study of the case of the current foreign policy of Turkey, with a particular focus on the Middle Eastern region as the key direction of the Turkish external relations in this decade.

There has been some literature (both monographs and journal articles) on the impact of the domestic factors on the Turkish foreign policy.[6] However, there is a lack of a thorough analysis of the influence of the domestic politics on foreign relations of this country after the so-called Arab Spring. The author has selected the case of Turkey as it enables to analyze the current process of increasing impact of the domestic factors (in particular, subjective domestic determinants) on foreign policy, observed in many countries. It can lead to the situation that the latter is becoming a function of the former – often with negative effects on the implementation of the foreign policy goals. The Middle Eastern policy is a very good example to study this phenomenon in the Turkish case as many current actions of Turkey in this region cannot be explained without taking into consideration domestic factors – more than it was the case in few previous decades. The empirical analysis can prove then the theoretical and methodological assumption that the analysis of the foreign policy requires a thorough study on the domestic issues.

The author wants to verify two hypotheses in this chapter. First, the Post-Arab Spring Middle Eastern policy of Turkey is to a large extent a function of domestic factors – current and short-sighted domestic politics, ideology and personal factor. Second, the combination of these domestic factors has a negative impact on the implementation of the goals of the Turkish Middle Eastern policy, including the ambition to be an influential regional power.

To verify these hypotheses, the following questions will be posed: What is the main characteristic of the Turkish foreign policy in general and Middle Eastern

5 See, e.g. Bruce M. Russet et al., *Grasping the Democratic Peace: Principles for a Post-Cold War World* (Princeton, NJ: Princeton University Press, 1992).

6 See, e.g. Semih İdiz, "Public Opinion as a Determinant of the New Turkish Foreign Policy," *SÜDOSTEUROPA Mitteilungen*, Vol. 50, No. 6 (2010), pp. 41–45; Jakub Wódka, *Polityka zagraniczna Turcji. Uwarunkowania wewnętrzne oraz podmioty decyzyjne* [Foreign Policy of Turkey. Domestic Determinants and Decision Makers] (Warszawa: Instytut Studiów Politycznych PAN, Wydawnictwo TRIO, 2012).

policy particularly in the 2011–2018 period? What has changed in this context in comparison to the first decade of the 21st century? What are the main domestic factors determining the current Middle Eastern policy of Turkey? What is the impact of these factors on the analyzed policy and is it changing in time?

The article is based on a qualitative approach. The author uses the elements of the current FPA (foreign policy analysis) which includes revisions of classical aspects as a result of critics and new approaches to studies on foreign policy. This article first of all takes into consideration the domestic structures and policy change.[7]

The article consists of three main parts. The first chapter is aimed at outlining the theoretical framework concerning the role of domestic factors in foreign policy. The next part is devoted to presenting the main stages of the Turkish foreign policy and Middle Eastern policy after the end of the Cold War. The last key chapter is the analysis of the impact of domestic factors on the Turkish Middle Eastern policy.

Foreign Policy Domestic Factors

Before discussing the foreign policy and the Middle Eastern policy of Turkey, it is worth outlining some important theoretical aspects of the issue of foreign policy domestic determinants.

"In moving away from a focus on the individual decision maker and the state bureaucracy FPA scholars began to show the interests in the domestic, societal sources of foreign policy."[8] The "domestic structure approach" has been developed in the literature, with a particular theoretical framework.

Different authors first of all presented classifications of the domestic determinants of foreign policy. The most popular one is the division into the objective (material) and subjective domestic determinants. The first group includes the following factors: the size of the country, its geographical location, demographic projections, economic, technological or military potential, transport infrastructure, etc. The catalogues of subjective determinants consist of: ideologies, doctrines, religions, elites' and society's perceptions of the international environment, awareness of the decision makers and personal factors as well as the nature of political institutions. The article will refer mainly to the

7 Alden and Aran, *Foreign Policy Analysis*, pp. 1–13.
8 Alden and Aran, *Foreign Policy Analysis*, p. 7.

group of the subjective factors which seems to be decisive in shaping the current Middle Eastern policy of Turkey (as argued below).[9]

Another classification is presented by James McCormick who distinguishes three main categories of the domestic sources of foreign policy: 1) societal environment (social determinants) – e.g. political culture, values, beliefs or self-perception; 2) institutional setting, i.e. constitutional system, division of power, political competition, etc. as well as 3) individual characteristics of decision-makers and policymaking positions.[10] All three categories will be crucial for this analysis because they include three main elements influencing nowadays the Turkish foreign policy and Middle Eastern policy.

Since the article is about the impact of domestic factors on the effectiveness of the Turkish Middle Eastern policy, it is important to refer to the international theory of cooperation, particularly to its part concerning the conditions of effective cooperation between the international actors. Helen Milner writes about six conditions (hypotheses) of cooperation that were indicated in the literature in the 1990s. It is, firstly, about the gains of international actors – absolute or relative (some scholars write about the necessity for balanced distribution of gains in negotiations as crucial to reach agreement) and as well as about the strategy of reciprocity which may be conductive to cooperation. The second issue is the number of actors. It can be said (with reservations) that the higher number of players, the less possible is the effective cooperation. According to the (third) iteration hypotheses, state's willingness to cooperate is influenced by whether they believe they will continue to interact indefinitely. The fourth condition is included in the international regimes hypotheses which refers to the facilitation of international cooperation thanks to the reduction of transaction and information costs by the international regimes. The fifth condition concerns the existence of epistemic communities of actors who share common beliefs, values, approaches, understanding of problems and their solutions. This condition is close to the fourth one. Both the international regime and epistemic community reduce uncertainty in relations. The difference lies in the type of the provided information – while the international regime gathers data on preferences and compliance of other partners, the epistemic community provides "expert" information which enables coordination of states' expectations. The sixth one refers

9 Zięba, *Uwarunkowania polityki zagranicznej*, pp. 21–28; Wódka, *Polityka zagraniczna Turcji*, pp. 30–32.

10 McCormick (ed.), *The domestic sources of American Foreign Policy*, pp. 1–18.

to the power asymmetries hypothesis according to which actors with different potential and capabilities may develop cooperation.[11]

However, Milner proves that these hypotheses have some weaknesses. For the purpose of this article, it is particularly important to emphasize one critical point, namely that the aforementioned conditions of the emergence of cooperation often depends on the domestic politics and factors (not necessary on structural issues). These factors are among others: interests and preferences of elites (bureaucratic groups), strategies of states and perceptions of decision makers. Milner adds that the domestic factors generally help to explain the international cooperation because they tell us much about the aggregation of preferences and construction of interests, adoption of strategies and the possibility of domestic ratification.[12] These arguments are important for the article because the domestic factors can explain what is actually needed for the effective implementation of the foreign policy goals.

Changes in Turkish Foreign Policy and Middle Eastern Policy after the Cold War

The development of the Turkish foreign policy and its Middle Eastern vector can be divided into three periods: the 1990s, the first decade of the 21st century (in the Middle Eastern case with additional distinguishing of 2008–2011 period) and the period after 2011.

In the 1990s the model of "coercive regional power" was implemented in the case of the Turkish foreign policy, which was reflected also in the relations with the Middle Eastern countries.[13] Although the redefinition of the foreign policy priorities took place in this period, it was a model based to a large extent on the principles from the Cold War period. In the 1990s Turkey kept then its traditional foreign policy doctrine based on: domination of the Western direction and lack of fully independent foreign policy, priority given to the national security dogma – in accordance with the Kemalist ideology, a substantial role of the

---

11 Milner, *International Theories of Cooperation*, pp. 470–80.

12 Milner, *International Theories of Cooperation*, pp. 489–96. Cf. Xinyuan Dai, Duncan Snidal and Michael Sampson, "International Cooperation Theory and International Institutions," in: *Oxford Research Encyclopedia of International Studies* (Oxford: Oxford University Press, 2010): 14 Jun. 2018, http://internationalstudies.oxfordre.com/view/10.1093/acrefore/9780190846626.001.0001/acrefore-9780190846626-e-93.

13 Ziya Öniş "Turkey and the Middle East after September 11: The Importance of the EU Dimension," *Turkish Policy Quarterly*, Vol. 2, No. 4 (2003), pp. 1–9.

army in shaping the foreign policy, keeping the *status quo* and a reactive, *ad hoc* approach as well as readiness to use hard power tools if necessary.[14]

It meant, with reference to the Middle East region, on the one hand, good relations with Israel but, on the other hand, the relations with other Middle Eastern countries, though in the state of development (starting with the Turgut Özal's era) but burdened with different tensions and conflicts, generated by the aforementioned model of foreign policy. Berna Süer wrote rightly with reference to the Turkish-Syrian relations that "the Cold war structure was a kind of insurance against the threats of the each country against another (…) Thus the disappearance of the bipolar rift uncovered the conflicts between the two countries."[15] In the 1990s, we could observe different problems in these bilateral relations – first of all issues of PKK and waters of the Euphrates and the Tigris as well as the Hatay territorial dispute. There was even a real possibility of the military conflict between the two states in 1998.[16] The situation did not look better in relation with other Middle Eastern neighbors of Turkey – Iran and Iraq. It was also obvious that the model of the Turkish foreign policy in the 1990s did not allow this country to play a substantial role in resolution of conflicts in the region.

At the beginning of the first decade of the 21st century we could observe a process of gradual transformation of foreign policy of Turkey – in general terms a change from focusing on the importance of military security and balance-of-power politics to the increasing appreciation of the value of civilian instruments of law, economics and diplomacy as well as multilateral international structures.[17] At that time, many scholars discussed the change of the Turkish foreign policy model from the "coercive regional power" to "benign regional power".[18] The change was associated with the Europeanization of the Turkish foreign policy – connected with the EU pre-accession process[19] as well as the AKP ruling (begun

14 For more, see, e.g. Adam Szymański, "Turkish Foreign Policy in 2007–2009: Continuity or Change?," *SInAN Working Paper*, No. 3 (2009), pp. 3–5.

15 Berna Süer, "Syria," in: *Turkey's Neighborhood,* ed. Mustafa Kibaroğlu (Ankara: Foreign Policy Institute, 2008), pp. 198–99.

16 Adam Szymański, "Turkish Policy Towards War in Syria," *TEKA of the Commission of Political Science and International Affairs*, Vol. 12, No. 1 (2017), pp. 68.

17 Michael Emerson and Nathalie Tocci, "Turkey as a Bridgehead and Spearhead. Integrating EU and Turkish Foreign Policy," *CEPS - EU-Turkey Working Papers*, No. 1 (2004), pp. 1–35.

18 Öniş *Turkey and the Middle East*, pp. 1–9.

19 Özlem Terzi, *The Influence of the European Union on Turkish Foreign Policy* (London: Routledge, 2010).

in 2002) and the implementation of the "strategic depth doctrine" of Ahmet Davutoğlu – with the use of the geostrategic position of Turkey and its historical experience of the Ottoman Empire era.[20] However, it began actually before 2002. Bülent Ecevit's government decided to pursue a regionally based foreign policy at the turn of the 21st century, which meant the development of contacts with all neighboring regions independently from the Western direction. As a result of the implementation of the new doctrine more civilian actors became involved in the decision-making process in the area of foreign policy, including civilian experts or civil society organizations.[21] Turkey started pursuing a more independent policy which became more balanced in terms of its main directions (not only the Western direction but also the Middle East, Russia, South Caucasus, Central Asia and the Balkans). It was a pro-active policy, with an extensive use of soft power tools, paying attention to good relations with neighbors (following the motto "zero problems with neighbors") and contributing to the stabilization of neighboring regions. The national security remained the priority but at the same time there were other important goals like democracy promotion.[22]

In the case of the Middle East, the model of the Turkish foreign policy was implemented particularly after 2003, when the Turkish parliament did not allow the US to open the second front of the Iraqi war on the Turkish territory. Turkey developed political, economic, social and cultural relations with many Middle Eastern countries, not only its neighbors, i.e. Syria, Iran and Iraq but also other states, including the Gulf countries, solving many bilateral problems. It became an active participant of regional organizations such as the Organization of Islamic Conference, OIC (the Turkish academic and politician Ekmeleddin Ihsanoğlu was its Secretary General in 2004–2014 period). It used many soft power instruments – first of all trade and diplomacy. It attempted to promote a specific economic and political model (market economy and democracy) in the region.[23] It tried to be more pro-active in the region – proposing some initiatives such as a two-stage plan for dealing with the Gaza issue (2008–2009).[24] Turkey

---

20 Alexander Murinson, "The Strategic Depth Doctrine of Turkish Foreign Policy," *Middle Eastern Studies*, Vol. 42, No. 6 (2006), pp. 945–64.

21 Kılıç Buğra Kanat, "AK Party's Foreign Policy: Is Turkey Turning Away from the West?" *Insight Turkey*, Vol. 12, No. 1 (2010), pp. 216–221.

22 Öniş *Turkey and the Middle East*, pp. 84–85.

23 Baskın Oran (ed.), *Türk Dış Politika. Kurtuluş Savaşından Bugüne Olgular, Belgeler, Yorumlar,* Volume III (İstanbul: İletişim, 2013), pp. 401–462; William Hale, "Turkey and the Middle East in the 'New Era,'" *Insight Turkey*, Vol. 11, No. 3 (2009), pp. 143–59.

24 Bülent Aras, "Turkey and the Palestinian Question," *SETA Policy Brief*, No. 27 (2009).

also began to contribute to the resolution of the regional conflicts. It played a role of an impartial "facilitator" of contacts between parts of conflicts – countries (Israel-Syria, Israel – Palestinian Autonomy) as well as actors within countries (e.g. Sunni and Shia groups in Iraq or Hamas and Fatah in the Palestinian Autonomy). [25]

However, the situation changed after 2008. The relations with Israel have deteriorated very clearly since that time as a result of such events as Israeli action in the Gaza Strip at the end of 2008 and the beginning of 2009, the Davos row between the then Prime Minister Recep Tayyip Erdoğan and Israeli President Shimon Peres in January 2009 and attack of Israeli commandos on Mavi Marmara ship in May 2010.[26] Turkey's sharpened position with regard to Israel put in question the continuation of Turkey's role as an intermediary in conflicts involving Israel. The same observation can be referred to the "Iran-West" mediation attempts concerning the issue of the Iranian nuclear program. Ziya Öniş wrote rightly that "by adopting active pro-Palestine and pro-Iran positions in these respective conflicts, Turkey progressively lost its ability to play a constructive role as a mediating power."[27] There was also a period of time when Turkey opted for one of the parties to the conflict in the Hamas-Fatah dispute. The so-called sectarian attitude began to be part of the Turkish Middle Eastern policy already at this time, in addition to other problems with the implementation of goals of this policy, connected with the "expectations-abilities" gap.[28]

In the last decade, after the events of the so-called Arab Spring, the Turkish foreign policy departed substantially from the European standards. It was reflected by the reference to the neighboring regions, particularly the Middle East. Some components of the old model of the "coercive regional power" came back, i.e. the securitization of the foreign policy (democracy promotion came to the background), more extensive use of the hard power tools – of course, without resigning from the variety of soft power instruments and reactive, *ad-hoc* regional policy deprived of any comprehensive foreign policy strategy. This was reflected in the activities of Turkey on the international arena generating

---

25 Adam Szymański, "Turkey's Role in Resolving the Middle East Conflicts," *International Issues and Slovak Foreign Policy Affairs,* No. 2 (2011), pp. 71–85.

26 See more Yusuf Ziya Bölükbaşı, "Türkiye-İsrail İlişkileri," in: *Değişen Dünyada Türk Dış Politikası,* ed. Murat Ercan (Ankara: Nobel Yayın Dağıtım, 2011), pp. 230–37.

27 Ziya Öniş, "Multiple Faces of the 'New' Turkish Foreign Policy: Underlying Dynamics and a Critique," *Insight Turkey*, Vol. 12, No. 1 (2010), p. 60.

28 Meliha B. Altunışık, "The Possibilities and Limits of Turkey's Soft Power in the Middle East," *Insight Turkey*, Vol. 10, No. 2 (2008), pp. 41–54.

frequent tensions and conflicts – also with almost all neighbors. The impartial attitude towards the regional conflicts was replaced by supporting clearly one party to a conflict. The failure of the "strategic depth doctrine" was noticeable.[29]

The change of the model of the Turkish foreign policy after 2011 and the partial return to the old traditions is clearly reflected in the Middle Eastern policy of Turkey. During the so- called Arab Spring the *ad-hoc*, reactive policy was revealed, e.g. in Libya and later Syria. Turkey after the period of supporting old regimes decided to take the side of the international coalition and opposition forces respectively. The radical change of position took place also with reference to the so-called Islamic State (ISIS) in Syria and Iraq after the period of lack of firm negative position towards ISIS followed by participation in actions against its militants.[30] The U-turns in the Turkish position proved the lack of long-term strategic thinking.

Besides, relations of Turkey with the Middle Eastern neighbors deteriorated after the so-called Arab Spring. Paradoxically, good relationship, based mainly on economic interests, was developed only with one neighboring partner – i.e. the Kurdish Regional Government (KRG) in northern Iraq.[31] The tensions with other Middle Eastern countries such as Egypt and some Gulf countries were a result of the pro-Islamist standpoint of the AKP governments and support for particular Islamist groups such as Muslim Brotherhood in Egypt or Hamas in the Palestinian Autonomy. The so-called Muslim Brotherhood Internationalism was noticeable also in 2017 when Turkey supported Qatar which shares the Turkish vision for the Sunni countries in the Middle East. Lebanon was another country with which Turkey's relations worsened due to the perception that the AKP government was pursuing a sectarian (pro-Sunni, anti-Shia and anti-Alawi)

---

29 Hüseyin Işıksal, "Turkish Foreign Policy under the AKP Era," in: *Turkish Foreign Policy in the New Millennium,* ed. Hüseyin Işıksal and Ozan Örmeci (Berlin: Peter Lang GmbH, 2015), pp. 15–28.

30 Hüseyin Işıksal, "Political Chaos in Iraq, ISIS, and Turkish Foreign Policy: The High Cost of the Westphalian Delusion," in: Turkey's Relations with the Middle East. Political Encounters after the Arab Spring, ed. Hüseyin Işıksal and Oğuzhan Göksel (Cham: Springer, 2018), pp. 83–103.

31 Mesut Özcan, "Turkey's Policy towards the Middle East and North Africa after the Arab Spring," *Turkey Policy Brief Series (TEPAV)*, No. 9 (2013), pp. 2–5: 25 Aug. 2018,http://www.tepav.org.tr/upload/files/1367496675-5.Turkeys_Policy_towards_the_Middle_East_and_North_Africa_after_the_Arab_Spring.pdf; Aydın Selcen, "Turkey's Relations with Iraq and the KRG," in: *The AKP and the Turkish Foreign Policy in the Middle East,* ed. Zeynep N. Kaya, Vol. 5 (London: LSE Middle East Center, 2016), pp. 37–40: 10 Sep. 2018, https://eprints.lse.ac.uk/66139/1/Kaya_AKPForeignPolicy_2016.pdf

foreign policy.[32] This policy was noticeable also in Iraq (support for Sunni political forces) or Syria, in which Turkey supported moderate Sunni opposition after the period of uncritical support for any groups being in opposition to Al-Assad regime. This meant the end of the role of "facilitator" in the resolution of regional conflicts.[33]

As a result of such a policy, by the end of 2013 Turkey was in isolation in the region, not having ambassadors to Egypt, Israel and Syria. The "splendid isolation" was a term used to describe the result of inflexible position of Turkey towards the conflict in Syria and Al-Assad regime. It showed losing the position of an influential regional power (the so-called central power, using Davutoğlu's term).[34]

In mid-2016 the new Turkish government led by Prime Minister Binali Yıldırım announced the improvement of relations with international partners. It must be admitted that the Turkish-Israeli relations have improved since that time but there are still tensions, connected mainly with the Palestinian issue. The improvement of relations with Iran and Iraq in 2017–2018 is a matter of necessity due to the situation in Syria and the Kurdish issue in its regional dimension. However, they are not based on solid ground, and there are many divergent positions taken by these states. At the same time, the relations with the KRG became worse due to the independence referendum of Iraqi Kurds.[35] Turkey has tried also to regain its regional position in 2017–2018 period. Because of this, it uses the diplomatic tools and, e.g. takes part in the so-called Astana process (together with Russia and Iran) and Sochi talks to resolve the Syrian conflict or makes bilateral arrangements with Russia on Idlib to prevent the attack of the Syrian forces. However, at least the multilateral meetings do not bring a substantial success.[36]

---

32 Burak Cop and Özge Zihnioğlu, "Turkish Foreign Policy under AKP Rule: Making Sense of the Turbulence," *Political Studies Review*, Vol. 15, No. 1 (2017), pp. 34–36.

33 Hüseyin Işıksal, "Turkish Foreign Policy, the Arab Spring, and the Syrian Crisis: One Step Forward, Two Steps Back," in: *Turkey's Relations with the Middle East,* ed. Işıksal and Göksel, pp. 13–31.

34 Ioannis Grigoriadis, "From 'Central Power' to 'Splendid Isolation': Turkish Foreign Policy's Declining Ambitions," *ELIAMEP Working Paper*, No. 67 (2015), pp. 1–10.

35 Nathaniel Handy, "Turkey's Evolving Relations with the Kurdish Regional Government (KRG) of Iraq Since the Arab Spring," in: *Turkey's Relations with the Middle East,* ed. Işıksal and Göksel, pp. 181–195.

36 Sevil Erkuş, "Turkey urges guarantors of Astana to 'accelerate political process,'" Hurriyet Daily News, 6 April 2018: 25 Aug. 2018, http://www.hurriyetdailynews.com/turkey-urges-guarantors-of-astana-to-accelerate-political-process-129922.

The involvement in these initiatives is determined not only by the goal of regaining the status of regional power but also the security concerns connected with the terrorist threat and refugee problem. The securitization of the Middle Eastern policy has come back. Turkey does not hesitate also to use hard power tools, if necessary, for security reasons – connected not only with the Islamic State but also with the problem of the Kurdish PKK in Iraq as well as the Democratic Union Party (PYD) and the People’s Protection Units (YPG) in Syria – all treated by Turkey as terrorist organizations. The best examples of using this kind of tools are the Turkish military operations on the Syrian territory – Euphrates Shield in 2016–2017 in northern Aleppo Governorate against so-called Islamic State and Kurdish Rojava, Olive Branch since 2018 in Afrin against the aforementioned Syrian Kurdish forces as well as operation in Idlib Governorate (since 2017).[37]

Impact of Domestic Factors on Turkish Middle Eastern Policy

The key question concerns the impact of domestic factors on the current Middle Eastern policy of Turkey. The domestic issues always belonged to the determinants of the Turkish foreign policy. Mustafa Aydın writes about the general determinants of the Turkish foreign policy. On the one hand, there are external determinants such as the geopolitical situation and current international affairs. On the other hand, there are many domestic sources of the Turkish foreign policy. The geostrategic location, historical experiences and state capacities belong to the objective factors. However, there are also cultural-ideological factors, systemic issues and the current affairs regarding the domestic politics.[38]

The aforementioned domestic factors played always a key role in the Middle Eastern policy of Turkey. The geographical location of Turkey between “the West and the East” was an asset with reference to the role in the Middle Eastern region. Turkey tried to play a role of the gate to the European continent for Arab countries in the political and economic dimension. For instance, during the first decade of the 21st century Turkey wanted to promote a specific economic and political model in the region and be a hub in the energy sector. The geostrategic

37 “Turkey after Afrin,” *Stratfor Worldview. Assessments*, 14 March 2018: 26 Aug. 2018, https://worldview.stratfor.com/article/turkey-afrin-syria-iran-kurds-ypg-pkk-olive-branch-invasion.

38 Mustafa Aydın, The Determinants of Turkish Foreign Policy, and Turkey’s European Vocation, in: *Analyzing Middle East Foreign Policies And the Relationship with Europe*, ed. Gerd Nonneman (London, New York: Routledge, 2005), pp. 197–216.

location was also a kind of dilemma when it comes to the regional identity and perception of Arabs.[39]

The historical experiences shaped the Turkish foreign policy towards the Middle East as well. It was both about the positive (constructive) and negative issues concerning different time periods. Examples in the former case are the Ottoman Empire heritage with reference to the position of the state, role of the military (also in foreign policy) or close contacts with the neighboring regions being parts of the Empire as well as process of Westernization and integration with the Euro-Atlantic structures. The negative issues concern usually bad relationships with countries in the past – conflicts, wars, border disputes, massacres, etc. The Ottoman times and events within World War I led to the animosities particularly between Turkey and Arab neighbors, being previously parts of the Ottoman Empire. On the one hand, Turkey did not forget the alliance between Arab countries and Allied forces. On the other hand, the Arabic states remember the "Ottoman imperialism" which is perceived by these countries as a reason for their underdevelopment as well as the Turkish actions against the Arab nationalists. The feeling of victimization on the Arab side is particularly strong in the case of Syria because of the Sanjak of Alexandretta (Hatay).[40]

A classical determinant of the Turkish foreign and Middle Eastern policy is the issue of the Turkish capacities, first of all when it comes to the human and economic/financial resources as well military strength. It is important for all countries in the Middle East region that Turkey is a country with about 82 million people, being a member of G20 and having the second largest army in the NATO. Of course, the Turkish capacities are limited. As already mentioned, this appeared to be one of the main problems in implementing the policy based on the use of soft power tools in the Middle East.

The influence of Kemalism has had an impact on the relations with Iran and the Arab neighbors of Turkey. In the 1990s, it primarily concerned the principles of nationalism (*milliyetçilik*) and secularism (*laiklik*) (except for a short period of the Welfare Party rule). The context of independence and sovereignty was important in the first case. Secularism played a role in relations with such countries as Iran, being an obstacle to the dynamic development of relations. However, it seemed that in the first decade of the 21st century these ideological factors, although still present and important, were not the key sources of the

39 Szymański, *Turkish Policy Towards War in Syria*, p. 65.

40 Meliha B. Altunışık and Özlem Tür, "From Distant Neighbors to Partners? Changing Syrian–Turkish Relations," *Security Dialogue*, Vol. 37, No. 2 (2006), p. 231.

Turkish foreign policy. Instead, religion and conservatism emerged as factors shaping to a certain extent the Middle Eastern policy of Turkey. The Sunni Islam (Hanafi school) which dominates in Turkey determined the development of the Turkish contacts with other Muslim countries and organizations (e.g. OIC or Arab League), particularly when the aforementioned sectarian politics of the government was developed.[41]

Systemic and short-term domestic developments were always important determinants of the Turkish Middle Eastern policy. The most important issues seem to be in this context: the political and economic system, the strategy in domestic politics (including electoral politics) and identity politics which can be referred both to the Kurdish issue and political competition/conflict along the secular-conservative line.[42]

The Middle Eastern policy of Turkey after the so-called Arab Spring is, of course, determined by the external factors such as the aforementioned geopolitical and regional situation (from the Turkish point of view, first of all the multidimensional conflict in Syria, presence of ISIS in Syria and Iraq and actions of PKK as well as PYD/YPG), which explains to a certain extent, e.g. the return to the securitization of the Middle Eastern policy of Turkey.[43] However, the author of this chapter argues that we can observe also a growing role of the domestic factors, mainly the subjective determinants in shaping the foreign policy. This occurs to such extent that the foreign policy is becoming, more than before, a function of domestic politics, at the cost of the effectiveness of the former.[44] This phenomenon could be called "domestication" of the foreign policy of Turkey.

We can distinguish three main domestic subjective factors which correspond very well to the three categories of domestic sources of foreign policy

41 For more, see, e.g. Husrev Tabak, "Manifestation of Islam in Turkey's Foreign Policy," in: *Domestic and Regional Uncertainties in the New Turkey*, ed. Husrev Tabak, Özgür Tüfekçi and Alessia Chiriatti (Cambridge: Cambridge Scholars Publishing, 2017), pp. 85–104.

42 Yücel Bozdağlioğlu, "Modernity, Identity and Turkey's Foreign Policy," *Insight Turkey*, Vol. 10, No. 1 (2008), p. 72.

43 Cf. Emirhan Yorulmazlar and Ebru Turhan, "Turkish Foreign Policy towards the Arab Spring: Between Western Orientation and Regional Disorder," *Journal of Balkan and Near Eastern Studies*, No. 3 (2015), pp. 337–52.

44 There are authors who claim that the Turkish foreign policy has been the extension of the domestic politics since 1923. However, the focus is usually on the identity politics and the impact of Kemalism on the external relations of Turkey in terms of the modernization process (as the key idea of Kemalism) being the driving force of both domestic and foreign policy. See Bozdağlioğlu, *Modernity, Identity*, pp. 55–76.

presented by McCormick. They are: the domestic strategy with particular goals, interests and policy making (issues connected with the institutional setting in broader sense), role of ideology and religion (societal environment) and decision-making process with the participation of few individuals (individual characteristics). Two of them belong also to the key domestic factors pointed out by Milner, which can decide about the effective international cooperation and as a result – foreign policy, i.e. domestic strategy, including interests and perceptions of decision makers.

When it comes to the domestic strategy and politics, it seems that the current foreign policy, particularly in the Middle Eastern region, is to a large extent its extension. The domestic politics after 2010 is clearly aimed to strengthen the domination of the AKP in the political/party system and the consolidation of power in the hands of its politicians – first of all Erdoğan and his loyal cadre. Therefore, it is important to pursue the effective politics in terms of gaining (or even increasing) the support of the electorate (as in the case of the June 2018 parliamentary and presidential elections) and, if necessary, other political forces. The measures taken in the foreign policy are becoming an instrument to achieve the aforementioned goals, apart from domestic tools such as: electoral malpractices, legal reforms, changes in the government – to increase the number of loyal politicians and of the governance system (parliamentary to presidential system), populist rhetoric and polarization.[45] Katerina Dalacoura speaks in this context about the policy of expediency and survival of the AKP – far from the previous ambition of being the great regional power.[46]

When it comes to the Middle Eastern region, the clearest example is the policy towards Syria and Iraq. Thinking about the support of electorate and keeping crucial alliance with the Nationalist Action Party (MHP, *Milliyetçi Hareket Partisi*) combined with the Kurdish policy on the national level and the national security policy determined Turkey's actions, including the military operations in Syria. The AKP government changed in 2015 its policy towards Kurds in Turkey – from dialogue with Abdullah Öcalan and positive attitude towards the pro-Kurdish

---

45 Menderes Çınar, "The Power Strategies of the AKP in Turkey," in: *The AKP and the Turkish Foreign Policy in the Middle East*, ed. Işıksal and Göksel, pp. 12–15.

46 Katarina Dalacoura, "A New Phase in Turkish Foreign Policy: Expediency and AKP Survival," *Future Notes*, No. 4 (2017), pp. 1–5: 28 Aug. 2018, http://www.iai.it/sites/default/files/menara_fn_4.pdf. Cf. Mehmet Şahin and Buğra Sarı, "Turkey in the Syrian Crisis: The Limits of a Middle Power Foreign Policy," in: *Turkey's Foreign Policy Towards the Middle East: Under the Shadow of the Arab Spring*, ed. Idris Demir (Cambridge: Cambridge Scholar Publishing, 2017), pp. 61–78.

People's Democratic Party (HDP, *Halkların Demokratik Partisi*) to a new conflict with the PKK and actions against the HDP treated as the terrorist organization as well. The HDP appeared to be a political force which could not bring electoral gains. Contrary to it, the June 2015 parliamentary elections showed that passing the 10 % electoral threshold by the HDP led to the insufficient result for the AKP to govern alone again. It began the policy far from the goal of solving the Kurdish issue, having definitely the impact on its regional dimension and attitude towards the PYD/YPG, shaped also by the generally more assertive Turkish national security policy based on fight against terrorism of different kind (in Turkey also Fethullah Gülen Movement – FETÖ).[47] As Marc Pierini rightly says, "to succeed in its current domestic strategy of crushing both the pro-Kurdish political party in Turkey, the Peoples' Democratic Party (HDP), and the insurgent PKK to win the upcoming referendum [in April 2017 on changes in the constitution aimed at introduction of the presidential system – AS], given the Kurds' opposition to the proposed constitution, the leadership in Ankara needs international support. That implies convincing Russia and Western powers to drop their support for the Syrian Kurds."[48] The policy towards the conflict in Syria has been driven by these goals of the domestic politics.

Moreover, the AKP needed an ally to achieve its domestic goal – introduction of the presidential system through constitutional changes and their implementation, including the presidential and parliamentary elections in June 2018. The nationalist MHP was the only option which required taking some steps in Syria and Iraq by the AKP government though. The assertive policy towards Kurds – not only in Turkey through stopping the so-called peace process but also in Iraq and Syria – was one of the main conditions to build a kind of coalition. The MHP leaders said clearly that the AKP government must form a security belt (also by military means) in the region to protect borders and security of Turkmens (old argument) as well as act against the Kurdistan belt from Iraq to the Mediterranean being a "chemical bomb."[49] The reference to still strong nationalist feelings in the

47 For more about this aspect, see: William Hale, "Turkey's domestic politics, public opinion and Middle East policy," Palgrave Communications, No. 2 (2016), pp. 5–6, doi:10.1057/palcomms.2016.81.

48 Marc Pierini, "Turkey's Domestically Driven Foreign Policy," *Carnegie Europe*, 27 February 2017: 28 Aug. 2018, http://carnegieeurope.eu/strategiceurope/68109.

49 Umut Erdem, "MHP presents conditions for formation of coalition with the AKP," Hurriyet Daily News, 17 June 2015: 29 Aug. 2018, http://www.hurriyetdailynews.com/mhp-presents-conditions-for-formation-of-coalition-with-the-akp--84129.

Turkish society was made both by the MHP and AKP politicians.[50] These are domestic factors that are to a large extent behind the decision about military operations in Syria and other measures taken to act against building the "Kurdistan belt." Their result makes the situation in Syria even more unstable, not to mention generating problems in relations with the Turkish main partners, such as the USA, which cooperates with PYD/YPG in fighting against ISIS.

The aforementioned issue shows that the impact of the domestic strategy and politics on foreign policy of Turkey goes hand in hand with another important domestic factor, i.e. the influence and instrumental use of the ideological and religious factors. When it comes to the nationalism and patriotism as the domestic source of the Middle Eastern policy of Turkey, it must be added to the last paragraph that the military operation in Afrin served in 2018 as one of the tools to develop the alternative Turkish history and mythology (as another tool to maintain the support of a substantial part of the society) based not only on martyrs from 15 July 2016 (coup attempt) but also on events outside the Turkish territory. To do it, the AKP government prepared the campaign, among other things, to compare the Afrin operation to the independence war after the First World War.[51]

---

50 According to the Konda survey on nationalism (*milliyetçilik*) from 2010, a substantial part of the Turkish society still share the opinion that the only nation which can be a friend of Turkey is the Turkish nation itself (48 percent "for", further 23 percent "certainly for") which reflects the traditional feeling of being surrounded by enemies. The patriotic feelings are also strong. It is proved by high support (48 percent "for", 23 percent "certainly for") for the claim that it would be equally honorable to "shoot the bullet and eat the bullet for the nation". See: "Konda Barometresi. Milliyetçilik and Ulusal Gurur Araştırması," December 2010, p. 6: 30 Aug. 2018, http://konda.com.tr/wp-content/uploads/2017/03/KONDA_1012_MILLIYETCILIK_VE_ULUSAL_GURUR.pdf. The results of Konda survey showing the strong nationalistic feelings in the Turkish society are confirmed by more current surveys such as Sabancı University's and Koç University's comparative research in 2014, in which, e.g. the opinion that the Turkish nation is the best in the world is shared by 71 percent of the society. Cf. Ali Çarkoğlu and Ersin Kalaycıoğlu, *Türkiye'de ve Dünya'da Milliyetçilik* (İstanbul: İstanbul Politikalar Merkezi, 2014), p. 27: 30 Aug. 2018, http://ipc.sabanciuniv.edu/wp-content/uploads/2014/06/Dunyada-ve-Turkiyede-Milliyetcilik-SON.pdf.

51 See, e.g. İsa Tatlıcan, "Çanakkale'de, 15 Temmuz'da, Afrin'de aynı ruh var," Sabah, 19 March 2018: 30 Aug. 2018, https://www.sabah.com.tr/gundem/2018/03/19/canakkalede-15-temmuzda-afrinde-ayni-ruh-var.

Religion/conservatism and instrumental use of religious feelings of the Turkish Sunni Muslims (about 70–85 % of Turks)[52] are also important factors determining the foreign policy of Turkey in the Middle East. It is behind the aforementioned sectarian support for Sunni groups in different countries, e.g. in Iraq and Syria or particular Islamist political forces – Muslim Brotherhood in Egypt among others which excludes (due to lack of impartiality) the possibility of playing a role of "facilitator" of contacts between parties to regional conflicts. In the period following the so-called Arab Spring, promoting the political and economic model in the region by the AKP government was replaced by the measures taken, first of all by Erdoğan, to create the image of Turkey as a leader of the Muslim (Sunni) community – in the Middle East and beyond (e.g. in Myanmar whose government persecutes the Muslim Rohingya community). In the first case, it was noticeable many times in the actions to defend the Palestinians and criticize harshly the Israeli policy. A good example is the extraordinary summit of the OIC in Istanbul in May 2018 convened in order to protest against the US decision to relocate its embassy from Tel Aviv to Jerusalem as well as condemn Israeli killings of Palestinian protesters. Before the summit, Istanbul also hosted a mass rally under the theme "Condemning Oppression, Supporting al-Quds [Jerusalem - AS]" at the Yenikapı with the participation of Erdoğan, the AKP and MHP politicians as well as foreign leaders of some Muslim countries.[53] As the Guardian journalists once wrote, "Turkey's president likes to portray himself as the global defender of Islam and has sought to position himself as a champion of Muslim causes and a leader of a solidarity movement for the oppressed faithful around the world, another stance that plays well with conservative voters."[54] The regional dimension of this policy cannot be neglected but Erdoğan gives first of all a clear message to the Turkish society, using the aforementioned religious

52 The research of Turkish scholars in the first and second decade of this century shows that the Turkish society is more and more conservative and religious, valuing highly the role of family and Islamic culture as well as applying the religious rules to the everyday life. For more, see, e.g. Hakan Yılmaz, "Türkiye'de Muhafazakarlık. Aile, Cinselik, Din," Ekim 2012: 30 Aug. 2018, http://www.aciktoplumvakfi.org.tr/pdf/muhafazakarlik/04.pdf.

53 "OIC summit on Palestine reject US decision on Jerusalem," Hurriyet Daily News, 19 May 2018: 31.Aug. 2018, http://www.hurriyetdailynews.com/oic-summit-on-palestine-reject-us-decision-on-jerusalem-132044.

54 Kareem Shaheen and Gökçe Saraçoğlu, "Turkey's Islamists and secularists join forces in bid to unseat Erdoğan," The Guardian, 18 June 2018: 31 Aug. 2018, https://www.theguardian.com/world/2018/jun/18/turkey-islamists-and-secularists-join-forces-in-bid-to-unseat-erdogan.

feelings to achieve the main goal of the domestic political strategy. He knows well that this policy can be much more effective in Turkey than in Arab countries, which do not necessarily accept the leading role of Turkey in the region (both governments and societies).

The third factor, which cannot be separated from the first two, is the "personalization" of the Turkish foreign policy, including the Middle East region.[55] It is, again, an extension of the domestic politics. The increasingly limited number of persons have a real impact on the decision-making process in the state. This process has also much do with the aforementioned goal of the domestic strategy, i.e. consolidation of power. The dominant position is taken by Erdoğan – particularly after the June 2018 elections and introduction of the presidential system within which the President uses extensively the right to issue decrees. It is a final stage of the process of narrowing the number of people who have an impact on the decision-making process. It was always a narrow group of the AKP politicians or people somehow connected with the party. However, in the current decade we could observe the process of replacing the people who could present sometimes a different position from the President by the loyal cadre. It was noticeable both on the party executive and the government level. The best example was the replacement of the Prime Minister Davutoğlu by Yıldırım in May 2016.[56]

It determines in the current decade also the foreign policy within which the process of narrowing the circles having the real impact on the external affairs is taking place – reversed to the one in the first decade of the 21st century when more civilian actors, including the civil society, participated in shaping the Turkish foreign policy. Even when besides Erdoğan some other politicians (having posts of presidents, prime ministers or foreign ministers) took part in pursuing the foreign policy in the Middle Eastern region, a negative impact on this policy of Erdoğan's actions based on emotions and personal perceptions rather than rational calculations was difficult to mitigate – as in the outlined case of relations with Israel in 2008–2009. In the situation of taking posts of prime ministers and foreign ministers by people very loyal to the President and presenting his position on different external affairs, this negative impact is even bigger. It is noticeable particularly with the reference to the policy towards Syria, Israel or Egypt within which the personal issues, perceptions and emotions of Erdoğan play a substantial role at the cost of state of relations with these Middle Eastern countries.

---

55 Ioannis Grigoriadis, Interview, Stiftung Wissenschaft und Politik (SWP), Berlin, 19 September 2016.

56 "Binali Yıldırım'dan ilk açıklama," Hürriyet, 19 May 2016: 1 Sep. 2018, http://www.hurriyet.com.tr/gundem/binali-yildirimdan-ilk-aciklama-40106163.

Conclusion

The article shows that after the Arab Spring we can observe another change of the model of the Turkish foreign policy and Middle Eastern policy. It seems to be now a mixture of traditional elements and the components developed during the implementation of "the strategic depth" doctrine. A partial return of the old model based on *ad hoc*, often reactive policy, its securitization, use of hard power tool and generating tensions with the Middle Eastern countries makes the achievement of goals and principles defined at the beginning of this century more problematic.

The key question posed in the article was about how important are domestic factors for shaping this kind policy after 2011. The two hypotheses formulated at the beginning of the article have been verified positively in this context. We can observe after the so-called Arab Spring the increasing significance of the domestic subjective determinants – to the extent which allows for claiming that the Middle Eastern policy of Turkey is to a large extent an extension of the domestic politics. This process can be called the "domestication" of the Turkish policy in the region. A particular role is played by three elements: the domestic political strategy, ideology/religion as well as personal factor, not neglecting the role of external – regional or global – determinants. The politics focused on achieving the domestic, short-sighted goals led by the consolidation of power by the AKP and Erdoğan, combined with the use of nationalism and (Sunni) Islam and personalization of the Turkish politics/decision-making process, make the Middle Eastern policy of Turkey less effective, depriving it of the long-term, comprehensive strategy.

This calls into question the key goal and ambition of Turkey to consolidate its position in the region as a strong, "central" regional power. However, the dysfunctional impact goes beyond the Middle East. On the one hand, it influences negatively the relations with the Western partners – the USA and the EU. The current tensions with the USA in the Middle East are to a large extent a result of moving the national security policy and policy towards Kurds in Turkey to the regional level (creating the PYD/YPG problem) and the sectarian, pro-Islamist position. The proposed inclusion of Turkey into the Common Foreign and Security Policy (CFSP) within the new formula of EU-Turkey relations seems to be problematic.[57] It would be very difficult for Turkey with its *ad hoc*, securitized policy to cooperate within the CFSP in the Middle Eastern region, among others

---

57 For more, see: Meltem Müftüler-Baç, "Turkey's future with the European Union: alternative model of differentiated integration," *Turkish Studies*, Vol. 18, No. 3 (2017), pp. 427–29.

to coordinate the external actions with the EU partners and be part of long-term initiatives (such as the EU regional strategies). On the other hand, the Middle Eastern policy of Turkey determined extensively by the short-sighted domestic politics contributes to limiting the independent foreign policy pursued in the first decade of the 21st century. It refers to a partial dependence on Russia in the Syrian case.

Bibliography

1. Alden, Chris and Amnon Aran. *Foreign Policy Analysis. New Approaches.* London and New York: Routledge, 2012.
2. Altunışık, Meliha B. "The Possibilities and Limits of Turkey's Soft Power in the Middle East." *Insight Turkey*, Vol. 10, No. 2, 2008, pp. 41–54.
3. Altunışık, Meliha B. and Özlem Tür. "From Distant Neighbors to Partners? Changing Syrian–Turkish Relations." *Security Dialogue*, Vol. 37, No. 2, 2006, pp. 229–48.
4. Aras, Bülent. "Turkey and the Palestinian Question." *SETA Policy Brief*, No. 27, 2009.
5. Aydın, Mustafa. "The Determinants of Turkish Foreign Policy, and Turkey's European Vocation." In: *Analyzing Middle East Foreign Policies and the Relationship with Europe*, ed. Gerd Nonneman. London and New York: Routledge, 2005, pp. 197–216.
6. Bozdağlioğlu, Yücel. "Modernity, Identity and Turkey's Foreign Policy." *Insight Turkey*, Vol. 10, No. 1, 2008, pp. 55–76.
7. Bölükbaşı, Yusuf Ziya. "Türkiye-İsrail İlişkileri." In: *Değişen Dünyada Türk Dış Politikası*, ed. Murat Ercan. Ankara: Nobel Yayın Dağıtım, 2011, pp. 197–243.
8. Buğra, Kanat Kılıc. "AK Party's Foreign Policy: Is Turkey Turning Away from the West?" *Insight Turkey*, Vol. 12, No. 1, 2010, pp. 205–25.
9. Cop, Burak and Özge Zihnioğlu. "Turkish Foreign Policy under AKP Rule: Making Sense of the Turbulence." *Political Studies Review*, Vol. 15, No. 1, 2017, pp. 28–38.
10. Emerson, Michael and Nathalie Tocci. "Turkey as a Bridgehead and Spearhead. Integrating EU and Turkish Foreign Policy." *CEPS - EU-Turkey Working Papers*, No. 1, August 2004, pp. 1–35.
11. Grigoriadis, Ioannis. "From 'Central Power' to 'Splendid Isolation': Turkish Foreign Policy's Declining Ambitions." *ELIAMEP Working Paper*, No. 67, 2015, pp. 1–10.

12. Grigoriadis, Ioannis. Interview, Stiftung Wissenschaft und Politik (SWP), Berlin, 19 September 2016.
13. Hale, William. "Turkey and the Middle East in the 'New Era.'" *Insight Turkey*, Vol. 11, No. 3, 2009, pp. 143–59.
14. Handy, Nathaniel. "Turkey's Evolving Relations with the Kurdish Regional Government (KRG) of Iraq Since the Arab Spring." In: *Turkey's Relations with the Middle East. Political Encounters after the Arab Spring*, ed. Hüseyin Işıksal and Oğuzhan Göksel. Cham: Springer, 2018, pp. 181–95.
15. Işıksal, Hüseyin. "Political Chaos in Iraq, ISIS, and Turkish Foreign Policy: The High Cost of the Westphalian Delusion." In: *Turkey's Relations with the Middle East. Political Encounters after the Arab Spring*, ed. Hüseyin Işıksal and Oğuzhan Göksel. Cham: Springer, 2018, pp. 83–103.
16. Işıksal, Hüseyin. "Turkish Foreign Policy, the Arab Spring, and the Syrian Crisis: One Step Forward, Two Steps Back." In: *Turkey's Relations with the Middle East. Political Encounters after the Arab Spring*, ed. Hüseyin Işıksal and Oğuzhan Göksel. Cham: Springer, 2018, pp. 13–31.
17. Işıksal, Hüseyin. "Turkish Foreign Policy under the AKP Era." In: *Turkish Foreign Policy in the New Millennium*, ed. Hüseyin Işıksal and Ozan Örmeci. Berlin: Peter Lang GmbH, 2015, pp. 15–28.
18. İdiz, Semih. "Public Opinion as a Determinant of the New Turkish Foreign Policy." *SÜDOSTEUROPA Mitteilungen*, Vol. 50, No. 6, 2010, pp. 41–45.
19. Lai, Hongyi. *Domestic Sources of China's Foreign Policy*. Abingdon and New York: Routledge, 2010.
20. McCormick, James M. (ed.). *The Domestic Sources of American Foreign Policy. Insights and Evidences*. Lanham: Rowman & Littlefield Publishers, 2017.
21. Milner, Helen. "International Theories of Cooperation Among Nations. Strengths and Weaknesses." *World Politics*, Vol. 44, No. 3, 1992, pp. 466–96.
22. Murinson, Alexander. "The Strategic Depth Doctrine of Turkish Foreign Policy." *Middle Eastern Studies*, Vol. 42, No. 6, 2006, pp. 945–64.
23. Müftüler-Baç, Meltem. "Turkey's future with the European Union: alternative model of differentiated integration." *Turkish Studies*, Vol. 18, No. 3, 2017, pp. 416–438.
24. Oran, Baskın (ed.). *Türk Dış Politika. Kurtuluş Savaşından Bugüne Olgular, Belgeler, Yorumlar*. Volume III. İstanbul: İletişim, 2013.
25. Öniş, Ziya. "Multiple Faces of the 'New' Turkish Foreign Policy: Underlying Dynamics and a Critique." *Insight Turkey*, Vol. 12, No. 1, 2010, pp. 47–56.
26. Öniş, Ziya, "Turkey and the Middle East after September 11: The Importance of the EU Dimension." *Turkish Policy Quarterly*, Vol. 2, No. 4, 2003, pp. 1–9.

27. Russet, Bruce M. *Grasping the Democratic Peace: Principles for a Post-Cold War World*. Princeton and NJ: Princeton University Press, 1992.
28. Süer, Berna. "Syria." In: *Turkey's Neighborhood*, ed. Mustafa Kibaroğlu. Ankara: Foreign Policy Institute, 2008, pp. 189–223.
29. Szymański, Adam, "Turkey's Role in Resolving the Middle East Conflicts." *International Issues and Slovak Foreign Policy Affairs*, Vol. 20, No. 2, 2011, pp. 71–85.
30. Szymański, Adam. "Turkish Foreign Policy in 2007–2009: Continuity or Change?" *SInAN Working Paper* (Center for European Studies, METU), No. 3, 2009.
31. Szymański, Adam. "Turkish Policy Towards War in Syria." *TEKA of the Commission of Political Science and International Affairs*, Vol. 12, No. 1, 2017, pp. 63–84.
32. Şahin, Mehmet and Sarı Buğra. "Turkey in the Syrian Crisis: The Limits of a Middle Power Foreign Policy." In: *Turkey's Foreign Policy Towards the Middle East: Under the Shadow of the Arab Spring*, ed. Idris Demir, Cambridge: Cambridge Scholar Publishing, 2017, pp. 61–78.
33. Tabak, Husrey, "Manifestation of Islam in Turkey's Foreign Policy." In: *Domestic and Regional Uncertainties in the New Turkey*, ed. Husrey Tabak, Özgür Tüfekçi and Alessia Chiriatti. Cambridge: Cambridge Scholars Publishing, 2017, pp. 85–104.
34. Terzi, Özlem. *The Influence of the European Union on Turkish Foreign Policy*. London: Routledge, 2010.
35. Wódka, Jakub. *Polityka zagraniczna Turcji. Uwarunkowania wewnętrzne oraz podmioty decyzyjne* [Foreign Policy of Turkey. Domestic Determinants and Decision Makers]. Warszawa: Instytut Studiów Politycznych PAN and Wydawnictwo TRIO, 2012.
36. Zięba, Ryszard. „Uwarunkowania polityki zagranicznej państwa" [Determinants of the Foreign Policy of a State], In: *Wstęp do teorii polityki zagranicznej państwa* [Introduction to the Theory of Foreign Policy of a State], ed. Ryszard Zięba. Toruń: Wyd. Adam Marszałek, 2007, pp. 17–36.

Internet Sources

1. "Binali Yıldırım'dan ilk açıklama." *Hürriyet*, 19 May 2016. http://www.hurriyet.com.tr/gundem/binali-yildirimdan-ilk-aciklama-40106163 (1 Sep. 2018).
2. Çarkoğlu, Ali and Ersin Kalayçioğlu. *Türkiye'de ve Dünya'da Milliyetçilik*, İstanbul: İstanbul Politikalar Merkezi, 2014, http://ipc.sabanciuniv.edu/wp-content/uploads/2014/06/Dunyada-ve-Turkiyede-Milliyetcilik-SON.pdf (30 Aug. 2018).

3. Çınar, Menderes. "The Power Strategies of the AKP in Turkey." In: *The AKP and the Turkish Foreign Policy in the Middle East*, ed. Zeynep N. Kaya. London: LSE Middle East Center, Vol. 5, 2016, pp. 12–5. https://eprints.lse.ac.uk/66139/1/Kaya_AKPForeignPolicy_2016.pdf (10 Sep. 2018).
4. Dai, Xinyuan, Duncan Snidal and Michael Sampson. "International Cooperation Theory and International Institutions." In: *Oxford Research Encyclopedia of International Studies*. Oxford: Oxford University Press, 2010. http://internationalstudies.oxfordre.com/view/10.1093/acrefore/9780190846626.001.0001/acrefore-9780190846626-e-93 (14 Jun. 2018).
5. Erdem, Umut, "MHP Presents Conditions for Formation of Coalition with the AKP." *Hurriyet Daily News*, 17 June 2015. http://www.hurriyetdailynews.com/mhp-presents-conditions-for-formation-of-coalition-with-the-akp--84129 (29 Aug. 2018).
6. Erkuş, Sevil. "Turkey Urges Guarantors of Astana to 'Accelerate Political Process.'" *Hurriyet Daily News*, 6 April 2018. http://www.hurriyetdailynews.com/turkey-urges-guarantors-of-astana-to-accelerate-political-process-129922 (25 Aug. 2018).
7. Hale, William. "Turkey's Domestic Politics, Public Opinion and Middle East Policy." *Palgrave Communications*, No. 2, 2016, doi:10.1057/palcomms.2016.81.
8. *Konda Barometresi. Milliyetçilik and Ulusal Gurur Araştırması*, December 2010, http://konda.com.tr/wp-content/uploads/2017/03/KONDA_1012_MILLIYETCILIK_VE_ULUSAL_GURUR.pdf (30 Aug. 2018).
9. "OIC Summit on Palestine Reject US Decision on Jerusalem." *Hurriyet Daily News*, 19 May 2018. http://www.hurriyetdailynews.com/oic-summit-on-palestine-reject-us-decision-on-jerusalem-132044 (31 Aug. 2018).
10. Özcan, Mesut. "Turkey's Policy Towards the Middle East and North Africa after the Arab Spring." Turkey Policy Brief Series (TEPAV), No. 9, 2013, http://www.tepav.org.tr/upload/files/1367496675-5.Turkeys_Policy_towards_the_Middle_East_and_North_Africa_after_the_Arab_Spring.pdf (25 Aug. 2018).
11. Selcen, Aydın. "Turkey's Relations with Iraq and the KRG." In: *The AKP and the Turkish Foreign Policy in the Middle East*, ed. Zeynep N. Kaya. London: LSE Middle East Center, Vol. 5, 2016, https://eprints.lse.ac.uk/66139/1/Kaya_AKPForeignPolicy_2016.pdf (10 Sep. 2018).
12. Shaheen, Kareem and Gökçe Saraçoğlu. "Turkey's Islamists and Secularists Join Forces in Bid to Unseat Erdoğan." *The Guardian*, 18 June 2018. https://www.theguardian.com/world/2018/jun/18/turkey-islamists-and-secularists-join-forces-in-bid-to-unseat-erdogan (31 Aug. 2018).

13. Tatlıcan, İsa. "Çanakkale'de, 15 Temmuz'da, Afrin'de aynı ruh var." *Sabah*, 19 March 2018. https://www.sabah.com.tr/gundem/2018/03/19/canakkalede-15-temmuzda-afrinde-ayni-ruh-var (30 Aug. 2018).
14. "Turkey after Afrin." Stratfor Worldview. Assessments, 14 March 2018. https://worldview.stratfor.com/article/turkey-afrin-syria-iran-kurds-ypg-pkk-olive-branch-invasion (26 Aug. 2018).
15. Yılmaz, Hakan. *Türkiye'de Muhafazakarlık. Aile, Cinselik, Din*. Ekim 2012, http://www.aciktoplumvakfi.org.tr/pdf/muhafazakarlik/04.pdf (30 Aug. 2018).

Sylwester Gardocki

Russian Contemporary Policy towards Syria

Abstract: Since many years, Russia has decided to regain its influence in the Middle East. In order to play a role with aspiration to be a superpower Russian leaders started to 'defend' its positions in the region. Thus Russia still collaborates with Iran which is facing the reimposition of sanctions and has involved its military forces in the war in Syria to support Bashar al-Assad regime. In the chapter the Russian policy in the Middle East is explained in the context of Syrian war in particular.

Keywords: Syria, Russian Foreign Policy, Bashar al-Assad, Middle East

Conflict in Syria lasting since 2011 has become quietened, but it is still not resolved. Russia, alongside with Islamic Republic of Iran, has played a major political and military role in standing by the Bashar al-Assad regime. Until, now, there is no possibility to resolve Syrian conflict with any Russian participation. After military involvement to help al-Assad to regain its control over Syrian territory, president of Russian Federation Vladimir Putin confirmed that Syria takes for him a very important place in a global rivalry between powers over the expansion of influence.

The main aim of this chapter is to explain the Russian policy in shaping the area of global and regional position what is correlated with the preservation and expansion of influence. Russian engagement in the war in Syria serves as an illustrative case of activity and securing its own position in relation to the U.S.

In the chapter the hypothesis is that Russia conducts global strategy of securing its interests in order to have an impact for any possible regional conflict resolution. For that reason, Syria plays a vital role for Russian interests in the Middle East but also for any other deals this state makes with U.S. especially or any different state throughout the world.

In order to verify proposed thesis some research questions have been raised. First, what is the concept of Russian strategy in the Middle East? Second, why did Russia decide to intervene in Syria in a military way to such an extent? Third, what is the role of Syria in the Russian policy in the Middle East?

A few methods and approaches have been applied in the chapter. Owing to Russian particular interest in relation to Syrian war and also in the whole Middle East, author based on realistic paradigm in international relations. It allows to explain all the mechanisms of rivalry in the case of Syrian conflict and also the conditions of temporary alliances.

Russian Strategy in the Middle East: Overview

After the collapsing of USSR, Russian strategy in the Middle East must have been redefined. Due to loss of great influence as USSR had spread in the Middle East, particularly in Iraq, Syria and also People's Democratic Republic of Yemen, Russia as inheritor of Soviet Union was facing new challenges. In the time of shaping its newborn political identity Russia faced with regaining its influence in the Middle East (replacing USSR) and tried to build a new form of relations based on non-ideological foundation and mutual interests. In the 1990s of the 20th century, during the Boris Yeltsin presidency Middle East was treated as same as other non-European regions towards which Russia could have not presented any coherent strategy mainly due to reorganizing itself in post-Soviet area.

Vladimir Putin who became a president of Russian Federation in December 1999 laid down the first step in ground preparations for real strategy towards Middle East. After stifling rebellion in Chechnya, he spread complete control over Chechnyan territory handing over the governing of the Republic to trusted Ramzan Kadyrov. For that reason Putin accomplished his mission, he declared before taking over the presidency, about resolving the situation in North Caucasus. Additionally resolving the problem of North Caucasus instability, Russia blocked any support given to Chechen rebels mainly from the Middle East. All actions taken by Russian military forces against Chechen rebels were justified the label of "war with international terrorism". Thus Russia effectively led to diminish the world opinion and criticism about their soldiers' inhuman actions[1].

In the beginning of the 21st century Russia decided to modify its politics related to Middle East. In the face of U.S. intervention in Iraq and toppling down Saddam Hussein's regime, Russia tried to work out a strategy which based not only on military and political goals but also on economic cooperation. Thus three elements combined together and shaped a new strategy toward the Middle East. It is been confirmed by Putin and then Dmitry Medvedev that 'Russian foreign policy is clearly focused on contributing to the goal of economic consolidation and the integral strengthening of Russia'. In this case the priority of geoeconomics over geopolitics has been emphasized[2].

---

1 Roland Dannreuther, Russia and the Middle East: A Cold War Paradigm?, "Europe-Asia Studies", vol. 64, No. 2, 2012, p. 546.

2 Dannreuther, Russia and the Middle East, p. 550.

In 2005 Russia increased its engagement in the Middle East. From 2005 to 2007 President Putin visited Egypt, Israel, Jordan, Oman, Saudi Arabia, Iran, Turkey and United Arab Emirates. In comparison to Boris Yeltsin who paid no official visit to Middle Eastern states, it was a great achievement. In particular, Putin's visit in Israel in 2005, which was the first ever by a Russian leader, showed the importance of Israel in the Russian policy in the Middle East[3]. During Putin's visit in Israel and meeting with Prime Minister Ariel Sharon one anecdote occurred. Putin described himself as "new man" in the Middle East and asked Sharon for the first advice to him. Sharon replied "never trust anyone". Later the situation was confirmed by current Minister of Foreign Affairs of Russian Federation Sergey Lavrov[4].

Tightening relations with Israel was motivated by economic factors. In 2009, the trade between Russia and Israel reached the amount of 3 billion USD, significantly more than with any Arab state. Russia developed economic ties with Israel to gain new technologies for improving and diversification of its own economy. Developing ties with Israel with synchronous close ties with Iran, Syria and even Palestinian Hamas was a unique achievement. Putin convinced Israeli leaders that all Russian engagement in the relation with Israeli enemies and involvement in a peace process is also beneficial for Israel's security[5].

In 2008 Israel and Russia signed agreement about mutual non-visa travel between two states. Hence, visiting Russian families of Jewish origin which settled down in Israel after the migration in the 1990s was much easier by the Russian citizens. On the wave of improving mutual relations in 2010, Russia and Israel signed military agreement on a long-term cooperation for the first time in history[6].

Basic result of contemporary Russia's strategy is to maintain positive relations with all the states in the Middle East even if they are in deep conflict with each other like Iran and Saudi Arabia or Syria, Iran with Israel. Inviting Russia as an observer to Organisation of Islamic Conference in 2005 heralded more friendly reception of Russia by Arab and Muslim states in the Middle East.

---

3 James Sladden, Becca Wasser, Ben Connable, Sarah Grand-Clement, RAND Perspectives No. 236, 24 Oct. 2018, https://www.rand.org/pubs/perspectives/PE236.html.

4 Alexey Vasiliev, Russia's Middle East Policy. From Lenin to Putin, New York 2018, p. 322.

5 Dannreuther, Russia and the Middle East p. 551.

6 The agreement resulted in Israeli licence handed over to Russia for drones production. Vasiliev, Russia's Middle East Policy, p. 327.

Russia is conscious that if one wants to be global player it must secure its own position at the table of negotiations and decisions. For this purpose improving relations with almost all Middle Eastern states has been initiated and decision on military involvement in Syria has been taken.

However, many analysts question if Russia has a strategy in the Middle East. According to expert of RAND there are three answers. First is that Russia has a Middle East strategy and it is mainly successful. Second is that Russian state has a regional strategy but it does not work as Russia had intended. Third is that Russia lacks a Middle East strategy. A verified answer of this issue might be based on the explanation of Russian specialists who cooperated with RAND and attended workshops, who declared that in the strategy of foreign policy of Russia towards Middle East mostly pragmatism is presented, aiming at reaching short-term requirements for stability and economic opportunity. This assumption dominated long-term perspectives with far-reaching objectives[7].

Peculiarities of Russian-Syrian Relations

Relations between Russia and Syria have a long history and a special meaning. During USSR time Syria was one of the key ally in Soviet foreign policy in the Middle East. Efraim Karsh described these type of connections as a "patron-client relationship" where USSR played a role of patron obviously[8]. Roy Allison in his analysis of Russian-Syrian relations pointed that during 'Cold War' times both parties needed each other and Syria under pan-Arab ruling of Hafiz al-Assad was one of the steadfast ally of USSR in the Middle East. This relationship based on strategic interdependence and the communist ideology, in this case, had no any meaning but was even contradictious with socialist and nationalist Syrian Ba'th Party regime[9].

Ideological differences were not an obstacle to sign the Treaty of Friendship and Cooperation between the Union of Soviet Socialist Republics and Syrian Arab Republic in 1980. Agreement based on common perception of the Middle East Cold War rivalry in the aspect of preventing forms of colonialism, imperialism including Zionism[10]. President H. al-Assad was reluctant to sign such

---

7 James Sladden, Becca Wasser, Ben Connable, Sarah Grand-Clement, op.cit., pp. 8–9.

8 Efraim Karsh, Soviet policy toward Syria since 1970, New York 1991, pp. 11–34.

9 Roy Allison, Russia and Syria: explaining alignment, "International Affairs", 2013, 89:4, p. 801.

10 The Treaty of Friendship and Cooperation between Union of Soviet Socialists Republics and Syrian Arab Republic, [in:] Efraim Karsh, op.cit., Appendix 1, pp. 212–214.

a treaty due to ideological discrepancies between Syria and USSR. However, necessity and perspective of Soviet support with military training and arms deals convinced him to follow this way. In fact, by the year of 2006 about 10000 Syrian officers received training at Soviet/Russian academies[11].

After collapsing of USSR Syria stayed as one of the important states in the spectrum of post-Soviet politics. Positive ties have been maintained although Russia had no such position as USSR in the Middle East. In December 1991 Syria recognized Russia as Soviet Union's successor. In September 1992 Minister of Foreign Affairs of Syria Faruk al-Shara visited Moscow and discussed about new vision of bilateral relations. Russian Foreign Minister Andrey Kozyriev told al-Shara that anti-Western ideological component of Russian-Syrian relations would be eliminated[12]. Afterwards, in September 1993 Russian Vice Foreign Minister Anatoly Adamishin paid a visit to Syria and discussed bilateral relations and also clearly stated about Russian willingness to engage in peace process. It meant that Russia in the period of self-organizing its statehood gave the U.S. free will to shape and control Israel-Palestinian issue[13].

In the 1990s of the 20th century Syrian-Russian relations, although they deteriorated because of obvious reasons, retained much importance due to four factors. First was connected with the Syrian army equipped mainly with Soviet weapons and needed a supply of spare parts. The second factor regarded Syrian debt rated at 11–17 billion USD what was a part of negotiations between two parts. The third factor referred to Russia's willingness to become a more important "player" in a peace process in the Middle East, and the last factor concerned deep personal relations between Russian and Syrian leaders[14].

However, the intensity of Russian-Syrian relations could not have been compared to that between Soviet Union and Syria. Russia was not able to "enter" into a peace process due to hard stand of Israel which blocked Russia in time of its converting and reorganizing policy. In 1999 president of Syria Hafiz al-Asad visited Russia, and this event would have been crucial. In fact, nothing special has been arranged and Syrian assumptions that Russia would restore Syria-Israel negotiations were miscalculated. At that time, Israel became a greater economic partner than Syria was. Even if there were obstacles at Israel's side in refraining

11 Allison, Russia and Syria: explaining alignment pp.801–802.

12 Andrej Kreutz, Russia in the Middle East: Friend or Foe?, Westport-London 2007, p. 18.

13 Kreutz, Russia in the Middle East: Friend or Foe?, p. 19

14 Kreutz, Russia in the Middle East: Friend or Foe?,

Russia from converging to Syrian interests, the developing Russian trade with Israel was considered an important factor[15].

When V. Putin became president, Russia started to purse the policy of resolving the instability in Caucasus and then regaining Russian position in post-Soviet territories and also in such regions as the Middle East. In 2005 President B. al-Assad visited Russia and meeting with Putin was considered a milestone. Russia annulated 73 % of Syrian debt and criticized Israeli and U.S. policy in the Middle East, however not taking any political actions against Israel. It was pointed that this al-Assad's visit laid a foundation of restoring Russian-Syrian ties as it was in the 1980s[16].

In the face of U.S. military presence in Iraq and Israeli offensive policy in the Middle East, Russia decided to secure its position in the region and extend its activity to have a possibility of playing an important "role" in the Middle East. Thus Russian-Syrian rapprochement was not coincidental and was an effect of Russian adjustment to changing political leverage between super powers and regional powers in the Middle East.

After 2005 political and economic ties between Russia and Syria were growing fast. Annual trade increased from 560 million USD to 2 billion USD in 2008. Among goods of Syrian import from Russia were mainly petrochemical products, engineering products – for oil and gas industry, tractors and trucks. Since 2005 Russian military advisers and officers started to serve and train Syrian military units. In 2006 Syria became equipped with Russian medium-range missile system. However, Russia did not accept Syrian requests for providing them S-300 missile system[17].

In May 2010 President Dmitry Medvedev paid a visit to Syria. Both sides agreed on common vision of Middle East process and even concluded a declaration of making the Middle East as a nuclear-free zone. During his visit to Syria, Medvedev also met with Hamas leader Khaled Mashal what strengthened the pro-Syrian standpoint[18].

Syria also manifested its pro-Russian attitude in the international politics. In 2008, alongside with Belarus, expressed its support for Russian military intervention in Georgia. In May 2018 Syria officially recognized two separatist republics – South Ossetia and Abkhazia and established diplomatic relations with them.

---

15 Kreutz, Russia in the Middle East: Friend or Foe?, pp.21–24.

16 See: Vasiliev, Russia's Middle East Policy, p. 387.

17 Vasiliev, Russia's Middle East Policy, pp. 387–388.

18 Vasiliev, Russia's Middle East Policy, p. 389.

Russian Engagement in the War in Syria

When the demonstrations in Syria turned into a civil war, Russia faced a big dilemma. It seemed that Syria became next in turn of a phenomenon called "Arab Spring" to demolish petrified government of Ba'th Party. The cases of Tunisia, Egypt, Yemen and particularly Libya showed that this option was taken seriously.

At the beginning, Russia feared of its position in the Middle East if Syria followed Tunisian, Egyptian or Libyan way of collapsing regimes. After years of restoration the friendly relations Syria became again one of the most important player in the Russian foreign policy in the Middle East. With Syria, Russia was able to make a counter-balance to U.S., Israeli and Saudi policy in the region. Additionally, having a large-scale access to military harbour in Tartus, Russia demonstrated its position not only in the Middle East but also in the area of the Mediterranean. If Syria was lost as an ally it would decline Russian position in the Middle East compared to the role of passive observer.

For that reason, Russia at once protested against considering Syrian case in the terms of conflict and its resolution in Libya. Foreign Minister of Russia Sergey Lavrov stated that reproducing Libyan experience, in particular military intervention, in other states like Syria was very dangerous, and in June 2011 he claimed that the situation in Syria did not pose a threat to the international peace and security[19].

In 2011 Russian position toward Syrian crisis was still ambiguous. President D. Medvedev announced even that Russia would not give a full shield to Syrian regime[20]. In that situation Russia was seeking balance between giving support to al-Assad regime and the West and Israel. However, there were limits to accept U.S. actions against Syria and in October 2011 Russia (along with China) vetoed draft resolution on Syria. It assumed condemnation of using military force against civilians by Syrian government and laid responsibility on Syrian regime for death of thousands of civilians[21]. Simultaneously Russia denied Arab League stance of imposing sanctions on Syria. Only two Syrian neighbours did not support the Arab League resolution – Lebanon and Iraq[22].

---

19 Allison, Russia and Syria: explaining alignment, p. 798

20 Allison, Russia and Syria: explaining alignment.

21 Full text of draft resolution: UN Security Council, 24 Oct. 2018. S/2011/612, https://www.securitycouncilreport.org/un-documents/document/syria-s2011-612.php.

22 Neil MacFarquhar, Nada Bakri, Isolating Syria, Arab League Imposes Broad Sanctions, "New York Times", November 27, 2011.

At the same time, initiated by U.S. and France and supported by Qatar and majority of states in the Arab League, "The Group of Friends of Syria" was established. Afterwards in February 2012 The Group recognized opposite to Al-Assad Syrian National Council (in November 2012 replaced by National Coalition for Syrian Revolution and Opposition Forces) as a legal representative of Syrian nation[23]. Russia opposed such formation of a group which might have decided about Syrian future and recognized Free Syrian Army (military representative of opposition) as a 'cover' for varied extremist groups.

Russian officials did not believe in U.S. arguments of military intervention in Syria after al-Assad extremely violated human rights. Instead, they perceived the U.S. intentions as geopolitically driven policy to eliminate the al-Assad regime which contradicts U.S. interest in the Middle East. The statement of Barack Obama in August 2011 about al-Assad stepping aside as official U.S. priority carried conviction to Russian leaders that it was the genuine purpose of U.S. activity[24].

In those circumstances Russia officially backed Syrian regime without any deliberation on U.S.-Russian rivalry but using basic arguments such as: international terrorism threat, anxiety for the territorial integrity of Syria and securing the status quo in the Middle East. Russian officials tried to match challenges and threats of their own state with those related to Syrian issue. Thus Sunni extremism in Syria was described by them as an extension of networks in the Islamic world[25]. Discussing the conflict in Syria Russia emphasized the possibility of large-scale involvement of Sunni radical group if the conflict would be more exacerbated and long-lasting. For sure, Russian leaders identified the radical groups' and movements' threat with the experience of Chechen war and the territory of North Caucasus still becoming a shelter for variable terrorists including "lone wolves".

Appearing of Jabhat al-Nusra, later associated with al-Qaeda and particularly Islamic State which became the most dangerous terrorist organization after the establishment of al-Qaeda, was a decent proof for Russian officials to use this argument as an explanation of its own interests in Syria. In the next years a lot of citizens of Russian Federation fascinated by the notions and ideology of Islamic State decided to join their ranks and fought in Syria.

23 Vasiliev, Russia's Middle East Policy, pp. 446–447.

24 Samuel Charap, Russia, Syria and the Doctrine of Intervention, "Survival" February-March 2013, Vol. 55, No. 1, p. 37.

25 Allison, Russia and Syria: explaining alignment, p. 810.

In 2017, according TASS (Russian News Agency) 2500 Russian citizens served in military units of Islamic State in Syria and Iraq[26]. Many of them originated from Chechnya and North Caucasus[27]. It also justified and labelled Russian activity in Syria.

When situation of B. al-Assad forces deteriorated and the fall of the regime became a real option, in 2015 President V. Putin decided to send Russian troops to Syria in order to help al-Assad to come out of the deadlock and reverse his position. Concentrated air strikes of Russian forces and using ground troops to fight rebel's position quickly came with result of taking the prevalence by al-Assad regime. Then government forces alongside with its allies (Russian troops, Iranian forces, Shia Hizballah and volunteers) finally regained the control over majority of territory including major cities like Aleppo.

In March 2016 Putin announced withdrawing Russian troops in Syria pointing that Russian military involvement was only a short-term action. Having in mind rigours of American military ground troops involvement in Iraq and Afghanistan and also Soviet long-lasting presence in Afghanistan and their repercussions, could not let Russian troops to stay officially in Syria any longer. Certainly, it did not mean Russians have withdrawn from Syria completely but they left indispensable amount of troops (jets, ground troops, military advisor) to control the situation in Syria. Currently Russian airplanes operate in the Hmeimim Air Base and they raid opposition's locations.

Role of Syria in the Russian Policy in the Middle East

Since decades Syria played a major role in Soviet and then Russian policy in the Middle East. In the 21st century Russia and Syria tightened mutual relations and hence with no exaggeration Syria can be described as one of the key elements in the Russian strategy in this region. However, it needs to be emphasized that Russia considers Syria as limited partner. In bilateral relations partnership is connected with trade and providing goods and military equipment for Syrian regime. Somewhat partnership is Russian granting an 'umbrella' for al-Assad government instead of having direct access to military bases and what's

26 Around 2500Russian citizens fighting alongside Islamic State – Civic chambers, 24 Oct. 2018. http://tass.ru/en/world/821862

27 See: Neil Hauer, Chechen and North Caucasian Militants in Syria, Atlantic Council, January 18, 2018, 24 Oct. 2018. https://www.atlanticcouncil.org/blogs/syriasource/chechen-and-north-caucasian-militants-in-syria.

even more important, to have Syria as instrument at the 'bargaining table' with U.S. and other states of the Middle East.

At the beginning of the war in Syria, Russian Foreign Minister S. Lavrov accurately pointed that all the western accusations of al-Assad are just a cover for grand geopolitical game[28]. The meaning of that was simple. The confusion over Syria was not about Syria exactly but Iranian or Russian influences. Russian officials were deeply conscious of that and they precisely knew U.S.' intentions behind toppling down al-Assad. Changing the regime in Syria would limit Iranian and also Russian position in the Middle East and their possibility to react in the region.

Samuel Charap confirmed this thesis in his paper pointing that "Russia's stance on international action on the Syria crisis has more to do with anxieties about the implications US power than it does with Syria itself"[29].

Then, one can notice that Syrian battlefield became a clear example of superpowers and regional powers rivalry. In the beginning Russia took restrained attitude to al-Assad regime. However, when the civil war in Syria turned into an international conflict Russia had no choice but to defend *status quo* and to keep al-Assad in power.

Russian military intervention conducted in the end of September was a clear proof of Russian strategy of securing its position in the Middle East. It was not coincidence that Putin chose such a time when U.S. and all Americans were absorbed in elections and the competition between Donald Trump and Hilary Clinton. At the time of presidential elections, international issues have a secondary meaning and U.S. citizens and politicians predominantly concentrate on internal affairs.

In result, helping to keep al-Assad in power Russia guaranteed itself a status of decisive state and secured its position in the Middle East. Currently any plan for Syrian conflict resolution needs to be discussed with participation of Russia. Due to the extent of Russian prevalence in Syria it was facilitated to engage separate states in a group resolving the Syrian conflict. Thus Russia encouraged Iran and Turkey to organize several summits of foreign ministers and ministers of defence under the umbrella of "Astana talks" into which U.S. was not invited.

What's more, in January 2018 in Sochi, Russia organized Syrian National Dialogue Congress in which participated representatives of government and

28 Allison, Russia and Syria: explaining alignment, p. 808.

29 Charap, Russia, Syria and the Doctrine of Intervention, p. 37.

opposition. On the assembly the final statement has been adopted in which participants arranged guidelines for the final normative act in Syria[30].

Having prevalence in Syria, Russia secured its place at the 'table of negotiations' but also has a valuable "bargain chip" at its disposal. Due to the fact of existence of diverse interdependencies in the relations between superpowers, Russia can play the Syrian card referring to the completely different issue even if it regards the location far away from the Middle East. For instance, unresolved conflict in the Eastern Ukraine can be negotiated by Russians with the Syrian card in their hands. This is the way the superpowers secure its position in case of opportunities to reach a compromise.

Conclusion

The expansion of conflict in Syria brought about taking extreme measures by Russia. Military involvement in the war and keeping the permanent control over the Syrian government policy secured Russian position in this state and in the Middle East. Nevertheless, financial assets or political justification of the taking part in the war directly, Russia guaranteed itself a prevalence over U.S. and its allies. With the capability of converging its interests with the interest of other states President Putin proved to be a serious 'geopolitical player' in the trouble area such as Middle East. Iran had no option but to rely on Russian assistance in the Syrian issue, and Turkey arbitrarily decided to cooperate with Russia in terms of Syrian conflict resolution even though it is a NATO member.

Bibliography

1. Allison, Roy. "Russia and Syria: Explaining Alignment", *International Affairs*, Vol. 89, No. 4, 2013. pp. 795–823
2. Charap, Samuel. "Russia, Syria and the Doctrine of Intervention", *Survival*, February-March, Vol. 55, No. 1, 2013. pp. 35–41
3. Dannreuther, Roland. "Russia and the Middle East: A Cold War Paradigm?", *Europe-Asia Studies*, Vol. 64, No. 2, 2012. pp. 543–560

30 Заключительное заявление Конгресса сирийского национального диалога, Сочи, 30 января 2018 года, http://www.mid.ru/en/foreign_policy/news/asset_publisher/cKNonkJE02Bw/content/id/3046246?p_p_id=101_INSTANCE_cKNonkJE02Bw&_101_INSTANCE_cKNonkJE02Bw_languageId=ru_RU, 24 Oct. 2018.

4. Karsh, Efraim. Soviet Policy toward Syria since 1970, Palgrave-Macmillan, New York 1991.
5. Kreutz, Andrej. Russia in the Middle East: Friend or Foe?, Praeger Security International, Westport-London 2007.
6. MacFarquhar, Neil, Bakri, Nada. “Isolating Syria, Arab League Imposes Broad Sanctions”, *New York Times*, November 27, 2011.
7. Vasiliev, Alexey. Russia’s Middle East Policy. From Lenin to Putin, Routledge, New York 2018.

Internet Sources

1. Around 2500Russian citizens fighting alongside Islamic State – Civic chambers, http://tass.com/world/821862 (24 Oct. 2018).
2. Hauer Neil, Chechen and North Caucasian Militants in Syria, Atlantic Council, January 18, 2018, https://www.atlanticcouncil.org/blogs/syriasource/chechen-and-north-caucasian-militants-in-syria (24 Oct. 2018).
3. Sladden James, Wasser Becca, Connable Ben, Grand-Clement Sarah, RAND Perspectives No.236, https://www.rand.org/pubs/perspectives/PE236.html (24 Oct. 2018).
4. UN Security Council, S/2011/612, https://www.securitycouncilreport.org/un-documents/document/syria-s2011-612.php (24 Oct. 2018).
5. Заключительное заявление Конгресса сирийского национального диалога, Сочи, 30 января 2018 года, http://www.mid.ru/en/foreign_policy/news/-/asset_publisher/cKNonkJE02Bw/content/id/3046246?p_p_id=101_INSTANCE_cKNonkJE02Bw&_101_INSTANCE_cKNonkJE02Bw_languageId=ru_RU (24 Oct. 2018).

Hana N. Hlaváčková

EU Small States and Their Fight against IS*

Abstract: Submitted chapter will focus at the theoretical level on the concept of small states and their possibilities to fight against terrorism. At the analytical level, it will show how selected small states of EU take activity in the common action of fight against terrorist group such as so-called Islamic state (IS). Author will focus on states of central (southeast) Europe: Poland, Czech Republic, Slovakia, Hungary and Slovenia. Main aim of the chapter is to show the importance of the activity of these small states. According to the concept of power of small states, it is obvious that the activity is not always active; however, also passive support is important to defeat IS. Author will show different ways of support by states in the fight against IS, both practical activities and political discussion. EU realizes the threat of IS, which is external to the security, the action must be taken abroad to defeat terrorism, far away from the EU borders or Schengen area. Great powers of Europe take action and initiative; however, small states also play their roles. The scope of activity and roles will be shown. Author has used qualitative methodology, specifically content analysis of created dataset composed of political declarations, media image and information about activity. Main research question is what roles and what range of activity is representative for selected states in the fight against IS.

Keywords: Terrorism, Islamic state, small states, role theory, Czech Republic, Poland, Slovakia, Slovenia, Hungary

Introduction

Now it is way harder to say whether terrorism is an external threat or an internal threat to European security. Islamic terrorism was for Europe an external threat coming inside; however, with Islamic State it is different. It has power to fight from outside. That is the reason, why the response also must be taken externally, not only internally, as was more usual. EU had to learn new strategies to fight a new form of terrorist organization such as Islamic state and had to understand, where exactly we can find the threats. Unfortunately, the

---

* This publication is the result of Metropolitan University Prague research project no. 68-02 'Territorial studies, Economy and International relations', which was conducted in 2019 under a grant from the Institutional Fund for the Long-term Strategic Development of Research Organisations.

way of learning was painful for European society, through terrorist attacks. Now, EU developed strategies, which are not 100 % safe; however, it is the only instrument EU has. Islamic state is a terrorist organization with its specificity. It is a new form of organization conquering the territory. It is different than Al-Qaeda. Terrorists seek for save-havens and when you are connected to exact territory, it is hard to hide. However it seems, that even in the situation, that the territory could be won back on the side of good, the good is still not winning. Islamic state has two faces: To conquer the territory and set up a caliphate outside EU; to conquer territory, spread fear and harm EU. In some respects, small states are not very different from medium-sized and large states. They exist in an interdependent world, and in many cases operate within a legacy from a colonial past. Their governments aspire to higher standards of living, but must struggle with limited material and human resources. European Union fails to solve the biggest problem in the history of integration. Whether security questions should be solved together or not together. There are EU missions in the unstable countries which should help stabilize the environment in the country.

Even small states of Europe are joining to coalition in the fight against IS. The fight must be waged in two front lines. First is inside Europe. Cooperation is done between information services, police, customs officers in the need to track suspicious persons, protection of important buildings, etc. The other front line is active or passive support outside Europe. Passive kind of cooperation is highly important in the fight against IS. Terrorists seek for safe-havens and when you are connected to exact territory, it is hard to hide. However it seems, that even in the situation, that the territory could be won back on the side of good, the good is still not winning. In some respects, small states are not very different from medium-sized and large states. They exist in an interdependent world, and in many cases operate within a legacy from a colonial past. Their governments aspire to higher standards of living, but must struggle with limited material and human resources. European Union fails to solve the biggest problem in the history of integration. Whether security questions should be solved together or not together. There are EU missions in the unstable countries which should help stabilize the environment in the country, so each state react as what is in his interest.

Aim of the chapter is to (1) *show different ways of support including political discussion around*; (2) *show the importance of the activity of these small states.* Main research question is *what roles and what range of activity is representative for selected states in the fight against IS*?

Theoretical and Methodological Framework

In my research I use social constructivism as a theoretical framework according to Checkel[1]. With constructivism we can speak about role theory as a one way of foreign policy analysis. Role theory is an instrument on how to study and analyze foreign policy behaviour of states. Authors of role theory also use constructivism, but often do not say how exactly. Some of them work with empirical research and some of them are more influenced by language and identity. Point is that with constructivism, you do not have to use one theory; there is more than one version and we can combine them. The same situation is with role theory. For example, L. Aggestam[2] (1999, 2006) combines rational positions of realism, foreign policy is based on maximization of gains, and however, role itself is socially constructed. In the role theory, there can be such combination.

In my research, role is socially constructed, and states learn roles according to rules inside institutions. I mean NATO and EU. Role is also based on material and non-material factors (norms, etc.).

Role conception is connected with the concept of identity. Identity is a part of role conception and has influence at its form. Creation of role is part of social reality and is formed by external and internal actors[3]. These actors put some expectations which can form the role itself. In some cases the role can be changed in time. It is connected with the norm and ideational changes. This is called process of socialization which for constructivists is very important. According to Elgström and Smith[4] role is constructed by the power in the international system

1 See Jeffrey T. Checkel, "International Norms and Domestic Politics: Bridging the Rationalist – Constructivist Divide." *European Journal of International Relations,* vol. 3, no. 4 (1997), pp. 473–495.; Jeffrey T. Checkel, "The Constructivism Turn in International Relations Theory. " *World Politics,* vol. 50, no. 2 (1998), pp. 324–348.; Jeffrey T. Checkel, "Theoretical Pluralism in IR: Possibilities and Limits". in: *Handbook of International Relations* In Walter Carlsnaes, Thomas Risse-Kappen, Beth Simmons, 2002, pp. 220–241.; Jeffrey T. Checkel, "Constructivism and EU Politics. " in: *Handbook of European Union Politics*. Knud E. Jørgensen, Pollack, M. A. Ben Rosamond, (London, Sage, 2006). 57–76.

2 Lisbeth Aggestam, "*Role Conceptions and the Politics of Identity in Foreign Policy*" (Centre for European Studies, 1999).; Lisbeth Aggestam, "Role theory and European foreign policy: a Framework of analysis. " in: *The European Union´s Roles in International Politics. Concepts and Analysis*. Ole Elgström, Michael Smith. (London, Routledge, 2006), pp. 11–29.

3 Martin Hollis, Sheila Smith, "Roles and Reasons in Foreign Policy Decision Making" *British Journal of Political Science,* vol. 16, no. 3 (1986), pp. 269–286.

4 Ole Elgström, Michael Smith, "Introduction" in: *The European Union´s Roles in International Politics. Concepts and analysis,* Elgström, Ole – Smith, Michael (Abingdon, Routledge, 2006), pp. 1–10.

or by the status of the actor. Small states are predetermined to different roles, without high goals or leadership. For example, typical roles are mentor, model, intermediary and bearer of values[5]. Role of small states is determined by the relationship to external environment.

We can name the role according to such specific relations and acting of actors[6]. There is a connection between the process of role conception and external expectations. Role is then influenced by norms and values which state accepts. Role conception consists of attitude frames, decisions, functions and commitments to community. Political decision makers fill the role with their own definitions, decisions, commitments, rules and activities. In this context, it is clear that the role has to be studied in a social context and the role is formed by intersubjective meanings. Role theory is a reflection of international context. Role conception and its role performance have to be seen in a broader context of how foreign policy is created[7]. In the schema below we can see concepts which create the role of state. First is conception of role that consists of internal shared expectation, external expectations and national role conception and then comes the role performance. There is also possibility for a change; however, change itself is not an easy process.

According to Lisbeth Aggestam[8] these conceptions have this meaning:

(1) Role expectations – can be external and internal. Internal expectations are formed by political culture, society, politicians themselves. External expectations are formed by institutional structure where the actor belongs.

5 See Ole Elgström, Michael Smith, "Introduction"pp. 1–10.

6 Sebastian Harnisch, Cornelia Frank, Hanns W. Maull, "Introduction" in: *Role Theory in International Relations. Approaches and analyses*, Sebastian Harnisch, Cornelia Frank, Hanns W. Maull, (New York, Routledge, 2011), pp. 1–4.; Sebastian Harnisch, "Role theory: Operationalization of key concepts" in: *Role Theory in International Relations. Approaches and analyses,* Sebastian Harnisch, Cornelia Frank, Hanns W. Maull, (New York, Routledge, 2011), pp. 7–15; P.G. Le Prestre, "Change and Continuity in Foreign Policy Role Conceptions after the Cold War" in: *Role Quests in the Post-Cold War Era. Foreign Policies in Transition*, P.G. Le Prestre, (ed.), (London, McGill-Queen´s University Press, 1997), pp. 251–232.

7 Kalevi Holsti, "National Role Conceptions in the Study of Foreign Policy" *International Studies Quarterly,* vol. 14, no. 3 (1970), pp. 246; Kalevi Holsti, "National Role Conceptions in the Study of Foreign Policy" in: *Role Theory and Foreign Policy Analysis,* Stephen G. Walker, (Durham, Duke University Press, 1987), pp. 5–43.

8 Lisbeth Aggestam, "Role theory and European foreign policy: a Framework of analysis. ", pp. 11–29.

Tab. 1: Differentiation of roles according to whether states act responsibly or not. Source: author according to Holsti (1970)

Role with responsibility	Role without responsibility
Regional leader	Independent state
Regional protector	Regional subsystem cooperator
Ideational protector	Developer
Mediator-integrator	Bridge
Leader	Role as an example
Promoter of security	Independent actor
	Role of internal development
	Isolated state
	Protected state
	Ally

(2) National role conception – it is a normative interpretation of actor. Conception is long term and shows what possibilities and strategies can actor play. It is formed by history, culture and societal characteristics.
(3) Role performance – is actual behavior of the actor. It can be influenced by specific situations. The actor plays its role.
(4) Role change – role is stable figure; it has to be consistent so politicians can fulfill it. Role can be changed in the context. The situation must be in severe condition – political instability, change of norms and speculation about role.

According to how role is constructed, I have divided my research. I will search for external expectations, internal expectations and national role conception towards fight against terrorism.

K. Holsti[9] showed 17 roles of states that can be played. In these 17 types are some types which are not suitable for this time period (he created it during the Cold War), and some of the types are not suitable for small states. Here in table are all of them. I will work only with some of them. I have divided them into two groups for easier determination. In this table are types of roles according to responsibility, whether such state needs to be responsible or not.

In this article qualitative methodology is used. As a method of research I have used critical content analysis.

9 Kalevi Holsti, "National Role Conceptions in the Study of Foreign Policy" *International Studies Quarterly*, vol. 14, no. 3 (1970), pp. 246.

Tab. 2: Types of aid towards states to fight IS

State	Iraq	Syria
Czech Republic	Military aid	Military aid
Hungary	Military aid	Military aid
Poland	Military	Humanitarian aid
Slovakia	Humanitarian aid	Humanitarian aid
Slovenia	Military aid	Humanitarian aid

Case Studies of EU Small States in the Fight against IS

In 2014 USA had launched an international coalition to counter an armed offensive of IS which threatened Iraqis' sovereignty. Some European countries have decided to join the coalition. Some of them are more active than others. It depends on the power of the states, the size and the wealth. Some states decided to stay more passive and support with humanitarian aid or money. However, some of the small states are active also in the field and have sent troops to Iraq to fight against IS.

In this section, I will focus on each state. I am interested in several questions: What each state does to fight against IS? Is it passive or active support of the coalition? What is the reason for what they do? I will focus on political discourse about the activity to see the role, if there are any external expectations? At the end, it will give the picture about role. In Tab. 2 we can see the types of aid donation from chosen EU small states.

Mentioned small states are examples of states which are not active in the fight against IS as much as it would be appropriate. Only Poland took part in action with its military contribution in Iraq; other states provide military aid in Iraq except Slovakia which provided only humanitarian aid. In Syria, two of five provided military aid, Czech Republic and Hungary, others provided humanitarian aid. In other states where we can find Islamic state no one participated. The question is, why are states such passive actors contrary to the threat. Is it because they are small states? The financial costs are so high that they cannot spend more? The answer lies in the political debate. Politicians do not want to spend more because it is not favourite among citizens. The same problem is with more activity. Not only military aid like weapons, but active role should be seen from them. Each state said that the question of terrorism is vital, some states have spoken about responsibility, but no one took the responsibility seriously.

It is interesting to ask, why EU did not take any common action so far against terrorism and IS. There are many examples where EU interest has and is active and participates or commands a mission. Why is it not active also in this field? We can speak about actions of small states, about their roles, however no one can win if the EU loses. When there is no common action, even hundred small states are not enough. In conclusion to their activities. I would expect more action from them, according to what politics say to their societies or at the EU level. Therefore, any smart EU approach to global terrorism would dedicate more time preparing for the advent of the next terrorist group, instead of focusing only on the existing ones like ISIS or past ones like al-Qaida. Summing up, the EU is not expected to have a prominent role in the ongoing struggle against ISIS in Iraq and Syria, but it should be prepared to take the lead in the next round of the fight against terrorism.

Now I will focus on the role which each state plays, and I will use the theoretical framework according to Aggestam.

External Expectations

External expectations are constructed according to what each state thinks that it should behave. Of course, it is constructed by high politicians such as presidents, prime ministers, ministers of roeigh affairs and others. External expectation is a concept which is also connected to international organization which creates the structure of behavior. Almost all five states have mentioned NATO as a leading organization. Under the NATO rules they feel obliged and fulfill NATO commitments. Czech Republic feels to fulfill expectations of a good NATO member. In Hungary politicians often mentioned NATO, however also often mentioned "to follow US stratégy." It has connotations with US President Trump, who does not criticize Hungary for its internal politics (on contrary to previous US President Obama). Polish politicians repeated, that Poland wants to be a good (Western) ally and good member of NATO. There was a game behind in the context of negotiations between Poland and USA about eastern partnership, where Poland promised to join the coalition when USA will take part in a stronger cooperation in eastern Europe. Slovak politicians mentioned that they feel the responsibility in the fight against terrorism and the threats that "pertains also to us". In Slovenia it was repeatedly mentioned in the context of war against IS, that Slovenia takes a responsible part of international community, and EU and NATO. Slovenia has an interesting start at this story (fight against IS), because when USA has formed alliance to fight against IS, on the list was also Slovenia, however without any asking whether they would like to be part or not. To sum up, it was expectable that all small states feel a pressure to be part of antiterrorist coalition.

Internal Expectations

Internal expectations refer to what is expected from politicians, government, president and prime minister and other ministers. Internal expectations is the prevailing opinion about what country should do and why. On the contrary, it is also the opinion of how others will react on what we do. In the Czech Republic politicians said, that it is "reasonable to be part of such coalition". In Hungary by their activity politicians expect the fulfilling of its international obligations. Polish politicians expected to be respected (by NATO members), when they participate in the fight against IS. Slovak and Slovenian politicians expected, that when they participate, they will be part of a coalition. It is visible, that small states (who are not in a great danger) do not participate, because they would like to beat terrorism, however because they know, that international community (NATO) wants this from them. It is also a good way how to tell their citizens the reason of participation and also that they do what they can.

Fight against Terrorism Part of Identity and Reasons to Fight Terrorism

In this section, I was interested in the discourse in each state, whether fight against terrorism (IS) is the reason to participate and whether it is part of states identity. However, the analysis shows that it is not part of identity and reasons are diversified from state to state. Of course, that fight against terrorism can bring prestige; it was visible in Slovenian and Czech discourse. In Slovak and Polish discourse I could find the justification that international community needs help to defeat the threat. In Poland politicians speak about sort of responsibility. In Hungary it was mentioned that terrorism threatens Christian values and they need to be secure. Focusing on the reasons, in all five states politicians have mentioned different reasons. Czech politicians speak about securing Europe and that participation is good. In the Czech case it was also mentioned, that aid is a good business, because Czech army sold airplanes to Iraqi army, those airplanes which are at the end of expiration date. Czech government count this "aid" in the total expenditure of donor aid. In Hungary and Slovenia, there are partly common reasons for antiterrorist activity. Both countries have experienced migration flows, and both take part in the action to stop it. In Poland politicians mentioned that partners (in fight terrorism) have suffered casualties, and they feel the need to help the partners. In Slovakia politicians speak about the only solution, which is humanitarian help. These reasons justify their (non)activity in the fight against IS. However, there are also other reasons that politicians speak about their limits. Common to almost all five countries is that they are small countries with limited sources. We can listen politicians speaking about doing their best in the fight against IS. The responsibility was shuffled to international community and other states. Only Poland was most active (due to a barter business with the USA).

Roles and Conclusions

To detect some role, I had to divide the role into smaller pieces, into processes that create the role (parts above). To name the roles, I take Holsti's table of roles and searched for the common activities of states. Now I can make some conclusions about the roles. Czech Republic can be called a developer. Such role is connected with stabilization and development of states who suffer terrorism (Iraq and Syria). Czech Republic also plays an independent actor for sure. This actor can or cannot join the action whether it chose, whether the action is worthy or not. No one can count on such an actor. Hungary, Slovakia and Slovenia also play as developers and independent actors. All of them can be also named as allies. So Poland is an ally. This role does not take the responsibility for an action. Poland plays also a role with responsibility; it can be called a promoter of security. Such role means that this actor takes responsibility in the promotion of security in the countries or region. Other actors can count on it for help.

To sum up the analysis, there are few facts that I would like to highlight in the discourses of these five states. (1) All countries call for common action and responsibility of international community and no one feels actually responsible for the fight against IS. (2) They connect NATO and fight against terrorism inside Coalition against Terrorism as a one action (which is not). All states see fight against terrorism as a commitment to international community (NATO). (3) States participate because partners of international community are involved too. Here is visible the strong reason, to be a good member of NATO. (4) Also in other countries (not only Slovenia and Hungary) were discussions that fight against IS should stop migration flows. (5) Politicians also argue that military action has to go hand in hand with political solutions. To sum up. I think that there is also other reason why small states of EU participate on the fight against terrorism. (6) They just want to show the flag and get the prestige. If this would not be true, they would help more than just aid. They would actually participate, except Poland who promised participation. But small states and their politicians are tied with this topic, because military participation is not popular. Politicians could lose their support and maybe lose their jobs.

Bibliography

1. Aggestam, Lisbeth. "Role Theory and European Foreign Policy: A Framework of Analysis" in: *The European Union's Roles in International Politics. Concepts and Analysis*, Elgström, O. – Smith, M. (ed.). London: Routledge, 2006, pp. 11–29.
2. Aggestam, Lisbeth. *Role Conceptions and the Politics of Identity in Foreign Policy* ARENA working papers, 99/08, Oslo: Centre for European Studies University of Oslo, 1999.
3. Checkel, Jeffrey T. "Constructivism and EU Politics" in: *Handbook of European Union Politics*, Jørgensen, Knud E. – Pollack, M. A. – Rosamond, B. (ed.). London: Sage, 2006, pp. 57–76.
4. Checkel, Jeffrey T. "International Norms and Domestic Politics: Bridging the Rationalist – Constructivist Divide" *European Journal of International Relations*, vol. 3, no. 4, 1997, pp. 473–495.
5. Checkel, Jeffrey T. "The Constructivism Turn in International Relations Theory" *World Politics*, vol. 50, no. 2, 1998, pp. 324–348.
6. Checkel, Jeffrey T. "Theoretical Pluralism in IR: Possibilities and Limits" in: *Handbook of International Relations*, Carlsnaes, W. – Risse-Kappen, T. – Simmons, B. (ed.). London: Sage, 2002, pp. 220–241.
7. Elgström, Ole, Smith, Michael "Introduction" in: *The European Union's Roles in International Politics. Concepts and Analysis*, Elgström, O. – Smith, M. (ed.). Abingdon: Routledge, 2006, pp. 1–10.
8. Harnisch, Sebastian "Role theory: Operationalization of Key Concepts" in: *Role Theory in International Relations. Approaches and Analyses*, Harnisch, S. – Frank, C. – Maull, H. W. (ed.). New York: Routledge, 2011, pp. 7–15.
9. Harnisch, Sebastian, Frank, Cornelia, Maull, Hanns W. "Introduction" in: *Role Theory in International Relations. Approaches and analyses*, Harnisch, S. – Frank, C. – Maull, H. W. (ed.). New York: Routledge, 2011, pp. 1–4.
10. Hollis, Martin, Smith, Sheila "Roles and Reasons in Foreign Policy Decision Making" *British Journal of Political Science*, vol. 16, no. 3, 1986, pp. 269–286.
11. Holsti, Kalevi. "National Role Conceptions in the Study of Foreign Policy" *International Studies Quarterly*, vol. 14, no. 3, 1970, pp. 233–309.
12. Holsti, Kalevi. "National Role Conceptions in the Study of Foreign Policy" in: *Role Theory and Foreign Policy Analysis*, Walker, S. G. (ed.). Durham: Duke University Press, 1987, pp. 5–43.
13. Le Prestre, P. G. "Change and Continuity in Foreign Policy Role Conceptions after the Cold War" in: *Role Quests in the Post-Cold War Era. Foreign Policies in Transition*, Le Prestre, P. G. (ed.). London: McGill-Queen's University Press, 1997, pp. 251–232.

Internet Sources (Corpus Consists of These Data)

1. "Hungary to send more troops fight in war against terror," http://abouthungary.hu/news-in-brief/hungary-to-send-more-troops-fight-in-war-against-terror/ (15 Nov. 2017).
2. "In coalition against IS," http://abouthungary.hu/news-in-brief/in-coalition-against-islamic-state-hungary-extends-mission-in-iraq-until-2019/ (15 Nov. 2017). Apnews, https://www.apnews.com/0b9b211f2c784ab1a5f5bda0f38b0acb (15 Nov. 2017).
3. Arteaga, Felix "The European Union's role in the fight against ISIS," http://www.europeanleadershipnetwork.org/the-european-unions-role-in-the-fight-against-isis_1955.html (15 Nov. 2017).
4. Bohuslav Sobotka „Proč Evropa musí pomáhat, "http://www.bohuslavsobotka.cz/proc-musi-evropa-pomahat-v-boji-proti-islamskemu-statu (15 Nov. 2017).
5. Česká televize "Česko pomáhá v boji proti islámskému státu," http://www.ceskatelevize.cz/ct24/domaci/1928384-cesko-pomaha-v-boji-proti-islamskemu-statu-po-vojenskych-expertech-vysle-i-lekare (15 Nov. 2017).
6. Daily News Hungary "Hungary´s foreign minister us can continue," https://dailynewshungary.com/hungarys-foreign-minister-us-can-continue-rely-hungary-fight-terrorism/ (15 Nov. 2017).
7. Defence talk "Poland to send F16 jets," http://www.defencetalk.com/poland-to-send-f-16-jets-soldiers-in-fight-against-isis-67663/ (15 Nov. 2017).
8. Foreign Policy "Who has contributed," http://foreignpolicy.com/2014/11/12/who-has-contributed-what-in-the-coalition-against-the-islamic-state/ (15 Nov. 2017). http://www.globaltimes.cn/content/885310.shtml (15 Nov. 2017).
9. Hungarian free press "Hungary sends troops to fight isis," http://hungarianfreepress.com/2015/04/14/hungary-sends-troops-to-fight-isis/ (15 Nov. 2017).
10. Idnes „Islámský stat zařadil českou republiku do koalice dablu, " http://zpravy.idnes.cz/islamsky-stat-zaradil-ceskou-republiku-do-koalice-dablu-p2p-/zahranicni.aspx?c=A151125_162154_zahranicni_ert (15 Nov. 2017).
11. Kormany.hu "Ministry of foreign affairs," http://www.kormany.hu/en/ministry-of-foreign-affairs-and-trade/news/peter-szijjarto-pledges-increased-and-extended-hungarian-military-participation-in-the-fight-against-terrorism (15 Nov. 2017).
12. Kormany.hu "Ministry of human recources," http://www.kormany.hu/en/ministry-of-human-resources/news/budapest-declaration (15 Nov. 2017).

13. Kormany.hu "Ministry of foreign affairs and Trade," http://www.kormany.hu/en/ministry-of-foreign-affairs-and-trade/news/the-threat-of-terrorism-is-a-global-phenomenon (15 Nov. 2017).
14. Kormany.hu "Prime ministers office," http://www.kormany.hu/en/prime-minister-s-office/news/hungary-can-never-fall-again (15 Nov. 2017).
15. Kormany.hu "Prime ministers office," http://www.kormany.hu/en/prime-minister-s-office/news/taking-care-of-persecuted-christians-is-a-natural-obligation-of-hungary (15 Nov. 2017).
16. Kormany.hu "Thousands of SIS fighters could try to return Europe," http://www.kormany.hu/en/news/thousands-of-isis-fighters-could-try-to-return-to-europe (15 Nov. 2017).
17. MSZ "Deputy minister Trzaskowski," http://www.msz.gov.pl/en/news/deputy_minister_rafal_trzaskowski_receives_delegation_of_us_congressmen (15 Nov. 2017).
18. MSZ "Foreign minister attends meeting," http://www.msz.gov.pl/en/news/foreign_minister_attends_meeting_of_the_global_coalition_to_counter_isil_in_washington_d_c_ (15 Nov. 2017).
19. MSZ "Minister waszczykowski," http://www.msz.gov.pl/en/news/they_wrote_about_us/minister_waszczykowski__poland_must_be_part_of_fight_against_isil__pap_dispatch_of_22_july;jsessionid=63CA0EC738FF7E11DF0D40748A0AB52D.cmsap1p (15 Nov. 2017).
20. MZV "Lajčák na stretnuti globalnej koalicije proti dais," https://www.mzv.sk/aktuality/detail/-/asset_publisher/Iw1ppvnScIPx/content/m-lajcak-na-stretnuti-globalnej-koalicie-proti-dais-vojenske-tazenie-musi-ist-ruka-v-ruke-s-politickym-procesom-veducim-k-zmiereniu-/10182 (15 Nov. 2017).
21. MZV "M Lajčák teroristov z dais možeme porazit len spolocnymi silami," https://www.mzv.sk/aktuality/detail/-/asset_publisher/Iw1ppvnScIPx/content/m-lajcak-teroristov-z-dais-mozeme-porazit-len-spolocnymi-silami/10182 (15 Nov. 2017).
22. MZZ "Novica," http://www.mzz.gov.si/si/medijsko_sredisce/novica/article/141/37526/ (15 Nov. 2017).
23. MZZ "Novica," http://www.mzz.gov.si/si/medijsko_sredisce/novica/article/141/38232/ (15 Nov. 2017).
24. MZZ "Zunanja politika," http://www.mzz.gov.si/si/zunanja_politika_in_mednarodno_pravo/mednarodna_varnost/boj_proti_terorizmu/ (15 Nov. 2017).
25. Pulaski.pl "New Strategy in the fight against ISIS,"https://pulaski.pl/en/new-strategy-in-the-fight-against-isis-what-role-for-poland/ (15 Nov. 2017).

26. Reuters "US ISIS Slovenia," https://www.reuters.com/article/us-isis-slovenia/slovenia-offers-military-instructors-equipment-to-fight-islamic-state-idUSKCN0VC0GK (15 Nov. 2017).
27. Slovenia Times "US placed Slovenia on the list," http://www.sloveniatimes.com/us-placed-slovenia-on-the-list-of-anti-isis-coalition-without-any-consultation (15 Nov. 2017).
28. Spectator.sme.sk "Slovakia considers aid to fight against SIS," https://spectator.sme.sk/c/20052236/slovakia-considers-aid-to-fight-against-isis.html (15 Nov. 2017).
29. Telegrapg.co.uk "Who is in the anti-Islamic state coalition," http://www.telegraph.co.uk/news/worldnews/middleeast/syria/11124070/Who-is-in-the-anti-Islamic-State-coalition-and-what-they-are-contributing.html (15 Nov. 2017).
30. The Global Coalition "Slovenia," http://theglobalcoalition.org/en/partners/slovenia/ (15 Nov. 2017).
31. Vlada.si "Slovenia active in efforts," http://www.vlada.si/en/media_room/newsletter/slovenia_weekly/news/article/slovenia_active_in_efforts_to_stabilise_the_situation_in_iraq_and_syria_50061/ (15 Nov. 2017).
32. WBJ.pl "Poland to send ut to 210 troops," http://wbj.pl/poland-to-send-up-to-210-troops-to-fight-against-isis/ (15 Nov. 2017).

Jiří Zákravský

Sports Diplomacy of the State of Qatar and Its (Lack of) Success in the Czech Republic: Analysis of the Czech Nationwide Press in 2016[1]

Abstract: The State of Qatar is a typical example of a small but rich country that uses sports diplomacy to promote itself all around the world. The main question of my chapter I try to answer is: Is Qatari sports diplomacy successful in the Czech Republic? This could be complicated, as the success of sports diplomacy is hard to measure. My idea of how to accomplish that is based on the analysis of the Czech nationwide dailies, meaning the analysis of the seven most read newspapers in the Czech Republic in 2016.

Keywords: Sports diplomacy, Qatar, media analysis, the Czech Republic

Introduction

The British sociologist Barrie Houlihan said, there is "[...] one of the common clichés associated with sport that 'sport and politics should not mix'"[2]. However, it is possible to observe a very close relationship between these two modern phenomena; they – sport and politics – are not autonomous spheres and politicians may have an effect on sports issues. For example, (professional) sporting activities are financed by the governments from the national budgets, the governing politicians have thus a huge influence on sport[3]. Nowadays, sport has become an important foreign policy tool that is used by the majority of countries, it does not matter whether they are democratic or not. As the American ex-ambassador in Finland Derek Shearer mentioned, "[i]n a globalized world, sport is a vital part of almost every country's soft power. It can increase national pride, spread national influence, and serve as a

1 This work was supported by the Institutional support for the long-term conceptual development of the research organization Department of Politics and International Relations, University of West Bohemia in 2019.
2 Barrie Houlihan, *The Government and Politics of Sport* (New York: Routledge 2014), p. 4.
3 Ivo Štulajter, Danka Barteková and Matyáš Štulajter. *Športová diplomacia* (Banská Bystrica: Belianum – Vydavateľstvo Univerzity Mateja Bela 2013), p. 18.

useful tool of public diplomacy, encouraging communication and international understanding"[4].

This means that so-called sports diplomacy – a specific subcategory of public diplomacy – is currently one of the most popular ways how states try to promote themselves in the international society. According to Stuart Murray, sports diplomacy "[…] uses sports people and sporting events to engage, inform, and create a favourable image amongst foreign publics and organisations to shape their perceptions in a way that is more conducive to achieving a government's foreign policy goals"[5]. In an ideal case, successful sports diplomacy and successful use of sports diplomacy tools should lead to a more positive image of the country. However, what does it mean to use sports diplomacy successfully? How could we measure the success of sports diplomacy?

I try to demonstrate the way how this could be done on the example of the State of Qatar and its image in the Czech Republic in 2016 concerning sports issues. Qatar is a typical example of a small but rich country that in the long term does not hesitate to work with sport in the context of Qatar's foreign relations and that uses sports diplomacy for foreign policy goals. The current *Qatar's Sport Sector Strategy (2011–2016)* openly mentioned that "[a]t the international level, sports events and athletes help raise Qatar's regional and global profile, and result in enhanced national pride. International sport is also a powerful tool for international engagement and diplomacy through tourism, aid and trade"[6].

In the next section, I introduce sports diplomacy tools used by Qatari politicians. Afterwards, I pay attention to the way how we can measure the success of sports diplomacy, first in general, and secondly on the example of the State of Qatar. In this section, I try to demonstrate that media analysis is one of the ways how it is possible to measure, or maybe better to say interpret, the (lack of) success of sports diplomacy. The description of media analysis is presented in this part as well. The third section is dedicated to the result of the analysis of the Czech nationwide dailies regarding Qatar's sports diplomacy. At this point, I would like to present the major arguments to respond to the main question of

4 Derek Shearer, "To Play Ball, Not Make War. Sports, Diplomacy and Soft Power," *Harvard International Review*, Vol. 36, No. 1 (2014), p. 56.

5 Stuart Murray, "The Two Halves of Sports Diplomacy," *Diplomacy & Statecraft*, Vol. 23, No. 3 (2012), p. 581.

6 "Qatar Olympic Committee, Qatar's Sport Sector Strategy (2011–2016)," Second edition – July 2011 http://www.aspire.qa/Document/Sports_sector_strategy_final-English.pdf.

this chapter: *Is Qatari sports diplomacy successful in the Czech Republic?* Before concluding the chapter, this question should be answered.

The main goal of this chapter is to present Qatar's sports diplomacy and its (lack of) success in the Czech Republic and analyze the ways how the Czech nationwide dailies framework Qatar's sports image through the analysis of the Czech nationwide press in 2016. This chapter should be a pilot study related to the broader research of "sports diplomacy measuring".

Qatar's Sports Diplomacy Tools

In general, four main sports diplomacy tools are being distinguished: 1) membership in international sports organizations, 2) hosting famous sporting events, 3) using sportsmen as "diplomats" and 4) sponsorship of famous sports clubs[7]. The State of Qatar has been using all of these sports diplomacy tools which should lead to the construction of a positive Qatari image.

Membership in international sports organization. If a nation wants to be active in the field of international sport, it must be also a member of a relevant international sports organization.[8] Qatar declared independence in 1971. Afterwards, as Luis Henrique Rolim Silva pointed out, Qatar's national sports associations "started to request for membership of their respective International Federations"[9]. During the 1970s, Qatari requests were successful. For example, in the Fédération Internationale de Football Association (FIFA), the Qatar Football Association is affiliated since 1972, the Qatar Olympic Committee was recognized as a member of the International Olympic Committee (IOC) in 1980, etc.

Hosting famous sporting events. Geoffrey Allen Pigman assumed that "[…] international sporting events have been viewed by many governments as an

7 Jiří Zákravský, "Sport a mezinárodní vztahy. Sportovní diplomacie jako součást zahraniční politiky," *Central European Journal of Politics*, Vol. 2, No. 2 (2016), pp. 25–32.

8 Many stateless nations and their sports federations want to become the members of the international sports organizations, and they perceive this step as a symbolic way of their international recognition. For example, this issue was very important for Kosovo's politicians, see Dario Brentin and Loïc Tregoures, "Entering Through the Sport's Door? Kosovo's Sport Diplomatic Endeavours Towards International Recognition," *Diplomacy & Statecraft*, Vol. 27, No. 2 (2016), pp. 360–378, and for the Basque nationalists as well, see Jiří Zákravský, *Baskové v ofsajdu. Sport jako nástroj politiky nestátních národů. Případová studie fotbalu v Baskicku* (Praha: Dokořán 2017).

9 Luis Henrique Rolim Silva, "The Establishment of the Qatar National Olympic Committee: Building the National Sport Identity," *The International Journal of the History of Sport*, Vol. 31, No. 3 (2014), p. 306.

ideal venue to showcase a country, its cities, and people to the world as attractive destinations for tourism and investment"[10]. Qatar has been frequently using this sports diplomacy tool. Currently, the Qataris host nearly a hundred international sporting events each year[11]. Some of them are annual (for example, ATP Tennis Tournament Doha, Qatar Masters Golf Tournament, or IAAF Diamond League); however, the most popular are the continental or world championships. For example, Qatar hosted the Asian Games in 2006, IHF World Handball Championships in 2015, UCI Road Cycling World Championships one year later, etc. In this sense, the greatest success of Qatar is hosting the FIFA World Cup in 2022[12]. A well-managed organization of sporting events on the Qatari soil should bear fruit to the country; that is to say, it should bring positive reactions from the international society.

In this context, Xinyu Yang quoted a source from the Qatar Administration who said: "Twenty years ago, people in other countries had no idea what Qatar was. We were a Middle Eastern country with a very strong economy but no prestige. It is sport that has changed the whole image. In 2006, we held the Asian Games and let Asia get to know us. From then on, we have been holding more and more events to let people from all over the world know about our country"[13]. This quotation shows the importance of hosting famous sporting events for Qatar.

Using sportsmen as "diplomats". Famous and successful sportsmen could help to present their country abroad. It could be one of the reasons why Qatar's politicians decided to invest a large amount of money in the development of sport. Qatar is characterized by "[…] a systematic policy of talent identification implemented in all Qatari schools and the Aspire academy for the promotion of male elite athletes at the core of its efforts"[14]. For instance, Mutaz Essa Barshim,

---

10 Geoffrey Allen Pigman, "International Sport and Diplomacy's Public Dimension: Governments, Sporting Federations and the Global Audience," *Diplomacy & Statecraft*, Vol. 25, No. 1 (2014), p. 100.

11 Xinyu Yang, "Why is Qatar investing so much money in sport?," *Association Internationale de la Presse Sportive*, 9 Feb. 2016 http://www.aipsmedia.com/index.php?page=news&cod=18109.

12 On the other hand, FIFA World Cup is connected to FIFA's corruption scandals and it could influence the international perception of the State of Qatar. See the section *Qatar and analysis of the Czech nationwide diaries*.

13 Yang, "Why is Qatar investing"

14 Danyel Reiche, "Investing in sporting success as a domestic and foreign policy tool: the case of Qatar," *International Journal of Sport Policy and Politics*, Vol. 7, No. 4 (2015), p. 494.

the current high jump world champion and the winner of two Olympic medals, is a "child" of the Aspire academy.

The naturalization of talented foreign sportsmen is a typical sign of Qatar's sporting policy as well. The Qatari national handball team was a runner-up in the IHF World Handball Championships (that took place on the Qatari soil) three years ago. However, the key part of the Qatar's squad was naturalized before the tournament, e.g. a goalkeeper Danijel Šarić was a representative of Serbia and Bosnia and Herzegovina, the second Qatar's keeper Goran Stojanović played for Yugoslavia and Montenegro, Bertrand Roiné won a world gold medal for France in 2011, Borja Vidal was born in Spain and he has been a citizen of Qatar since 2013. However, the handball players are just the tip of the iceberg. As Rook Campbell mentioned, nearly 40 Kenyan athletes became Qatari citizens in 2005[15]. In 2003, the Kenyan runner Stephen Cherono switched his citizenship to Qatari and changed his name to Saif Saeed Shaheen. Reportedly, he received $1 million for taking this step and "[...] he will be paid $1,000 a month for the rest of his life"[16], although he disclaimed the statement. The Bulgarian weight-lifter Angel Popov won a bronze Olympic medal in 2000 but the official results did not include Popov's name, at that time he was the citizen of Qatar named Said Saif Asaad and he became the second Olympic medallist in the Qatari history.

Sponsorship of famous sports clubs. In the same vein, Qatar works with famous sports clubs. If you have a huge amount of money, however you do not have your own famous sportsmen, you can buy them without the need for changing their citizenships; this means that Qatar, their Foundation or the state-owned firms, could be the sponsors of the world famous sports clubs, for example the Catalan football club FC Barcelona. For a very long time, Barcelona's footballers did not have their sponsor's logo displayed on the shirts, the first commercial kit sponsor became the Qatar Foundation in 2011. It was replaced by the Qatar Airways in 2013 and the Qatar's state-owned flag carrier sponsored the Catalan football club until 2017.

Similarly, Qatar Sports Investment which is "a key actor for Qatar's global acquisitions [...]"[17] owns the French football club Paris Saint-Germain. Currently,

---

15 Rook Campbell, "Staging globalization for national projects: Global sport markets and elite athletic transnational labour in Qatar," *International Review for the Sociology of Sport*, Vol. 7, No. 4 (2015), p. 57.

16 Jere Longman, "Track and Field; A Runner Changes His Flag for Cash," *New York Times*, 23 Aug. 2003 http://www.nytimes.com/2003/08/23/sports/track-and-field-a-runner-changes-his-flag-for-cash.html.

17 Reiche, "Investing in sporting success," p. 495.

PSG is one of the main actors on the football transfer market. Last year, Paris Saint-Germain bought a football star from FC Barcelona, the Brazilian striker Neymar, for nearly $263 million[18], making him the most expensive player in the football history. Other famous football players that came to PSG after Qatar started to own the club are the forward Edinson Cavani from Uruguay, Argentine Ángel Di María, a young French footballer Kylian Mbappé, the Swedish Zlatan Ibrahimović, or the well-renowned ex-captain of England, David Beckham.

How Can We Measure the Success of Sports Diplomacy (on the Example of the State of Qatar in the Czech Republic)?

All of these facts could show that the State of Qatar is very active in the context of sports diplomacy but there is still the question if Qatar is successful in it. It is possible to say, the success of sports diplomacy is hard to measure: How can we (try to) measure the success of sports diplomacy, or how can we (try to) get the data?

I assume there are two possible ways how we can do it. The first is a systematic and sophisticated sociological research, however it could be very expensive to prepare, distribute to the respondents and then get authentic data. The second way is media analysis. Media have a huge impact on the public opinion; they set agenda and framework the topics. That is to say, media help to form people's thoughts and opinions. Missing a profound sociological research, we cannot learn what exactly people think about a certain country; however, this way we can see how the media present their own views which have the power to influence the readers, viewers and listeners. In other words, the way how the topics of the articles are selected and how these articles are written probably influences the public opinion.

In this chapter, I try to "measure" the success of Qatar's sports diplomacy based on the articles published in the Czech nationwide dailies during 2016. In the Czech Republic, there are seven main dailies. *Blesk* is the most read Czech daily (see Tab. 1) and it is considered a tabloid. Another example of a Czech tabloid is *Aha!*, however it is not as popular as *Blesk*. The second most read newspaper in the Czech Republic is *MF Dnes*, a respectable daily that was owned

18 Alaa Shahine and Charles Penty, "Qatar Makes a $263 Million Statement With Proposed Neymar Deal," *Bloomberg*, 3 Aug. 2017 https://www.bloomberg.com/news/articles/2017-08-03/neymar-seen-bringing-more-than-trophies-to-psg-s-qatari-owners.

Tab. 1: The most read statewide newspapers in the Czech Republic in 2016. "Čtenost: Deníky potvrdily své pozice, vede Blesk," *MediaGuru*, 9 Feb. 2017 https://www.mediaguru.cz/clanky/2017/02/ctenost-deniky-potvrdily-sve-pozice-vede-blesk.

Daily	Readers per day in the first half of 2016 (in thousands)	Readers per day in the second half of 2016 (in thousands)
Blesk	967	995
MF Dnes	611	609
Sport	287	289
Právo	281	278
Aha!	223	223
Lidové noviny	211	208
Hospodářské noviny	147	150

by Andrej Babiš,[19] the second richest Czech, a leader of his own political party ANO and a minister of finance at that time. In the Czech Republic, the question of Babiš's influence on his media has been much discussed since he was also the owner of *Lidové noviny* daily as well. Daily *Sport* is Czech's third most read daily. Its name suggests it is a sport daily newspaper, the only one in the Czech Republic. Other Czech dailies are *Právo* and *Hospodářské noviny*.

The statewide newspaper analysis is composed of the following steps. I used the database of Czech media called Anopress and found all the articles published in seven Czech dailies in 2016 that included the word *Katar* (Qatar in the Czech language). Afterwards, I divided these articles into two main categories: *the articles that mentioned Qatar in the context of sport*, and *the rest*. Then, I worked only with the first category and sorted the articles into three groups: positive, neutral and negative articles.

In general, the *positive articles* in the context of sports diplomacy admire the results, performances and winnings of the sportsmen or the country that hosted the sporting event for their stadiums, infrastructure or background, etc. The *neutral articles* inform about the sporting events, clubs or results, describe them and do not evaluate them. The *negative articles* could be connected to the doping scandals of the sportsmen that are linked to their country as well. They can inform about the insufficient background for sportsmen, fans and journalists

19 Currently, Andrej Babiš is not an owner of these newspapers as he was forced to transfer them into a trust fund. However, there is still a public debate about his influence on "his" media.

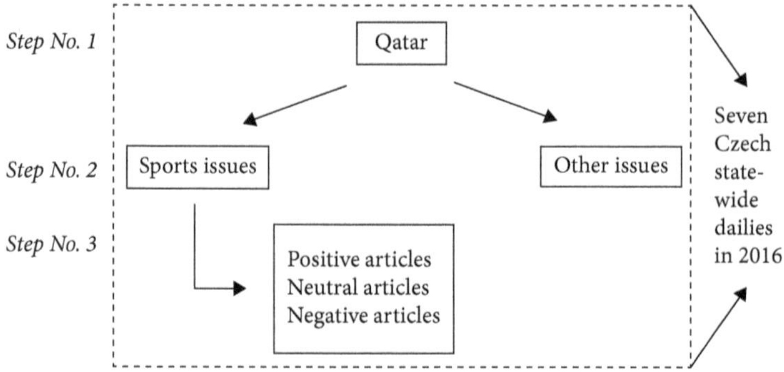

Fig. 1: The steps of the analysis

during the sporting events hosted by a country. These articles can also openly evaluate the level of corruption in the international sports organizations or in the professional sport in general and criticize selected countries, etc.

Qatar('s Sports Diplomacy) and the Czech Statewide Dailies

What are the results of the media analysis I described in the previous section? Generally, Qatar was mentioned in 319 articles in seven Czech nationwide dailies in 2016. From those 158 articles mentioned this Gulf monarchy from a non-sport perspective, especially in connection with the political situation in the Middle East or with the economic issues. More than half of the articles (161) informed about the State of Qatar in the context of sport.

In general, the majority of sports articles (128) was neutral and described the Qatari activity in the international sport environment only. Eight positive articles were found, five were published in daily *Právo*, the others in *Aha!*, *MF Dnes* and *Sport*. Their authors mainly appreciated the preparation of Qatar's hosting of the FIFA World Cup in 2022. The exceptions were *Sport* that applauded Qatar national under-23 football team playing very well in the AFC U-23 Asian Cup[20], and *MF Dnes* that informed about the football tournament for the workers being involved in the preparations of Qatari infrastructure; however, the article mentioned the poor working conditions as well[21].

20 "Zlín doma potvrdí formu," *Sport*, 26 January 2016, p. 25.
21 Miroslav Němý, "Katar už šampionát má. Zatím ale jen pro dělníky," *MF Dnes*, 28 April 2016, p. 18.

The readers of the Czech nationwide dailies were able to read 25 negative articles, in other words, 15.5 % of the articles about the sport and Qatar were negative. Just the *Aha!* daily did not publish any text criticizing the State of Qatar, the other tabloid *Blesk* published just one critical article in connection to the Czech ambitions in the Olympic Games in Rio de Janeiro. In the text, *Blesk*'s columnist called the Qatar national handball team "the soldiers of fortune" and mentioned their "controversial silver medal from the World Cup"[22]. However, the majority of negative articles is openly connected to the corruption scandals, especially in the context of bidding for hosting the international sporting events, mainly the FIFA World Cup in 2022. The published texts labelled the 2022 World Cup in Qatar as a "controversial"[23], and they openly informed about the (possible) corruption[24]. Furthermore, the Czech journalists wrote about road cycling and the UCI Road Cycling World Championships hosted by Qatar and called it "a really bad idea"[25], criticized Qatar's policy of naturalizing the sportsmen (not only in *Blesk*)[26], or, as mentioned above, focused on the harsh working conditions. For example. *Lidové noviny* published the English article "Foreign workers deserve respect", his author said that "[d]ozens of construction workers from Nepal and India were charged recruitment fees by agents in their home countries, housed in squalid accommodation and barred from leaving the country by employers in Qatar who confiscated their passport [...]"[27].

All in all, Qatar was mentioned in a negative way 11 times in the context of sport in *Lidové noviny*; it means that in this newspaper, every second article about Qatar and sport was critical. Four times Qatar was criticized in the context of sport in *MF Dnes* and *Sport*. Three negative articles were published in *Právo* and two in *Hospodářské noviny*. However, *Hospodářské noviny* did not inform about Qatar and sport in general very often and two negative texts are 40 % of

22 Petr Žaloudek, "Kdy se zrodí česká," *Blesk*, 4 August 2016, p. 16.

23 For example, see Miroslav Němý, "Jak padla říše kmotra atletiky," *MF Dnes*, 19 January 2016, p. 18; Miroslav Němý, "Nejhorší kmotr sportovního světa," *Lidové noviny*, 19 January 2016, p. 18.

24 For example, see "Ve zkratce," *Právo*, 19 January 2016, p. 23; Radek Malina, "Terminátor Blatter vyhrožuje návratem," *Právo*, 18 February 2016, p. 21; "Je tu válka kontinentů, jde o Blatterovů trůn," *Hospodářské noviny*, 22 February 2016, p. 40; Pavel Kalina, "Architektura za časů globalizace," *Lidové noviny*, 6 April 2016, p. 9; Luděk Mádl, "Jak Infantino opravuje světový fotbal," *MF Dnes*, 24 October 2016, p. 20.

25 Tomáš Macek, "Jak se dá okrást sport o duši," *MF Dnes*, 17 October 2016, p. 12.

26 Jaroslav Šindelář, "Cizinec do české repre nepatří," *Lidové noviny*, 24 November 2016, p. 24.

27 Tom Finn, "Foreign workers deserve respect," *Lidové noviny*, 8 April 2016, p. 4.

Tab. 2: Czech statewide dailies and the State of Qatar in 2016

	All articles where Qatar was mentioned	**Articles that mentioned Qatar in the context of sport**	**Positive articles (in the context of Qatar and sport)**	**Neutral articles (in the context of Qatar and sport)**	**Negative articles (in the context of Qatar and sport)**	**% of positive articles/ sports articles**	**% of negative articles/ sports articles**
Aha!	11	8	1	7	0	12.5 %	-
Blesk	10	6	0	5	1	-	16.7 %
Hospodářské noviny	67	5	0	3	2	-	40 %
Lidové noviny	61	22	0	11	11	-	50 %
MF Dnes	48	32	1	27	4	3.1 %	12.5 %
Právo	69	35	5	27	3	14.3 %	8.6 %
Sport	53	53	1	48	4	1.9 %	7.5 %
	319	**161**	**8**	**128**	**25**	**5 %**	**15.5 %**

the articles that mentioned Qatar regarding sport. Together, the Czech tabloids (*Aha!* and *Blesk*) published just one negative text, though it did not speak about corruption, the most frequently discussed topic in this sense. For more detail, see Tab. 2.

Conclusion: The (Lack of) Success of Qatar's Sports Diplomacy in the Czech Republic?

Before I try to answer the major question asked in the beginning of this chapter, I focus on the positive and negative aspects of Qatar's sports diplomacy in the Czech Republic. I assume the first positive aspect for Qatari sports diplomacy is the fact that more than half of the articles about Qatar in seven Czech nationwide dailies mentioned this monarchy in the context of sport. Preferably (from Qatar's point of view), that should lead the public to the conclusion that Qatar is closely connected with sport, which is being perceived as something positive by the majority of the world population, and it could help create a more positive Qatari image. At the same time, some articles mentioning the State of Qatar and its activity in the international sport are positive, nevertheless a very small minority, that is only 5 % of them. On the other hand, the most negative aspect for sports diplomacy of the State of Qatar, that the analysis of the Czech nationwide dailies in 2016 showed, is that nearly every sixth article about the State of

Qatar and sport was negative as well as every second article in *Lidové noviny* and 40 % of the articles in *Hospodářské noviny*.

What does it mean for Qatar's sports diplomacy in the Czech environment? Or better to say: *Is the Qatari sports diplomacy successful in the Czech Republic?* Given the fact that this chapter is based solely on data from nationwide dailies collected during one-year period, it is difficult to answer this question. Even though, we can see some aspects that should lead us to responding 'yes' to that question, we could consider the negative answer as well.

The major conclusion is the following: As long as Qatar avoids scandals on the sport pitch, there is a precondition of Qatar's successful sports diplomacy not only in the Czech Republic. This means that Qatari sports diplomacy could be a very useful tool of their foreign policy. This conclusion is not valid only for the State of Qatar in the Czech environment. Generally, sports diplomacy formula says that fewer scandals linked to a country and their sports issues equals a more positive image of the country.

Bibliography

1. "Je tu válka kontinentů, jde o Blatterovů trůn." *Hospodářské noviny*. 22 February 2016, p. 40.
2. "Ve zkratce." *Právo*. 19 January 2016, p. 23.
3. "Zlín doma potvrdí formu." *Sport*. 26 January 2016, p. 25.
4. Brentin, Dario and Loïc Tregoures. "Entering through the sport's door? Kosovo's sport diplomatic endeavours towards international recognition," *Diplomacy & Statecraft*, Vol. 27, No. 2, 2016, pp. 360–378.
5. Campbell, Rook. "Staging globalization for national projects: Global sport markets and elite athletic transnational labour in Qatar," *International Review for the Sociology of Sport*, Vol. 7, No. 4, 2015, pp. 45–60.
6. Finn, Tom. "Foreign workers deserve respect." *Lidové noviny*. 8 April 2016, p. 4.
7. Houlihan, Barrie. *The Government and Politics of Sport*. New York: Routledge, 2014.
8. Kalina, Pavel. "Architektura za časů globalizace." *Lidové noviny*. 6 April 2016, p. 9.
9. Macek, Tomáš. "Jak se dá okrást sport o duši." *MF Dnes*. 17 October 2016, p. 12.
10. Mádl, Luděk. "Jak Infantino opravuje světový fotbal." *MF Dnes*. 24 October 2016, p. 20.
11. Malina, Radek. "Terminátor Blatter vyhrožuje návratem." *Právo*. 18 February 2016, p. 21.

12. Murray, Stuart. "The two halves of sports diplomacy," *Diplomacy & Statecraft*, Vol. 23, No. 3, 2012, pp. 576–592.
13. Němý, Miroslav. "Jak padla říše kmotra atletiky." *MF Dnes*. 19 January 2016, p. 18.
14. Němý, Miroslav. "Katar už šampionát má. Zatím ale jen pro dělníky." *MF Dnes*. 28 April 2016, p. 18.
15. Němý, Miroslav. "Nejhorší kmotr sportovního světa." *Lidové noviny*. 19 January 2016, p. 18.
16. Pigman, Geoffrey Allen. "International sport and diplomacy's public dimension: governments, sporting federations and the global audience," *Diplomacy & Statecraft*, Vol. 25, No. 1, 2014, pp. 94–114.
17. Reiche, Danyel. "Investing in sporting success as a domestic and foreign policy tool: the case of Qatar," *International Journal of Sport Policy and Politics*, Vol. 7, No. 4, 2015, pp. 489–504.
18. Rolim, Silva and Luis Henrique. "The establishment of the Qatar national Olympic committee: building the national sport identity," *The International Journal of the History of Sport*, Vol. 31, No. 3, 2014, pp. 306–319.
19. Shearer, Derek. "To play ball, not make war. Sports, diplomacy and soft power," *Harvard International Review*, Vol. 36, No. 1, 2014, pp. 53–57.
20. Šindelář, Jaroslav. "Cizinec do české repre nepatří." *Lidové noviny*. 24 November 2016, p. 24.
21. Štulajter, Ivo, Danka Barteková and Matyáš Štulajter. *Športová diplomacia*. Banská Bystrica: Belianum and Vydavateľstvo Univerzity Mateja Bela, 2013.
22. Zákravský, Jiří. "Sport a mezinárodní vztahy. Sportovní diplomacie jako součást zahraniční politiky," *Central European Journal of Politics*, Vol. 2, No. 2, 2016, pp. 15–36.
23. Zákravský, Jiří. *Baskové v ofsajdu. Sport jako nástroj politiky nestátních národů. Případová studie fotbalu v Baskicku*. Praha: Dokořán, 2017.
24. Žaloudek, Petr. "Kdy se zrodí česká." *Blesk*. 4 August 2016, p. 16.

Internet Sources

1. "Čtenost: Deníky potvrdily své pozice, vede Blesk." MediaGuru. 9 February 2017. https://www.mediaguru.cz/clanky/2017/02/ctenost-deniky-potvrdily-sve-pozice-vede-blesk (18 Jan. 2018).
2. "Qatar Olympic Committee, Qatar's Sport Sector Strategy (2011–2016)." Second edition – July 2011. http://www.aspire.qa/Document/Sports_sector_strategy_final-English.pdf (16 Jan. 2018).

3. Longman, Jere. "Track and Field; A Runner Changes His Flag for Cash." New York Times. 23 August 2003. http://www.nytimes.com/2003/08/23/sports/track-and-field-a-runner-changes-his-flag-for-cash.html (18 Jan. 2018).
4. Shahine, Alaa and Charles Penty. "Qatar Makes a $263 Million Statement With Proposed Neymar Deal." Bloomberg. 3 August 2017. https://www.bloomberg.com/news/articles/2017-08-03/neymar-seen-bringing-more-than-trophies-to-psg-s-qatari-owners (18 Jan. 2018).
5. Yang, Xinyu. "Why is Qatar investing so much money in sport?" *Association Internationale de la Presse Sportive*. 9 February 2016. http:// www.aipsmedia.com/index.php?page=news&cod=18109 (16 January 2018).

Part III – Economy and Energy Policy

Rafał Ulatowski

The Paradox of the Shale Oil Market. The Middle East and the Global Oil Market

Abstract: The energy revolution in the United States at the turn of the first and second decades of the 21st century has caused a tsunami on the global oil market and raised questions about the economic and political consequences of the new energy abundance in the United States. One would expect the Middle East to be the biggest victim of this new American strength, yet paradoxically, the shale revolution is not hurting Middle East oil producers most of all. The additional supply is moderating oil prices in the long term, and moderate prices benefit Middle East producers. Although in the short term they lose some potential revenue, in the long term their large reserves require a large market. The main challenge for Middle Eastern countries is to improve the structure of their economies and lower the dependence of their economies on oil. Internal reform should be put at the top of their agendas. The main losers in the shale revolution are high-cost producers. There is no sign that the rise of oil production in the United States will cause a geopolitical rebalancing of the Middle East.

Keywords: Middle East, OPEC, resource curse, rentier state, shale oil

The energy revolution in the United States at the turn of the first and second decades of the 21st century has caused a tsunami on the global oil market and raised questions about the economic and political consequences of the new energy abundance in the United States. The storyline of the energy market has evolved from one of resource wars[1] towards a new energy abundance[2]. One would expect the Middle East to be the biggest victim of this new American strength, because oil and gas are the lifeblood of the regional economy and politics. The United States is now in a position to gain "energy independence"[3] and

1 Michael Klare, *Blood and Oil. The Dangers and Consequences of America's Growing Dependency on Imported Petroleum* (New York: Metropolitan Books 2005).

2 Rex Tillerson, "Capitalizing on the coming era of energy abundance," *Address to Texas Alliance of Energy Producers*, Houston, 2 Apr. 2013: 11 Oct. 2018 https://corporate.exxonmobil.com/news/newsroom/speeches/2013/0402_capitalizing-on-the-coming-era-of-energy-abundance/; Michael Klare, "From Scarcity to Abundance: The Changing Dynamics of Energy Conflict," *Penn State Journal of Law & International Affairs*, Vol. 3, Issue 2 (2015) pp. 10–41.

3 Edward L. Morse, et al., *Energy 2020: Independence day. Global Ripple Effects of the North American Energy Revolution* (Citi GPS, 2013); Simon Lack,

withdraw its military from the Middle East[4], while oil prices should be "lower for longer". The United States should became a new swing supplier[5].

It is argued in this chapter that, paradoxically, the shale revolution is not hurting Middle East oil producers most of all. The additional supply is moderating oil prices in the long term, and moderate prices benefit Middle East producers. Although in the short term they lose some potential revenue, their large reserves require a large market. Long-term high prices harm demand and cause the development of production in high-cost areas. When prices are moderate, production in high-cost areas is reduced. The main challenge for Middle Eastern countries is to improve the structure of their economies and lower the dependence of their economies on oil. Internal reform should be put at the top of their agendas. The main losers in the shale revolutions are high-cost producers. The shale revolution will not cause the Middle East to lose importance in the oil market, nor will it cause any geopolitical change in the region.

This chapter consists of four sections. Section 1 discusses the role of energy in theories of international relations. Section 2 looks into the development of the oil market in the 21st century. Section 3 analyzes the economic consequences of the shale revolution. Section 4 looks into the political consequences of the new market balance of power.

This chapter is based on the analysis of three groups of sources. The first group is statistical data and documents. The second group is publications issued by international organisations. The third consists of the relevant literature.

Energy – between Conflict and Cooperation

Although many publications on energy neglect the importance of theoretical rigour and have been "descriptive, atheoretical and noncumulative"[6], all theories of international relations offer interesting suggestions about the role of energy

---

"America's Path To Energy Independence: The Shale Revolution," *Forbes*, 4 Jun. 2018: 11 Oct. 2018 https://www.forbes.com/sites/simonlack/2018/06/04/americas-path-to-energy-independence-the-shale-revolution/#5b035edf7554.

4 Mark Boris Andrijanič, "The American energy revolution: challenging Europe and the Middle East," *European View*, Vol. 14, Issue 2 (2015), pp. 263–273; "The Petrostate of America," *The Economist*, 15 Feb. 2014: 11 Oct. 2018 https://www.economist.com/leaders/2014/02/15/the-petrostate-of-america.

5 Ed Morse, "US set to become swing oil supplier," *Financial Times*, 15 Feb. 2018: 11 Oct. 2018 https://www.ft.com/content/49354866-117d-11e8-8cb6-b9ccc4c4dbbb.

6 Ernest J. Wilson, "World politics and international energy markets," *International Organization*, Vol. 41, Issue 1 (1987), pp. 125–149.

in international relations, about the participants in the energy market and their behaviour. The four most important perspectives are presented below.

Most of the literature related to energy is dominated by realist thinking. Energy-related literature was born mostly out of the energy crisis of 1973. The experience of the oil embargo put energy security at the top of state priorities. Realists see in energy resources a strategic good. States are the principal actors determined to provide energy security. Realists recognise that there is a danger of conflict between states over scarce energy resources. Energy issues are a zero-sum game. Unlike the realists, scholars belonging to the school of liberalism see states as principal actors, but also acknowledge the importance of other actors such as companies and international organisations. Liberals treat energy resources like other commodities. They also question the idea of non-cooperative behaviour between states. They argue that cooperation is not only possible, but does actually take place, and they underline the role of international regimes and international organisations. Authors working within liberal framework argue that the trade in energy creates various interdependencies, mostly between producers and consumers. For liberals, the economic dimension of energy is also much more important than it is for realists. The third theory is Marxism. In the context of the energy market, Marxists argue that producers of natural resources are locked into the role of suppliers of primary resources for the developed countries. They argue that producing countries receive only a fraction of the income from the extraction of natural resources; they are exploited and disadvantaged in international system. Western governments and companies maintain close relations with local elites. From the Marxist perspective, the wars in the Middle East reflect the need of capitalist countries to ensure their access to the petroleum resources of the region. The fourth research agenda is constructivism. Authors of this school look behind the material power relations and argue that the world is socially constructed. For such scholars, ideas, norms, values and identities play a crucial role, including in the energy market.[7]

Despite the growing literature on cooperation in the energy sector, competition between states still dominates. This is only occasionally broken by short-term periods of closer cooperation. Middle East countries, especially, try to keep control over their most important strategic asset – oil – in the hands of the

---

7 Thijs Van de Graaf, Benjamin K. Sovacool, Arunabha Ghosh, Florian Kern and Michael Klare, "States, markets, and institutions: integrating international political economy and global energy politics," in: *The Palgrave handbook of the international political economy of energy*, ed. Thijs Van de Graaf, Benjamin K. Sovacool, Arunabha Ghosh, Florian Kern and Michael Klare. (London: Palgrave Macmillan UK, 2016), pp. 15–16.

government. The attempt by these countries to take control over the oil market in the 1970s was short-lived, and unsuccessful. Cooperation among them proved to be ineffective. OPEC[8], the most important tool in their hands, proved to be ineffective as a cartel. Jeff Colgan's study clearly indicates that OPEC brings its members very limited economic benefits and that its actual role is limited to bringing political benefits, mainly international prestige. OPEC members cultivate the "rational myth" that they are able to steer the global oil market[9]. Middle Eastern powers are unwilling to cede control over their energy policies to global bodies, and are not willing to participate in international agreements; McGowan calls this the "paradox of sovereignty". States have less control over the energy market in a globalised world, yet are unwilling to act jointly[10]. This weak international cooperation in the energy sector has an impact on the governance of energy at the global level. There is no single organisation that manages this field, but a broad group forming a "regime complex"[11]. As K. Westphal argues, the narrative of energy is "permanent conflict". As she shows, "What has become apparent (again) over recent years is the fact that energy governance takes place in a field of tension between governance based on market and institutions (and the rule of law) on the one hand, and state-centred, power-based geopolitics on the other"[12].

The Oil Market in the 21st Century

At the beginning of the 21st century, the oil market was oversupplied. Prices were low. OPEC and non-OPEC producers tried to curb production to prop up prices. Despite the efforts of both groups of suppliers, in the period 1998–2001 the market remained unstable. Exporters were unable to find the right level of production and faced the problem of how to implement the agreed production

---

8 Four out of five founding OPEC member states are from the Middle East: Saudi Arabia, Kuwait, Iran, and Iraq. Only Venezuela is not a Middle Eastern country. Today, Middle Eastern countries continue to dominate in OPEC.

9 Jeff D. Colgan, "The Emperor Has No Clothes: The Limits of OPEC in the Global Oil Market," *International Organization*, Vol. 68, Issue 3 (2014), pp. 599–632.

10 Francis McGowan, "International regimes for energy: Finding the right level for policy" in: *Energy for the Future: A New Agenda*, ed. Ivan Scarse and Gordon MacKerron (Basingstoke: Palgrave Macmillan, 2009), pp. 20–34.

11 Thijs Van de Graaf, *The Politics and Institutions of Global Energy Governance*, (Basingstoke: Palgrave Macmillan, 2013), pp. 44–63.

12 Kirsten Westphal, "Energy Policy between Multilateral Governance and Geopolitics: Whither Europe?," *IPG*, No. 4 (2006), p. 58.

quotas[13]. First, with the dynamic rise of Chinese imports after it joined the WTO and rapid global economic growth, the demand side of the market helped to push prices up. Also, the consequences of a long period of low levels of investment became visible. Producers were unable to raise production, despite growing demand. Spare capacity started to fall, the market tightened and prices started to rise[14]. In the early 21st century, the world entered a super-cycle on the commodities market that was fuelled by rising demand from emerging markets. Oil was only one of the commodities whose prices rose dramatically, hitting a record level[15]. Despite certain expectations, the supply side did not react immediately. Oil companies and oil-producing countries were not immediately convinced that the price growth was sustainable and justified investments. Most exporting countries were also heavily indebted and not capable of increasing their investments. The absence of a reaction on the supply side gave rise to speculation about a coming peak in the oil supply. Publications anticipating that the world would soon start to run out of oil began to snowball. Even the country with the biggest reserves of conventional oil – Saudi Arabia – was not excluded from these predictions[16]. The Middle East's image as a leading exporter was further damaged by fast-growing local consumption that restricted export capacity. The problems of high energy intensity, high levels of energy subsidies and the inefficiency of local economies was not resolved[17]. Interestingly, the decision makers in Saudi Arabia also showed little interest in increasing production quickly. They expected the value of oil to rise over time, and so did not view the rapid exploration of resources as economically and politically rational[18].

---

13 Wilfried L. Kohl, "OPEC behavior, 1998–2001," *The Quarterly Review of Economics and Finance*, Vol. 42, Issue 2 (2002), pp. 209–233.

14 Lutz Kilian, and Bruce Hicks, "Did Unexpectedly Strong Economic Growth Cause the Oil Price Shock of 2003–2008?," *Journal of Forecasting*, Vol. 32, Issue 5 (2013), pp. 385–394.

15 John Baffes, M. Ayhan Kose, Franziska Ohnsorge, and Marc Stocker, *The Great Plunge in Oil Prices: Causes, Consequences, and Policy Responses*, (World Bank, 2015, PRN/15/01).

16 David Goodstein, *Out of Gas: The End of the Age of Oil* (New York London: W.W.Norton & Company, 2004); Matthew R. Simmons, *Twilight in the Desert: The Coming Saudi Oil Shock and the World Economy* (New Jersey: Wiley, 2006).; See Tab. 3 and Tab. 4.

17 Glada Lahn, Paul Stevens, *Burning Oil to Keep Cool. The Hidden Energy Crisis in Saudi Arabia*, (Chatham House, 2011); Laura El-Katiri, Bassam Fattouh, *A Brief Political Economy of Energy Subsidies in the Middle East and North Africa*, (OIES Paper, 2015).

18 James D. Hamilton, "Causes and Consequences of the Oil Shock of 2007–08," *Brookings Papers on Economic Activity, Economic Studies Program, The Brookings Institution*, Vol. 40, No. 1 (2009), p. 239.

After the strong growth in oil prices and demand in the first decade of the 21st century, there was a temporary hiatus in 2009 as a result of the global financial crisis. Oil prices stayed at a stable level of around 100 USD/b in the period 2011–2014, guaranteeing exporters record income from petroleum exports and a positive current account balance. The Saudi Arabian minister of Petroleum and Mineral Resources, Ali Al-Naimi, believed that 100 USD/b was the new normal price for oil. But in 2014, the oversupply of the market became apparent. Once again, voices were clearly heard calling OPEC to cut production[19]. There were two main reasons for the growing oversupply, both well known from the history of the oil market. Every period of high prices is followed by a period when the oil intensity of the economy falls and the oil supply grows. The 21st century has been no exception. Global growth in oil consumption has been relatively slow in the second decade of the 21st century. In some countries and regions it has even fallen. And supply has grown.[20] The oil industry in the United States developed the competence to exploit unconventional hydrocarbon resources. First, shale gas exploration began, followed by shale oil. The situation on the oil market started to change. Leonardo Maugeri argued that the United States was the country with the biggest potential for increasing production, while other production leaders should be Canada, Brazil and Iraq. Only the last of these is in the Middle East. The long-standing period of high prices caused an investment boom and technological improvements in oil extraction. The market situation was going to change, to the detriment of traditional oil producers[21].

The growing focus on climate policy in the 21st century raised questions about the future role of oil. Was oil to become a stranded asset? The idea that oil demand could one day peak as a result of climate policy and technological progress is a nightmare for Middle East policy makers. As James Smith, the U.S. ambassador to Riyadh, wrote in a 2010 memo to U.S. Energy Secretary Steven Chu: "Effectively, peak oil arguments have been replaced by peak demand."[22]

---

19 Ali Al-Naimi, *Out of the Desert: My Journey From Nomadic Bedouin to the Heart of Global Oil* (Penguin, 2016).; See: Tab. 1 and Tab. 2.

20 Christiane Baumeister, Lutz Kilian, "Understanding the Decline in the Price of Oil since June 2014," *Journal of the Association of Environmental and Resource Economists*, Vol. 3, No. 1 (2016), pp. 131–158.

21 Leonardo Maugeri, *Oil: The Next Revolution*, (Discussion Paper - Belfer Center for Science and International Affairs, Harvard Kennedy School, 2012).

22 "Saudi Arabia was worried about a danger much bigger than shale when it blindsided oil markets," *Financial Post*, 13 Apr. 2015: 11 Oct. 2018 https://business.financialpost.com/commodities/energy/

Within a few years, the discussion moved from a peak in oil supply to a peak in oil demand.[23]

The shale oil revolution questioned certain "truths" about the oil market. The first was that oil is an exhaustible resource. Of course, essentially, oil is an exhaustible resource. But the recent discoveries and technological improvements have pushed this natural limit into the unforeseeable future. Today, the total known oil reserves are almost two-and-a-half times greater than what was known in 1980. The second popular "truth" was that oil demand and supply curves are steep. This idea resulted from the fact that conventional oil exploration involves a significant time lag between an investment decision and the start of production. But with shale oil, things are different. The time lag between an investment decision and oil production is counted in weeks, not years. Additionally, the life of a shale oil well is much shorter than that of a conventional oil field. Consequently, the "responsiveness of shale oil to price changes will be far greater than that for conventional oil. (…) Shale oil acts as a form of shock absorber for the global oil market." The third "truth" that became questioned was that oil flows from East to West, that is, from the Middle East to Europe and the United States. Currently, demand in the West is (generally) falling and production in the USA is growing, so this part of the world requires less oil from the Middle East. At the same time, oil demand in the east (Asia) is growing rapidly. The fourth "truth" was that OPEC stabilises oil prices. Spencer Dale argues that OPEC has the capacity to manage temporary shocks, but not a structural one. And the shale revolution changed nothing in this respect. So, from OPEC's perspective it was logical not to reduce supply in 2014–2015. This would have been ineffective due to the structural change in the market that shale oil caused.[24]

In the first decade of the 21st century, a discussion began about the need to better govern global energy issues. The term global energy governance was coined in 2005 during the G8 summit in Gleneagles. The three main reasons behind this process were the growing importance of climate change in the energy debate, geopolitical changes (the decline of the bipolar world and the rise of emerging markets) and the growing volatility of energy

saudi-arabia-was-worried-about-a-danger-much-bigger-than-shale-when-it-blindsided-oil-markets.

23 Spencer Dale, Bassam Fattouh, *Peak Oil Demand and Long-Run Oil Prices*, (Energy Insight, 2018).

24 Spencer Dale, "New Economics of Oil, Society of Business Economists Annual Conference," *BP*, 13 Oct. 2015: 11 Oct. 2018 https://www.bp.com/content/dam/bp/pdf/speeches/2015/new-economics-of-oil-spencer-dale.pdf.

markets[25]. All of these processes directly affect Middle East countries, which are dependent on the oil industry. Their decades-long struggle to diversify their economies had not brought the results expected. They are still almost fully dependent on oil for export income and fiscal income. The terms 'resource curse', 'rentier state' and 'rent-seeking' still well describe them[26].

Another important aspect that has to be indicated is the collapse and rebuilding of oil prices in the period 2014–2018. In contrast to 2008/2009, OPEC was not ready to unilaterally cut production to secure the stability of oil prices. Saudi Arabia, which is the unofficial leader of OPEC, demanded that exporters from outside the organisation should also make production cuts. Ali Al-Naimi indicated that his country was not ready to unilaterally stabilise prices. Yet there was no readiness on the part of other countries in 2014 to participate. The production surge provoked a price collapse. The policy of Saudi Arabia was intended to protect its market share. Ali Al-Naimi declared that, as a low-cost producer, the Kingdom was not going to "subsidise higher cost supplies". He confirmed that "Anything we can do to make downward cycles shorter and less extreme is beneficial. (…) This includes seeking to allow markets to work with a minimum of meddling."[27] The main problem for Ali Al-Naimi was the behaviour of Russia. Two questions were crucial from his point of view: 1) Was Russia going to participate in an agreement restricting production, and 2) Was it going to keep its promises? Previous experience had made Al-Naimi sceptical about both issues[28]. The self-confident declarations of Saudi politicians that their country was not concerned about prices were rooted in the fact that, in late 2014, Saudi Arabia had over 700 billion USD of financial reserves. Saudi Arabia was not ready to sacrifice its market share. Memories of the early 1980s and its unilateral production cut resurfaced, and the country was not ready to repeat that mistake. In fact, since the mid-1980s, Saudi Arabia had avoided any unilateral activities on the

25 Thijs Van de Graaf, Jeff Colgan, "Global energy governance: a review and research agenda," *Palgrave Communications*, 26 Jan. 2016: 11 Oct. 2018 https://www.nature.com/articles/palcomms201547, pp. 2–3.

26 Mohamed Sami Ben Ali, Lara Cockx, Nathalie Francken, "The Middle East and North Africa: Cursed by Natural Resources?," in: *Economic Development in the Middle East and North Africa*, ed. Mohamed Sami Ben Ali, (London: Palgrave Macmillan, 2016), pp. 71–93.

27 Ali Al-Naimi, Speech, *CERAWEEK 2016*, 23 Feb. 2016: 11 Oct. 2018 http://fingfx.thomsonreuters.com/gfx/ce/1/482/482/NAIMI%20AT%20CERA%20WEEK.pdf.

28 Ali Al-Naimi, *Out of the Desert*.

oil market. Robert Mabro had noticed that expectations of this type are unjustified[29]. Although many sub-periods may be identified in Saudi oil policy and that policy has change over time, since the 1980s it has not featured any readiness to take unilateral action. Consequently, the policy of OPEC has also evolved. Robert D. Cairns and Enrique Calfucura argue that OPEC's policy "has too many facets for a tractable mathematical model"[30]. During the period analysed, the policy also evolved because of the dramatic fall in income from oil exporters. In 2016, a discussion started about a freeze in production, and in November and December the OPEC+ agreement was signed. OPEC and eleven non-OPEC oil exporting countries joined together to reduce production and inventories and thereby raise prices[31].

Economic Consequences of the Shale Revolution

The oil price collapse caused by the shale revolution has had a profound impact on the economies of petroleum exporting countries. Revenue from petroleum exports was reduced and the stability of these economies put into question. But the effects of the price collapse have differed between regions.

The shale revolution has a wide range of possible economic consequences. These include a long period of low oil prices ("lower for longer"), the ability of the United States to achieve energy independence and the idea that the United States may play the role of a swing producer in the oil market. All of these consequences could be profound for the Middle East.

The first issue that should be discussed is the price of oil. In the aftermath of the oil price collapse of 2014, the belief emerged that the world is entering a sustained period of low oil prices: "lower for longer". But unexpectedly, in 2018 oil price again rose rapidly[32]. In September 2018, the price of oil surpassed 80 USD/b, the highest it had been in four years. During 2016, OPEC and the non-OPEC exporters negotiated an agreement about a production freeze, and later a

29 Giacomo Luciani, "Saudi Arabia and the limits of signalling," *OIES Forum*, No. 100 (2015), p. 17

30 Robert D. Cairns, Enrique Calfucura, "OPEC: Market failure or power failure?," *Energy Policy*, Vol. 50, Issue C (2012), p. 571.

31 Andreas Economou, Bassam Fattouh, *5+1Key Facts about the OPEC Declaration of Cooperation*, (OIES Oxford Energy Comment, 2018).

32 Amrita Sen, Yasser Elguindi, "Era of 'lower for longer' oil prices is dead," *Financial Times*, 22 May 2018: 11 Oct. 2018 https://www.ft.com/content/60412154-5da1-11e8-9334-2218e7146b04.

cut. After months of negotiations, the OPEC+ agreement was signed; it foresaw a 1.8 million b/d production cut. Faced with a dramatic fall in the value of oil exports and OPEC's unwillingness to take unilateral action, a wider group of producers agreed on cooperation[33]. The countries participating in the agreement did not target any specific price, but concentrated on the level of inventories. Suhail Al Mazroui, the United Arab Emirates' Minister of energy and industry and OPEC president, argued that the organisation serves the "noble goal" of rescuing the oil market. He summarised this policy as follows: "I don't think we ever said that we're targeting a price. We all remember what happened two years ago — the market was over-flooded, and it wasn't OPEC who over-flooded the market. And no one intervened to do anything about it. (…) OPEC and non-OPEC (countries) came together, they sacrificed some of their production to try and fix the imbalance in the market. So the objective of OPEC was, I would say, a noble goal to rescue the market (from) a long over-supply"[34]. This agreement, orchestrated by Saudi Arabia and Russia, allowed a reduction in oil stocks and a consequent rise in prices. Although some of the production cuts were in fact involuntary, the general picture of disciplined cooperation was presented to the outside world. The participating countries worked on extending cooperation. Production cuts in Saudi Arabia, Kuwait, the UAE and Iraq were smaller than intended. These countries filled the gap caused by the dramatic involuntary production cuts in Venezuela, Mexico and Angola[35]. The rising prices caused a diplomatic reaction from the United States. The period of lower prices caused a dramatic fall in upstream investments, and the current stagnation and decline in production in many regions is a consequence of this development. Lower prices also strengthen demand. The current market conditions confirm the old truth about the cyclical nature of the market[36]. Rising demand assures Middle East

33 "OPEC and non-OPEC Ministerial Meeting," *OPEC*, No. 25 (2016): 11 Oct. 2018 https://www.opec.org/opec_web/en/press_room/3944.htm.

34 Yen Nee Lee, "OPEC is acting with 'noble goal' of rescuing the oil market, says organization's president," *CNBC*, 23 Apr. 2018: 11 Oct. 2018 https://www.cnbc.com/2018/04/23/uae-energy-minister-suhail-al-mazrouei-on-opec-production-cuts-oil-prices.html.

35 Brian Wingfield, Samuel Dodge, Cedric Sam, "OPEC Can't Shake Over-Compliance on Oil Cuts," *Bloomberg*, 17 Sep. 2018: 11 Oct. 2018 https://www.bloomberg.com/graphics/opec-production-targets/.

36 Christiane Baumeister, Lutz Kilian, "Forty Years of Oil Price Fluctuations: Why the Price of Oil May Still Surprise Us," *Journal of Economic Perspectives*, Vol. 30, No. 1 (2016), pp. 139–160.

producers that it is worth expanding production capacity. Kuwait is planning to increase its capacity up to 4 million b/d in 2020, and the UAE up to 3.5 million b/d, keeping a spare capacity of 0.5 million b/d. Iraq as well, which in the last decade has demonstrated a huge potential for cooperating with foreign companies, plans to further expand production[37]. Saudi Arabia plans to invest 20 billion USD to maintain, and possibly expand, its sustainable oil production capacity from the current level of 12 million b/d up to 13 million b/d.[38]

The reduced direct dependence of the United States on the Middle East oil supply has created a discussion about a reduction in the American interest in the region. This idea reflects the concept of US energy independence. Promoted by President Richard Nixon in the aftermath of the first oil crisis, this concept has never become reality. Although levels of imports were occasionally reduced, in the long term a rising dependence on imports was observed. However, this trend was put to an end by the shale revolution. Local production started to grow. Initially imports were reduced, but it soon proved difficult for the domestic market to absorb the additional supply of light shale oil. The decades-long ban on exports imposed because of the 1973 oil crisis was finally lifted in late 2015. The ability to export strengthened the domestic oil industry, enabling it to access the global market and achieve higher prices. Exports began to reach record levels. Although the United States is still a net oil importer, it has also become an important exporter[39], to such an extent that, during the administration of President Barack Obama, Amos J. Hochstein (Special Envoy, Bureau of Energy Resources) called for the "leadership" of the United States in energy issues[40], and

37 Nick Butler, "The dangers of Iraq's oil law," *Financial Times*, 30 Apr. 2018: 11 Oct. 2018 https://www.ft.com/content/da2b5cae-46d7-11e8-8ee8-cae73aab7ccb.

38 Denis Pinchuk, Dmitry Zhdannikov, Olesya Astakhova, "Saudi Arabia to invest $20 billion in spare oil production capacity," Reuters, 04 Oct. 2018: 11 Oct. 2018 https://www.reuters.com/article/us-oil-opec-falih-investment/saudi-arabia-to-invest-20-billion-in-spare-oil-production-capacity-idUSKCN1ME111.

39 Patti Domm, "US oil exports boom to record level, surpassing most OPEC nations," *CNBC*, 27 Jun. 2018: 11 Oct. 2018 https://www.cnbc.com/2018/06/27/us-oil-exports-boom-to-record-level-surpassing-most-opec-nations.html.

40 Amos J. Hochstein, "Remarks of Special Envoy, Bureau of Energy Resources," *Dentons 2016 Energy Outlook Event*, 02.08.2016: 11 Oct. 2018 https://2009-2017.state.gov/e/enr/rls/260845.htm.

President Donald Trump went even further in June 2017. The goal should not be energy independence, but "American energy dominance"[41].

The increase in domestic production in the United States did not alter its being an integral part of the global energy market. The fact that the United States imports less oil from the Middle East does not mean that other countries also import less. In fact, the shale revolution may increase, and not reduce, the world's energy dependence on the Middle East. Middle East producers enjoy the lowest production costs in the world, giving them a competitive advantage over exporters from other parts of the world. Low prices squeeze out high-cost producers, something which can be already observed. The dramatic fall of production in Venezuela – and also in countries like Mexico and Angola – is a sign of possible development in the future. The current rise in prices was not high enough to bring investments in the oil sector to the pre-price collapse level[42]. In the late 1980s, the collapse in oil prices created an expectation of growing dependence on the Middle East, and today as well the world should have similar expectations. The Crown Prince of Saudi Arabia, Mohammed bin Salman, said that the rise in prices in September 2018 was due to unsatisfactory production levels in Canada, Libya, Venezuela and Mexico at the same time trying to play down falling exports from Iran.[43] When, in May 2018, the United States announced its withdrawal from the nuclear agreement with Iran (the Joint Comprehensive Plan of Action), it was clear that, in keeping with tradition, the oil sector would be one of the main targets of the new US sanctions[44], and this strategy has proved very effective. Even before the formal imposition of sanctions on 5 November 2018, Iranian oil exports are falling, and oil companies are bailing out of deals with Iran. The new approach of the administration of the United States is killing Iran's hope of re-emerging as a top oil producer and exporter. Plans for join projects with international oil companies have had to be put off. The readiness of Arab oil producers antagonistic toward Iran (especially Saudi Arabia) to increase exports

41 Donald J. Trump, "Remarks by President Trump at the Unleashing American Energy Event," *White House*, 29.06.2017: 11 Oct. 2018 https://www.whitehouse.gov/briefings-statements/remarks-president-trump-unleashing-american-energy-event/.

42 IEA, *World Energy Investment 2018*, (IEA, 2018).

43 Stephanie Flanders, et al., "Saudi Crown Prince Discusses Trump, Aramco, Arrests: Transcript," *Bloomberg*, 05 Oct. 2018: 11 Oct. 2018 https://www.bloomberg.com/news/articles/2018-10-05/saudi-crown-prince-discusses-trump-aramco-arrests-transcript.

44 David Ramin Jalilvand, *The US Exit from the JCPOA: What Consequences for Iranian Energy?*, (OIES Oxford Energy Comment, 2018).

is reducing Iran's importance on the market. Currently, the only hope for Iran to keep production stable is cooperation with China and Russia, two countries able to resist US sanctions[45]. The Middle East has the biggest concentration of oil reserves in the world. The case of Iran shows how geopolitical constraints present the biggest challenge to production expansion. With stagnating or even declining exports to the West, the region can compensate for these losses by increasing exports to the East. China, India and the smaller (but not small) economies of Asia offer an incredible demand potential for decades to come. Also, falling production in mature regions such as the North Sea and high-cost areas provides an opportunity to strengthen position. As the IEA predicts, "Once US tight oil plateaus in the late 2020s and non-OPEC production as a whole falls back, the market becomes increasingly reliant on the Middle East to balance the market."[46] Crown Prince Mohammed bin Salman hopes that, for his country, the best time is yet to come: "(…) we believe that the other side will be a lot of producers disappearing. So, for example, we believe that China will be decreased sharply if not disappeared after five years from today. And other countries will continue every day to disappear as countries producing oil. Nineteen years from today, Russia will have declined heavily if not disappeared with 10 million barrels. So comparing the rise of the demand for oil and the disappearing supplier, Saudi Arabia needs to supply more in the future."[47]

An important aspect of the energy market is the capacity to balance it in the short term. Spare capacity is kept by certain producers to limit price hikes. In the history of the oil industry, different players have acted as swing producer, but in the last decade only Saudi Arabia has had enough spare capacity to allow take on that role. Although this does not mean that the kingdom actually was a swing producer, it had the potential, and this gave it substantial market power. But the elasticity of the shale industry has raised the question of a possible swing role for the US industry, favoured by the fact that investments and shale production are price sensitive, and the investment cycle is short. On the other hand, there is no single management centre that could decide production levels.

The reduction in the importance of Middle East oil for the global economy and the long period of low prices discussed during the early phase of the shale

---

45 Clifford Krauss, "Trump Hit Iran With Oil Sanctions. So Far, They're Working," *The New York Times*, 19 Sep. 2018: 11 Oct. 2018 https://www.nytimes.com/2018/09/19/business/energy-environment/iran-oil-sanctions.html.

46 IEA, *World Energy Outlook-2017*, (IEA, 2017).

47 Stephanie Flanders, et al., "Saudi Crown Prince Discusses Trump, Aramco, Arrests: Transcript."

revolution could have disastrous consequences on local economies in the region dependent on oil income. Some of them are directly dependent, some indirectly enjoy economic support from oil exporting countries. The region remains strongly integrated with the global economy through the oil market. The level of global economic growth, interest rates, an open trade system and geopolitical stability all remain crucial for the countries of the region. But the price of oil is the single most important parameter for the Middle East economies[48]. As the authors of the IMF report "Middle East and Central Asia Regional Economic Outlook Update: Middle East and Central Asia" (dated May 2018) argue: "The outlook for oil prices remains highly uncertain". Despite decades of investments and plans to diversify their economies, they are still highly dependent on oil income and the generation of oil rents. Many economies of the region are still characterised as rentier states. The challenges created for them by falling oil prices are mainly visible in two areas: first, the oil income needed to balance the national budget (the break-even price of oil). Second, the oil income needed to balance the current account (the external break-even price). During the oil price collapse of 2014–2015, the tightening of the fiscal position affected even the richest local economies and pushed the local authorities to raise income and limit expeditors. In consequence, in January 2018 value added tax (VAT) was introduced in the UAE and Saudi Arabia. Also, the government of Iraq introduced sales and excise taxes on some goods and services in 2018.[49] On the expenditure side, the efficiency of public spending should be increased, and energy subsidies eliminated. Changes in social security and pension systems are also required. Benefits have to be reduced and the retirement age raised in the face of budget deficits. The most visible consequence of low oil prices is mounting public debt. IMF researchers take a pessimistic view of development. "Although public debt remains manageable for most MENAP oil exporters, the rapid build-up of debt in many of them is a cause for concern. Debt has increased by an average of 10 percentage points of GDP each year since 2013, with countries financing large fiscal deficits through a combination of drawdowns of buffers (where available) and increased domestic and foreign borrowing (…). Looking ahead, several factors are likely to continue to drive debt upward in MENAP oil exporters. These include the slower pace of fiscal consolidation, weak growth prospects, and the possibility of higher financing costs given the expected monetary policy tightening in advanced

48 Tab. 5.
49 "Iraq Corporate - Other taxes", PWC, 15 Nov. 2018: 14 May 2019, http://taxsummaries.pwc.com/ID/Iraq-Corporate-Other-taxes.

economies. Given anticipated financing needs—cumulative overall fiscal deficits are projected to be $294 billion in 2018–22, (...)—countries are increasingly vulnerable to a sudden tightening of global financial conditions."[50] But the rise in oil prices may change the economic situation, and these pessimistic predictions will not necessarily materialise[51]. As the Crown Prince of Saudi Arabia argues, the reforms are paying off, and higher oil prices of course support a more balanced budget. The planned budget of the Kingdom of Saudi Arabia for 2019 foresees spending of 1 trillion and 100 billion riyals. Non-oil income has increased by 300 percent, from 100 billion riyals to 300 billion riyals, as a result of the reforms of recent years. Still, the balancing of the national budget is forecast for 2023. This goal will be achieved much faster in the UAE, by 2019. This combination of economic reforms, higher prices and higher demand for Middle East oil gives hope for the architects of economic policies in the region[52].

The Political Consequences of the Shale Revolution

Despite its economic impact, the shale revolution should not dramatically change the US foreign policy towards the Middle East. Although the idea of a US withdrawal from the Middle East has emerged, it was noted early on that such a prospect is not very probable. However, lower oil prices and a lower level of dependence on imports have created more foreign policy options for the US administration, and have weakened the position of oil exporters[53].

The reduced reliance of the United States on Middle East oil should allow the U.S. to redefine, or even reverse, its decades-long engagement in the Middle East. The rise in U.S. domestic production should switch off the oil-for-security mechanism. Although up until 1971 the United Kingdom was the guarantor of stability in the Persian Gulf, the United States was already active in the region as early as 1945. The famous meeting between President Franklin D. Roosevelt and King Ibn Saud marked the beginning of the United States'

---

50 IMF, *Regional Economic Outlook Update: Middle East and Central Asia,* (IMF, May 2018), p. 6.

51 IMF, *Regional Economic Outlook: Middle East and Central Asia*, (IMF, October 2015).

52 Jonathan Wheatley, "Gulf economies rebound as oil price rises," *Financial Times*, 11 Oct. 2018: 11 Oct. 2018 https://www.ft.com/content/0c525d0e-bcbc-11e8-8dfd-2f1cbc7ee27c.

53 Ed Crooks, Geoff Dyer, "Energy security: Strength in reserve," *Financial Times*, 05 Sep. 2013: 11 Oct. 2018 https://www.ft.com/content/916a6744-0f14-11e3-8e58-00144feabdc0.

political presence in the region. In the following decades, Iran also became a close ally of the U.S. During the 1970s America followed twin pillars strategy, supporting Iran and maintaining its strategic partnership with Saudi Arabia. With the revolution in Iran and the Soviet invasion of Afghanistan, the United States strengthened its ties with Saudi Arabia. President Jimmy Carter clearly stated this in his State of the Union Address on 23 January 1980. "Let our position be absolutely clear: an attempt by any outside force to gain control of the Persian Gulf region will be regarded as an assault on the vital interests of the United States of America, and such an assault will be repelled by any means necessary, including military force"[54]. Ronald Reagan continued Carter's policy of strengthening relations with Saudi Arabia[55], and the U.S. kept its promise to protect the Persian Gulf. As Secretary of State James Baker explained: "The economic lifeline of the industrial world runs from the Gulf and we cannot permit a dictator such as this to sit astride that economic lifeline"[56]. When Iraq invaded and occupied Kuwait, the United States was determined to liberate the country. It built a coalition of countries and successfully restored order in the region. The United States also kept up a military presence in the region. As various reports show, the U.S. has spent trillions of US dollars in the Middle East since 11 September 2001.[57]

The political consequences of the reduced dependence of the United States on imported oil can differ for each country of the Middle East. As Meghan O'Sullivan argues, the number of barrels imported from the Middle East is not the only driver of the United States' interest in the region. Fighting terrorism, countering the proliferation of weapons of mass destruction and supporting Israel all remain top foreign policy priorities. The United States is also interested, more broadly, in keeping very unstable region stable. Withdrawing from the

---

54 Jimmy Carter, "The State of the Union Address Delivered Before a Joint Session of the Congress," *The American Presidency Project*, 23 Jan. 1980: 11 Oct. 2018 http://www.presidency.ucsb.edu/ws/?pid=33079.

55 Tyler Priest, "The Dilemmas of Oil Empire," *Journal of American History*, Vol. 99, Issue 1 (2012), pp. 236–251.

56 Thomas L. Friedman, "Mideast Tensions; U.S. Jobs at Stake in Gulf, Baker Says," *The New York Times*, 14 Nov. 1990: 11 Oct. 2018 https://www.nytimes.com/1990/11/14/world/mideast-tensions-us-jobs-at-stake-in-gulf-baker-says.html.

57 Neta C. Crawford, "United States Budgetary Costs of Post 9/11 Wars Through FY 2018," *Watson Institute Brown University*, Nov. 2017: 11 Oct. 2018 https://watson.brown.edu/costsofwar/files/cow/imce/papers/2017/Costs%20of%20U.S.%20Post-9_11%20NC%20Crawford%20FINAL%20.pdf.

region could strengthen Iran's hand against other countries and make it easier for Iran to develop weapons of mass destruction. But as discussed earlier, the administration of President Trump has no intention of taking such a step; in fact, it is moving in the opposite direction. Trump's tough line on Iran is 180 degrees opposed to the policy of the Obama administration.

The rise in production in the United States and the reduction of its dependence on the supply of oil from the Middle East may change relations between Saudi Arabia, the UAE or Kuwait and the United States. For decades, those relations have been symmetrical (oil for security), but as Meghan O'Sullivan argues, they may became more asymmetrical. She argues that, in an energy-abundant environment, Saudi Arabia's reserves will lose some of their importance and its spare capacity will lose its political leverage. In consequence, with the United States reducing its interest in the region, new alliances may emerge and new powers may fill a power vacuum in the region. It is also a question of the political regimes in the region. Meghan O'Sullivan called the correlation between falling oil income and rising prospects for democracy, developed by Thomas Friedman, the First Law of Petropolitics[58]. But a reduction in production in some non-Middle East exporting countries increases the importance of Middle East producers. The tough line taken toward Iran also means strengthening ties with Saudi Arabia, which has to fill the gap after Iran is pushed out of the market. Following the summit in 2017, the U.S. and Saudi Arabia agreed to strengthen their cooperation on security. Saudi Arabia also agreed to buy American weaponry, at a record level. But fast rising oil prices during 2018 again led to growing pressure from the United States on oil producers to increase production and lower prices. During his remarks on 25 September 2018 to the 73rd Session of the United Nations General Assembly, President Trump argued that "OPEC and OPEC nations, are, as usual, ripping off the rest of the world, (…). We defend many of these nations for nothing, and then they take advantage of us by giving us high oil prices."[59]

---

58 Meghan L. O'Sullivan, *Windfall: How the New Energy Abundance Upends Global Politics and Strengthens America's Power* (New York, London, Toronto, Sydney, New Delhi: Simon&Schuster, 2017) pp. 249–282.

59 Donald Trump, "Remarks by President Trump to the 73rd Session of the United Nations General Assembly," *White House*, 25 Sep. 2018: 11 Oct. 2018 https://www.whitehouse.gov/briefings-statements/remarks-president-trump-73rd-session-united-nations-general-assembly-new-york-ny/.

A few days later, Trump pointed to the logic of oil for security deals, arguing that the king of Saudi Arabia might not last two weeks without U.S. support[60]. Such statements show that cooperation in one field does not exclude confrontation in another. Producers and American allies in the region such as Saudi Arabia, Kuwait or UAE have to be more sensitive to the priorities of the United States. But their importance in the market is also growing. They, also, should not be interested in pushing prices towards 100 USD/b. It is in this context that we can understand the statement of Crown Prince Mohammed bin Salman that OPEC is working to keep oil prices down[61].

Conclusions

When the shale oil revolution in the United States started, there was a general expectation that Middle East oil would lose its importance to the global economy and that Middle Eastern countries would lose the political leverage that oil had given them. But the paradox of the situation is that, after only a few years, we can observe that Middle East oil is more, not less, important to the global economy. Unexpectedly, the shale revolution did not cause a diversification of oil production in the world, but a concentration in the most economically efficient areas.

The shale revolution provoked a price collapse that was quietly observed by Saudi Arabia, Kuwait and other key Middle East producers in late 2014 and 2015. Then, through 2016, an agreement on a production freeze, and later on a cut, was negotiated between OPEC and non-OPEC producers. It was concluded in December 2016. The price of oil then began to increase, again achieving the relatively high level of over 80 USD/b. Credit for this success is due to, among other players, the Kingdom of Saudi Arabia (KSA), the UAE and Kuwait. The Saudi Minister Khalid A. Al-Falih, together with his colleague Alexander Novak, led the efforts of both groups of countries to stabilise the market and raise income. Saudi Arabia, Kuwait and the UAE – but also Iraq – play a crucial role in the market. As some high-cost producers face falling production

60 Tamara Qiblawi, "Trump says Saudi King wouldn't last 'two weeks' without US support," *CNN*, 07 Oct. 2018: 11 Oct. 2018 https://edition.cnn.com/2018/10/03/politics/trump-saudi-king-intl/index.html.

61 Stephen Cunningham, Vivian Nereim, "Oil Price Isn't Spurring Enough Investment, Saudi Minister Says," *Bloomberg*, 22 Mar. 2018: 11 Oct. 2018 https://www.bloomberg.com/news/articles/2018-03-22/oil-price-isn-t-spurring-enough-investment-saudi-minister-says.

Tab. 1: Value of petroleum exports (millions of USD). Source: OPEC, *Annual Statistical Bulletin*, 2018.

	2000	2001	2002	2003	2004	2005	2006	2007	2008
Iran	18 821	21 420	19 219	26 124	34 289	48 306	57 719	69 248	89 855
Iraq	18 319	11 585	11 246	7 526	17 730	23 579	30 299	39 412	61 111
KSA	70 866	59 788	63 815	82 272	110 746	161 871	190 468	205 452	280 998
Kuwait	18185	14 969	14 060	19 005	26 675	42 440	53 160	59 006	82 672
UAE	26 148	23 909	22 806	29 183	38 801	55 079	70 100	73 827	102 087
	2009	**2010**	**2011**	**2012**	**2013**	**2014**	**2015**	**2016**	**2017**
Iran	55 746	72 228	114 751	101 468	61 923	53 652	27 308	41 123	52 728
Iraq	39 307	51 589	83 010	94 090	89 403	84 303	49 211	43 684	59 730
KSA	161 613	214 897	317 614	337 480	321 888	284 558	152 910	136 194	159 742
Kuwait	48 914	61 753	97 373	108 534	107 543	94 324	48 444	41 461	50 683
UAE	67 876	74 638	79 573	86 016	85 640	88 855	53 836	45 559	65 641

due to underinvestment, Middle Eastern countries are enjoying low production costs and access to finance, and are making plans to expand production in the future. Of course, this sweeping, optimistic picture cannot hide the fact that some producers are facing geopolitical challenges in the region. Iran is the most visible case. In 2016–2017, discussion centred on Iran regaining its market share after the period of sanctions. Today, Iranian production is again falling due to US sanctions.

Middle East oil producers have survived the oil price plunge thanks to financial buffers accumulated during the oil price bonanza. Due to falling spare production capacity in the world supply, the region is again gaining in economic and political importance. The shale revolution that was to weaken Middle East producers has in fact strengthened them by eliminating high-cost producers.

The shale revolution has changed very little in the United States' engagement in the Middle East. The U.S. is present in the region, and there are no signs that anything is going to change in this regard. The geopolitical consequences of the emergence of shale oil seem to be limited. Of course, Middle East producers are developing their relations with China, India and other Asian countries; these are becoming their biggest clients. But this process had already begun well before shale oil became an issue. There are no signs that the rise of oil production in the United States will cause a geopolitical rebalancing of the Middle East.

Tab. 2: Current account balances of OPEC Members (millions of USD). Source: OPEC, *Annual Statistical Bulletin*, 2018.

	2000	**2001**	**2002**	**2003**	**2004**	**2005**	**2006**	**2007**	**2008**
Iran	9 271	1 731	1 920	-622	-216	15 392	20 585	32 594	22 838
Iraq	-8 169	-15 410	-782	-935	-2 404.6	1 917.8	7 095.6	19 991.7	32 344.4
KSA	14 317	9 353	11 873	28 048	49 295	89 990	98 934	93 329	132 322
Kuwait	14 757	8 376	4 315	9 491	15 509	30 070	45 312	41 331	60 240
UAE	12 144	9 589	3 014	7 153	10 573	24 369	36 045	19 641	22 278
	2009	**2010**	**2011**	**2012**	**2013**	**2014**	**2015**	**2016**	**2017**
Iran	9 477	27 555	58 507	23 362	25 105	13 571	1 237	16 388	16 063
Iraq	-1142,5	6 477	26 129	29 542	22591.4	24427,9	1 913	5 404	15 744
KSA	20 955	66 751	158 545	164 764	135 442	73 758	-56 724	-27 551	11 519
Kuwait	28 278	36 991	66 148	79 124	70 471	53 966	8 587	640	4 684
UAE	7 249	7 241	50 948	79 564	71 192	54 471	17 525	13 197	27 491

Tab. 3: Oil production in the Middle East (1,000 b/d). Source: BP, *Statistical Review of World Energy 1965–2017*.

2000	**2001**	**2002**	**2003**	**2004**	**2005**	**2006**	**2007**	**2008**
23657	23 189	21 919	23 582	24 868	25 576	25 802	25 440	26 517
2009	**2010**	**2011**	**2012**	**2013**	**2014**	**2015**	**2016**	**2017**
24818	25 834	28 082	28 523	28 194	28 496	30 023	31 849	31 597

Tab. 4: Middle East and world crude oil exports by country (1,000 b/d). Source: OPEC, *Annual Statistical Bulletin*, 2018.

	2000	**2001**	**2002**	**2003**	**2004**	**2005**	**2006**	**2007**	**2008**
Middle East	16 027.1	15 092.6	13 738.0	14 533.1	16 314.7	16 860.7	16 911.5	16 669.6	17 386.0
World Total	38 886.3	38 021.1	37 024.2	38 730.9	42 156.6	43 009.9	42 485.3	42 921.7	42 242.6
	2009	**2010**	**2011**	**2012**	**2013**	**2014**	**2015**	**2016**	**2017**
Middle East	15 308.2	15 987.5	17 772.3	18 076.8	17 497.2	16 792.8	17 037.3	19 321.1	18 746.4
World Total	40 748.9	41 399.9	41 280.3	42 038.5	40 827.5	40 201.6	41 551.5	44 249.1	44 753.3

Tab. 5: MENAP region: Selected economic indicators, 2000–2019, (Percent of GDP, unless otherwise indicated). Source: IMF, *Regional Economic Outlook Update: Middle East and Central Asia*, (IMF, May 2018), p. 19.

	Average				Projection	
MENAP (2011–2019 data exclude Syrian Arab Republic)	2000–2014	2015	2016	2017	2018	2019
Real GDP (annual growth)	4.8	2.5	4.9	2.6	3.4	3.7
Of which non-oil growth	5.9	1.6	1.9	3.2	3.6	3.9
Current Account Balance	8.8	-4.0	-4.2	-0.9	0.5	-0.3
Overall Fiscal Balance	3.5	-8.6	-9.4	-5.6	-4.4	-3.5
MENAP oil exporters						
Real GDP (annual growth)	5.0	1.9	5.4	1.7	2.8	3.3
Of which non-oil growth	6.6	0.3	0.8	2.6	3.2	3.4
Current Account Balance	12.6	-3.8	-3.6	1.2	3.0	1.8
Overall Fiscal Balance	6.7	-9.2	-10.6	-5.2	-3.8	-2.8

MENAP oil exporters: Algeria, Bahrain, Iran, Iraq, Kuwait, Libya, Oman, Qatar, Saudi Arabia, the United Arab Emirates and Yemen.

Bibliography

1. Al-Naimi, Ali. *Out of the Desert: My Journey from Nomadic Bedouin to the Heart of Global Oil*. London: Penguin, 2016.
2. Ali, Mohamed Sami Ben, Lara Cockx and Nathalie Francken. "The Middle East and North Africa: Cursed by Natural Resources?" In: *Economic Development in the Middle East and North Africa*, ed. Mohamed Sami Ben Ali. London: Palgrave Macmillan, 2016, pp. 71–93.
3. Andrijanič, Mark Boris. "The American Energy Revolution: Challenging Europe and the Middle East." *European View*, Vol. 14, No. 2, 2015, pp. 263–273.
4. Baffes, John, M. Ayhan Kose, Franziska Ohnsorge and Marc Stocker. *The Great Plunge in Oil Prices: Causes, Consequences, and Policy Responses*. Washington, D.C. : World Bank, 2015, PRN/15/01.
5. Baumeister, Christiane and Lutz Kilian. "Understanding the Decline in the Price of Oil since June 2014." *Journal of the Association of Environmental and Resource Economists*, Vol. 3, No. 1, 2016, pp. 131–158.
6. Baumeister, Christiane and Lutz Kilian. "Forty Years of Oil Price Fluctuations: Why the Price of Oil May Still Surprise Us." *Journal of Economic Perspectives*, Vol. 30, No. 1, 2016, pp. 139–160.

7. Cairns, Robert D. and Enrique Calfucura. "OPEC: Market Failure or Power Failure?" *Energy Policy*, Vol. 50, No. C, 2012, pp. 570–580.
8. Colgan, Jeff D. "The Emperor Has No Clothes: The Limits of OPEC in the Global Oil Market." *International Organization*, Vol. 68, No. 3, 2014, pp. 599–632.
9. Dale, Spencer and Bassam Fattouh. *Peak Oil Demand and Long-Run Oil Prices*. Oxford: Energy Insight, 2018.
10. Economou, Andreas and Bassam Fattouh. *5+1Key Facts About the OPEC Declaration of Cooperation*. Oxford: OIES Oxford Energy Comment, 2018.
11. El-Katiri, Laura, Bassam Fattouh. *A Brief Political Economy of Energy Subsidies in the Middle East and North Africa*. OIES Paper, 2015.
12. Goodstein, David. *Out of Gas: The End of the Age of Oil*. New York, London: W.W.Norton & Company, 2004.
13.Simmons, Matthew R. *Twilight in the Desert: The Coming Saudi Oil Shock and the World Economy*. New Jersey: Wiley, 2006.
14. Hamilton, James D. "Causes and Consequences of the Oil Shock of 2007–08." *Brookings Papers on Economic Activity, Economic Studies Program, The Brookings Institution*, Vol. 40, No. 1, 2009, pp. 215–261.
15. IEA. *World Energy Outlook-2017*. IEA, 2017.
16. IEA. *World Energy Investment 2018*. IEA, 2018.
17. IMF. *Regional Economic Outlook: Middle East and Central Asia*. IMF, October 2015.
18. IMF. *Regional Economic Outlook Update: Middle East and Central Asia*. IMF, May 2018.
19. Jalilvand, David Ramin. *The US Exit from the JCPOA: What Consequences for Iranian Energy?* OIES Oxford Energy Comment, 2018.
20. Kilian, Lutz and Bruce Hicks. "Did Unexpectedly Strong Economic Growth Cause the Oil Price Shock of 2003–2008?" *Journal of Forecasting*, Vol. 32, No. 5, 2013, pp. 385–394.
21. Klare, Michael. *Blood and Oil. The Dangers and Consequences of America's Growing Dependency on Imported Petroleum*. New York: Metropolitan Books, 2005.
22. Klare, Michael. "From Scarcity to Abundance: The Changing Dynamics of Energy Conflict." *Penn State Journal of Law & International Affairs*, Vol. 3, No. 2, 2015, pp. 10–41.
23. Kohl, Wilfried L. "OPEC Behavior, 1998–2001." *The Quarterly Review of Economics and Finance*, Vol. 42, No. 2, 2002, pp. 209–233.

24. Lahn, Glada, Paul Stevens. *Burning Oil to Keep Cool. The Hidden Energy Crisis in Saudi Arabia*. London: Chatham House, 2011.
25. Luciani, Giacomo. "Saudi Arabia and the Limits of Signalling." *OIES Forum*. Vol. 100, 2015. pp. 16–19.
26. Maugeri, Leonardo. *Oil: The Next Revolution*. Discussion Paper - Belfer Center for Science and International Affairs, Harvard Kennedy School, 2012.
27. McGowan, Francis. "International Regimes for Energy: Finding the Right Level for Policy." In: *Energy for the Future: A New Agenda*, ed. Ivan Scarse and Gordon MacKerron. Basingstoke: Palgrave Macmillan, 2009, pp. 20–34.
28. Morse, Edward L., et al. *Energy 2020: Independence Day. Global Ripple Effects of the North American Energy Revolution*. Citi GPS, 2013.
29. O'Sullivan, Meghan L. *Windfall: How the New Energy Abundance Upends Global Politics and Strengthens America's Power*. New York, London, Toronto, Sydney, New Delhi: Simon & Schuster, 2017.
30. Priest, Tyler. "The Dilemmas of Oil Empire." *Journal of American History*, Vol. 99, No. 1, 2012, pp. 236–251.
31. Tillerson, Rex. "Capitalizing on the Coming Era of Energy Abundance." *Address to Texas Alliance of Energy Producers*. Houston, 2 April 2013. https://corporate.exxonmobil.com/news/newsroom/speeches/2013/0402_capitalizing-on-the-coming-era-of-energy-abundance/ (11 October 2018).
32. Van de Graaf, Thijs. *The Politics and Institutions of Global Energy Governance*. Basingstoke: Palgrave Macmillan, 2013.
33. Van de Graaf, Thijs, Benjamin K. Sovacool, Arunabha Ghosh, Florian Kern and Michael Klare. "States, Markets, and Institutions: Integrating International Political Economy and Global Energy Politics." In: *The Palgrave Handbook of the International Political Economy of Energy*, ed. Thijs Van de Graaf, Benjamin K. Sovacool, Arunabha Ghosh, Florian Kern and Michael Klare. London: Palgrave Macmillan UK, 2016, pp. 3–44.
34. Westphal, Kirsten. "Energy Policy between Multilateral Governance and Geopolitics: Whither Europe?" *IPG*, No. 4, 2006, pp. 44–62.
35. Wilson, Ernest J. "World Politics and International Energy Markets." *International Organization*, Vol. 41, No. 1, 1987, pp. 125–149.

Internet Sources

1. Al-Naimi, Ali. "Speech." CERAWEEK 2016. 23 February 2016. http://fingfx.thomsonreuters.com/gfx/ce/1/482/482/NAIMI%20AT%20CERA%20WEEK.pdf (11 Oct. 2018).

2. Butler, Nick. "The Dangers of Iraq's Oil Law." Financial Times. 30 April 2018. https://www.ft.com/content/da2b5cae-46d7-11e8-8ee8-cae73aab7ccb (11 Oct. 2018).
3. Carter, Jimmy. "The State of the Union Address Delivered Before a Joint Session of the Congress." The American Presidency Project, 23 January 1980. http://www.presidency.ucsb.edu/ws/?pid=33079 (11 Oct. 2018).
4. Crawford, Neta C. "United States Budgetary Costs of Post 9/11 Wars Through FY 2018." Watson Institute Brown University. November 2017. https://watson.brown.edu/costsofwar/files/cow/imce/papers/2017/Costs%20of%20U.S.%20Post-9_11%20NC%20Crawford%20FINAL%20.pdf (11 Oct. 2018).
5. Crooks Ed and Geoff Dyer. "Energy Security: Strength in Reserve." Financial Times. 5 September 2013. https://www.ft.com/content/916a6744-0f14-11e3-8e58-00144feabdc0 (11 Oct. 2018).
6. Cunningham, Stephen and Vivian Nereim. "Oil Price Isn't Spurring Enough Investment, Saudi Minister Says." Bloomberg. 22 March 2018. https://www.bloomberg.com/news/articles/2018-03-22/oil-price-isn-t-spurring-enough-investment-saudi-minister-says (11 Oct. 2018).
7. Dale, Spencer. "New Economics of Oil, Society of Business Economists Annual Conference." BP. 13 October 2015. https://www.bp.com/content/dam/bp/pdf/speeches/2015/new-economics-of-oil-spencer-dale.pdf (11 Oct. 2018).
8. Domm, Patti. "US Oil Exports Boom to Record Level, Surpassing Most OPEC Nations." CNBC. 27 June 2018. https://www.cnbc.com/2018/06/27/us-oil-exports-boom-to-record-level-surpassing-most-opec-nations.html (11 Oct. 2018).
9. Flanders, Stephanie et al. "Saudi Crown Prince Discusses Trump, Aramco, Arrests: Transcript." Bloomberg. 5 October 2018. https://www.bloomberg.com/news/articles/2018-10-05/saudi-crown-prince-discusses-trump-aramco-arrests-transcript (11 Oct. 2018).
10. Friedman, Thomas L. "Mideast Tensions; U.S. Jobs at Stake in Gulf, Baker Says." The New York Times. 14 November 1990. https://www.nytimes.com/1990/11/14/world/mideast-tensions-us-jobs-at-stake-in-gulf-baker-says.html (11 Oct. 2018).
11. Hochstein, Amos J. "Remarks of Special Envoy, Bureau of Energy Resources." Dentons 2016 Energy Outlook Event. 2.8.2016. https://2009-2017.state.gov/e/enr/rls/260845.htm (11 Oct. 2018).
12. "Iraq Corporate - Other taxes", PWC, 15 Nov. 2018. http://taxsummaries.pwc.com/ID/Iraq-Corporate-Other-taxes (14 May 2019)

13. Krauss, Clifford. “Trump Hit Iran with Oil Sanctions. So Far, They're Working.” The New York Times. 19 September 2018. https://www.nytimes.com/2018/09/19/business/energy-environment/iran-oil-sanctions.html (11 Oct. 2018).
14. Lack, Simon. “America's Path to Energy Independence: The Shale Revolution.” Forbes. 4 June 2018. https://www.forbes.com/sites/simonlack/2018/06/04/americas-path-to-energy-independence-the-shale-revolution/#5b035edf7554 (11 Oct. 2018).
15. Lee, Yen Nee. “OPEC Is Acting with ‘Noble Goal’ of Rescuing the Oil Market, Says Organization's President.” CNBC. 23 April 2018. https://www.cnbc.com/2018/04/23/uae-energy-minister-suhail-al-mazrouei-on-opec-production-cuts-oil-prices.html (11 Oct. 2018).
16. Morse, Ed. “US Set to Become Swing Oil Supplier.” *Financial Times*. 15 February 2018. https://www.ft.com/content/49354866-117d-11e8-8cb6-b9ccc4c4dbbb (11 Oct. 2018).
17. “OPEC and non-OPEC Ministerial Meeting.” OPEC. No. 25. 2016. https://www.opec.org/opec_web/en/press_room/3944.htm (11 Oct. 2018).
18. Pinchuk, Denis, Dmitry Zhdannikov and Olesya Astakhova. “Saudi Arabia to Invest $20 Billion in Spare Oil Production Capacity.” *Reuters*. 4 October 2018. https://www.reuters.com/article/us-oil-opec-falih-investment/saudi-arabia-to-invest-20-billion-in-spare-oil-production-capacity-idUSKCN1ME111 (11 Oct. 2018).
19. Qiblawi, Tamara. “Trump Says Saudi King Wouldn't Last ‘Two Weeks’ without US Support.” CNN. 7 October 2018. https://edition.cnn.com/2018/10/03/politics/trump-saudi-king-intl/index.html (11 Oct. 2018).
20. “Saudi Arabia Was Worried about a Danger Much Bigger than Shale When It Blindsided Oil Markets.” Financial Post. 13 April 2015. https://business.financialpost.com/commodities/energy/saudi-arabia-was-worried-about-a-danger-much-bigger-than-shale-when-it-blindsided-oil-markets (11 Oct. 2018).
21. Sen, Amrita and Yasser Elguindi. “Era of ‘Lower for Longer’ Oil Prices Is Dead.” Financial Times. 22 May 2018. https://www.ft.com/content/60412154-5da1-11e8-9334-2218e7146b04 (11 Oct. 2018).
22. “The Petrostate of America.” The Economist. 15 February 2014. https://www.economist.com/leaders/2014/02/15/the-petrostate-of-america (11 Oct. 2018).
23. Trump, Donald J. “Remarks by President Trump at the Unleashing American Energy Event.” White House. 29.6.2017. https://www.whitehouse.gov/briefings-statements/remarks-president-trump-unleashing-american-energy-event/ (11 Oct 2018).

24. Trump, Donald. "Remarks by President Trump to the 73rd Session of the United Nations General Assembly." White House. 25 September 2018. https://www.whitehouse.gov/briefings-statements/remarks-president-trump-73rd-session-united-nations-general-assembly-new-york-ny/ (11 Oct. 2018).
25. Van de Graaf, Thijs and Jeff Colgan. "Global Energy Governance: A Review and Research Agenda." Palgrave Communications. 26 January 2016. https://www.nature.com/articles/palcomms201547 (11 Oct. 2018).
26. Wheatley, Jonathan. "Gulf Economies Rebound as Oil Price Rises." Financial Times. 11 October 2018. https://www.ft.com/content/0c525d0e-bcbc-11e8-8dfd-2f1cbc7ee27c (11 Oct. 2018).
27. Wingfield, Brian, Samuel Dodge and Cedric Sam. "OPEC Can't Shake Over-Compliance on Oil Cuts." Bloomberg. 17 September 2018. https://www.bloomberg.com/graphics/opec-production-targets/ (11 Oct. 2018).

Fazli Doğan and Erdem Özlük

Success of Integration Initiatives in the Islamic World: The Case of D-8

Abstract: The Developing 8 Organization for Economic Cooperation (D-8) was founded in 1997 for improving member states' (Bangladesh, Egypt, Indonesia, Iran, Malaysia, Nigeria, Pakistan, and Turkey) position in the global economy. However, since the very beginning of the foundation, D-8 has not been able to meet the expectations that it set for itself in the charter of the organization. This chapter discusses the failure of the organization over seven parameters. These parameters can be listed as follows: i. Absence of *raison d'etre* that reinforces the integration level between members, ii. Lack of hegemonic support for deeper integration, iii. Absence of great power among the members, iv. Problem of geographical proximity, v. Different understanding of the role of religion in determining the foreign policies, vi. Different political and societal structures between members, and vii. Limited partnership capabilities between member states.

Keywords: Developing 8, integration, Islamic World, Turkey

Introduction

The Developing 8 Organization for Economic Cooperation (D-8) was established under the leadership of Turkey at the Presidential Summit at Istanbul on June 15th 1997.[1] The member states and founders of D-8 are Bangladesh, Egypt, Indonesia, Iran, Malaysia, Nigeria, Pakistan, and Turkey. All members of D-8 are also members of the Organization of Islamic Cooperation (OIC). D-8 was established for the purpose of improving the standings of member states in world economy, creating new opportunities and improving commercial relations of the member states.[2] The member states aim to improve their capacities in some cooperation themes by working together. Trade, transportation, agriculture and food security, industrial cooperation, energy and minerals, health and tourism are not only the priority areas of the D-8 but also the themes of cooperation.[3]

Although, since the very beginning of the foundation, all cooperation and priority areas were determined for a stronger cooperation between member states, D-8 has not been able to meet the expectations that it set for itself in the

1 https://developing8.org/image/DocumentandResouce/9297091.pdf (3 Apr. 2018).

2 *D8 internet platform*, 17 May 2018. http://developing8.org/.

3 03 Apr. 2018 http://developing8.org/about-d-8/purposes-objectives/.

charter. For example, as stated in D-8 Economic Outlook 2016/2017, "in 2012, intra-D-8 exports were recorded at US$ 69 billion, but it decreased to US$ 48 billion in 2015. Despite the major fall in export volume, the total amount can still be considered substantial when compared to total intra-D-8 exports of US$ 34 billion in 2009 and US$ 21 billion in 2005. The share of intra-D-8 exports in total D-8 exports continued to decrease since 2012 and reached 7,2 % in 2015. Similarly, the share of intra-D-8 imports has decreased from 8,3 % in 2012 to 6,4 % in 2015".[4]

This chapter discusses the possibilities and limits of the integration initiatives in the Islamic world focusing specifically on the case of D-8. D-8 was founded on the objectives of founding a deeper and stronger integration in the Islamic world. The founding father of the project was the late Necmettin Erbakan, the prime minister of Turkey between 1996 and 1997, whose main aim was to establish political and economic unions in the Islamic world in order to challenge the current international system which has been highly western oriented and capitalist. However, more than 20 years after the foundation, it is claimed that D-8 as a deep and strong integration model failed due to the some structural problems such as political and economic crises in member states and the dynamics or constrains of the international system.

The failure of the organization can also be summarized as follows: limitations of the organization's own capacity and common and structural problems in the Islamic world. To clearly and unambiguously display the problems, this chapter is divided into two principal sections. The first section discusses on purpose, principles, and organizational structure of the D-8. In the second section, D-8 as an integration model in the Islamic world is analyzed over the seven parameters which are considered as the main reasons of the failure of the organization. These parameters are: i. Absence of *raison d'etre* that reinforces the integration level between members, ii. Lack of hegemonic support for deeper integration, iii. Absence of great power among the members, iv. Problem of geographical proximity, v. Different understanding the role of religion in determining the foreign policies, vi. Different political and social structures between members, and limited partnership capabilities between member states.

4 *D-8 Economic Outlook 2016/2017:* 03 Apr. 2018 *"Enhancing Productivity and Competitiveness"*, p. 30, http://developing8.org/image/Booklet/D8-EconomicOutlook.pdf.

Section I

A The Organizational Structure and Purposes of the D-8

The establishment of D-8 was announced officially through the Istanbul Declaration of Summit of Heads of State on June 15, 1997.[5] D-8 is a global organization rather than a regional one, as the composition of its members reflects. The Charter[6] of the organization which signed in 2012 in Pakistan also articulates that D-8, as an intergovernmental organization, shall enjoy a legal personality and capacity. Founding members established a mechanism for development cooperation in many areas such as trade, industry, finance, and so forth. D-8 cooperation encompasses all areas including political consultation and coordination at the international fora.[7] According to the first Summit Declaration in 1997, and Charter of the organization (Article 2 declares principles and scope of cooperation) the main objective of D-8 is declared to be socio-economic development in accordance with following principles: "-Peace instead of conflict. -Dialogue instead of confrontation. -Cooperation instead of exploitation. -Justice instead of double-standard. -Equality instead of discrimination. -Democracy instead of oppression."[8]

The objectives of D-8 are set forth in the Charter in article 1.[9] These objectives are:

"(a) To promote and enhance joint efforts towards achieving sustainable socio-economic development through effective utilization of economic and social potentials of D-8 countries;

(b) To promote welfare, alleviate poverty, and to improve quality of life of the people of D-8 countries,

(c) To further strengthen economic, social, technical and scientific ties within the D-8 community;

(d) To promote private sector activity, through, inter alia, encouraging cooperation between chambers of commerce and industry, joint investments between private companies and public-private partnership, towards achieving the long-term goal of balanced national development in the D-8 countries;

---

5 27 Mar. 2018 http://developing8.org/about-d-8/brief-history-of-d-8/.

6 For the Charter of D-8, 3 Apr. 2018 https://developing8.org/image/Otherdocument/8388836.pdf.

7 Dipo Alam, "A Glimpse at D-8 Achivements", *Uluslararası Ekonomik Sorunlar Dergisi*, No. 32, (2008), p. 8.

8 *D-8 Journal: Special Edition*, 2017, p. 6.

9 Charter of the Developing-8 Organization for Economic Cooperation, Article 1; 11 May 2018 https://developing8.org/image/Otherdocument/8388836.pdf.

(e) To strengthen cooperation with other countries, regional and international organizations, as well as non-governmental organizations, with a view to promoting the concerns and interests of the developing countries;
(f) To work towards playing an effective role in the global economy commensurate with its collective potential and capacity."

The principal organs of D-8, regulated in article 5 of the Charter, are the Summit of Heads of State or Government (regulated in article 6), Council of Ministers (article 7), Commission (article 8), and Secretariat (article 9).[10]

The Summit, as the supreme organ of D-8, is composed of the heads of state/government of member states. It is convened once in every two years in one of the members, by alphabetical rotation. The main function of the Summit is to provide overall guidance for the work and activities of the organization towards achieving its objectives.

The Council of Ministers, as the principal decision-making organ of D-8, is composed of the ministers of foreign affairs of member states. In principle, it is convened at least once a year. Functioning in accordance with the general policy of the organization and the overall directives of the Summit, the Council acts as a forum for the thorough and comprehensive consideration of the issues.

The Commission is the executive organ of D-8. Working under the direct supervision of the Council, and guided by the decisions and directives of both the Council and the Summit, the Commission is responsible for in-depth discussion and consideration of all issues and aspects of the work of the organization, including the preparation the agenda of the Council and the Summit. The Commission is composed of senior officials appointed by their respective governments as commissioners. The Commission meets twice a year.[11]

The Secretariat is responsible for initiating, coordinating, and monitoring the implementation of all D-8 activities and meetings related to the principal organs and technical meetings. The Secretary-General is appointed on recommendation by the Council of Ministers by consensus from among the nationals of member states and approval by the Summit for a non-renewable four-year term in accordance with the principle of rotation in alphabetic order.

10 Charter of the Developing-8 Organization for Economic Cooperation, Article 5, 18 Apr. 2018 https://developing8.org/image/Otherdocument/8388836.pdf.
11 *D-8 15th Anniversary Booklet*, 05 Apr. 2018 https://developing8.org/image/Booklet/Booklet.pdf.

B General Overview of the D-8

One of the main targets of the founding fathers of the organization in the long run was to enlarge the organization with new member states from the Islamic world. Therefore, membership in D-8 is open to other developing states subscribing to the purposes and principles of the D-8.[12]

Since the foundation of the organization, D-8 has made some achievements such as Preferential Trade Agreement (PTA) between members. At the 5th D-8 summit held in Bali in 2006, PTA was signed by all members.[13] The implementation of the PTA is seen as one of the most important achievements of the organization to develop trade based on free trade principles among member states.[14] Additionally, at the meeting of the Council of Ministers held in Islamabad on December 19, 2013, the members agreed on the importance of establishing a Wise Men Group (WMG) for evaluating the organization in general and provide recommendations for the future vision.[15] Besides the PTA and WMG, other important frameworks such as Agreement on Visa Facilitation, Cooperation on Customs, and Memorandum of Understanding on Civil Aviation have been concluded. Forums have also been created to promote institutional linkages among the member states.[16]

Besides, the draft resolution on granting "Observer Status to the Organization of the Developing Eight Countries (D-8) at the General Assembly" adopted on October 2014 at the Sixth Committee under UN General Assembly's 69th session was adopted by the UN General Assembly without voting on December 2014.[17]

As shown in Tab. 1, all members except Malaysia have a population of over 80 million. The total population of member states is always seen as a great potential and advantage of the organizations since its foundation. While the world population is over 7 billion, total population of member states of D-8 is over 1

12 *D8*, 03 Apr. 2018 http://www.mfa.gov.tr/_d-8_.en.mfa.

13 *D8*, 03 Apr. 2018 http://www.mfa.gov.tr/_d-8_.en.mfa.

14 D-8 Fifth Summit Meeting, Bali, 13 May 2006, 5 May 2018 https://developing8.org/image/Booklet/Reports-of-5th-and-6th-Summits.pdf.

15 *D8*, 17 Apr. 2018 http://www.mfa.gov.tr/_d-8_.en.mfa.

16 Khalid Iqbal, "The Developing Eight: Functions, Challenges and Prospects", *IPRI Journal XIII*, No. 2, (Summer 2013), p. 147.

17 *Official Documents System of the United Nations*, 13 Apr. 2018 https://documents-dds-ny.un.org/doc/UNDOC/GEN/N14/559/41/PDF/N1455941.pdf?OpenElement.

Tab. 1: Basic indicators of the member states. Data excerpted from https://www.cia.gov/library/publications/the-world-factbook/ and https://data.worldbank.org/ 3 April 2018

D-8 members	Population (2017 est.)	Gross domestic product (GDP) (2016 est.)	GDP-Per capita (2016 est.)	Stock of direct foreign investment at home (billion $ in 2016)	Military expenditures (%of GDP in 2016 or 2015)	Export (billion in 2016 est.)	Import (billion in 2016 est.)
Bangladesh	157,826,578	$629.7 billion	$3,900	$13.24	1.44 %	$34.14	$40.37
Egypt	97,041,072	$1.132 trillion	$12,600	$97.14	1.67 %	$20.02	$56.71
Indonesia	260,580,739	$3.031 trillion	$11,700	$229.1	0.88 %	$144.4	$129
Iran	82,021,564	$1.549 trillion	$19,300	$46.02	2.69 %	$83.98	$63.14
Malaysia	31,381,992	$863.3 billion	$27,300	$121.6	1.41 %	$165.3	$140.9
Nigeria	190,632,261	$1.09 trillion	$5,900	$113.4	0.43 %	$34.7	$35.24
Pakistan	204,924,861	$986.3 billion	$5,100	$39	3.56 %	$21.71	$41.62
Turkey	80,845,215	$1.994 trillion	$25,000	$133.2	1.73 %	$150.2	$191

billion. Total GDP of members is over $11 trillion and world total GDP is over $127 trillion.[18] Taking this data into consideration, D-8 generates only 8 % of the world's economy output of $127 trillion while generating 15 % of the world's population. Additionally, in terms of GDP per capita, each member state is below developed countries' average.

Considering the foreign direct investment (FDI) rate which is a very important indicator for understanding any economy's place in the world, it is not easy to say D-8 members are the attraction points.[19] The flows of FDI into D-8 members can help them to accelerate the process of development. However, the flow of capital and investment needs an integrated and efficient capital and

18 *The World Factbook*, 10 Apr. 2018 https://www.cia.gov/library/publications/the-world-factbook/geos/xx.html.

19 Mumtaz Hussain Shah, Saima Samdani, "Impact of trade liberalization on FDI inflows to D-8 countries", *Global Management Journal for Academic & Corporate Studies*, Vol. 5, No 1, (2015), pp. 30–37.

Tab. 2: Land of area and energy resources of D-8 members. Data excerpted from https://www.cia.gov/library/publications/the-world-factbook/ and https://data.worldbank.org/ 10 May 2018

D-8 Members	Proven oil reserves (bbl in 2017, est.)	Natural gas (cubic meters in 2017, est.)	Area: land + water (sq. km)
Bangladesh	28 million	205.4 billion	148,460
Egypt	4.4 billion	2.186 trillion	1,001,450
Indonesia	3.23 billion	2.775 trillion	1,904,569
Iran	158.4 billion	33.5 trillion	1,648,195
Malaysia	3.6 billion	1.183 trillion	329,847
Nigeria	37.06 billion	5.284 trillion	923,768
Pakistan	350.6 million	542.5 billion	796,095
Turkey	388.5 million	18.49 billion	783,562
Total	207.46 billion	45.752 trillion	7.535.946

financial markets.[20] Because the positive effect of foreign direct investment on economic growth depends on absorbing capacities of member states and one of the most important capacities is financial development.[21] As shown in Tab. 2, in terms of land areas, and energy resources, D-8 states have a great potential. As discussed in the section two, the geographical factors and geopolitical potential are in fact much more important if all the member states are located in the same region. D-8 members are spread across three continents, and this is a very big hurdle to make integration between members stronger and deeper.

According to D-8 Economic Outlook of 2017, as we see in Fig. 1, over the last 5 years, D-8 countries have increased their share in the world output only by 0.1 percentage point to reach 9.0 % in 2015. Considering the organization's potential, it can be stated that the contribution of the D-8 members as a group to the world output is below their potential. On the other hand, the share of the D-8 countries in the total GDP of developing countries has declined steadily and was

20 Alireza Kazerooni and Somayeh Razzaghi, "Assessing the Feasibility of Common Currency Area among D-8 Group Members: Structural VAR Model Approach", *The International Journal of Applied Economics and Finance*, Vol. 8, No. 1, (2014), p. 18.

21 Marzieh Esfandyari, "The Role of Financial Markets Development in the Foreign Direct Investment Effect on Economic Growth (The case of D8 with Emphasizing on Iran)", *International Journal of Academic Research in Business and Social Sciences*, Vol. 5, No. 10, (2015), p. 247.

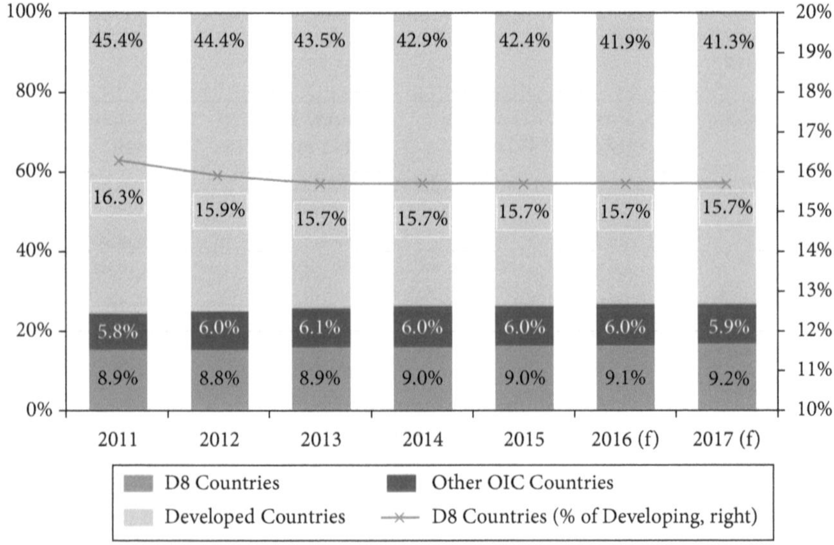

Fig. 1: Gross Domestic Product (PPP Current USD). Source: __*D-8 Economic Outlook 2016/2017,* p. 12, http://developing8.org/image/Booklet/D8-EconomicOutlook.pdf

recorded at 15.7 % in 2015, a decrease by 0.6 percentage points over the five-year period under consideration.[22]

Section II

A Testing the Success of the D-8 over Seven Parameters

Although it has a great potential in terms of population, geographical size and energy resources, we can argue that D-8, as an integration model in Islamic world, has not been a successful integration. We can discuss the failure of the D-8 over seven parameters.[23] The main reasons for the failure of the organization can be listed as follows:

22 __*D-8 Economic Outlook 2016/2017,* pp. 11–12, 03 Apr. 2018 http://developing8.org/image/Booklet/D8-EconomicOutlook.pdf.

23 It is important to bear in mind that while setting forth these parameters for evaluating the D-8, we take into consideration successful integration models such as EU and NATO.

First and foremost, there is no *raison d'etre* that reinforces the integration level between members. Deeper and stronger integration requires a common ground between member states.[24] If there is no reason of existence such as common enemy or threat, the organization will probably fail in the long run. It is therefore safe to say that the stronger the reason of existence is, the deeper the integration is. Every organization is a product of searching for collective action and larger cooperation. Any state that takes part in any organization seeks to reduce the cost either in political aims or security or economic aims. As Mitrany argued in his famous doctrine of ramification, development of cooperation in one field will help the proliferation of international collaboration in other technical fields.[25] The historical evolution of the integration in Europe is the most important example of the ramification. Additionally, NATO as the most successful integration model in the field of collective defense was an outcome of the very strong common ground (Soviet threat for the West Europe) for the member states.

The origin of the D-8 was the outcome of searching for the Islamic union within the area of economic cooperation between developing countries. Prime Minister Erbakan, conservative political figure and architect of the D-8 project, considered D-8 as a cooperation and development model for the developing Islamic countries. According to Erbakan, many states would take part in D-8 in the long run and the organization would be the symbol of the Islamic solidarity across the world. As Makovsky argued Erbakan's major diplomatic initiative was to establish a grouping of the eight most populous Islamic states, intended to foster economic cooperation, as well as political consultations, and serve as a Muslim counterweight to the industrialized G-7.[26] However, we can easily claim that there is no consensus between member states about the *raison d'etre* of the D-8. Although the only and the most powerful common ground between the members is Islam, the place and role of the religion in member states' both domestic and foreign policy differs significantly. The lack of a tangible common

---

24 Ernst B. Haas, "The Balance of Power: Prescription, Concept, or Propaganda", *World Politics*, Vol. 5, No. 4, (1953), p. 442.

25 David Mitrany, *A Working Peace System: An Argument for the Functional Development of International Organization*, (London: Royal Institute for International Affairs, 1943) p. 6. See also David Mitrany, "The Functional Approach to World Organization", *International Affairs*, Vol. 24, No. 4, (1948), pp. 350–363.

26 Alan Makovsky, "How to Deal with Erbakan", *Middle East Quarterly*, Vol. 4, No. 1, (March 1997), pp. 3–8.

ground between Islamic countries all over the world in general shows itself in the D-8 in particular, and affects the success of the D-8 as an integration.

Another reason that has led to the failure of the D-8 is the lack of a hegemonic support for stronger integration. Hegemony is a contested concept in international relations. In this study, we define hegemony as a capacity of a single state holding dominant position in terms of power to dominate international system.[27] As Cox argued, hegemony is defined as an economic, social, and political structure.[28] Hegemonic power sees international organizations as the indispensable part of the international order based on the non-violence and consent rather than coercion.[29] For example, United States has led to foundation of many international organizations. NATO, World Trade Organization, IMF, World Bank can be seen as a sign of the US.[30] The US also supported the integration initiatives in the Western Europe after the Second World War.[31] Today's European Union would not have been successful without the support of the United States.

D-8 had no hegemonic support from major international actors such as the US or EU during the establishment of the organization. In this sense D-8 can be considered as an initiative which was founded by the states dissatisfied with the current international order. Although some members of the organization were willing to set up an alternative order, their capacities and potential were

---

27 Kanti Bajpai and Varun Sahni, "Hegemony and Strategic Choice", in: *War, Peace and Hegemony in a Globalized World: The Changing Balance of Power in the Twenty-First Century,* ed. Chandra Chari, (New York: Routledge, 2007), pp. 93–107.

28 Robert W. Cox, "Gramsci, Hegemony and International Relations: An Essay in Method", in: *International Relations: Critical Concepts in Political Science,* Vol. III, ed. Andrew Linklater,/London: Routledge, 2000), pp. 1207–1217.

29 Cox, "Gramsci, Hegemony…", p. 1218.

30 Johan Lindeque and Steven McGuire, "The United States and Trade Disputes in the World Trade Organization: Hegemony Constrained or Confirmed?", *MIR: Management International Review,* Vol. 47, No. 5, (2007), pp. 725–744; Christoph Scherrer, " 'Double Hegemony'? State and Class in American Foreign Economic Policymaking", *Amerikastudien/American Studies,* Vol. 46, No. 4, (2001), p. 573; Mark Beeson, Alex J. Bellamy, "Globalisation, Security and International Order After 11 September", *Australian Journal of Politics and History,* Vol. 49, No. 3, (2003), pp. 347–348; Robert Hunter Wade, "US Hegemony and the World Bank: The Fight over People and Ideas", *Review of International Political Economy,* Vol. 9, No. 2, (2002), pp. 201–229.

31 Arnold Wolfers, "National Security as an Ambiguous Symbol", *Political Science Quarterly,* Vol. LXVII, No. 4, (1952), pp. 481–502; Barton J. Bersntein, "Containment", in: *Encyclopedia of American Foreign Policy,* eds. Alexander Delonde, et al., (New York: Charles Scribnes's Sons, 2002), pp. 345–362.

limited for establishing a new order. The inability on the part of the organization to garner the support of the great powers in the international arena has led to its failure.

Thirdly, there is no great power among the members to lead and convince the others for a strong integration. All D-8 members can be classified as developing countries. None of eight members is the permanent member of the UN Security Council. As mentioned in the first part, even though member states have a great potential and are very important actors in their own region, they have limited capacity to solve important problems even in their neighborhood. This is so because some of the members suffer from deep and structural political and economy instability. D-8 has thus far performed far worse than expected due largely to political and economic crisis on the one hand, and to the lack of commitment on the part of governing elites in member countries on the other.[32] In addition to these problems, after the two decades, we can assert that D-8 was never a priority for the member states' foreign policy agendas. Furthermore, none of the members has tendency to accept a leadership position of the other states within the organization. The main problem of the Islamic world is that states tend to have culture of rivalry rather than cooperation. This culture of rivalry can cause negative effects on the possibility of cooperation even between member states, and the lack of cooperation thus makes integration weak and fragile.

D-8 members, as shown in Tab. 3, also ranked between 59 and 152 among 188 countries in terms of their Human Development Index (HDI) value. For example, Turkey, as a candidate member for the EU and a member of NATO, has an HDI of 0.576, ranked 71st among 188.[33] The higher rank shows the level of development of states. None of the member states of the D-8 is ranked top 50 in the index.

The problem of geographical proximity between member states is yet another reason that has led to the failure of the D-8. D-8 members are located in three different continents. In fact, it can be said that it is a global organization rather

32 Berdal Aral, "An Inquiry into the D-8 Experiment: An Incipient Model of an Islamic Common Market?", *Alternatives: Turkish Journal of International Relations*, Vol. 4, No. 1&2 (Spring & Summer 2005), p. 90.

33 Human Development Index which is a composite index measuring average achievement in three basic dimensions of human development – a long and healthy life, knowledge and a decent standard of living is an important date for understanding the place of the any state in the international system, 03 Apr. 2018 http://hdr.undp.org/en/content/human-development-index-hdi.

Tab. 3: Human development index of D-8 (2016 from UNDP)

Members of D-8	HDI Rank	Value of HDI	Group of HDI
Bangladesh	139	0.579	MHD
Egypt	111	0.549	MHD**
Indonesia	113	0.528	MHD
Iran	69	0.572	HHD
Malaysia	59	0.643	HHD*
Nigeria	152	…	LHD***
Pakistan	147	0.404	MHD
Turkey	71	0.576	HHD

*HHD=high human development; **MHD=Medium human development; ***LHD=low human development

than a regional organization. From Indonesia to Nigeria, the organization covers a large geographical area. Some members have no common borders with other members such as Nigeria or Egypt. Compared to EU where all member states are located in the same European geography, D-8 members are scattered from South Asia to West Africa. Although Vasquez argued that geographical proximity is one of the most important conditions or cause of war,[34] geographical proximity is very important to create a deep integration and security complex. For example, according to Buzan, security complex is a set of states whose major security perceptions and concerns are so interlinked that their national security problems cannot reasonably be analyzed or resolved apart from one another.[35] D-8 in this sense has no potential to create a security complex.

Geographically located in distant areas creates a constraint that prevents member states from focusing on any specific problem. While states like Malaysia and Indonesia have different foreign policy agendas and priorities, Nigeria located in the Western Africa may have a totally different geopolitical agenda. Therefore, it becomes difficult for member states to meet on a common ground.

34 John A. Vasquez, *The War Puzzle Revisited*, (Cambridge: Cambridge University Press, 2009), p. 317.

35 Barry Buzan, *People, States and Fear*, (Sussex: Wheatsheaf Books, 1983). See also Barry Buzan and Ole Waever, *Regions and Powers, The Structure of International Security*, (Cambridge: Cambridge University Press, 2003), p. 51; Barry Buzan, "Regional Security Complex Theory in the Post-Cold War World", in: *Theories of New Regionalism*, eds. Fredrik Söderbaum and Timothy M. Shaw, (London: Palgrave Macmillan, 2003).

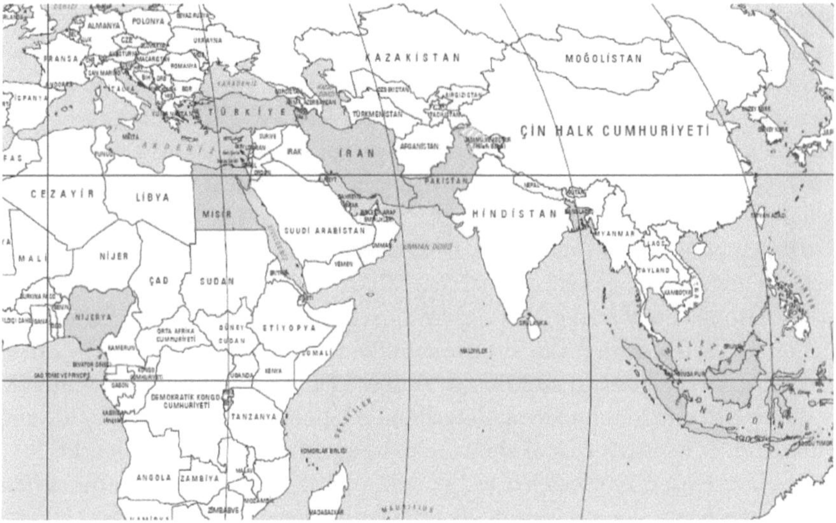

Fig. 2: D-8 Member States. Source: http://sdam.org.tr/image/foto/2017/12/15/Islam-Dunyasinda-Bir-Ittifak-Projesi-Olarak-D-8_1513346070.pdf

As Ozkan notes, the priorities of the members participating in any organization are as critical as the common aim of the organization. If each member's motivations stem from different considerations and those considerations cannot be articulated through a common channel, the chances of success of such organizations are less.[36] Regional diversity also negatively affects the effectiveness of the D-8's objectives in addition to the difficulty of creating a common agenda for members. Due to geopolitical disadvantage of the organization even cooperation in the economic development area, transportation and communication costs will be relatively higher.

The fifth reason for the failure of the D-8 is understanding of the role of religion in determining foreign policies of the members is quite different. D-8 can be classified as an international organization of eight Muslim-majority countries focused on socioeconomic development.[37] Although Islam is a common ground for all the members, each member has different understanding of religion and

36 Mehmet Ozkan, "Turkey in the Islamic World: An Institutional Perspective", *Turkish Review of Middle East Studies*, Vol. 18, (January 2007), p. 182.

37 Raymond W. Baker, *One Islam, Many Muslim Worlds*, (New York: Oxford University Press, 2015), p. 117.

Islamic culture. Additionally, there are sectarian differences in Islam as well. The sectarian differences between Sunni and Shiite Muslims bring about a distinct political divide or even conflict between member states. For example, Turkey and Iran each follow one of the two main sects in Islam namely Iran is largely Shia, while Turkey is Sunni Muslim state. In other words, there is no single interpretation of Islam in the Muslim world in general and within D-8 members in particular. Due to these differences, the place and role of Islam in political scene is also different in each member state. D-8, in this context, cannot be regarded as a pure Islamic project, despite the fact that Erbakan's most important driving force to establish the organization was clearly the religion. As a matter of fact, locating D-8 as a religious project can also weaken the integration's capacity rather than make it more efficient. In addition to all these factors, D-8 which is composed of states with different understanding about religion's role in policy making and with different sects has lack of ability to represent the whole Islamic world.

Another reason that has led to the failure of the organization is the difference in the political, economic, and social structures of member states. All D-8 members have a different social and political structure. The level of development varies sharply among member states, and this difference has also negative effect on the integration.[38] While trade between D-8 members is expected to increase substantially, differences between members have tended to weaken the potential trade capacity of the organization.[39] Huge differences between members in terms of political and social structure may also weaken integration and differentiate the members' foreign policy priorities. D-8 is thus negatively affected by these differences. For a successful integration, member countries must share as many values as possible. Members that have a common political and social language are less likely to conflict with one another. The more shared values there are, the more successful the integration will be. As in the case of the EU, the integration deepens if the member countries are convinced that the change will be carried out with peaceful means.

Finally, limited partnership capability between the member states is another reason for the failure of the organization. The European Coal and Steel Community (ECSC), origin of the EU, was formed in 1951 with the aim of organizing free movement of coal and steel and free access to sources of production.

---

38 Naved Ahmad and Fareed Ahmed, "Does Government Size Matter? A Case Study of D-8 Member Countries", *Pakistan Economic and Social Review*, Vol. 43, No. 2, (Winter 2005), p. 200.

39 Mohim Sheihaki Tash, "An Analysis of Bilateral Trade between Iran and D-8 Countries", *Global Journal of Management and Business Research*, Vol. 12, No. 2, (2012), p. 33.

Founding of ECSC and pooling Franco-German coal and steel production were not only economical but also political. The underlying political objective was to strengthen Franco-German solidarity, banish the possibility of war, and open the way to the future European integration.[40] Over time, the benefits of cooperation in coal and steel have spread to other areas, and today there is a strong integration of social, economic, and political dimensions. In the case of D-8, it can be seen that there is no interdependence in terms of the foreign trade partners of the member states. Tab. 4 shows that member states' first foreign trade partner is not any of D-8 member. The member states do not trade with or invest in one another' economy as much as they do with the developed or other developing states.[41] This situation also negatively affects the success of the D-8.

Conclusion

D-8 was founded with the motto of cooperation in development in 1997. The member states, members of the OIC at the same time, are among the leading states in terms of their technological and economic development levels, commercial potentials, and population within the OIC. Given their position in the OIC, D-8 members have high potentials in economic field. For example, D-8 as a major global market for agricultural and food products, is one of the largest producers and importers of food and feed grains in the world.[42] As Hassan pointed aptly, the D-8 should focus energies together for building the common future by making best use of potentials of the member states, to pursue good governance, and to upgrade social and economic conditions of the people.[43]

With its potential capacity, D-8 can be a global actor with the condition of deepening the integration process among the members in the field of economic cooperation. D-8 members have a similarity of patterns such as trade openness, financial sector growth, and stability of the exchange rate which is the initial

40 *Treaty establishing the European Coal and Steel Community, ECSC Treaty*, 03 Apr. 2018 http://eur-lex.europa.eu/legal-content/RO/TXT/?uri=LEGISSUM%3Axy0022.

41 Yaghoob Jafari, et al., "Determinants of Trade Flows among D-8 Countries: Evidence from Gravity Model", *Journal of Economic Cooperation and Development*, Vol. 32, No. 3, (2011), p. 22.

42 V. Shahabinejad and A. Akbari, "Measuring Agricultural Productivity Growth in Developing Eight", *Journal of Development and Agricultural Economics*, Vol. 2, No. 9, (September 2010), p. 326.

43 M. Kabir Hassan, "Economic Performance of the OIC Countries and the Prospect of an Islamic Common Market", *Economic Research Forum*, Working Paper No. 461, (2009), p. 20.

Tab. 4: Major import and export partners of the member states (2016). Data excerpted from https://www.cia.gov/library/publications/the-world-factbook/ and https://data.worldbank.org/ 3 April 2018

Turkey	Export	Germany 9.8 %, UK 8.2 %, Iraq 5.4 %, Italy 5.3 %, US 4.7 %, France 4.2 %
	Import	China 12.8 %, Germany 10.8 %, Russia 7.6 %, US 5.5 %, Italy 5.2 %
Iran	Export	China 30.1 %, India 16.7 %, South Korea 9.7 %, **Turkey 9.5 %,** Japan 6.8 %
	Import	UAE 27.4 %, China 13.2 %, **Turkey 7.8 %,** South Korea 4.3 %, Germany 4 %
Indonesia	Export	China 11.6 %, US 11.2 %, Japan 11.1 %, Singapore 7.8 %, India 7 %, **Malaysia 4.9 %,** South Korea 4.8 %
	Import	China 22.9 %, Singapore 10.8 %, Japan 9.6 %, Thailand 6.4 %, US 5.4 %, **Malaysia 5.4 %,** South Korea 5 % (2016
Egypt	Export	UAE 12.5 %, Saudi Arabia 7.7 %, Italy 6.5 %, **Turkey 6.3 %,** UK 4.6 %, US 4.5 %
	Import	China 12.9 %, Germany 8.7 %, US 5.3 %, Italy 4.5 %, **Turkey 4.3 %,** Saudi Arabia 4.1 % (2016)
Bangladesh	Export	US 13.1 %, Germany 12.7 %, UK 8.6 %, France 5.1 %, Spain 5 %
	Import	China 24.3 %, India 13.4 %, Singapore 5.1 %, Japan 4.5 % (2016)
Malaysia	Export	Singapore 14.7 %, China 12.6 %, US 10.3 %, Japan 8.1 %, Thailand 5.7 %, Hong Kong 4.8 %, India 4.1 %
	Import	China 19.4 %, Singapore 9.8 %, Japan 7.7 %, US 7.6 %, Thailand 5.8 %, South Korea 5 %, **Indonesia 4 %**
Nigeria	Export	India 34 %, US 9 %, Spain 5.9 %, France 5.8 %, South Africa 5.5 %, Canada 5.1 %
	Import	China 20.3 %, US 8.3 %, Belgium 7.6 %, UK 4.4 %, Netherlands 4.1 %
Pakistan	Export	US 16.3 %, China 7.6 %, UK 7.4 %, Afghanistan 6.5 %, Germany 5.7 %
	Import	China 29.1 %, UAE 13.2 %, **Indonesia 4.4 %,** US 4.3 %, Japan 4.2 %

condition necessary to build a stronger economic cooperation.[44] In order to make better use of these advantages in the long term, members require undertaking

44 Lukman Hakim, et al., "The Pattern of Macroeconomics and Economics Integration: Evidence on D-8 Economic Cooperation", *Journal of Organisational Studies and Innovation*, Vol. 2, No. 2, (2012), p. 8.

a certain set of economic reforms and ensuring that macroeconomic stability. When these conditions are fulfilled, the D-8 will have the ability to design and realize substantial projects related to trade and investment facilitation among its members and achieve higher global competitiveness.[45]

On the other hand, there are some structural problems inherited from the other problems in the Islamic world that prevent the real potential of the organization. D-8 members also have some particular problems regarding their own national features. For example, in Turkey during the foundation of the organization, military and civil bureaucracy strongly opposed to Erbakan's policies mainly because they alienated Turkey from West and Erbakan's Islamic foreign policy conflicted with the secular foundation of the modern Turkey.[46] Because D-8 had depended on Erbakan's personal idea and initiatives and found it difficult to carry on following his resignation until Justice and Development Party came to power in 2002.[47]

To overcome all these problems and obstacles, democratic consolidation should be seen as a path to reach the main objectives of the D-8 articulated in the charter. If the organization's integration capacity gets deeper and stronger in the long run, democracy should be "the only game in the town"[48] within the member states. There is a strong link between democracy and level of success of integration because democratic regimes by speaking the same political language, share many common features to develop the cooperation in any field.[49] However, democratic regimes in the D-8 are not consolidated except Turkey and Malaysia. Democratic consolidation in all member states will also facilitate the D-8's long-term aims such as pursuing good governance, rule

---

45 Altay Atli, "Islam as a Catalyst for Economic Integration? The Case of the Developing-Eight", *International Congress of Asian and North African Studies*, ICANAS 38, (Ankara, September 2007), p. 158.

46 William M. Hale, *Turkish Foreign Policy, 1774–2000*, (London: Frank Cass, 2002), p. 298.

47 Kohei Imai, *The Possibility and Limit of Liberal Middle Power Policies: Turkish Foreign Policy toward the Middle East during the AKP Period (2005–2011)*, (Lanham: Lexington Books, 2018), p. 71.

48 Adam Przeworski, *Democracy and the Market: Political and Economic Reforms in Eastern Europe and Latin America*, (Cambridge: Cambridge University Press, 1991), p. 26.

49 Michael Doyle, "Kant, Liberal Legacies, and Foreign Affairs, Part I," *Philosophy and Public Affairs*, Vol. 12, No. 3, (1983). See also, Chansoo Cho, "Explaining Cooperation among Illiberal States: A Social Constructivist Challenge", *The Korean Journal of International Studies*, Vol. 10, No. 2, (2012), pp. 157–185.

of law, sound economic policies, and political stability as prerequisites for a smooth process of long-term development and improvement in standards of living in the member states.[50]

Bibliography

1. *D-8 Journal: Special Edition*, 2017.
2. Ahmad, Naved and Fareed Ahmed. "Does Government Size Matter? A Case Study of D-8 Member Countries." *Pakistan Economic and Social Review*, Vol. 43, No. 2, Winter, 2005.
3. Alam, Dipo. "A Glimpse at D-8 Achivements." *Uluslararası Ekonomik Sorunlar Dergisi*, Vol. 8, No. 32, 2008.
4. Aral, Berdal. "An Inquiry into the D-8 Experiment: An Incipient Model of an Islamic Common Market?." *Alternatives: Turkish Journal of International Relations*, Vol. 4, No. 1&2 Spring & Summer, 2005.
5. Atli, Altay. "Islam as a Catalyst for Economic Integration? The Case of the Developing-Eight." *International Congress of Asian and North African Studies*, ICANAS 38, Ankara, September, 2007.
6. Bajpai, Kanti and Varun Sahni. "Hegemony and Strategic Choice." In: *War, Peace and Hegemony in a Globalized World: The Changing Balance of Power in the Twenty-First Century*, ed. Chandra Chari. New York: Routledge, 2007.
7. Baker, Raymond W. *One Islam, Many Muslim Worlds*. New York: Oxford University Press, 2015.
8. Beeson, Mark and Alex J. Bellamy. "Globalisation, Security and International Order after 11 September." *Australian Journal of Politics and History*, Vol. 49, No. 3, 2003.
9. Bersntein, Barton J. "Containment." *Encyclopedia of American Foreign Policy*, eds. Alexander Delonde, et al. New York: Charles Scribnes's Sons, 2002.
10. Buzan, Barry and Ole Waever, *Regions and Powers, The Structure of International Security*. Cambridge: Cambridge University Press, 2003.
11. Buzan, Barry. "Regional Security Complex Theory in the Post-Cold War World." In: *Theories of New Regionalism*, eds. Fredrik Söderbaum and Timothy M. Shaw. London: Palgrave Macmillan, 2003.
12. Buzan, Barry. *People, States and Fear*. Sussex: Wheatsheaf Books, 1983.

---

50 For the full text of the official D-8 Global Vision (2012–2030), https://developing8.org/image/Otherdocument/7258441.pdf 17 May 2018.

13. Cho, Chansoo. "Explaining Cooperation among Illiberal States: A Social Constructivist Challenge." *The Korean Journal of International Studies*, Vol. 10, No. 2, 2012.
14. Doyle, Michael. "Kant, Liberal Legacies, and Foreign Affairs, Part I." *Philosophy and Public Affairs*, Vol. 12, No. 3, 1983.
15. Esfandyari, Marzieh. "The Role of Financial Markets Development in the Foreign Direct Investment Effect on Economic Growth (The case of D8 with Emphasizing on Iran)." *International Journal of Academic Research in Business and Social Sciences*, Vol. 5, No. 10, 2015.
16. Haas, Ernst B. "The Balance of Power: Prescription, Concept, or Propaganda." *World Politics*, Vol. 5, No. 4, 1953.
17. Hakim, Lukman et al. "The Pattern of Macroeconomics and Economics Integration: Evidence on D-8 Economic Cooperation." *Journal of Organisational Studies and Innovation*, Vol. 2, No. 2, 2012.
18. Hale, William M. *Turkish Foreign Policy, 1774–2000*. London: Frank Cass, 2002.
19. Hassan, M. Kabir. "Economic Performance of the OIC Countries and the Prospect of an Islamic Common Market." *Economic Research Forum*, Working Paper No 461, 2009.
20. Imai, Kohei. *The Possibility and Limit of Liberal Middle Power Policies: Turkish Foreign Policy toward the Middle East during the AKP Period (2005–2011)*. Lanham: Lexington Books, 2018.
21. Iqbal, Khalid. "The Developing Eight: Functions, Challenges and Prospects." *IPRI Journal*, Vol. 13, No. 2, Summer 2013.
22. Jafari, Yaghoob et al. "Determinants of Trade Flows among D-8 Countries: Evidence from Gravity Model." *Journal of Economic Cooperation and Development*, Vol. 32, No. 3, 2011.
23. Kazerooni, Alireza and Somayeh Razzaghi. "Assessing the Feasibility of Common Currency Area among D-8 Group Members: Structural VAR Model Approach." *The International Journal of Applied Economics and Finance*, Vol. 8, No. 1, 2014.
24. Lindeque, Johan and Steven McGuire. "The United States and Trade Disputes in the World Trade Organization: Hegemony Constrained or Confirmed?." *MIR: Management International Review*, Vol. 47, No. 5, 2007.
25. Makovsky, Alan. "How to Deal with Erbakan." *Middle East Quarterly*, Vol. 4, No. 1, March, 1997.
26. Mitrany, David. "The Functional Approach to World Organization." *International Affairs*, Vol. 24, No. 4, 1948.

27. Mitrany, David. *A Working Peace System: An Argument for the Functional Development of International Organization*. London: Royal Institute for International Affairs, 1943.
28. Tash, Mohim Sheihaki. "An Analysis of Bilateral Trade between Iran and D-8 Countries." *Global Journal of Management and Business Research*, Vol. 12, No. 2, 2012.
29. Ozkan, Mehmet. "Turkey in the Islamic World: An Institutional Perspective." *Turkish Review of Middle East Studies*. Vol. 18, January 2007.
30. Przeworski, Adam. *Democracy and the Market: Political and Economic Reforms in Eastern Europe and Latin America*, Cambridge: Cambridge University Press, 1991.
31. Cox, Robert W. "Gramsci, Hegemony and International Relations: An Essay in Method." In: *International Relations: Critical Concepts in Political Science*, ed. Andrew Linklater. London: Routledge, 2000.
32. Scherrer, Christoph. "'Double Hegemony'? State and Class in American Foreign Economic Policymaking." *Amerikastudien/American Studies*, Vol. 46, No. 4, 2001.
33. Shah, Mumtaz Hussain and Saima Samdani. "Impact of Trade Liberalization on FDI Inflows to D-8 Countries." *Global Management Journal for Academic & Corporate Studies*, Vol. 5, No. 1, 2015.
34. Shahabinejad, Vahid and A. Akbari. "Measuring Agricultural Productivity Growth in Developing Eight." *Journal of Development and Agricultural Economics*, Vol. 2, No. 9, September 2010.
35. Vasquez, John A. *The War Puzzle Revisited*, Cambridge: Cambridge University Press, 2009.
36. Wade, Robert Hunter. "US Hegemony and the World Bank: The Fight over People and Ideas." *Review of International Political Economy*, Vol. 9, No. 2, 2002.
37. Wolfers, Arnold. "National Security as an Ambiguous Symbol." *Political Science Quarterly*, Vol. LXVII, No. 4, 1952.

Internet Sources

1. *D-8 Economic Outlook 2016/2017*, http://developing8.org/image/Booklet/D8-EconomicOutlook.pdf (3 April 2018).
2. *D-8 Economic Outlook 2016/2017: "Enhancing Productivity and Competitiveness"*, http://developing8.org/image/Booklet/D8-Economic Outlook.pdf (3 April 2018).
3. Information about Human Development Index http://hdr.undp.org/en/content/human-development-index-hdi (3 Apr. 2018).

4. D8 documents, http://developing8.org (5 Apr. 2018).
5. *Treaty establishing the European Coal and Steel Community, ECSC Treaty* http://eur-lex.europa.eu/legal-content/RO/TXT/?uri=LEGISSUM%3Axy0022 (3 Apr. 2018).
6. *The World Factbook by CIA* https://www.cia.gov/library/publications/the-world-factbook/ (3 Apr. 2018).
7 .*D8 internet platform*, http://developing8.org/ (17 May 2018).
8. *D8*, http://www.mfa.gov.tr/_d-8_.en.mfa (3, 17 Apr. 2018).
9 .*Data from worldbank* https://data.worldbank.org/ (3 Apr. 2018).
10. *Official Documents System of the United Nations* https://documents-dds-ny.un.org/doc/UNDOC/GEN/N14/559/41/PDF/N1455941.pdf?OpenElement (13 Apr. 2018).

Iwona Sobol and Gabriela Mieczkowska

Islamic Banking Development in GCC Region on the Examples of the Kingdom of Saudi Arabia and the United Arab Emirates

Abstract: The purpose of this chapter is to present and clarify routes of Islamic banking development in the Gulf region on the example of the Kingdom of Saudi Arabia (KSA) and the United Arab Emirates (UAE). The countries' Islamic banking market financial picture is presented against conventional banking development in the region. Further perspectives for development of the industry in the region are also indicated, including factors negatively influencing possible future growth. Although Gulf region is being perceived as the origin of whole Islamic finance industry, there are still some factors working against the development of Islamic banking there. The chapter presents also a short introduction to Islamic banking principles, giving theoretical setup onto further analysis.

Keywords: Islamic banking, GCC Region, Saudi Arabia, United Arab Emirates, future of Islamic banking

Introduction

Significance of Islamic banking has been increasing in the last few decades. Since the 1970s, assets of Islamic banks have been growing dynamically and in June 2016 reached almost US$ 1.5 trillion[1]. Islamic banks operate in over 75 countries, not only Muslim ones but also those where Muslim minority live, such as the UK, the USA or France. The reasons why such institutions were established across the world are connected with the neo-revivalist movements among Muslim societies on one hand and the raising wealth of some Middle East countries on the other. One of the most influential movements was the Muslim Brotherhood, established in Al-Ismailijja (Egypt) in 1928 by Hasan al-Banna. The Muslim Brotherhood criticised interest-based financial system in Egypt and other parts of the Muslim world and argued that since Islam provides its followers with a comprehensive ideological framework for all aspects of life, the economic affairs should be also included within that framework[2]. This is the reason why all

1 Islamic Financial Services Board, "*Islamic Financial Services Industry Stability Report 2017*" (Kuala Lumpur, May 2017).

2 Abdullah Saeed, *Islamic Banking and Interest: A Study of Prohibition of Riba and its Contemporary Interpretation* (Leiden: E. J. Brill, 1996), p. 9.

interest-based activities, including banking operations, should not be allowed[3]. The opinions of Muslim Brotherhood and other Muslim movements found followers in academic world as well as among market practitioners.

But if it were not the wealth of the Gulf states, which was the result of oil crisis and the enormous increases in the oil prices, the development of Islamic finance probably would have been much slower. Almost all the Islamic banks that were established in the 1970s were partly or even totally funded by oil-linked wealth coming from Gulf Cooperation Council (GCC) countries, mainly Saudi Arabia, the United Arab Emirates and Kuwait. The banks which were established at the time include: Islamic Development Bank, Dubai Islamic Bank, Kuwait Finance House, Bahrain Islamic Bank, Qatar Islamic Bank and Faisal Islamic Bank of Bahrain. Up to now GCC region, along with Iran and Malaysia, is the leader in the Islamic banking market. At the end of June 2016, assets of Islamic banks operating in this region accounted for 43.6 % of total global Islamic banking assets. And such countries, as the Kingdom of Arabia and the United Arab Emirates took 2nd and 4th place, respectively, in the world ranking of countries with the largest Islamic banking assets[4]. The Islamic banking markets of those two countries as the most important Islamic banking markets in the GCC region, were chosen for the analysis in this chapter. The main purpose of the chapter is to present their evolution and current state of development as well as perspectives for their further development. The analysis conducted in the article is based mainly on scientific literature and market reports.

Evolution and Current State of Islamic Banking in Saudi Arabia

Saudi Arabia is a country situated in the Arabian Peninsula. It is inhabited by around 28.5 million people (2017). The country is religiously homogenous. Most of its population are Sunni Muslims (85–90 %). There is also a Shia minority (10–15 %)[5]. Non-Muslim presence is virtually absent and without any influence

3 The prohibition of usury (arab. *riba*), which is understood as any sort of increase over the principal amount, is the main principle which has to be followed by Islamic banks. But it is not the only one. Other principles include: avoidance of uncertainty (*gharar*), prohibition of speculation (*maysir*), prohibition of trading in illegal (*haram)* products (e.g. alcohol, pork, pornography, tobacco), reliance on the participation model of banking. See more I. Sobol, "Islamic banking in the European Union countries", *European Integration Studies,* No. 9 (2015), pp. 184–197.

4 Islamic Financial Services Board, *Islamic Financial Services Industry Stability Report 2017*, (Kuala Lumpur, May 2017).

5 CIA, https://www.cia.gov, 09 Sept. 2017.

in the country. The Muslim society mainly represents Hanbali school of shariah jurisprudence (*fiqh*), which is considered to be the most rigorous of all schools of shariah law. Saudi Arabia is the birthplace of Islam, which is a crucial element in the country's identity and religious beliefs and practices[6].

Saudi Arabia has been a country which has been instrumental in bringing about Islamic banking. The first Islamic banks which were established in the 1970s in Muslim countries were financed by the Saudi capital coming from the export of oil[7]. The establishment of Islamic banks was also influenced by the pan-Islamic movement, which assumed the unification of the Muslim world and which gained significance in the 1970s with the increasing income in the countries of the Middle East. Faisal, the King of Saudi Arabia, became the leader of this movement[8]. One of the important initiatives of King Faisal, which proved to be an important step in the creation of Islamic financial institutions, was the establishment of the Organisation of Islamic Conference – OIC[9]. The organisation was established in 1970 and in 1972, its charter was adopted, according to which the governments of Muslim countries should cooperate closely and provide mutual assistance in the political, economic, scientific, cultural and social spheres. In the field of economics, one of the first steps taken by OIC was the establishment of the first Islamic international bank. Islamic Development Bank (IDB) was founded in July 1975. The governments of Muslim countries, members of the OIC, became its shareholders[10]. The main objective of the bank was to support the economic and social development of the Member States and the Muslim community in accordance with shariah. Jeddah in Saudi Arabia became the headquarters of the bank.

It should be noted that up to now Saudi Arabia along with other GCC countries remain the primary financiers of Islamic finance industry worldwide.

Despite of all the Saudi initiatives and the support for Islamic banking industry and the very religious society, Saudi Arabia was one of the least hospitable countries to Islamic banks. It has lagged behind some other Muslim

---

6 Ibrahim Warde, *Islamic Finance in the Global Economy* (Edinburgh: Edinburgh University Press, 2000), p. 15.

7 The biggest financiers were Prince Muhammad b. Faisal Al-Saud and Sheikh Saleh Kamel.

8 King of Saudi Arabia in the years 1964–1975.

9 Since 2011, the organisation has been called Organisation of Islamic Cooperation – OIC. In 2017, 57 countries were members of OIC, http://www.oic-oci.org/, 20 Aug. 2017.

10 Ahmed El-Ashker and Rodney Wilson, *Islamic Economics: A Short History* (Leiden: Brill, 2006) p. 331–332.

countries in terms of promoting Islamic banking in its own country. This was due to the fact that even before the Islamic banks were established, Saudi Arabia was a rich country that lived off of oil export and revenues from foreign investment and interest income. Thus, the economy of this country depended, to a large extent, directly or indirectly on interest. Establishing Islamic banks would make existing banks un-Islamic, which could be a problem in a country where the rulers repeatedly had to fend off accusations of impiety[11]. The first Islamic financial bank, Al Rajhi Bank, was established in 1988[12]. However, it was only allowed to operate on the condition of not using the word "Islamic" in its name. At the beginning of the 2000s, excess liquidity in Saudi Arabia (resulted from high oil prices and repatriation of funds from the United States after the terrorist attack on 11 September 2001) was migrating to Dubai and Bahrain – which became competing centres of Islamic banking in the GCC region, and where Islamic banking products started to be provided by such global financial institution as Citi, HSBC, Credit Suisse, UBS, etc. In order to retain those funds, Saudi Arabia finally allowed to Islamise its banking system[13].

It should be also mentioned that the development of Islamic banking in Saudi Arabia is supported by the presence of educational institutions where Islamic finance is taught and which were established even before Islamic banks started to operate in the country. The first Islamic finance education centre, Islamic Research Centre (now Islamic Economic Institute), was established at the King Abdulaziz University in 1977. In 1981, the second educational institution Islamic Research and Training Institute (IRTI) was founded by Islamic Development Bank[14]. Those two institutions are renowned worldwide especially due to extensive research that is conducted there.

Apart from those two most famous institutions, Islamic finance is taught and researched in the following Saudi universities: Effat University, King Saud

---

11 Ibrahim Warde, "Status of the Global Finance Industry," in: *Islamic Finance: Law and Practice*, ed. C. R. Nethercott and D. M. Eisenberg (Oxford: Oxford University Press, 2012), p. 10.

12 Al Rajhi Bank, http://www.alrajhibank.com, 09 Aug. 2017.

13 Mahmoud A. El-Gamal, *Islamic Finance in the Middle East*, Statement prepared for US Senate Committee on Banking, Housing and Urban Affairs' hearing: "Money Laundering and Terror Financing Issues in the Middle East", 13 July 2005.

14 Khalid Alotaibi and Fayaz Ahmad Lone, "Islamic Banking and Finance Education: A Comparative Study of Saudi Arabia and the UK," *International Journal of Economic Research*, Vol. 13, No. 7 (2016), pp. 2651–2662.

University, King Fahad University of Petroleum and Minerals and Al Imam Muhammad Ibn Saud Islamic University[15].

Currently out of 12 domestic commercial banks in Saudi Arabia, four are fully-fledged Islamic banks. These are: Al Rajhi Bank, Alinma Bank, Al Bilad Bank and Bank Al Jazira. The largest conventional bank, National Commercial Bank, is in the transition to become also a fully shariah-compliant bank. The rest of banks are conventional banks which provide a mix of shariah-compliant and conventional banking products and services[16].

It should be noted that Islamic banks in Saudi Arabia are subject to the same regulations as their conventional counterparts: the Banking Control Law (BCL), issued by Royal Decree No. M/5 on 11 June 1966 and the Charter of Saudi Arabian Monetary Agency (SAMA) issued by a Royal Decree No.23 on 15 December 1957. The BCL is considered to be the main legislation regulating all banking services in the country. According to this act, as well as Charter of SAMA, the Saudi central bank, SAMA, is responsible for the regulation and the supervision of the banking system. The fact that Islamic banks have no special regulations in Saudi Arabia, can be considered an obstacle in the development of Islamic banking in this country. It results in lack of uniformity and decreases the confidence of the market participants.

Nevertheless, Saudi Arabia is the country with the largest Islamic banking assets in the world, only after Iran. At the end of June 2016, assets of Islamic banks operating in this country amounted to US$ 307.64 billion and accounted for 20.6 % of total global Islamic banking assets[17].

Saudi Arabia is also one of the leaders when it comes to market penetration of Islamic banking. At the end of June of 2016, Islamic banking assets had a 51.1 % share in total banking assets of the country. The only countries ahead of Saudi Arabia are Iran and Sudan, which completely Islamised their financial system (100 % share of Islamic banks) and Brunei where Islamic banking assets now account for 57 % of the domestic market share[18]. It should also be pointed out that the Saudi Islamic banking sector grows faster than the conventional one, which can indicate that in the near future the penetration of Islamic banking in Saudi Arabia will be even higher.

It should be also noted that the largest Islamic bank in the world is the bank operating in Saudi Arabia – Al Rajhi Bank. At the end of 2015, its assets

15 Alotaibi and Lone, "Islamic Banking". pp. 2651–2662.

16 Fitch Ratings, 02 Feb. 2016, *Islamic Banking is Dominant in Saudi Arabia.*

17 Islamic Financial Services Board, *Islamic Financial.*

18 Islamic Financial Service Board, *Islamic Financial.*

Tab. 1: Top Islamic banks/Islamic banking windows globally by total assets. Source: ICD Thomson Reuters, *Islamic Finance Development Report 2016*.

Name of the Bank	**Country**	**Total Assets (US$ Mn, FYE 2015)**
Al Rajhi Bank	Saudi Arabia	84,120
National Commercial Bank	Saudi Arabia	62,518
Kuwait Finance House	Kuwait	54,490
Bank Mellat	Iran	51,800
Bank Melli Iran	Iran	51,711
Dubai Islamic Bank	UAE	40,826
Bank Saderat Iran	Iran	39,242
Maybank Islamic Berhad	Malaysia	36,446
Qatar Islamic Bank	Qatar	34,881
Bank Tajerat	Iran	33,792

amounted to US$ 84,120 million. If Islamic financial services offered by conventional banks are also taken into account, also the second biggest bank comes from Saudi Arabia (Tab. 1).

The perspectives of further development of Islamic banking in Saudi Arabia seem to be bright, mainly due to high demand for Islamic banking products from the very religious Saudi society. Also the country's authorities plan to support this sector within its Vision 2030 program, aiming at the development of the country's non-oil sector. There are however a few obstacles that need to be overcome if Saudi Islamic banking industry wants to use its high potential. Apart from already mentioned lack of regulations dedicated to Islamic finance, the biggest problems which Saudi Islamic banks need to overcome concern risk management, especially the management of liquidity risk and insufficient deposit base. Problems of liquidity management are faced by Islamic banks in all countries, where they operate, which is the result of insufficient supply of short-term instruments and lack of well-developed secondary market[19]. There is also a big problem with the deposit base, which come in large extent from the government and rely mainly on oil sector. When in 2016, the Saudi government withdrew large amounts of deposits, SAMA immediately needed to respond through capital injections into the banking system[20]. But despite of the above-mentioned

19 Iwona Sobol, "Liquidity Management Practices in Islamic Banking," *Journal of Management and Finance*, Vol. 11, No. 2, Part 1 (2013), pp. 566-576 .

20 Islamic Financial Services Board, *Islamic Financial.*

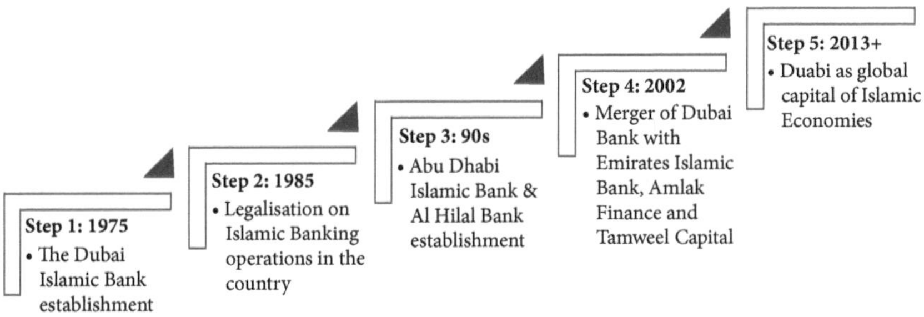

Fig. 1: Islamic banking evolution in the United Arab Emirates. Source: Authors' compilation.

problems Saudi Islamic banking sector faces, it can be expected that its share in the banking system of the country will even more increase within next few years, leading to gradual Islamisation of the whole banking system.

Evolution and Current State of Islamic Banking in the United Arab Emirates

The United Arab Emirates are known as Islamic banking hub, as well as the 4th biggest Islamic banking market in the world. Demographically, the population of the country is about 9.5 million people (est. 2017), majority (76 %) is declared Muslim, followed by Christians (13 %). From Islamic finance and banking perspective, 15.4 % of global assets are located in the country and about 20–30 % of banking industry is Islamic with the annual growth of circa 8 %.

The history of Islamic banking subindustry can be described in five steps (Fig. 1).

One of the first Islamic banking institutions in the world was established in 1975 in the United Arab Emirates – Dubai Islamic Bank. The bank was initially state owned, further transferred to semi-private hands.

A decade after, regulation legalising Islamic banking operations in the country was set up, being a significant driver for further growth[21]. The regulation of Federal Law #6 regarding Islamic banks, financial institutions and investment companies includes:

21 Annam Hashmi, "An Analysis of United Arab Emirates Banking Sector," *International Banking & Economics Research Journal*, No. 6 (2007), pp. 77-88.

- Industry setup regulations;
- Legal requirements for business operations;
- Operations character;
- Supervisory and audit requirements, including Shariah Law Boards[22].

Further development in the field was continued in the 1990s, when Abu Dhabi Islamic Bank and al-Hilal Bank were established. Abu Dhabi Islamic Bank was the first fully-fledged Islamic bank. The structure was public joint stock company, with ratio of 71 % of public ownership. As opposite, Al-Hilal Bank was established as a fully government-owned bank, with no shares being listed at any stock exchange. Both of the banks offer similar products and services of personal (including private), business and corporate banking, as well as treasury, and investment. Core operations are on-going locally, and globally in few offices across North Africa, Europe and Asia.

Merger of Dubai Bank with Emirates Islamic Bank in 2002 to create Dubai-based Emirates NBD[23], was an important step in the development of Islamic finance in the country. The banks have created financial institution offering unique combination of Islamic products and services. The period of time was considered as slowdown in the economy, and the merger of those institutions helped them to survive and create strong subset for further Islamic banking sector in the country. What is more, two mortgage institutions of Amlak and Tamweel were added to the process to bring even more specialised services in strictly Islamic banking area[24]. Initially, Almak joined Dubai Bank and Tamweel joined with Emirates Islamic, prior to creating institution of Emirates Islamic. According to one of the local media commentators – "This move came within the new economic vision of the Government of Dubai, aimed at merging small and medium banking units into major institutions capable of competing with other banks"[25].

Finally, the most recent step of Islamic banking evolution in the UAE was establishment of Dubai as the global capital of Islamic economies in 2013 and

22 Central Bank of U.A.E., "Federal Law No. 6 of 1985 regarding Islamic Banks, Financial Institutions and Investment Companies", 26 Jul. 2017.

23 Emirates 24/7, "Two Dubai Banks Approve Merger", 9 Oct. 2017, http://www.emirates247.com.

24 Babu Das Augustine, "Emirates Islamic Bank in Talks to Merge with Dubai Bank", *Gulf News*, (2015): 03 Oct. 2017 https://gulfnews.com/business/sectors/banking/emirates-islamic-bank-in-talks-to-merge-with-dubai-bank-1.690988.

25 Emirates 24/7, "Two Dubai Banks Approve Merger", 09 Oct. 2017, http://www.emirates247.com.

undertaking two strategic legal initiatives for the Islamic banking industry. Institution of Dubai Islamic Economy Development Centre was established to support role of Dubai as a global capital of Islamic finance. Central Bank of the United Arab Emirates has officially considered separation of conventional and Islamic banking, driven by strong growth in Islamic banking field. Another step was publishing of "Standards of Issuing, Acquiring and Trading Sukuk" in 2013 by Dubai Financial Markets (DBM)[26], being a step towards development in the area of commercial trade and asset management subsectors. The document has outlined rule of security issuance, shariah supervisory requirements, guarantees and detailed sukuks' rules[27].

There was a noticeable increase in the market share of Islamic banking at the country economy after 2010. The process was mainly supported by factors like surging real estate market and also rapid growth in the banking assets across the country.

The United Arab Emirates are considered a pioneer for Islamic banking. It has about 20 financial institutions offering either fully-fledged Islamic banking or Islamic windows. These are historically mentioned Al Hilal Bank, next to Islamic windows offers such as Credit Agricole Corporate and Investment Bank[28].

Looking at the size of regional[29] Islamic banking assets (Fig. 2), the numbers are increasing year-on-year bringing very positive forecast for the future.

An average annual growth is around ~16 %. General banking overlook at the region shows that compared to ASEAN, South Asia, Turkey and some other countries where Islamic banking services are provided like Jordan, Egypt, Sudan and South Africa, the share of Islamic banking in the total banking assets is the highest in GCC – 34 %. Country-specific results show that the Kingdom of Saudi Arabia has the highest share – over 50 %, while UAE is on the level of 20–30 %, which is very high comparing it to the countries such as Egypt or Indonesia.

The United Arab Emirates are considered to be the fourth biggest Islamic banking market in the world (Fig. 3). From a global perspective, 9 % of Islamic

26 Dubai Financial Markets (DFM), "Dubai Financial Market Standards on Shari'a-Compliance. Standard No.2. Issuing, Acquiring and Trading Sukuk", 10 Oct. 2017, http://www.dfm.ae/.

27 PriceWaterhouseCoopers, "Islamic Finance. Creating Value", 09 Aug. 2017, https://www.pwc.com.

28 *Shariah Complaint Banking Providers in UAE*, 10 Aug. 2017, https://www.islamicfinance.com/.

29 Regional is considered as Gulf Cooperation Council (GCC) countries, including: Qatar, Saudi Arabia, United Arab Emirates, Kuwait, Oman, Bahrain.

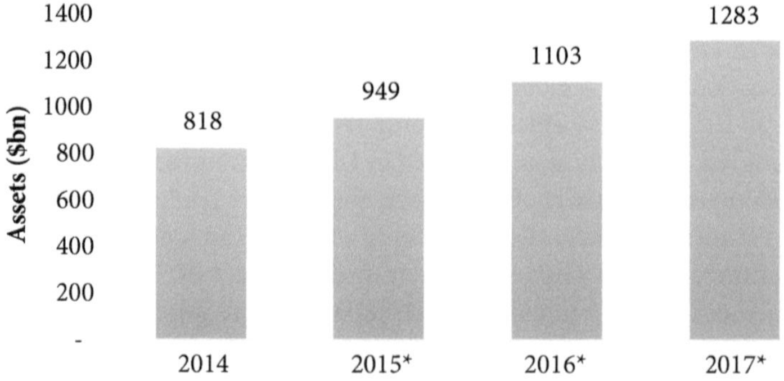

Fig. 2: Islamic banking assets in GCC region. *Calculations based on CAGR. Source: Authors' compilation based on EY, "World Islamic Banking Competitiveness Report 2016", 16 Aug. 2017 www.ey.com.

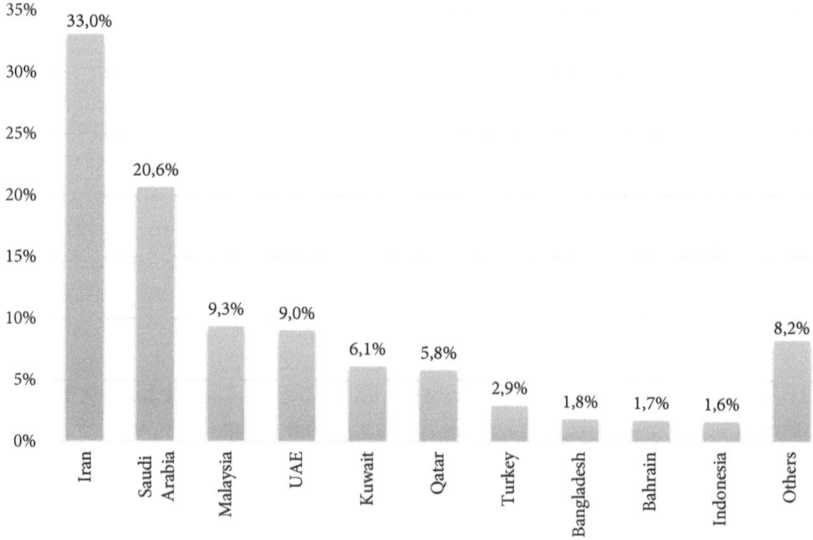

Fig. 3: Islamic Banking assets globally in 2016. Source: Authors' compilation based on Islamic Financial Services Board, *Islamic Financial Services Industry Stability Report 2017*, Kuala Lumpur 2017.

banking assets is located there. Looking at the national banking assets size in the UAE, 21.6 % in 2016 was accounted for that category.

The median growth of Islamic banking sector is ~8 %. Historically growth levels of conventional banking were more than 50 % smaller than Islamic banking. In 2014, both sub-industries' growth is on the similar level of 18–19 %. The same level of Islamic banking growth was observed in the Kingdom of Saudi Arabia, being the strongest Islamic banking economy globally.

Moreover, Emirates Islamic has launched a new initiative – Islamic Banking Index, allowing to measure economically and strategically the effectiveness of shariah-compliant banking[30]. The most recent result shows very positive internal situation country-wise with increasing demand and penetration for the products and services. Islamic banks are considered as trustworthy and financially strong institutions. Referring to Fig. 4, it is observed that more customers associate Islamic banking institutions with factors such as:

- Innovation; mainly in mobile/online banking and technology;
- Better quality and faster service;
- Product and service customisation;
- Easy to understand procedures;
- Local community support.

Although, in comparison to conventional banking, there is still a lot of space for innovation and better customer service.

According to World Islamic Banking Competitiveness Report, the future of the sector is bright for the nine biggest Islamic banking economies. On particular case of the United Arab Emirates, the forecast for 2020 shows that Islamic banking assets will increase to the level of ~ US$ 290 billion, keeping the 4th global position, just after Iran, the Kingdom of Saudi Arabia and Malaysia. In addition, the United Arab Emirates are next to Saudi Arabia, Qatar, Pakistan and Turkey as a key player on the account of level of average annual growth rate and size of banking sector assets.

The main mid-term growth drivers are:

- Average growth of banking sector assets;
- Increase in the market share of Islamic banking in global economy.

30 Emirates Islamic, "Islamic Banking Index by Emirates Islamic," 15 Aug. 2017, https://www.emiratesislamic.ae/.

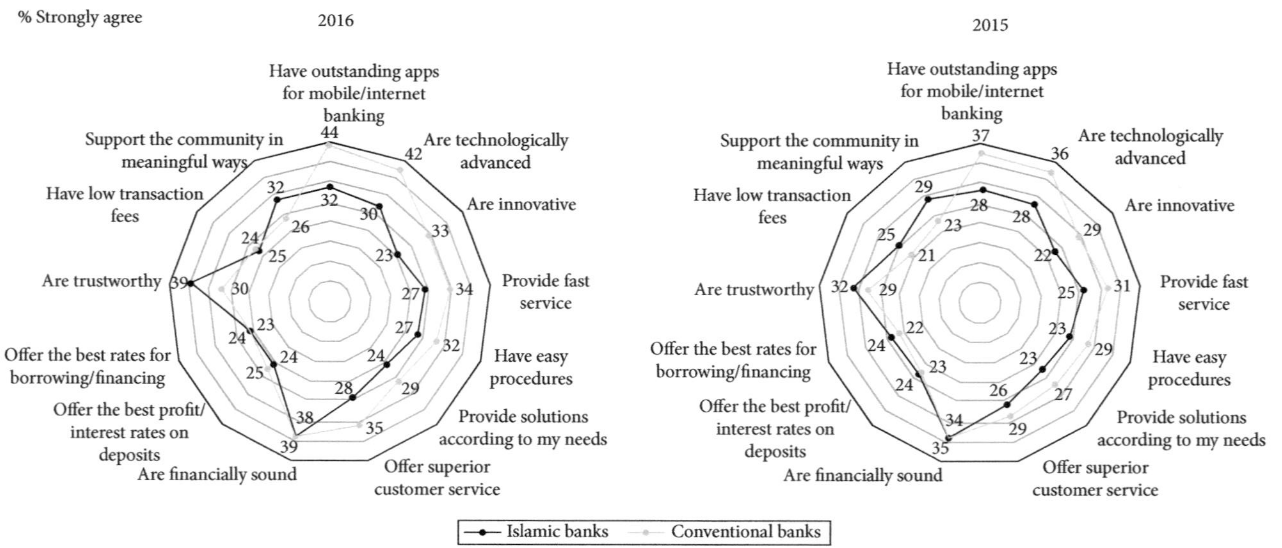

Fig. 4: Islamic banking perception in United Arab Emirates. Source: Authors' compilation based on "*Islamic Banking Index by Emirates Islamic*," 16 Aug. 2017 https://www.emiratesislamic.ae/.

Banking sectors assets are forecasted to grow due to focus on regionalisation in the industry, together with massive improvements in technology and digital acceleration globally as well as very innovative character of business models and financial structures coming from emerging markets in both conventional and Islamic banking fields. Additional factors, such as ongoing diversification of the economies, falling oil prices and policies called 'jobs-for-nationals', are influencing strong regionalisation and transforming the role of financial institutions. Technological developments will allow to achieve detailed identification of customer needs. It is strongly needed at that point, when personalisation and customisation of products and services is crucial to achieve the success in the long term[31].

Market share of Islamic banking within global economy shows that pool of potential profit will increase at least twice in 2020[32].

On the other hand, there are still some obstacles and current issues, which need to be tackled globally to ensure smooth pace of development of Islamic banking. First one is lack of unified, globally accepted regulations and clear interpretations of what shariah principles mean. This creates a barrier for development of innovation plus issue with cross-border Islamic finance transactions and operations. Lack of standardisation is still observed, influencing banking transparency and limiting the attractiveness of Islamic banking among new potential Muslim and non-Muslim customers[33].

There is a positive future for Islamic banking in the country, which can be summarised by words of Dubai ruler Sheikh Mohammed bin Rashid Al Maktoum "We have a clear vision for this vital sector and we want it to contribute significantly to our national economy and to help bolster our position as the world's capital for Islamic economy[34]." The country is considered as a well-established hub for Islamic economy globally and strong features of infrastructure,

31 Issac John, "UAE Islamic Banking to Hit $263b by 2019", *Khaleej Times* (2015): 20 Jul. 2017, https://www.khaleejtimes.com/business/banking-finance/uae-islamic-banking-to-hit-263b-by-2019.

32 EY, *"World Islamic Banking Competitiveness Report 2016,"* 27 Jul. 2017, http://www.ey.com/.

33 Hussain Al-Qemzi, "Innovation is key to the future of Islamic banking", *Gulf News,* (2015):3 Aug. 2017. https://gulfnews.com/business/sectors/banking/innovation-is-key-to-the-future-of-islamic-banking-1.1512208.

34 Andy Sambidge, "UAE has what it takes to be Islamic finance hub", *Arabian Business,* (2013): 20 Aug. 2017, https://www.arabianbusiness.com/uae-has-what-it-takes--be-islamic-finance-hub-488788.html.

strategic location in the centre of Islamic world mixed together with knowledge and experience in the field are strengthening its position even more.

Conclusions

The chapter is a study of evolution, current state and perspectives of development of Islamic banking in Saudi Arabia and the United Arab Emirates. The analysis covers the period since the very initial development of the industry in those two countries. Scientific papers and market research reports were used to prepare the chapter. The results of the study show that Islamic banking is a steadily established subsector of whole banking industries in both of the countries. The establishment and further development processes originated around the 1970s and continued in the 1980s and 1990s with setups of first Islamic banking institutions in both Saudi Arabia and the United Arab Emirates. The route of development in the United Arab Emirates was slightly different from Saudi Arabia. First legal regulations regarding Islamic finance and banking operations were already set up in the 1980s in the United Arab Emirates and fully cover operations and supervision of the institutions. While in Saudi Arabia, there is not direct regulatory framework for Islamic banking until today and the operations are covered by general banking law. It is worth mentioning that educational institutions have an important role in development of Islamic banking mainly in Saudi Arabia, but have some supportive role also in the United Arab Emirates.

The future of Islamic banking sectors is considered to be bright. Significant connection with local economic growth, steadily increasing demand for the products and services and widening positive opinions about innovative character of the industry are just a few of the features allowing to assume positive further image. On the other hand, there are some obstacles for the global development of the sector, including lack of unified global regulation with regards to operations, supervisory and crucial risk management.

Bibliography

1. Alotaibi, Khalid and Lone, Fayaz Ahmad. "Islamic Banking and Finance Education: A Comparative Study of Saudi Arabia and the UK", *International Journal of Economic Research*, Vol. 13, No. 7. 2016, pp. 2651–2662.
2. Al-Qemzi, "Innovation Is Key to the Future of Islamic Banking", *Gulf News*, 2015.
3. El-Ashker, Ahmed and Rodney, Wilson. *Islamic Economics: A Short History*, Leiden: Brill, 2006.

4. El-Gamal, Mahmoud A., "Islamic Finance in the Middle East" Statement prepared for US Senate Committee on Banking, Housing and Urban Affairs' hearing: "Money Laundering and Terror Financing Issues in the Middle East", 13 July 2005.
5. Hashmi, Annam. "An Analysis of United Arab Emirates Banking Sector," *International Banking & Economics Research Journal*, No. 6, 2007, pp. 77-88.
6. John, Issac. "UAE Islamic Banking to Hit $263b by 2019", *Khaleej Times*, 2015.
7. Saeed, Abdullah. *Islamic Banking and Interest: A Study of Prohibition of Riba and Its Contemporary Interpretation*, Leiden: E. J. Brill, 1996.
8. Sambidge, Andy. "UAE Has What it Takes to Be Islamic Finance Hub", *Arabian Business*, 2013.
9. Sobol, Iwona. "Islamic Banking in the European Union Countries," *European Integration Studies*, No. 9, 2015, pp. 184–197.
10. Sobol, Iwona. "Liquidity Management Practices in Islamic Banking," *Journal of Management and Finance*, Vol. 11, No. 2, Part.1, 2013, pp. 566-576.
11. Warde, Ibrahim. *Islamic Finance in the Global Economy*, Edinburgh: Edinburgh University Press, 2000.
12. Warde, Ibrahim. *Status of the Global Finance Industry*, in: *Islamic Finance: Law and Practice*, ed. C. R. Nethercott, D. M. Eisenberg, Oxford: Oxford University Press, 2012.

Internet Sources

1. Al Rajhi Bank, http://www.alrajhibank.com. (9 Aug. 2017).
2. Central Bank of U.A.E., *Federal Law No. 6 of 1985 Regarding Islamic Banks, Financial Institutions and Investment Companies*, source: https://www.centralbank.ae. (26 Jul. 2017).
3. CIA, https://www.cia.gov, (9 Sept. 2017).
4. Dubai Financial Markets (DFM), *Dubai Financial Market Standards on Shari'a-Compliance. Standard No.2. Issuing, Acquiring and Trading Sukuk*, http://www.dfm.ae/. (10 Oct. 2017).
5. Emirates 24/7, *Two Dubai Banks Approve Merger*, http://www.emirates247.com, (15 Aug. 2017).
6. EY, *World Islamic Banking Competitiveness Report 2016*, http://www.ey.com/. (27 Jul. 2017).
7. Fitch Ratings, *Islamic Banking Is Dominant in Saudi Arabia*, (2 Feb. 2017).

8. ICD Thomson Reuters, *Islamic Finance Development Report 2016*.
9. *Islamic Banking Index by Emirates Islamic, Emirates Islamic*, https://www.emiratesislamic.ae/. (16 Aug. 2017).
10. Islamic Financial Services Board, *Islamic Financial Services Industry Stability Report 2017*, Kuala Lumpur, May 2017.
11. OIC, http://www.oic-oci.org/ (20 Aug. 2017).
12. PriceWaterhouseCoopers, *Islamic Finance. Creating Value*, https://www.pwc.com. (9 Aug. 2017).
13. *Shariah Compliant Banking Providers in UAE*, https://www.islamicfinance.com/. (10 Aug. 2017).

Martina Ponížilová

China's Risk-Averse Middle East Policy: Protecting Economic Interests While Staying Out of Conflicts[1]

Abstract: The strategic map of the Middle East is slowly changing with traditional powers retreating from the regional management, power vacuum expanding and emerging powers, such as China, playing increasingly important role in regional trade and economic relations. However, the question is if China as the most powerful of emerging powers and an important trade partner of Mideast countries is willing and capable to take on the role of an extra-regional leader that will stabilize the regional order. This article explains motivations behind China's Mideast policy and shows that although China increases its presence in the region, it is not yet ready to become a major force in shaping regional politics.

Keywords: Middle East, China, emerging power, energy security, risk-averse policy

Introduction

The strategic and energetic significance of the Middle East is long well-known. The traditional powers such as Great Britain, France, the USA or Russia (and earlier USSR) have been trying to secure their economic, geopolitical and security interests in the Middle East for decades and therefore have been engaging in the regional politics. Lately, also emerging powers such as China, India, Brazil or South Korea got involved in Mideast politics with increased intensity. This is especially true since the beginning of the 1990s.

Emerging powers, specifically China, can be seen as new economic powers in the international system, but not as political and military centres capable and/or willing to act as global leaders or "world's policemen" by performing a role as peace guarantors, mediators in conflicts and enforcers of the rules of

1 This text was partially based on the article by Martina Ponížilová titled "Foreign Policy Activities of China in the Middle East: Establishing Energy Security or Being a Responsible Emerging Power?", which was published in the Journal of Balkan and Near Eastern Studies in 2018 (https://www.tandfonline.com/doi/full/10.1080/19448953.2018.1506292).

This work was supported by the Institutional support for the long-term conceptual development of the research organization Department of Politics and International Relations, University of West Bohemia in 2019.

international politics. According to some scholars, we are witnessing slow and partial withdrawal of the United States from the Middle East in last years[2] and cooling of relations with some of their regional allies (Egypt and Saudi Arabia above all)[3]. This creates a leadership vacuum which could (should?) be filled by emerging powers such as China. In the environment where neither regional nor international institutions are able to manage conflicts effectively, external powers are restricting their involvement in regional politics, and regional powers represent mutual rivals, the threats to other actors' interests increase. If China wants to secure their economic interests in the future, it will need to engage more in Mideast politics and help to stabilize it. However, the question is if China as the most powerful of contemporary emerging powers and an important trade partner of Mideast countries is willing and capable to become a political leader that will stabilize the regional order.

The principal reason for greater engagement of China in the Middle East from the beginning of the 1990s is an increased need of energy supplies and an interest in strengthening trade relations with local countries. Even though

---

2 See: Michael Singh, "Chinese Policy in the Middle East in the Wake of the Arab Uprisings," in: *Toward Well-Oiled Relations: China's Presence in the Middle East Following the Arab Spring*, ed. Niv Horesh (Basingstoke, New York: Palgrave Macmillan, 2016), pp. 169–70. However, not all authors agree that the presence of the US in the Middle East is failing. Bronson argues that "America will remain militarily and politically engaged in the Middle East; this is key to the realization of a primary U.S. national strategic goal: economic growth and development." (Rachel Bronson, "The United States in the Middle East: Bound by Growing Energy Demand," *Middle East Policy Council*, Vol. XXI, No. 2, 2014, p. 38). Economic and energy interests are not the only ones important to the USA, though. As Luft explains, "[a]ny suggestion that U.S. foreign policy is 'all about oil' ignores the complexity and multitude of U.S. interests. Geography, Cold War legacies, Israel, terrorism, religion, nuclear proliferation, and democracy promotion are just some of the factors guiding U.S. thinking on the Middle East" (Gal Luft, "Will energy-rich America depart from the Middle East and Eurasia?," *Turkish Policy Quarterly*, Vol. 12, No. 4, 2014: 17 Sep. 2018 http://turkishpolicy.com/dosyalar/files/vol_12-no_4-luft.pdf, p. 82).

3 E.g. Jonathan Fulton, "China is trying to pull Middle East countries into its version of NATO," *The Washington Post*, 21 Jun. 2017: 31 Jul. 2017 www.washingtonpost.com/news/monkey-cage/wp/2017/06/21/how-china-is-shifting-toward-the-middle-east; Niv Horesh, "Introduction," in: *Toward Well-Oiled Relations: China's Presence in the Middle East Following the Arab Spring*, ed Niv Horesh (Basingstoke, New York: Palgrave Macmillan, 2016), p. 2; Shannon Tiezzi, "China Seeks Expanded Role in Middle East," *The Diplomat*, 04 Jun. 2014: 16 Jun. 2017 www.thediplomat.com/2014/06/china-seeks-expanded-role-in-middle-east.

Chinese involvement in the region reflects also some of its security and geopolitical concerns, the analysis of China's activities shows that its geopolitical and security efforts are mainly risk-averse and are incomparable with those of USA, Russia or European powers. China is not yet ready and/or willing to become a major force in shaping regional politics which would articulate a new vision for the Middle East providing a credible alternative to the Western-designed (US-designed) regional order. Even though there is a long and intense debate about the declining power of the traditional powers on one hand, and the rise of emerging powers on the other, the latter are "not yet ready to take on roles as global powers"[4] and their engagement in the Mideast politics in the last three decades is a proof of that.

Chinese behaviour and policies in the region cannot be viewed as a case *sui generis*, on the contrary, it points out to recently not unusual phenomenon which is a greater significance of geoeconomics in foreign policy of states and emerging powers, above all. The term *geoeconomics* indicates systematic exploitation of economic foreign policy tools employed to reach geopolitical objectives and to engage in geopolitical power struggle.[5] Contemporary emerging powers tend to use economic tools in order to achieve geopolitical goals quite often. Even though they still exploit military power and diplomatic instruments, their relatively strong economic power position in the international system predestinates them to benefit from economic rather than military instruments in obtaining geopolitical objectives. China is one of the largest economic powers in contemporary international politics and, at the same time, it uses geoeconomic instruments in its foreign policy intensely – when its economic power increases, so does its willingness to use mainly economic tools and policies in order to ensure not only economic interests goals but also strategic interests.

The aim of this chapter is, first, to introduce foreign-policy interests and activities of China in the Middle East from the beginning of the 1990s up to the present; second, to show that its role in the regional politics is largely limited to the role of economic partner (trade partner, importer of strategic energy sources, investor, receiver of FDIs, exporter of goods, etc.), but not political leader and security stabilizer. These roles still rest on the shoulders of traditional and, increasingly, regional powers.

---

4 Harsh V. Pant, "India and the Middle East: Before and After the Arab Spring," in: *The International Politics of the Arab Spring: Popular Unrest and Foreign Policy*, ed. Robert Mason, (New York: Palgrave Macmillan, 2014), p. 158.

5 Robert D. Blackwill and Jennifer M. Harris, *War by Other Means: Geoeconomics and Statecraft* (Cambridge: The Belknap Press of Harvard University Press, 2016), p. 1.

Chinese Energy and Economic Interests in the Middle East

The fact that China is the world's largest energy consumer and importer is well-known. China is, just after the USA, the second largest importer and consumer of oil and one of the world's biggest consumers of natural gas and electricity[6]. Since the Middle East is rich in energy resources, it is not surprising that Chinese Mideast policy has been influenced by China's energy demands. It is probable that China's energy demands will continue to increase in the future as its economy and industry will keep growing[7] and thus also its dependence on energy supplies from the Middle East will likely rise.

Chinese Mideast policy has been influenced by the interests of three state-owned energy companies (Sinopec, China National Petroleum Corporation and China National Offshore Oil Corporation) for which the government's economy-focused policy of finding new investment opportunities and trade partners in the region is highly suitable. The aim of this policy is nothing else than to ensure that sufficient energy supplies from oil-rich states will not stop flowing to China. However, Middle Eastern countries are not only oil and natural gas suppliers but also foreign investors in China (primarily Gulf states), receivers of China's investments, receivers of large number of Chinese migrant workers[8] and partners in non-energy trade (e.g. with military equipment). The biggest part of region's imports come from China, and the country itself represents the largest trade partner of nine Middle East countries (Algeria, Egypt, Kuwait, Lebanon, Libya, Qatar, Saudi Arabia, Turkey, UAE)[9].

Middle Eastern countries represented important economic partners of China already in the 1980s and at the beginning of the 1990s when their mutual trade was based mostly on arms sales which were crucial to China's economic modernization. China, for example, sold intermediate-range ballistic missiles to Saudi Arabia, and during the Iran-Iraq war Beijing provided both Tehran and Baghdad with arms and military technology because it wanted to maintain good

---

6 CIA The World Factbook, "China," 11 Jul. 2017: 18 Jul. 2017 www.cia.gov/library/publications/the-world-factbook/geos/ch.html.

7 E.g. Singh, "Chinese Policy in the Middle East," p. 163.

8 A high number of Chinese workers live in several Middle Eastern states – predominantly in the Gulf or Egypt and before 2011 in Libya and Yemen, too.

9 John Calabrese, "China's Role in Post-Hegemonic Middle East," *Real Clear World*, 1 May 2017: 18 Jul. 2017 .<www.realclearworld.com/articles/2017/05/01/how_china_and_america_can_share_the_mideast_burden.html>. CIA The World Factbook, "Imports – Partners," 24 Aug. 2017 <www.cia.gov/library/publications/resources/the-world-factbook/fields/2061.html#ag>.

relations with both countries[10]. Especially newly established Islamic Republic was grateful for China's decision to sell them weapons which they desperately needed because of the Iraqi threat and the impossibility to gain armaments on the global market at the same time. During the 1990s and 2000s, Beijing assisted Tehran with building its defence capabilities by providing armaments and Iran became the biggest importer of Chinese weapons in the Middle East. China also delivered to Iran some components crucial for the development of Iranian nuclear program even though they supported international sanctions against the Islamic Republic[11].

After 1993, when China became a net oil importer, the Middle East got the attention of Chinese government also as an oil-rich area, and fossil fuels have played a pivotal role in mutual Sino-Mideast relations since. Subsequently, economic cooperation with many local producers was established (e.g. with Oman, Iraq, Egypt, Libya, Algeria); however, soon it turned out that it will be Iran, Saudi Arabia and smaller Gulf Cooperation Council (GCC) countries as the biggest oil producers in the region which will be of the most significance for meeting Chinese energy demands. In the 2010s, China imported more than half of their oil supplies and a third of their natural gas supplies from the Middle East.

Trade relations with states on the Arabian Peninsula, especially Saudi Arabia, date back to the 1990s. Already in 1999, Chinese and Saudi representatives agreed on extensive cooperation in oil trade and in 2002, the kingdom got to the position of the biggest provider of oil and petrochemical products for China[12]. In addition, the volume of foreign investments from Saudi Arabia to China increased, and *vice versa*. Chinese investments grew in the UAE, Qatar, Iran, Egypt, Jordan and Algeria, as well[13]. Saudi Kingdom and the United Arab Emirates count for the biggest trade partners in the whole region and Qatar represents the biggest supplier of natural gas[14]. China and the states of the GCC are also planning to

10 Flynt Leverett and Jeffrey Bader, "Managing China-U.S. Energy Competition in the Middle East," *The Washington Quarterly*, Vol. 29, No. 1 (2006), p. 188.

11 "A History of Iran's Nuclear Program," *Iran Watch*, 09 Apr. 2016: 28 Jul. 2017 www.iranwatch.org/our-publications/weapon-program-background-report/history-irans-nuclear-program.

12 Owen Daniels and Chris Brown, for The Diplomat "China's Energy Security Achilles Heel: Middle Eastern Oil," *The Diplomat*, 8 September 2015: 21 July 2017 <www.thediplomat.com/2015/09/chinas-energy-security-achilles-heel-middle-eastern-oil>.

13 Geoffrey Kemp, *The East Moves West: India, China, and Asia's Growing Presence in the Middle East* (Washington: Brookings Institution Press, 2010), pp. 12–13.

14 Fulton, "China is trying to pull Middle East countries".

create a free-trade zone. Also Iran is highly important for China's energy strategy since it has the largest gas reserves and the fourth biggest oil reserves in the world and, therefore, it can become a main exporter of energy sources to China in the long-term period[15]. In 2002, China received 15 % of its oil imports from Iran, and nowadays, oil represents about 80 % of the overall import from the Islamic Republic; however, the export to Iran is more diverse containing high technology, manufactured goods and engineering services[16].

Sino-Middle Eastern cooperation is also a necessary part of the Chinese "One Belt, One Road" initiative (2013) which is a reflection of Chinese ambitions to change the international trade system and to connect its ports with ports in South and East Asia, the Middle East, Africa and Europe. This initiative is important to the Arab states and Iran because it promises deeper economic cooperation with China, and also to Beijing for whose plans the Middle East is indispensable because of its strategic location. Therefore, it is desirable or even necessary for China to engage more in regional politics and to deal with local security problems more actively in order to eliminate any possible threats to "One Belt, One Road" initiative. According to Cafiero and Wagner, Beijing is determined to cooperate with Mideast countries in the fight against terrorism and extremism as two potential sources of security threats to the OBOR initiative;[17] however, counterterrorism solely cannot safeguard Chinese economic and geopolitical interests in the region because intra-regional rivalry and civil wars destabilize regional order as well. Beijing is very cautious about taking sides in regional disputes and wars as will be described in the next part of the text, nevertheless China's Mideast foreign policy seems to be slowly changing due to expanding business ties and deepening economic cooperation.

China's Risk-Averse Policy and Avoiding Conflicts Resolution

Communist China during Mao Zedong's rule supported liberation movements in the Arab world in their anticolonial struggle; however, it did not have any

15 Manochehr Dorraj, "The Future of Sino-Iran Relations" in: *Toward Well-Oiled Relations: China's Presence in the Middle East Following the Arab Spring*, ed. Niv Horesh (Basingstoke, New York: Palgrave Macmillan, 2016), p. 209.

16 Dorraj, "The Future of Sino-Iran Relations," pp. 208–209.

17 Giorgio Cafiero and Daniel Wagner, "What the Gulf States Think of 'One Belt, One Road': Saudi Arabia, UAE, Qatar, and Oman have mixed feelings about China's ambitious project," *The Diplomat*, 24 May 2017: 15 Jan. 2018 https://thediplomat.com/2017/05/what-the-gulf-states-think-of-one-belt-one-road/.

diplomatic relations with many Arab states and Israel for a long time and "it was too weak and poor to be a significant force in the region's numerous conflicts."[18] That is why China stayed largely outside Mideast politics. This changed slightly in the second half of the 1970s when Beijing inclined to more pragmatic policy less influenced by ideology. Establishing diplomatic and trade relationships with all states in the region suited China's modernization plans better. During the 1980s and even more from the beginning of the 1990s, we can observe a more intense involvement of China in the Middle East whose goal was to achieve new economic interests and support its modernization through arms deals. At present, China maintains diplomatic ties with all states in the region and tries to preserve steady and strategic partnerships with all countries and also non-state actors like Hizballah, Hamas or Muslim Brotherhood[19].

What is symptomatic for contemporary Mideast policy of China is its pragmatism, i.e. China's desire to have friendly and economically fertile relations with all countries, even with mutual rivals. However, as Horesh and Xu point out, "[i]n order to secure access to oil and gas, China aims to befriend all, but avoids formal alliance with any country in the Middle East."[20] Beijing can economically benefit from close ties with various Middle Eastern states and therefore it is pragmatic not to get involved in regional rivalries and not to establish a security partnership with any particular country. This means that China is hesitant to take sides in regional conflicts because siding with some countries might antagonize others which could harm China's economic interests.

However, Beijing's long-term effort to keep its distance from regional conflicts is quite surprising, since China's economic growth depends, to a high degree, on uninterrupted and sufficient energy supplies from conflict-prone Middle East. For quite some time, China's proactive Mideast policy has then been based mainly on economically-focused and politically "harmless" projects such as establishing China-Arab States Cooperation Forum (2004) and China-Gulf Forum or engaging in peacekeeping operations such as the one in Lebanon. Nevertheless, Beijing starts to realize that regional disputes and wars can negatively influence its investments and trade and endanger Chinese workers and emigrants. China is

---

18 Hoong Ng. Weng, "China, the wild card in the Israel-Palestine peace process," *Asia Times*, 4 Mar. 2017: 27 Jul. 2017 www.atimes.com/china-wild-card-israel-palestine-peace-process.

19 Singh, "Chinese Policy in the Middle East," pp. 166, 168.

20 Niv Horesh and Ruike Xu, "Conclusion: China's Growing Presence in the Middle East," in: *Toward Well-Oiled Relations: China's Presence in the Middle East Following the Arab Spring*, ed. Niv Horesh (Basingstoke, New York: Palgrave Macmillan, 2016), p. 217.

also aware of its vulnerability to oil and gas supply reduction or outage as a result of conflicts. Therefore, for several years, China's Navy has been combating piracy in the Gulf of Aden in order to stabilize waters around Somalia and Yemen. Also Chinese representatives proclaim that non-proliferation of weapons of mass destruction and anti-terrorism combat are a part of China's Mideast policy. Apart from few exceptions[21], these efforts remain mostly rhetorical even though it is greatly concerned with the spread of extremist Islamist ideology and terrorism from the Middle East to Central Asian states.[22]

The Arab Uprisings slightly changed Beijing's perspective of its involvement in conflict solving because they endangered close diplomatic ties with Middle Eastern countries, and the overall instability as a result of the revolutions could have jeopardized China's investments and economic interests. After all, civil wars outbreak in Libya and Syria caused China the loss of millions of dollars in investments[23]. Eventually, Beijing recognized new regimes in order to maintain good relationships with Arab countries regardless of who holds power, and has engaged more intensively to the solution of some security and political disputes. Beijing realized that their inactivity and disconcern could induce negative consequences for Chinese energy interests in case the region's unstable security situation caused serious distortion of energy supplies[24]. But still, as we could observe, Chinese policies were mainly wary and risk-averse than proactive – for example, Chinese government criticized the NATO-led military intervention in Libya in 2011 even though China enabled this intervention when abstained from voting in the UN Security Council. China supported UNSC Resolution 1970 calling for the termination of violence Libyan regime used against rebels and civilians because China had to protect and evacuate its tens of thousands inhabitants in Libya (not to mention its estates)[25]. However, it did not want to accept the UNSC Resolution 1973 because it gave the international community

21 E.g., China approved series of UNSC resolutions regarding non-proliferation of WMD and helped to arrange the Joint Comprehensive Plan of Action in 2015.

22 In Weng's opinion, it is one of the reasons why China might deepen its cooperation with Arab states and Israel (Weng, "China, the wild card"). It actually has already started in 2016 when China underwent first counterterrorism exercises with Saudi Arabia.

23 Massoud Hayoun, "China's Approach to the Middle East Looks Familiar," *The Diplomat*, 29 Nov. 2016: 28 Jul 2017 www.thediplomat.com/2016/11/chinas-approach-to-the-middle-east-looks-familiar.

24 Daniels and Brown, for The Diplomat "China's Energy Security Achilles Heel".

25 Singh, "Chinese Policy in the Middle East," p. 172.

an authorization for military intervention in Libya. Beijing itself, though, did not propose its own viable non-military solution of the Libyan crises.

The intervention in Libya changed the way how Beijing dealt with the civil war in Syria. China was not sure about Western states' interests anymore, therefore it vetoed several drafts of resolutions regarding the solution of this conflict in the UN Security Council and criticized Western powers' policies in Syria, but again, it did not propose any exact plan for a ceasefire and peace. Chinese representatives repeatedly declared that peace negotiations is the only option but again, as in the Libyan case, China knows what it wants (to prevent military intervention of Western powers resulting in overthrowing al-Assad's regime) but it does not have an exact plan how to achieve a ceasefire and lasting peace in Syria (China's Four-Point Plan for Syria[26] from 2012 has not received much attention, nor support, partially because it was too vague).

In spite of more intense involvement in solving Syrian civil war by vetoing UNSC resolutions, this event did not change the overall Beijing's approach to Middle Eastern politics which is still far from typical, more proactive great-power policies based on the role as security arbiter and peacemaker which has been traditionally exerted by the USA, European powers or even Russia. There are several proofs that China is trying to get more involved in Middle Eastern issues which can be explained by both their economy interests and also diplomatic aspiration to find "its way as an emerging great power newly capable of exercising influence around the world"[27] and to become regional "honest broker". Yet, its initiatives regarding the Syria civil war and the Israeli-Palestinian conflict ended with mixed results. And thus, China tends to leave the solution of Middle Eastern problems to other great powers. Even though Beijing has been taking part in negotiations about the Syria civil war since the conflict started, the

26 China's Four-Point Plan for Syria suggested the following: (1) the immediate ceasefire and active cooperation of all fighting parties with Lakhdar Brahimi, the joint special representative of the United Nations and the Arab League for Syria, in his mediation efforts, (2) empowerment of interlocutors that would help Syria to establish a transitional governing body and to create a roadmap of political transition, (3) greater responsibility in the resolution of the crisis and in the support of Brahimi's mediation efforts on the part of the international community, (4) mitigation of the humanitarian crisis in Syria and larger humanitarian assistance to the Syrian people (Lina Yang, "China announces new proposal on Syria," *English.gov.cn* (The State Council, The People's Republic of China), 31 Oct. 2012: 17 Sep. 2018 http://www.gov.cn/misc/2012-10/31/content_2255082.htm).

27 Singh, "Chinese Policy in the Middle East," p. 162.

USA and Russia played a central role and China mostly took the back seat[28]. And it is the same with most other disputes and conflicts in this region in last years.

Greater Participation of China in the Middle East Politics – Desired, or Not?

It is well-known that to great powers' concerns belongs, among other things, the preservation of stability of any region where the particular power has economic, political or security interests. Since the Mideast countries and institutions have been traditionally too weak and poorly functioning, various external powers took up the management of regional economic and security regimes in order to ensure subsystem's stability and safeguard their interests.

On the contrary to the USA who uses extensive military presence, military and economic support of allies, diplomatic engagement and exceptionally also military intervention, China seeks to maintain friendly relations with every state in the region, to avoid military solution of security problems and interference in internal affairs of states, to expand investment opportunities and trade exchanges but also to elude direct military and economic assistance. Thus, China endeavours to achieve their economic and geopolitical goals mostly by economic tools and by supporting development and diplomacy. That is why Beijing often did not react when a conflict broke out or limited its response to either support or rather disapprove of other powers' policies.

So even if China regularly resists military interventions of external powers to the region, Beijing itself often does not offer its own solution to particular Mideast problems. Therefore, it is not in Beijing's interest to undermine the US position as regional leader and destroy the US-created security architecture even though we can observe that some Chinese activities in the Middle East should balance the power of the USA. China, in certain respects, still benefits from the active engagement of the USA[29] in the region since it lowers China's financial expenses and potential political costs[30].

As events of recent years showed, Beijing will not be able to rely on the US security architecture forever. Despite some identical interests, certain approaches

28 Tiezzi, "China Seeks Expanded Role in Middle East".

29 E.g. U.S. efforts to stabilize the security environment, to preserve free navigation across the Strait of Hormuz, to deal with conflicts and to fight against extremism and terrorism, etc.

30 Daniels and Brown, for The Diplomat "China's Energy Security Achilles Heel"; Horesh, "Introduction," pp. 1–2; Singh, "Chinese Policy in the Middle East," p. 166.

to Mideast politics differ and leaving solutions to all problems purely on the United States or, on the contrary, the US disengagement from the region can harm Chinese interests. Apart from this, there are several factors that push China more into its greater engagement in the Middle East – ever-increasing dependency on Middle Eastern oil, growing amount of Chinese investments in the area, high number of Chinese workers employed in the Gulf and elsewhere, "One Belt, One Road" initiative, worsening security situation in the region, and fragile political nature of many countries which create chaotic and unpredictable environment leading to rise of new threats to Chinese interests.

For the above-mentioned reasons, it would be desirable for China itself if it participated more in the Middle East's management in order to prevent an unwanted development of regional politics. Yet, Horesh correctly states that "China's supplanting of the US as the world's leading superpower or even as the Middle East's security arbiter is far from certain."[31] This can be explained in two ways. First, it is not possible just to replace the USA by China as a new leader because Beijing is still not able and/or willing to become the great power with all duties that belong to this role. This can be illustrated by its inability to provide security guarantees to its allies, by its reluctance to vote always in favour of its allies in international organizations, or by its unwillingness to be the regional peacemaker. China lacks a grand strategy for the Middle East along the lines of traditional great powers. Rather, it is adapting somehow *ad hoc* to the events that break out in the region. After all, "strategic caution"[32] is characteristic for current Beijing's Mideast policy. Chinese capabilities enable China to play a much bigger role in managing regional crises but nowadays, its policy is too risk-averse and cautious.

The second reason why China cannot simply and quickly take over the leadership in the Middle East from the USA is the fact that even though the greater involvement of China in regional politics might represent an opportunity to diversify security relationships for some Middle Eastern countries in the times when there are rumors about US leadership declining, it does not pose a real alternative to the security partnership with the USA. American allies do not want to replace the US with China as a security guarantee. The Mideast (above all GCC) states are satisfied to do business with China but are suspicious of China being their security ally since it cooperates closely with Iran who is the major threat for GCC countries[33].

31 Horesh, "Introduction," p. 2.

32 Calabrese, "China's Role in Post-Hegemonic Middle East".

33 Daniels and Brown, for The Diplomat "China's Energy Security Achilles Heel".

Conclusions

The strategic map of the Middle East has been changing again. Even though it is still Western powers (the USA above all) who dominate the Middle Eastern region, China is increasingly present there and the same can be said about other Asian emerging powers (India or South Korea). At the same time, the United States, the European powers and also Russia are slowly losing influence in favour of new power centres in the international system. Dorraj and Pethiyagoda agree that China's economic and diplomatic relationships with states in the Middle East – above all Iran and the GCC states – will sooner or later change regional geopolitics and thus influence world affairs[34]. Yet, the question if China is be able and/or willing to become a leading power in the Middle East or at least one of the powers who account for the management of the region, stays unanswered.

From time to time, Beijing proposes a plan to solve one of many Mideast conflicts, cautiously reacts to regional disputes, occasionally criticizes other powers (mainly the US) for their political missteps and tries to balance between regional rivals. But only rarely their peace proposals and other diplomatic initiatives attract more attention, and they basically have no real impact. Beijing is aware of all risks that come with greater involvement in regional politics and that their economic and trade accomplishments do not have to translate automatically into successful diplomacy and security policy. The next few years will show whether China's grand strategy for the Middle East lies in its current wary and risk-averse policy, or whether the Chinese government is still evolving and will soon declare a real grand strategy regarding this highly strategic region.

Bibliography

1. Blackwill, Robert D. and Jennifer M. Harris. *War by Other Means: Geoeconomics and Statecraft*. Cambridge: The Belknap Press of Harvard University Press, 2016.
2. Bronson, Rachel. "The United States in the Middle East: Bound by Growing Energy Demand." *Middle East Policy Council*, Vol. XXI, No. 2, 2014, pp. 34–39.

34 Dorraj, "The Future of Sino-Iran Relations" p. 206; Kadira Pethiyagoda, "India-GCC Relations: Delhi's Strategic Opportunity," *Brookings Doha Center Analysis Paper*, No. 18, 2017: 15 Jun. 2017 www.brookings.edu/wp-content/uploads/2017/02/india_gcc_relations.pdf, p. 4.

3. Dorraj, Manochehr. "The Future of Sino-Iran Relations." In: *Toward Well-Oiled Relations: China's Presence in the Middle East Following the Arab Spring*, ed. Niv Horesh. Basingstoke, New York: Palgrave Macmillan, 2016, pp. 206–215.
4. Horesh, Niv and Ruike Xu. "Conclusion: China's Growing Presence in the Middle East." In: *Toward Well-Oiled Relations: China's Presence in the Middle East Following the Arab Spring*, ed. Niv Horesh. Basingstoke, New York: Palgrave Macmillan, 2016, pp. 216–231.
5. Horesh, Niv. "Introduction." In: *Toward Well-Oiled Relations: China's Presence in the Middle East Following the Arab Spring*, ed Niv Horesh. Basingstoke, New York: Palgrave Macmillan, 2016, pp. 1–4.
6. Kemp, Geoffrey. *The East Moves West: India, China, and Asia's Growing Presence in the Middle East*. Washington: Brookings Institution Press, 2010.
7. Leverett, Flynt and Jeffrey Bader. "Managing China-U.S. Energy Competition in the Middle East." *The Washington Quarterly*, Vol. 29, No. 1, 2006, pp. 187–201.
8. Pant, Harsh V. "India and the Middle East: Before and After the Arab Spring." In: *The International Politics of the Arab Spring: Popular Unrest and Foreign Policy*, ed. Robert Mason. New York: Palgrave Macmillan, 2014, pp. 155–175.
9. Singh, Michael. "Chinese Policy in the Middle East in the Wake of the Arab Uprisings." In: *Toward Well-Oiled Relations: China's Presence in the Middle East Following the Arab Spring*, ed. Niv Horesh. Basingstoke, New York: Palgrave Macmillan, 2016, pp. 169–170.

Internet Sources

1. "A History of Iran's Nuclear Program," *Iran Watch*. 9 April 2016. www.iranwatch.org/our-publications/weapon-program-background-report/history-irans-nuclear-program (28 July 2017).
2. Cafiero, Giorgio and Daniel Wagner. "What the Gulf States Think of 'One Belt, One Road': Saudi Arabia, UAE, Qatar, and Oman Have Mixed Feelings about China's Ambitious Project," *The Diplomat*. 24 May 2017. https://thediplomat.com/2017/05/what-the-gulf-states-think-of-one-belt-one-road/ (15 January 2018).
3. Calabrese, John. "China's Role in Post-Hegemonic Middle East," *Real Clear World*. 1 May 2017. www.realclearworld.com/articles/2017/05/01/how_china_and_america_can_share_the_mideast_burden.html (18 July 2017).
4. CIA The World Factbook. "China," 11 July 2017. www.cia.gov/library/publications/the-world-factbook/geos/ch.html (18 July 2017).

5. CIA The World Factbook. "Imports – Partners," www.cia.gov/library/publications/resources/the-world-factbook/fields/2061.html#ag (24 August 2017).
6. Daniels, Owen and Chris Brown. "For the DiplomatChina's Energy Security Achilles Heel: Middle Eastern Oil," *The Diplomat*. 8 September 2015. www.thediplomat.com/2015/09/chinas-energy-security-achilles-heel-middle-eastern-oil (21 July 2017).
7. Fulton, Jonathan. "China Is Trying to Pull Middle East Countries into Its Version of NATO," *The Washington Post*. 21 June 2017. www.washingtonpost.com/news/monkey-cage/wp/2017/06/21/how-china-is-shifting-toward-the-middle-east (31 July 2017).
8. Hayoun, Massoud. "China's Approach to the Middle East Looks Familiar," *The Diplomat*. 29 November 2016. www.thediplomat.com/2016/11/chinas-approach-to-the-middle-east-looks-familiar (28 July 2017).
9. Luft, Gal. "Will Energy-Rich America Depart from the Middle East and Eurasia?" *Turkish Policy Quarterly*, Vol. 12, No. 4, 2014 pp. 77–84. http://turkishpolicy.com/dosyalar/files/vol_12-no_4-luft.pdf (17 September 2018).
10. Pethiyagoda, Kadira. India-GCC Relations: Dehli´s Strategic Opportunity. *Brookings Doha Center Analysis Paper*, No. 18. Doha: Brookings Doha Center, 2017. www.brookings.edu/wp-content/uploads/2017/02/india_gcc_relations.pdf (15 June 2017).
11. Tiezzi, Shannon. "China Seeks Expanded Role in Middle East," *The Diplomat*. 4 June 2014. www.thediplomat.com/2014/06/china-seeks-expanded-role-in-middle-east (16 June 2017).
12. Weng, Hoong Ng. "China, the Wild Card in the Israel-Palestine Peace Process," *Asia Times*. 4 March 2017. www.atimes.com/china-wild-card-israel-palestine-peace-process (27 July 2017).
13. Yang, Lina. "China Announces New Proposal on Syria," *English.gov.cn* (The State Council, The People's Republic of China), 31 October 2012. http://www.gov.cn/misc/2012-10/31/content_2255082.htm (17 September 2018).

Part IV – Regional Studies

Yuriy Skorokhod

"Consociational Democracy": The Model of the Democratization of Deeply Divided Arab Societies?

Abstract: The chapter examines the prospects of applying the model of "consociational democracy" to the deeply divided Arab societies in order to ensure their democratic transition after the "Arab Spring". The main attention is devoted to the impact of external factors on how the model of "consociational democracy" could operate. Based on the case study of Lebanon, we can outline at least three models demonstrating the impact of external factors.

The first model implies the existence of a "center of power" outside of Lebanon which has played a significant (and sometimes dominant) role in the balancing of the interests of subcommunities and, in some cases, acted as mediator (the period of Mount Lebanon *mutasarrifiyya*), Greater Lebanon (under the French mandate), and post-Taif period (particularly in 1990–2005). The external centers of dominant influence were the Ottoman Empire, France, and Syria, respectively.

The second model also stipulates a high level of influence of the external environment on the Lebanese political system, with no dominance of a single international (regional or non-regional) actor (the period of the Civil War (1975–1990), and, to some extent, the period following the Cedar Revolution in 2005).

The third model is characterized by a relatively low degree of external influence on the consociational system. This model was applied during the period of "confessional democracy" in the first decade after Lebanon gained independence, in which consensus-building was more of a problem for the Lebanese politicians themselves.

The study also suggests that based on the dynamics of international relations in the Middle East in the XXI century, the successful establishment of "consociational democracy" in the countries of the region, which could stabilize deeply divided Arab-Muslim societies and ensure their transition to a stable representative democracy, in the nearest future is unlikely.

Keywords: Arab East, Lebanon, democratization, "consociational democracy", deeply divided societies

Introduction

The democratization of the Arab East has become a major challenge for scholars who investigate the problems of democratic transition throughout the world. "Transitologists", as Laura Guazzone and Danióla Pioppi emphasize, have always "considered the Arab countries as latecomers and/or exceptional with respect to the much more advanced transitions taking place in most other parts of the world"[1]. Despite the diversity of approaches and concepts, the capacity of the Arab-Muslim world to absorb democratic ideas and introduce democratic forms of government as they are understood in the western world has been and still remains a central motion in the debate on the democratization of Arab countries. Some researchers, including Raymond Hinnebusch, have pointed out that "If one looks at actual existing democratization in the Middle East, two historical roads or models are apparent. "Consociational democracy", adapted in Lebanon, is a model for democratizing multi-communal society" and "*political liberalization without democratization*", which began to spread throughout the region in the 1990s[2].

At the same time, the continuous civil war in Lebanon (1975–1990), inability of the system of "consociational democracy" to prevent the outbreak of war, according to many scholars, have demonstrated "the limits of "consensual democracy" as mode of government and non-violent conflict management in multi-confessional society capable of leading to its development and reform while maintaining the balance of the political system"[3]; that is, they have questioned the ability of this model to ensure stability of multi-confessional societies. Scientists cautioned against "viewing the Lebanese formula as a panacea for resolving sectarian tensions in transitional societies"[4].

It is noteworthy that the catalysts of scientific and political discussions on democratization in the Middle East mostly were the events which had a significant impact on the development of the Middle East region. Among the latter, a crucial role was played by the Arab Spring, which led to a change (in Egypt, Yemen, Libya, Tunisia), or a significant weakening (in Syria) of a number of authoritarian political regimes in the Middle East but did not launch a democratic transition in those countries. The Arab Spring has renewed discussion within the scientific community on the prospects and possible ways of democratizing Arab

1 Laura Guazzone, Daniyla Pioppi, "Interpreting Change in the Arab World," in: *The Arab State and Neo-Liberal Globalization. The Restructuring of State Power in the Middle East,* ed. Laura Guazzone and Daniyla Pioppi (Reading: Ithaca Press, 2009), p.3.

2 Raymond Hinnebusch, "Prospects for democratization in the Middle East", in: *Democratization in the Middle East. Dilemmas and Perspectives*, ed. Birgitte Rahbek (Aarhus: Aarhus University Press, 2005), p. 38.

3 Karam Karam, "An Analysis of Political Change in Lebanon in the Light of Recent Mobilization Cycles", in: *The Arab State and Neo-Liberal Globalization. The Restructuring of State Power in the Middle East,* ed. Laura Guazzone and Daniyla Pioppi (Reading: Ithaca Press, 2009), p. 50.

4 Tamirace Fakhoury, "Do Power-Sharing Systems Behave Differently amid Regional Uprisings? Lebanon in theArab Protest Wave," *Middle East Journal*, Vol. 68, No. 4 (Autumn 2014), p. 509.

societies, on the causes of the "deficit of democracy" in Arab countries, on the relationship between the phenomena of democracy and stability, compatibility of Islam with democracy, and so on.

One of the aspects of this debate was to reassess the possibility of applying Lebanese experience in non-Western, deeply divided societies that have an authoritarian political culture and suffer from problems similar to ones of Lebanon. The core question here is whether the system of "consociational democracy", which according to the founders of this theory is most suitable for multi-confessional and multi-ethnic societies, is capable of bringing about stability in deeply divided Arab-Muslim societies and, in the long run, facilitating their transition to a stable representative democracy. This, in turn, puts before the researchers a number of fundamental questions, namely: The problems of the confessional system in Lebanon are generated by the defects of the model of "confessional democracy" or by the peculiar nature of Lebanese social reality? The failure of "confessional democracy" in Lebanon **is** caused more by endogenous or exogenous factors? This study is devoted to the analysis of the impact external factors laid upon the functioning of the Lebanese political system.

The impact of external factors on Lebanon's "confessional democracy" and its sources. Lebanon's experience enables us to outline main characteristics of "consociational democracy" system and the conditions indispensable for its operation. In our opinion, main features of "consociational democracy" are as follows:

1. ***Recognition*** of the autonomy of the subcommunity (sociocultural group) and of its role as a subject of political process.
2. ***Proportionality*** as a key principle of the representation of confessional communities in all bodies of power across the country.
3. ***Different interests*** and goals of the system's main components.
4. ***The potential for a lasting conflict*** in society, which is a reflection of the present contradictions that underlie the relations between subcommunities and are perceived by members of sociocultural groups at the emotional and moral level as a threat to subcommunal interests. Consequently, the process of confessional balancing can only be aimed at limiting the scale and intensity of conflict situations arising as a result of the contentious interactions between subcommunities. "The goal of the confessional balancing process is not to destroy communal power, - Enver Koury pointed out - but to control it so that it become a stabilizing rather than de stabilizing factor"[5].

5 Enver Koury, *The Crisis in Lebanese System. Confessionalism and Chaos* (Washington: American Enterprise Institute for Public Policy Research, 1976), p. 19.

5. ***Absolute relativity*** of the power potential of a subcommunity. The potential of this power, on the one hand, is determined through its comparison with the power potential of other subcommunities, and on the other hand, through their ability to achieve their aspirations.
6. To a certain extent, ***the power policy*** is designed not to gain any benefits, but to neutralize the opponent's strategy. All other options can pose a threat to the very existence of the system itself.
7. ***Lack of uniform value orientations*** at the national level. For typical Lebanese society, it is a common practice that institutions function at the national level without being backed up by shared values and incentives at the individual level.

Thus, the confessional system introduced in Lebanon was intended to contribute to the establishment of stability, security, order, and equilibrium in society. In other words, the system of confessionalism was to prevent the expansion of conflicts beyond controllable limits, that is, to preclude them from turning into a genuine threat to the very existence of the system itself.

Lebanese experience gives ground to distinguish the following conditions necessary for the functioning of "consociational democracy":

- Most components of the system (especially the political elite of the main sociocultural groups) must be equally interested in preservation of the system and reaching a principle agreement on that.
- Autonomous religious and ethnic communities have to recognize the necessity of the system's preservation as a prerequisite for establishing relations of interdependence between them, which would make the process of achieving a balance of power possible.
- Sociocultural groups must have a clear vision of what benefits the functioning of this system brings, and, on the contrary, they must realize that any community within other systems would be in a more disadvantaged position.
- The system itself must be able to evolve through adapting transformation processes that take place within society.
- The president must be guided by secular considerations while adopting a particular domestic policy; he must stay aside the interests of communities, clans, and families when making key decisions, and observe only the interests of the state.
- There must be no destructive influence of external factors.

The model of "confessional democracy" in Lebanon has taken a corporate form of power sharing which enabled some scholars to refer to it as a "corporate consociationalism"[6]. According to this model, balancing of power and a certain reconciliation of interests takes place at the level of the elite representing a subcommunity, and the political process itself is personalized.

The most important prerequisite for this interconfessional interaction at the leadership level was the Lebanese elite's consensus on such a key issue as an agreement concerning the very existence of the sociopolitical system itself within which the Lebanese elite itself operates. In Lebanon, the political system of "confessionalism" "....guarantees political power to a fixed group of elites who actively work to exclude challenges to their communal domination or to the system that maintains it"[7].

In turn, solving of this problem requires efforts aimed at minimizing the conflicts occurring within the system. The success of these endeavors can be ensured only through interconfessional interaction at the elite level. On the other hand, the leaders of subcommunities simultaneously fulfill the functions of "limitation" and "deterrence" with respect to each other since the Lebanese elite has been segmental in its nature. Its interests consist in protecting and asserting its positions within a certain section of society (family, clan, subcommunity, etc.), as well as in maintaining a kind of system which would be the most suitable option for completing the first task. These limited interests have been for a long time a way of guaranteeing political stability in Lebanon – it has arranged the environment necessary for the functioning of the system as a whole. In this context, any attempts by certain local leaders (regardless of their confessional affiliation) to take up the role of a strategic elite (that is, to act as a national leader or to identify themselves with certain external powers, which in turn would increase their status in the system of the Lebanese elite) were perceived by other subjects as endangering political stability and even the very existence of a system as such.

The Lebanese model of "confessional democracy" can be viewed as a conflict model of society's development. The instability of the system a priori results from the way autonomous segments (communities and subcommunities) are combined, from the contradictions between the dynamics of the relationship between autonomous segments and the rigid structure of the system (that is the legislation which has stipulated fixed proportions of subcommunal representation in

6 Imad Salamey, "Failing Consociationalism in Lebanon and Integrative Options," *International Journal of Peace Studies*. Vol. 14, No. 2 (Autumn/Winter 2009), p. 85.

7 Benjamin MacQueen, "Lebanon's Electoral System: Is Reform Possible?" *Middle East Policy*, Vol. XXIII, No. 3 (Fall 2016), p. 71.

the bodies of power). Consequently, the resolution of these contradictions has gone through a large-scale conflict, as an apparent threat to the very existence of the system has loomed.

The weakness of the Lebanese political system in conjunction with, according to Georges Corm, the "minority complex" of the Lebanese society[8], which manifests itself in an inadequately exaggerated reaction to any events perceived as a challenge to the interests of a subcommunity, has laid foundation for further expansion of the impact external factors exert on the ongoing political processes in Lebanon. The mobilization of the support of foreign powers served as an integral part of the Lebanon's response to the alleged threats to subcommunal interests.

In case of Lebanon, it is possible to outline at least two essential factors that had a decisive affect on the development of political processes and the functioning of the system of "confessional democracy". **The first factor** was a high probability of the outbreak of an orientation crisis in the Lebanese foreign policy. According to Meir Zamir, the National Pact of 1943 "was essentially an attempt to bridge the gap between the two contradictory conceptions of national identity of Lebanese state, namely, Lebanese Christian or Arab Muslim"[9]. The civilizational division between the Muslims and the Christians has led to a sharp sensitivity of the Lebanese society to external influence. As a result, significant changes in the balance of power at the regional and global levels, as well as the necessity to respond to new challenges on the international scene, for Lebanon could potentially bring about an internal conflict. **The second factor** was the settlement of the military and political bodies of the Palestinian Liberation Organization (PLO) in Lebanon, which has served as a catalyst for regional and global actors' engagement in the Lebanese affairs. There is also a peculiar process of "lebanonization" of the Palestinian problem going on, which essentially has been manifested through the attempts of some regional powers to enlist Lebanese actors in stepping up the pressure against the leadership of the PLO. Since the second half of the 1970s, there has been a steady tendency towards expansion of the range of states and organizations involved in the Lebanese events (Syria, Israel, Iraq, Iran, the PLO, the USA, France, Great Britain, the USSR, etc.). Thus, Lebanon has gradually turned into a battlefield where other powers fought for leadership in the Middle East.

---

8 Georges Corm, *Fragmentation in the Middle East: The Last Thirty Years* (London, Sydney: Hutchinson, 1983), p. 155.

9 Meir Zamir, *The Formation of Modern Lebanon* (London, Sydney : Croom Helm, 1985), p. 221.

On the other hand, the enlargement of the scale of influence from the outside has led to a disturbance in the balance of power in Lebanon, with the Lebanese political system having failed to overcome the excess burden. In the past it was within the system of "confessional democracy" that subcommunal forces could ensure the realization of their interests using the existing mechanisms for achieving a balance of power, but now they opted for establishing "special relations" with external actors that were strategic in their nature and aimed at protecting subcommunities. As a result, not only the traditional Christian-Muslim contradictions have deepened, but also there has been activated a process of differentiation of political forces that sought to offer their own vision of ways to protect subcommunities and focused on different regional actors. This tendency has been most clearly observed since the second half of the 1980s. At that time, several armed conflicts between the leading Shiite factions – "Hezbollah" and "Amal" – occurred; the Christian community faced hostilities between troops of General Michel Aoun and the military-political organization called "Lebanese Forces" under the command of Samir Geagea. Thus, if earlier the instability in Lebanon was a consequence of structural relations between Lebanese autonomous "centers of power" (communities – subcommunities), then with the onset of the Civil War the instability was also a function of structural relations at the level of the inter-Arab and Middle Eastern systems of international relations in general. For a long time, Lebanon has been a concentration of a number of problems pertaining to both the Lebanese and the inter-Arab regional and global contradictions.

The models of the influence external factors exert on the functioning of "confessional democracy" in Lebanon. It should be noted that the very establishment of the consociational system in Lebanon to a certain extent has resulted from the impact of external factors. The emergence of confessional democracy was not a consequence of autochthonous development of the Lebanese society (only some of its elements were imminent, for example, the experience of reaching consensus among the multi-confessional feudal elite during elections of emir); in fact, it was a result of applying the West European idea of democratic pluralism to Lebanon's sociopolitical environment and of reconciling the interests of various subcommunities, which means that establishment of confessional democracy was made possible through the import of formal institutions to Lebanon.

The political stability of deeply divided societies largely depends on the way external factors affect their development. The experience of Lebanon allows for distinguishing the following models of the influence external factor exert on the functioning of confessional democracy:

The first model implies the existence of a "center of power" outside of Lebanon which had a significant (and sometimes dominant) influence on the process of balancing the interests of subcommunities and, in some cases, served as a mediator. This type of influence was typical for the period of Mount Lebanon (*mutasarrifiyya*), Greater Lebanon (the period of the French mandate), and post-Taif period (particularly in 1990–2005). The external centers of dominant influence were the Ottoman Empire, France, and Syria, respectively. At the same time, while the influence of the Ottoman Empire was to some extent counterbalanced by the European powers which acted not only as the initiators but also the guarantors of the newly-formed system of power and even the Lebanese autonomy, the influence of France and Syria in Lebanon had no significant limitations.

In the last two cases there was a consensus within the international system regarding the recognition of the dominant status those states had enjoyed in Lebanon: either an officially documented consensus – as in case of France which obtained a mandate for the administration of Lebanon and Syria, or a tacit consent – as it was in case when a number of leading actors such as the United States, Saudi Arabia, Egypt, etc., recognized the pretensions of Syria.

We would like to point out that in the context of implementation of this model, the implications for the system of "consociational democracy" in Lebanon depended exclusively on the goals which the most dominant state set forward with regard to its Lebanese policy. While France was interested in strengthening the institutes of "consociational democracy", the Lebanese course of Syria in the 1990s and early 2000s was oriented towards forging a political regime in Lebanon which would serve as an instrument for establishing the hegemony of Damascus in the country. In this period, which was described as the period of "indirect rule" of Syria[10], there was a tendency towards "Syrianization" of the Lebanese state bodies and of the Lebanese society as a whole. It was also manifested through the total influence of Damascus upon most aspects of the development of Lebanese society. Almost any key domestic policy problem could not be solved without prior agreement with the Syrian leadership. The new political elite was critically interested in the existence of such a political regime as it developed client-patron relations with Damascus and was unilaterally dependent on him.

Theodor Hanf has pointed out that "This dependent political system has evolved its own client-patron structures, in which Syrian government has

10 Taku Osoegawa, *Syria and Lebanon. International Relations and Diplomacy in the Middle East* (London: I.B.Tauris, 2013) pp. 91–148.

assumed the role of supreme *za'im*, keeping order among both traditional *zu'ama'* and warlords turned politicians"[11]. Despite the external attributes of democracy, in particular organization of parliamentary elections in Lebanon in 1992, 1996, and 2000, the international nongovernmental organization Freedom House which assesses the level of freedom throughout the world has lowered the position of Lebanon in the ranking to "Not Free" during the era when Syria dominated Lebanon[12].

The second model also stipulates a high level of influence of the external environment on the Lebanese political system, with no dominance of a single international actor. This type of influence was seen during two periods: the period of the Civil War (1975–1990), and, to some extent, during the period following the Cedar Revolution ("the Independence Intifada") in 2005.

The defining features of the political system of Lebanon during the period of the Civil War, which can be characterized as a period of *militia fragmentation*, were as follows:

- The division of the Lebanese territory into confessional cantons, controlled by militia, and the institutionalization of disintegration mechanisms. At the same time, the process of disintegration was still not fully completed.
- The formation of a new configuration of connections and relationships between separate segments of the Lebanese elite (*zu'ama'* and military leaders); the ability of the traditional political elite to fulfill the functions of harmonizing the interests of subcommunities (at the level of *zu'ama'*) was substantially limited; its positions in subcommunities were largely dependent on military leaders.
- The source of the strength of a military formation was not so much the support from a subcommunity, but the blocking of the police along with certain foreign powers who provided them with financial and other assistance. In particular, the Christian militants received assistance from Israel, Saudi Arabia, Jordan, Egypt, and Iraq during those periods, while the Muslim militias – from the PLO, Libya, Iran, and Syria.

Hence in the period of the Civil War, the mechanism of balancing the forces of subcommunities in the Lebanese society has been shaped in a complex multilevel

---

11 Theodor Hanf, *Coexistence in Wartime Lebanon. Decline of a State and Rise of a Nation* (London: The Centre for Lebanese Studies in association with I.B.Tauris & Co Ltd, 1993), p. 642.

12 Iliya Harik, Democracy, "Arab Exceptionalism" and Social Science," *Middle East Journal*, Vol. 60, No. 4 (Autumn 2006), p. 670.

configuration, an indispensable element of which was the coordination of the interests of international actors.

After the Cedar Revolution, the political processes in Lebanon have developed under the significant influence of the external factor, multi-dimensional in its orientation. During this period, two political camps were formed in Lebanon: the March 8 Alliance (pro-Syrian) and the March 14 Alliance (anti-Syrian), whose positions differed fundamentally on such important issues as the withdrawal of Syrian troops from the Lebanese territory and future relations with Syria, the disarming of the Hezbollah military wing, the establishment of the International Independent Investigation Commission into the assassination of Rafiq Hariri. In a broader context, the basis of the conflict between the two camps was the problem of the country's foreign policy orientation and vision of the ways to further develop Lebanon. In particular, Hezbollah, a leading actor in the March 8 Alliance, saw Lebanon as part of resistance axis against Israel, which included Syria, Iran, and Hamas, while the representatives of the March 14 Alliance were more focused on the West and moderate Arab countries, in particular Saudi Arabia and Egypt[13]. In later years, the core contradiction in Lebanon appeared to be the confrontation between the Sunni and Shi'a, which has been a reflection of the struggle between Iran and Saudi Arabia for leadership in the Middle East.

Thus, after the withdrawal of the Israeli (2000) and Syrian (2005) troops from Lebanon, the Lebanese political elite has failed to unite. The problem of priorities in the foreign relations of Lebanon and the establishment by the Lebanese elite of alliances with external actors have discouraged the formation of the necessary prerequisites for the restored process of stabilization and democratization of a deeply divided Lebanese society.

The third model was characterized by a relatively low degree of external influence on the social system. This type of influence was typical of a "confessional democracy" model during the first decade after Lebanon's independence, in which consensus-building was more of a problem for the Lebanese politicians themselves.

Conclusion

The experience of Lebanon shows to the special receptiveness of the "consociational democracy" model to the external influence. The analysis of the models of the external factor influence on the Lebanese political system proposed in

---

13 Ohannes Geukjian, "Political Instability and Conflict after the Syrian Withdrawal from Lebanon," *Middle East Journal*, Vol. 68, No. 4 (Autumn 2014), p. 529.

this chapter allows us to conclude that the Third Model (which assumes a low level of external influence) and the First Model (which assumes the presence of a regional or extra-regional actor that has a dominant influence on balancing the interests of ethnic and religious groups, but only while this actor is focused on ensuring stability by strengthening consociational democracy institutions), in general, create favorable external conditions for the functioning of the "consociational democracy" system.

The dynamics of international relations in the Middle East in the 21st century questions the likelihood of the near future successful implementation in the countries of the region of a "consociational democracy" model that can guarantee stability in deeply divided Arab-Muslim societies and ensure their transition to a stable representative democracy. In the aftermath of the Arab Spring significantly increases the role of non-state actors, as relatively independent elements in the power balance at the regional level. As a result, an important part of Middle Eastern strategies of the Arab states as well as extra-regional countries, aimed at strengthening their influence in the region, becomes direct or indirect links with non-governmental actors. In the situation of weakness of a number of Arab states, the internal political struggle (both between non-state actors and political regimes, and between non-state groups themselves) is often seen as a reflection of a struggle for influence in the Middle East. This suggests that in the conditions of reformatting the regional balance of power in the Middle East after the Arab Spring, the impact of the external environment on Arab states trying to implement the "consociational democracy" model will generally fit into the framework of the Second Model, which is characterized by a high level influence of regional and extra-regional forces, which are tough competitors by their nature.

Bibliography

1. Corm, Georges. *Fragmentation in the Middle East: The Last Thirty Years.* London, Sydney: Hutchinson, 1983.
2. Fakhoury, Tamirace. "Do Power-Sharing Systems Behave Differently amid Regional Uprisings? Lebanon in the Arab Protest Wave." *Middle East Journal*, Vol. 68, No. 4, 2014, pp. 505–520.
3. Geukjian, Ohannes. "Political Instability and Conflict after the Syrian Withdrawal from Lebanon." *Middle East Journal*, Vol. 68, No. 4, 2014, pp. 521–545.
4. Guazzone, Laura, Pioppi, Daniyla. "Interpreting Change in the Arab World." In: *The Arab State and Neo-Liberal Globalization. The Restructuring of State Power in the Middle East*, ed. Laura Guazzone and Daniyla Pioppi. Reading: Ithaca Press, 2009, pp. 1–15.

5. Hanf, Theodor. *Coexistence in Wartime Lebanon. Decline of a State and Rise of a Nation*. London: The Centre for Lebanese Studies in association with I.B.Tauris & Co Ltd, 1993.
6. Hinnebusch, Raymond. "Prospects for Democratization in the Middle East." In: *Democratization in the Middle East. Dilemmas and Perspectives*, ed. Birgitte Rahbek. Aarhus: Aarhus University Press, 2005, pp. 31–40.
7. Iliya, Harik. "Democracy, "Arab Exceptionalism" and Social Science," *Middle East Journal*, Vol. 60, No. 4, 2006, pp. 664–684.
8. Karam, Karam. "An Analysis of Political Change in Lebanon in the Light of Recent Mobilization Cycles." In: *The Arab State and Neo-Liberal Globalization. The Restructuring of State Power in the Middle East*, ed. Laura Guazzone and Daniyla Pioppi. Reading: Ithaca Press, 2009, pp. 47–72.
9. Koury, Enver. *The Crisis in Lebanese System. Confessionalism and Chaos*. Washington: American Enterprise Institute for Public Policy Research, 1976.
10. MacQueen, Benjamin. "Lebanon's Electoral System: Is Reform Possible?" *Middle East Policy*, Vol. XXIII, No. 3, 2016, pp. 71–83.
11. Osoegawa, Taku. *Syria and Lebanon. International Relations and Diplomacy in the Middle East*. London: I.B.Tauris, 2013.
12. Salamey, Imad. "Failing Consociationalism in Lebanon and Integrative Options," *International Journal of Peace Studies*, Vol. 14, No. 2, 2009, pp. 83–105.
13. Zamir, Meir. *The Formation of Modern Lebanon*. London, Sydney: Croom Helm, 1985.

Vladimír Naxera

"Islamophobia without Muslims": Anti-Muslim and anti-Arab Attitudes in Czech Society (Introductory Remarks)

Abstract: The issue of Islam is a crucial one in current Czech politics. These topics can be found in everyday social conversation, debates held in political institutions, and in the media. This critically poised essay consists of three main parts. Firstly, the author deals with Czech President Miloš Zeman's attitudes towards Islam. Secondly, text comments on Czech party programs and their statements related to immigration, Islam (especially in the context of political populism), etc. And finally, study shows some example of Czech "haters" and their hateful perception of Islam and immigration.

Keywords: Islamophobia, Czech politics, populism, anti-Muslim attitudes, immigration

Introduction

The issue of Islam is a crucial one in current Czech politics. It also represents a certain paradox (in light of the number of Muslims living in the Czech Republic and in terms of the contact and only sporadic experiences that the Czech Republic and most Czechs have had with the Islamic world). Although the proportion of Muslims in the country's population is negligible, the link between Islam, politics, and security has become one of the central points of political and social debate in the Czech Republic in recent years.[1] The topics of Islam and immigration can be found in everyday social conversation, debates held in political institutions, and in the media.[2] This issue of Islam, which is surprising in light of the actual number of Muslims living in the country, was fundamentally

---

1 See Bronislav Ostřanský, *Islamofobie po česku: Český odpor vůči islámu, jeho východiska, projevy, souvislosti, přesahy i paradox* (Prague: Vyšehrad, 2017); Ondřej Beránek and Bronislav Ostřanský, *Stíny minaretů. Islám a muslimové jako předmět českých veřejných polemik* (Prague: Academia, 2016); Ondřej Slačálek and Eva Svobodová, "Professionalised "civil society" vs. grassroots "uncivil society"? The "Little Czech" 20 years later," *Socio.hu*, No. 5 (2017), pp. 23–52.

2 See Viera Žúborová and Ingrid Borárosová, "Migrácia v médiách: utečenci verzus migranti. Chápanie migrantov a utečencov v mediálnom priestore v kontexte pozitívnej a negatívnej mediatizácie," *Central European Journal of Politics*, Vol. 2, No. 1 (2016), pp. 1–15.

reflected in the Czech parliamentary elections in 2017 and also in presidential elections in early 2018 (this text was completed shortly before they took place).[3]

The discussion on Islam in the Czech environment (and elsewhere) is significantly related to the so-called migration crisis. Issues of migration have long been a consistent thread woven into European political discourse. This "crisis" is a phenomenon that political parties (both relevant and wholly marginal) feel the need to react to, and the same applies to public discourse. In this regard, the Czech Republic is not an exception. The issue of migration can be associated with a wide range of areas that it enters into. The issue is commonly discussed in the context of economics,[4] security,[5] identity, or – more widely – religion, culture, or the nation.[6] In these contexts of security, culture, or civilization, the issue of migration in Czech public and political discourses is often linked to the topic of Islam – the same topic that this text focuses on. At the same time, Islam and migration are placed in the wider context of the relationship toward foreigners in the Czech Republic in general. There are relatively few Muslims – and foreigners at all for that matter – living in the Czech Republic. According to statistics from the Ministry of the Interior, foreigners make up only 4 % of the Czech Republic's population (with the largest communities from Slovakia, Ukraine, and Vietnam). These foreigners commit only 0.4 % of all illegal activities and the share of illegal migration in the overall increase in the number of foreigners is negligible (statistics on the numbers and makeup of foreign arrivals is dealt with below). Despite this fact, this issue is clearly the "hottest" topic in current public debate.

This critically poised essay consists of three main parts. It contains a sketch of the three lines of discourse relating to the topic of Islam. These lines are seemingly different, but they are related to each other. On the other side, this study does not aspirate to include all cases and anti-Islamic attitudes in the Czech Republic. It means that text must be seen as probe to several different anti-Islamic

3 This text was finished at the beginning of 2018. During editing in the autumn of 2018, some minor changes have been made.

4 Žúborová and Borárosová, "Migrácia v médiách", pp. 1–15.

5 Compare Jarmila Androvičová, "Sekuritizácia migrantov na Slovensku – analýzy diskurzu," *Sociológia*, Vol. 47, No. 4 (2015), pp. 319–339; Philippe Bourbeau, *The securitization of migration. A study of movement and order* (London: Routledge 2011); Petr Krčál and Vladimír Naxera, "Populistická konstrukce národa ohroženého migrací: CAQDAS volebního diskurzu českých parlamentních voleb 2017," *Sociológia*, Vol. 50, No. 5 (2018), pp. 491–523.

6 Compare Agnes Czajka, "Migration in the Age of Nation-State: Migrants, Refugees, and the National Order of Things," *Alternatives*, Vol. 39, No. 3 (2014), pp. 151–163.

contexts within Czech politics and society, not as an evaluation of all aspects of this problem. The first section will focus on analyzing statements made by Czech President Miloš Zeman and his stance on Islam. In regard to the fact that the president can be considered without doubt to be a moral authority or a "moral entrepreneur",[7] the labels that he creates and introduces into dominant political and social discourse (in the sense of the imagination of how things should be) are a highly relevant topic of research. The Czech President (as an institution and a specific individual) has long held a high position in terms of public approval ratings carried out by the Public Opinion Research Centre under the Czech Academy of Sciences. For this reason, it can be assumed that the messages of the president are seen by a large portion of Czech society as "truth" or "objective reality", which is further mediated and amplified by the media.[8] The analysis of presidential speeches has a strong tradition in political science,[9] which stems from the symbolic importance of the function on which certain expectations are based. Through his speeches, the president creates certain narratives – in this sense, presidential speeches are understood as an integral part of the public sphere, which is also linked to the construction of the shape of democracy in a given country.[10] The contribution of this part of the study lies in the interpretation of original and heretofore unanalyzed data (see below) and in the contextualization of the phenomenon of Islam as a security threat from Miloš Zeman's point of view, which opens a new and original window in the research terrain.

The second level will deal with the discourse created by political parties as a part of the election programs in the campaign leading up to the 2017 parliamentary elections. These elections, which were clearly influenced by the topic of Islam, were clearly reflected in the fundamental change in the structure of the Czech party system. These elections primarily led to the loss of "traditional"

7 Compare Stanley Cohen, "Whose side were we on? The Undeclared Politics of Moral Panic Theory," *Crime, media, culture*, Vol. 7, No. 3 (2011), pp. 237–243.

8 David Altheide, *Creating Fear: News and Construction of Crisis* (Piscataway: Transaction Publishers. 2002).

9 See James Meernik and Michael Ault, "The tactics of foreign policy agenda-setting: Issue choice and the president's weekly radio address," *International Area Studies Review*, Vol. 16, No. 1 (2013), pp. 74–88; or Miloš Gregor and Alena Macková, "Euroscepticism the Czech way: An analysis of Václav Klaus's speeches," *European Journal of Communication*, Vol. 30, No. 4 (2015), pp. 74–88.

10 Martin Reisigl, "Analysing political rhetoric," in: *Qualitative Discourse Analysis in the Social Science*, eds. Ruth Wodak and Michal Krzyznowski (New York: Palgrave Macmillan, 2008), pp. 96–120.

political parties and the emergence of new parties and movements, many of which have defined themselves as protest groups. Many of them were able to sound out a certain existing social demand and, using populism, artificially exaggerated all problems relating to migration.

The third level will focus on examples of the relatively indiscriminate anti-Islamic – or more generally anti-foreigner – discourse that has strongly permeated Czech society. In this section, I present several interesting examples of this debate and highlight the factors that underlie it.

President Zeman and His Perception of Islam as a Security Threat for the Czech Republic and Europe

Miloš Zeman's view on the issue of Islam can be framed into the President's stance on the issue of security, as this method will help us to reveal the true nature of how Zeman truly perceives Islam. The following section is based on broader research of Miloš Zeman's rhetorical strategies, which I carried out with my colleague Petr Krčál. Methodologically speaking, this part of my essay has been conceived as a CAQDAS of dataset, which is made up of complete interviews, statements, speeches, and other expressions made by Miloš Zeman in the first four years (March 2013–March 2017) of his first presidential election period. All documents were taken from the official website of the President of the Republic (http://www.zemanmilos.cz/cz/). The total extent of the dataset is 675 539 words. The dataset was processed using MAXQDA11+ software. The search subject included words that are linked to the phenomenon of corruption, specifically: security/danger, endangerment/endanger, threat, risk. Found occurrences were subjected to manual refining. During this refining process, occurrences of terms that 1) were not linked to the topic of security (e.g., "securing [in the sense of providing conditions for] the course of the event") and that 2) were not linked to the conventional concept of security but fell into the wider concept of it (e.g., "ensuring the security of miners") were deleted. After refining, I identified a total of 292 codes, i.e., the results of the key word search, which were then divided into several subcategories that followed the logic of the research intention. For this essay, the category[11] dealing with what Zeman views as a source of danger or threat is crucial – a total of 121 cases were found in this category.

11 For more details about other categories see Vladimír Naxera and Petr Krčál, ""This is a Controlled Invasion": The Czech President Miloš Zeman's Populist Perception of Islam and Immigration as Security Threats," *Journal of Nationalism, Memory & Language Politics*, Vol. 12, No. 2 (2018), pp. 192–215.

If we read the individual codes relating to Zeman's understanding of what the source of danger is, we find one central theme that is linked to Islam, Islamism, jihad, migration, terrorism, etc. This topic clearly dominated in Zeman's speeches. In the beginning of his presidential mandate, it was possible on several occasions to find other topics – e.g., Russia as a security threat in light of the conflict in Ukraine (e.g., "We see the situation in Ukraine and what threats exist there, that is, a certain reinstallation of Russian power that had been somewhat forgotten."). Over the course of time, however, he began to relativize the issue of Russia and finally ceased to talk about Russia as a source of danger altogether ("I refuse the opinion that there is danger in the East."); he did, however, begin to emphasize the threat of migration and Islamic terrorism ("I have long contended that these attributes are endangered by Islam, primarily by its radical branch, which has several times declared its intent to conquer Europe and subject it to its own culture."), which he explicitly placed above the "Russian problem": "Decades ago I had already realized that individual nation states are exposed to external danger. At that time, I saw Russian imperialism as the primary danger. Well, it turned out that the real enemy wasn't forming to the east, but to the south in the form of the Islamic State and its branches such as the Taliban, Al-Qaeda, or the Muslim Brotherhood. In the meantime, the number of these organizations has grown considerably. Sometimes they fight amongst themselves, because – as Charles Darwin wrote – the greatest aggression is of an internal nature. On the other hand, they are willing to unite in the interest of creating one Islamic State, a caliphate."

Zeman contextualizes Islam/migration as a source of danger on several levels. Firstly, it is a potential source of terrorism: "The danger has come closer to our borders and, by the way, it is naïve to assume that there is no connection between the wave of migration and terrorism, because that would mean assuming that this wave of migration does not include potential jihadists, the number of which we naturally cannot estimate precisely, but some of them [...] have taken part in the Paris attacks mentioned previously." In terms of migrants, Zeman repeatedly mentions their illegal behavior: "The term refugee evokes various associations within us, but in reality these are people who have continually broken the law by not applying for asylum in the first safe country." According to Zeman, empathy with refugees itself is a problem. The president does not see these individuals as real refugees, but as invasive armies: "Through his indecisiveness and a number of other seemingly conciliatory and seemingly humanitarian gestures, which in my opinion do not appreciate the true danger, because, contrary to him, I see the migration crisis as an organized invasion." Zeman sees manifestations of Islam as such as a source of danger: "I have made the objection – and this is linked to religion – that Islamic migration is dangerous because it is not possible to assimilate it into European culture." "[…] it's not possible to carry on a discussion with the Islamic State; it's not possible to debate with those who, like a social cancer, want to destroy existing civilizations. If we are going to close our eyes in our discussions and say that they're all peaceful and they want to cooperate, then it will be too dangerous. Because anti-civilizations are destroyed with weapons and not dialogues."

If we were to quantify a result from the 121 codes found in which Zeman discusses the source of danger, 92 (i.e., more than three quarters) deal with Islamic terrorism. Mention of other types of danger (primarily Russia) have appeared only in roughly the first year of his mandate; over the course of four years, Zeman mentioned other sources of danger sporadically and only in single-digit occurrences. Thus Zeman's concept of the sources of danger has been evidently monothematic in past years.

It is possible to make these conclusions about Zeman's perception of Islam and security:[12] It is obvious from the text that Miloš Zeman's "topic number one" in regard to security is Islam and also the migration, Islamism, terrorism, jihad, etc., that is linked to it. However, it should be said that Zeman does not differentiate much between these terms in his speeches and creates an implicit link (or in some cases an "equal sign") between them. Although in the beginning of his presidential function he labeled Russia a security problem on several occasions, he later reframed this point of view, relativizing the issue of Russia (in connection with events in Ukraine) and ultimately denying it completely. After Zeman ceased to thematize Russia as a source of danger, Islam as a whole remained in his view of security issues for the Czech Republic and Europe as the only threat worth mentioning (any mention of other sources of danger were wholly incidental and inexplicit in Zeman's speeches – e.g., the statement that a source of danger "might be propaganda").

The way in which Zeman refers to Islam as a threat targets the very roots of this faith, which is understood as something wholly incompatible with Europe and its culture. Thus it is not only radical Islam and the terrorism connected to it that is a problem and a security issue; it is also Islam as such. This concept of the endangerment of security is then linked to suggested methods to remedy the situation, which in the majority of cases are aimed at the fight against Islamic

12 See also Petr Krčál, "Sociální konstrukce extremismu v sociální imaginaci Miloše Zemana," *Acta Fakulty filozofické Západočeské univerzity v Plzni*, Vol. 9, No. 3 (2017), pp. 73–92.

organizations or preventing immigrants from stepping onto European (and thus Czech) soil.

Islam as a Theme of the 2017 Parliamentary Elections

The 2017 Czech parliamentary elections had two pivotal themes. The first was the relationship of parties to possible post-election cooperation with the ANO movement led by billionaire Andrej Babiš, who combines political, economic, and media power in a problematic manner and is a typical example of a "political entrepreneur".[13] Babiš is facing a number of corruption-related problems and even prosecution by the police. Despite this fact, however, he represents an interesting alternative to Czech voters to the other "traditional" political parties. The second topic was clearly the issue of migration and the issues of the threats to the nation, Islam, and terrorism that accompany it.

A total of 31 parties and movements took part in the elections, with at least 14 of them building their program solely or at least predominantly on topics concerning the need to protect the Czech nation, which is supposedly being threatened by Islamic threats, an "invasion" of Muslims, and so forth. Most of these parties (e.g., the Order of Nation, the Workers' Party of Social Justice, the Czech National Front, etc.) are completely marginal, making up only 2.6 % of all votes. On the other hand, the Freedom and Direct Democracy Party (SPD), led by Czech-Japanese entrepreneur Tomio Okamura, won over 10 % of all votes, giving the party 22 seats in the 200-member Chamber of Deputies. This party can be characterized as a far-right party. At the same time, there are anti-Islamic attitudes in other political parties that are commonly perceived as democratic (in both right-wing and left-wing parties).[14]

From the results of the analysis of the party programs of all nine parties that gained seats in these elections, it is clear that for most of them the issue of migration became one of the primary points in their election program or they deemed migration to be such a serious and important phenomenon that it must be dealt with in their election program. This fact was supported by a certain "people's demand" for a solution to the problem (i.e., only an ostensible problem in light

---

13 See Lubomír Kopeček, ""I'm Paying, So I Decide": Czech ANO as an Extreme Form of a Business-Firm Party," *East European Politics and Societies*, Vol. 30, No. 4 (2016), pp. 725–749; Petr Just and Jakub Charvát, "Business-Firm Parties and the Czech Party System after 2010," *Politics in Central Europe*, Vol. 12, No. 3 (2016), pp. 83–110.

14 See Miroslav Mareš, *Ne islámu! Protiislámská politika v České republice* (Brno: CDK, 2015).

of the statistics on the actual number of migrants coming to the Czech Republic) and the firm anchoring of the issue of migration in public discourse as a security threat. The only parties that resisted this discourse were the Czech Pirate Party and the Mayors and Independents Party, the programs of which show only isolated references to migration. Furthermore, these references are made on lines that highlight the need to address the issue constructively, ideally through prevention and action at the site of the problem. A number of other parties perceived issues of migration and Islam as clear threats – this was reflected clearly in the victorious ANO movement. In the following statement from the party's program, we can see the interconnection of a whole score of interesting topics, primarily the explicit link between migration and physical threat (i.e., terrorist attacks) and between migration and an identity threat:[15] "In light of the endless migration crisis and terrorist attacks in Europe, the safety of our citizens is paramount. The protection of national identity is a priority for us." Most of the parties agreed in the same manner on the problematic nature of EU migrant quotas for the redistribution of refugees. Anti-Muslim and anti-immigrants positions of individual parties are in several cases related to populist political strategies that became part of Czech political mainstream[16] during last several years.[17] Populism stands on distinguishing of two homogenous and antagonistic groups – "the pure people" and "the corrupt elite".[18] Politicians using this strategy create images of enemies of "pure people" (or of nation in our case) – these enemies are not limited to "corrupt elite" but include also European Union, foreign financial circles, NGOs, or immigrants.[19] Permanent need for political enemies leading to legitimization of "non-standard" practices is one of main characteristic points of political populism.

15 Compare Aleksandra Grzymala-Kazlowska, "Social Anchoring: Immigrant Identity, Security and Integration Reconnected?," *Sociology*, Vol. 50, No. 6 (2016), pp. 1123–1139.

16 We can say the same about Czech President Miloš Zeman – Naxera and Krčál, "This Is an Controlled Invasion".

17 Krčál and Naxera, "Populistická konstrukce národa ohroženého migrací", compare Věra Stojarová, "Populist, Radical and Extremist Political Parties in Visegrad countries vis a vis the migration crisis. In the name of people and the nation in Central Europe," *Open Political Science*, Vol. 1, No. 1 (2018), pp. 32–45.

18 Cas Mudde, *The Populist Radical Right in Europe* (Cambridge: Cambridge University Press, 2007), p. 23.

19 Atilla Antal, "The Political Theories, Preconditions and Dangers of the Governing Populism in Hungary," *Czech Journal of Political Science*, Vol. 24, No. 1 (2016), p. 16.

The greatest emphasis on the issue of migration was undoubtedly put forth by SPD's Tomio Okamura, a matter we will deal with briefly here. As such, the party is an interesting one. Tomio Okamura himself is not a newcomer to Czech politics. In 2013, he entered the Chamber of Deputies as the chief of the Dawn of Direct Democracy, which can be considered to be an extreme populist right-wing party.[20] During the election period, however, Okamura was forced to leave the party due to his manipulations with party funding. He then formed the new SPD, which he led to success in the 2016 regional elections, when in most regions he ran in a coalition with the Party of Civic Rights linked to President Miloš Zeman. This campaign was led under slogans of "stop the EU, stop terrorists", etc. The party succeeded with similar slogans in the 2017 parliamentary elections.

In order to illustrate, I have added several statements from the party's election program that are typically populist[21] and show the SPD's attitude toward Islam, migration, security, multiculturalism, the EU, etc.: "No to parasites, no to immigrants." "No to Islam, no to terrorists, the security of our citizens means more." "A plan is being carried out for a multicultural European superstate in which the Czech Republic will be only an insignificant administrative unit. We cannot be content with the future of this modern-day protectorate where third-party wages are paid for work on assembly lines for international corporations and under conditions that would never have gone unpunished in their home countries." "We reject positive discrimination and preferential treatment of citizens based on their race, ethnicity, or religion." "Ongoing illegal immigration is the initial phase of a conflict that will ultimately endanger freedom, democracy, and the very existence of the Czech Republic and our nation." "We want strict conditions for the Czech Republic's immigration policy. We do not want immigrants unable to adapt, nor do we want the advent of Islamic religious fanatics." These examples show the direction in which the SPD is oriented.

Before moving to the next topic, the issue of the 2017 election can be placed into the context of the Czech Republic's migration policy. Tab. 1 to 4 clearly show the number and country of origin of asylum seekers arriving from the beginning of 2017 until the end of September (i.e., until just before elections). Over a thousand people applied for asylum in this period, of which only 125 individuals were granted asylum or other legal forms of protection. Taking into account that there were 2,228 candidates running for 14 openly anti-migration

---

20 See Vlastimil Havlík, "Protiislámská politika populistické radikální pravice," in: *Ne islámu! Protiislámská politika v České republice*, ed. Miroslav Mareš (Brno: CDK, 2015), pp. 125–145.

21 Krčál and Naxera, "Populistická konstrukce národa ohroženého migrací".

Tab. 1: Numbers of applications for international protection in 2017 by months (January–September)

Month	Applications total
January	132
February	103
March	119
April	96
May	140
June	122
July	142
August	120
September	112
TOTAL	**1086**

Tab. 2: Applications for international protection in September 2017

Citizenship	Applications total	*-of which: females*	*-of which: minors*
Armenia	**14**	7	5
Azerbaijan	**8**	4	4
Belarus	**1**	-	-
Cuba	**3**	1	-
Ethiopia	**1**	-	-
Georgia	**14**	2	3
Ghana	**1**	-	-
Iraq	**2**	2	-
Kazakhstan	**7**	3	3
Macedonia	**1**	-	-
Moldova	**4**	-	-
Nigeria	**2**	-	-
Pakistan	**6**	2	3
Russian Federation	**2**	-	-
Sri Lanka	**1**	-	1
Stateless	**1**	-	1
Syria	**4**	1	3
Tunisia	**2**	-	-
Turkey	**4**	-	-
Ukraine	**26**	7	4
Viet Nam	**8**	-	-
TOTAL	**112**	**29**	**27**

Tab. 3: International protection proceedings in 2017 – numbers of decisions of the Ministry of the Interior and numbers of pending cases in 2017 (January–September)

Month	Decisions total	*-of which: asylum granted*	*-of which: subsidiary protection granted*
January	**109**	5	6
February	**124**	9	18
March	**122**	2	15
April	**122**	3	9
May	**126**	4	4
June	**102**	-	15
July	**111**	-	9
August	**120**	-	13
September	**192**	3	10
TOTAL	**1128**	**26**	**99**

parties and movements, there was an unbelievable number of more than 17 anti-refugee candidates for each accepted refugee, with SPD gaining 22 parliamentary mandates.

Examples of Folk Discourse in Relation to Islam

The final section of this text will focus in brief on examples of anti-Islamic discourse among the Czech public. Anti-Islamic or anti-migrant stances are not only found on the political level, but also in everyday social debate. An example of a consequence of this can be seen in the most popular competition for the best Czech singers in the country. For two years now, the competition has selected the music group Ortel, whose frontman (with a neo-Nazi past) has called for Europe to be saved from the Muslim invasion and supports resistance to politicians who succumb to pressure from Brussels and the protection of the nation. A whole score of similar singers (often of very dubious quality) has also emerged in recent years.

Public debates on social networks or posts under online news articles, which show a growing frequency of posts condoning or even encouraging violence, make up a specific category. This is not happening only in marginal neo-Nazi media, but on mainstream sites as well. I have chosen two examples that seem most representative. The first concerns two articles on the Rohingya refugee crisis in Myanmar from the Novinky.cz daily news site. Both articles dealt with violence by government soldiers on children, women, etc. Posts that received

Tab. 4: Decisions of the Ministry of the Interior on international protection in September 2017. Source of all tables: Ministry of the Interior. Ministry of the Interior, "International Protection in the Czech Republic 2017", 15 Dec. 2017, www.mvcr.cz/soubor/cs-stat-zari-2017-pdf.aspx.

Citizenship	Decisions total	*-of which: asylum granted*	*-of which: subsidiary protection granted*
Afghanistan	**4**	-	-
Albania	**1**	-	-
Algeria	**5**	-	-
Armenia	**10**	-	-
Azerbaijan	**24**	-	-
China	**3**	-	-
Cuba	**12**	-	5
Georgia	**23**	-	-
Ghana	**2**	-	-
Iraq	**1**	-	-
Israel	**1**	-	-
Kazakhstan	**2**	-	-
Lebanon	**1**	-	-
Mongolia	**2**	-	-
Nigeria	**2**	-	-
Russian Federation	**10**	-	-
Stateless	**2**	-	-
Syria	**6**	3	2
Turkey	**3**	-	-
Ukraine	**68**	-	2
Viet Nam	**9**	-	-
Yemen	**1**	-	1
TOTAL	**192**	**3**	**10**

the highest ratings from other readers included: "At least somewhere they're not taking any crap from Muslims." "At least I know where to escape from the Muslims when they overrun Europe." "I approve of a higher principle: violence against a Muslim is not violence." On the contrary, the most negative reactions were made toward comments that criticized violence, for example: "It's sad that they're also kidnapping children." "Poor people, poor children. Good Lord, there's so much evil in this world."

The second example chosen is focused on one regional daily newspaper published in the North Bohemian town of Teplice. This daily newspaper regularly prints photos of first grade elementary school students throughout the region. Recently, the paper printed a photograph of a school class. The majority of its pupils were Vietnamese, Roma, and Arabs. The pupils, however, were not immigrants – even the Arab children are predominantly the offspring of Arabs who have lived in the region for decades, many of whom are doctors in local hospitals, etc. Here are some of the comments that appeared below the photo shortly after it was printed: "A class full of terrorists. A grenade would be in order. Shoot them on the spot." "Okamura, get them out of here." "Lucky for them their primary school is in Plynárenská (*Czech: Natural Gas Utility*) Street." This last comment obviously refers to the use of gas for the mass destruction of Jews and Roma during World War II and implicitly offers the same solution. Regardless of the moral swamp that debates have sunk into, the local deputy elected for Okamura's SPD de facto legitimized them by declaring that she "understands the people's indignation."

Similar social debates are thus legitimated by politicians and also supported by a number of media outlets. Many Czech media outlets have strong anti-immigrant attitudes, which are often linked to an attempt to maximize profit in terms of viewer numbers. Leaving aside various conspiracy-theory sites and web portals providing fake news that widely comment on Islam and migration (many of which are, according to security service reports, linked to Russian funding), even a number of standard media outlets (including the most widely read site Novinky.cz from which the aforementioned comments on Myanmar were taken from) show an ostensible and instrumental use of the topic of refugees.

To conclude this section, we can return to the very beginning of the chapter in which I mention that the so-called migration crisis is often associated with economic,[22] security,[23] and identity[24] issues. All these levels are found in Czech public debate. On the economic level, we are confronted with claims such as "migrants will take our jobs or social benefits", "the state pays for migrants but not for sick children," etc. On a security level, the arrival of migrants, especially Muslims, is associated with the threat of terrorist attacks, a topic that political representatives speak about regularly (the example of President Zeman, see above). A very commonly mentioned concern is the fear of sexual violence.

---

22 Žúborová and Borárosová, "Migrácia v médiách", pp. 1–15.

23 Androvičová, "Sekuritizácia migrantov na Slovensku", pp. 319–339.

24 Czajka, "Migration in the Age of Nation-State", pp. 151–163.

Regardless of the astounding number of rapes in the Czech Republic, which are met with relatively high tolerance and the belief that it is the woman's fault for being raped, the image of foreigner/rapist as a danger to "our" women is suddenly and instrumentally construed. The level of identity mainly concerns views that Islam is incompatible with European culture, that "Muslims will force us to veil our women," that "Muslims will cancel Christmas", and so forth.

I believe several causes for this state of affairs can be identified. The first are economic problems and the economic deprivation of the population in a number of Czech regions (especially peripheral ones). Many people without work or poorly paid work can easily heed the call of politicians who say "this is an immigrant and he wants to take your job." The second problem is that Czech society is very homogeneous and many Czechs have no experience with anything foreign. Thus the image of a foreigner as something unknown easily incites fear.[25] The last cause that can be mentioned is the role of specific politicians and media outlets that foster the growth of this fear.

Conclusions

Looking at the social debate, the structure of media output (from some media outlets more than others), and the shape of the election campaign and election results in 2017, it might seem that the Czech Republic is a country that is endangered by the influx of thousands of Muslims who want to destroy the state, its institutions, people, and culture by ransacking and conquering it. The aim of this chapter is to point out the nature of this debate, which leads to the creation of a similar picture – one that is not, however, founded on any realistic basis. The many structural problems Czech society suffers from (economic deprivation, education, media, inexperience with anything foreign or different, etc.) result in the negative attitudes of a large portion of the Czech public toward the few incoming refugees who have chosen to come to the Czech Republic for various reasons. This mixture of fear and hatred is firmly anchored in the structures of the Czech public's attitude toward foreigners as such. The situation has been instrumentally exploited by various populist political actors, including President Zeman or SPD Chairman Tomio Okamura. We can easily characterize both politicians as "fear mongers". Using instrumental fears and creating an image of the Czech Republic's endangerment via open lies, manipulation of facts or hoaxes, these politicians have succeeded in inciting the anti-immigration

25 Compare Petra Košťálová, *Stereotypní obrazy a etnické mýty* (Prague: SLON, 2012).

tendencies of Czech society and strengthened them in such a way that only 125 asylum seekers became the pivotal factor for elections. There is no doubt that this suits a portion of the country's political actors – not only has it allowed them to gain political points (e.g., Okamura), it has also helped them hide other topics (adoring Russia in Zeman's example or, in Andrej Babiš's case, concealing his own problems with corruption). As a symbol of the greatest evil that has come to the Czech Republic, Islam (brought along by migrants) has served as a suitable instrument of political gain for various political actors.

In addition, over the last few years the nature of the social debate on this whole issue has changed. In posts under mainstream media discussions, it is easy to find requests such as "I want all Muslim children to die", which are given hundreds and hundreds of "plus points" from other readers. With the help of a portion of the political elite, fear of things foreign has been transformed into hate for things foreign. Although – for the time being – it is still on a rhetorical level, it is as if this hatred knows no bounds. However, the number of real attacks on foreigners has begun to increase. The stance held by a number of political elites toward foreigners, including their inappropriate choice of words and purposeful fabrications, may lead to more such attacks in the future. This is because the ones committing these acts will feel legitimized and consecrated to do so by political power. It is not my opinion that the stances condoning violence and the primitive nature of the discussion noted in this chapter are a problem among the majority of the Czech population. The problem lies in the fact that the silent majority does not protest against this and, by doing so, silently condones the positions of the outspoken minority supported by various politicians. As a result, their requests and behavior slowly creep into the realms of social norms. Statements that twenty years ago would have come from the mouths of marginal neo-Nazis are now coming from the mouths of "decent Czechs" who are defending their culture and daughters against "Muslim barbarians".

Bibliography

1. Altheide, David. *Creating Fear: News and Construction of Crisis*. Piscataway: Transaction Publishers, 2002.
2. Androvičová, Jarmila. "Sekuritizácia migrantov na Slovensku – analýzy diskurzu." *Sociológia*, Vol. 47, No. 4, 2015, pp. 319–339.
3. Antal, Atilla. "The Political Theories, Preconditions and Dangers of the Governing Populism in Hungary." *Czech Journal of Political Science*, Vol. 24, No. 1, 2016, pp. 5–20.

4. Beránek, Ondřej and Bronislav Ostřanský, eds. *Stíny minaretů. Islám a muslimové jako předmět českých veřejných polemic*. Prague: Academia, 2016.
5. Bourbeau, Philippe. *The Securitization of Migration. A Study of Movement and Order*. London: Routledge, 2011.
6. Cohen, Stanley. "Whose Side Were We on? The Undeclared Politics of Moral Panic Theory." *Crime, Media, Culture*, Vol. 7, No. 3, 2011, pp. 237–243.
7. Czajka, Agnes. "Migration in the Age of Nation-State: Migrants, Refugees, and the National Order of Things." *Alternatives*, Vol. 39, No. 3, 2014, pp. 151–163.
8. Gregor, Miloš and Alena Macková, "Euroscepticism the Czech Way: An Analysis of Václav Klaus's Speeches," *European Journal of Communication*, Vol. 30, No. 4, 2015, pp. 404–417.
9. Grzymala-Kazlowska, Aleksandra. "Social Anchoring: Immigrant Identity, Security and Integration Reconnected?" *Sociology*, Vol. 50, No. 6, 2016, pp. 1123–1139.
10. Havlík, Vlastimil. "Protiislámská politika populistické radikální pravice." In: *Ne islámu! Protiislámská politika v České republice*, ed. Miroslav Mareš. Brno: CDK, 2015, pp. 125–145.
11. Just, Petr and Jakub Charvát. "Business-Firm Parties and the Czech Party System after 2010." *Politics in Central Europe*, Vol. 12, No. 3, 2016, pp. 83–110.
12. Kopeček, Lubomír. ""I'm Paying, So I Decide": Czech ANO as an Extreme Form of a Business-Firm Party." *East European Politics and Societies*, Vol. 30, No. 4, 2016, pp. 725–749.
13. Košťálová, Petra. *Stereotypní obrazy a etnické mýty*. Prague: SLON, 2012.
14. Krčál, Petr and Vladimír Naxera. "Populistická konstrukce národa ohroženého migrací: CAQDAS volebního diskurzu českých parlamentních voleb 2017." *Sociológia*, Vol. 50, No. 5, 2018, pp. 491–523.
15. Krčál, Petr. "Sociální konstrukce extremismu v sociální imaginaci Miloše Zemana." *Acta Fakulty filozofické Západočeské univerzity v Plzni*, Vol. 9, No. 3, 2017, pp. 73–92.
16. Mareš, Miroslav, ed. *Ne islámu! Protiislámská politika v České republice*. Brno: CDK, 2015.
17. Meernik, James and Michael Ault. "The Tactics of Foreign Policy Agenda-Setting: Issue Choice and the President's Weekly Radio Address." *International Area Studies Review*, Vol. 16, No. 1, 2013, pp. 74–88.

18. Mudde, Cas. *The Populist Radical Right in Europe*. Cambridge: Cambridge University Press, 2007.
19. Naxera, Vladimír and Petr Krčál. ""This is a Controlled Invasion": The Czech President Miloš Zeman's Populist Perception of Islam and Immigration as Security Threats." *Journal of Nationalism, Memory & Language Politics*, Vol. 12, No. 2, 2018, pp. 192–215.
20. Ostřanský, Bronislav, ed. *Islamofobie po česku: Český odpor vůči islámu, jeho východiska, projevy, souvislosti, přesahy i paradox*. Prague: Vyšehrad, 2017.
21. Reisigl, Martin. "Analysing Political Rhetoric." In: *Qualitative Discourse Analysis in the Social Science*, eds. Ruth Wodak and Michal Krzyznowski. New York: Palgrave Macmillan, 2008, pp. 96–120.
22. Slačálek, Ondřej and Eva Svobodová. "Professionalised "Civil Society" vs. Grassroots "Uncivil Society"? The "Little Czech" 20 Years Later. " *Socio.hu*, No. 5, 2017, pp. 23–52.
23. Stojarová, Věra. "Populist, Radical and Extremist Political Parties in Visegrad countries vis a vis the Migration Crisis. In the Name of People and the Nation in Central Europe." *Open Political Science*, Vol. 1, No. 1, 2018, pp. 32–45.
24. Žúborová, Viera and Ingrid Borárosová. "Migrácia v médiách: utečenci verzus migranti. Chápanie migrantov a utečencov v mediálnom priestore v kontexte pozitívnej a negatívnej mediatizácie." *Central European Journal of Politics*, Vol. 2, No. 1, 2016, pp. 1–15.

Internet Sources

1. Ministry of the Interior, "International Protection in the Czech Republic 2017," www.mvcr.cz/soubor/cs-stat-zari-2017-pdf.aspx (15 Dec. 2017).

Magdalena Ickiewicz-Sawicka

Balkan Muslims – Origin, Structure, Identity

Abstract: Balkan Muslims are an extraordinary example of the functioning of Islamic religious communities in this part of the European continent. Abstraction from the main discourse on the existence of Islam in Europe (it has a decidedly negative character and focuses mainly on its radical factions), while the Muslim Muslims are an excellent example of a different, religious Muslim tradition. The chapter consists of five parts. The first one contains a general description of Balkan Muslims as a separate phenomenon in this part of Europe. The second contains contemplation about the historical roots of Balkans, the original religiosity in the form of a community of bogomils. The third one shows the mystical Balkan Islam in the form of Bectan religious communities. The next part was devoted to reflections on the subject of the esoteric order of Dervish dancing. The last part of the chapter presents a brief description of the smallest Islamic religious group inhabiting the Balkans – Goran. The text has an introduction and ending.

Keywords: Balkan Muslims, liberal Islam, faith, religion, Ottoman religious tradition, culture, ethnicity

Introduction

Islam appeared very early in the Balkans, even before Ottoman domination. The development of Islam in the Balkans was further strengthened by a progressive (over 500 years) dominance in these areas of the Ottoman Empire. The heyday of culture and Islam in the Balkans is at the height of the reign of Suleiman the Magnificent (1520–1566)[1]. At that time, as part of the peaceful process of Islamization of Slavic lands, a specific group of Slavonian Muslims emerged, building the foundations of the following Muslim communities in the Balkans:

a) Bosnian-Herzegovina (currently Bosnian culture),
b) Pomackiej (Pomaks) – (Bulgarian Muslims),
c) Torbesz (Torbeši) – (Macedonian Muslims),
d) Goranska (Gorani) – Highlander Muslims and small communities of Croatian and Serbian Muslims.

---

1 Miriam Greenblatt, *Süleyman the Magnificent and the Ottoman Empire* (New York: Benchmark Books Pinson, 2003), Mark Pinson, *The Muslims of Bosnia-Herzegovina: Their Historic Development from the Middle Ages to the Dissolution of Yugoslavia* (Harvard University Press, 1994).

Balkan Muslims – The Picture of the Phenomenon

The process of shaping Muslim religious communities begins already in the seventh century and continues to our times. Although the date of the emergence of Islam in the Balkans is considered to be 1463, the year of the final liking of these areas by the Ottomans and their incorporation into the border of the empire. However, some sources[2] indicate that Islam already existed in these areas much earlier before the Ottoman domination.

Afterwards, this religion was popularized in Bosnia peacefully, but the process was two-fold – Islamization was sometimes associated with Turkmenistan. On the other hand, this Islamization of the Balkans is wrongly identified only and exclusively with the turkmenization of the autochthonous population. Cultural and religious transfers worked both ways, just as the Slavic population took over Ottoman customs, so ethnic Turks succumbed to Christian (Slavic) influences. Although the Ottoman Empire gained further areas by means of aggression and force, the process of Bosnia's Islamization took place peacefully and started before the Turkish domination, while during this the Slavic population switched to Islam mainly for economic reasons (e.g., tax exemption, fast career path, higher income, free access to education, prestige and willingness to join the Ottoman elite). Pure pragmatism and the prospect of material status, the reason for the transition to Islam was definitely less than the authentic conversion and desire to participate in the Muslim community.

The Balkans have gone through three stages of Islamization: pre-Ottoman, early-Ottoman, and proper Islamization. The first and the second were associated with the Islamization of Bosnian bogomilia, and the third is the intense Islamization of the southern Slavs, especially during the heyday of the Ottoman Empire [3].

Bosnian Bogomils [4] and Balkan Islam

The Bosnian Middle Ages were characterized by the existence of a dualistic religion practiced by the bogomilic sect, religious group that spread throughout the

---

2 H. T. Norris, *Islam in the Balkans: Religion and Society between the Arab World* (University of South Carolina Carolina Press, 1993).

3 JohnVan Antwerp Fine, *The Early Medieval Balkans: Late Twelfth Century*, (University of Michigan Press, 1991), p. 171.

4 "**Bogomil** - member of a dualist religious sect that flourished in the Balkans between the tenth and fifteenth centuries. It arose in Bulgaria toward the middle of the tenth century from a fusion of dualistic, neo-Manichaean doctrines imported especially from the Paulicians, a sect of Armenia and Asia Minor, and a local Slavonic movement

Balkans. Traces of the functioning of this community date back to the tenth century, although its bloom falls on the twelfth century (ibidem). At that time the Bogomil worship developed into the true Ecclesia Bosensis, later called Ecclesia Slavonicae. The bogomiłs were a peculiar link that was to combine different Balkan religious traditions. Nevertheless, Bosnian bogomils (especially in the time of Turkish domination in Bakana) made the conversion to Islam, and the heirs of their traditions are the center of Islamic presence in the areas described [5].

As part of Turkish Islamization, numerous Muslim communities have emerged and dynamically developed in Bosnia, which in turn have absorbed other Muslims from various parts of the vast empire. In this way, godliness spread in the Balkan territory, and from 1222 Bosnia became the real center of this dualistic denomination. On the other hand, the adoption by Islamists of the bogomili has become one of the most important stages in the process of Islamization of Bosnia. Cultural syncretism, which in turn was characteristic of this group, was a factor conducive to conversion to Islam. The religious doctrine of bogomils, intertwined with Islam, led to the emergence of a new, Bosniac-Muslim ethnic identity. The mixing of Muslims with bogomils resulted in a specific variation of the liberal Islam, adapted to the Slavic realities. Bogomilskie traces are also found in Arabic sources. The following examples serve to support this thesis, both Ebul-Feth es Sahristani (1153) and Ali Ibn Ahmed ez-Zahiri (1064) mention this religious group in their work entitled El-mileu venihal[6].

Christian historian Seid Ibn Bitrik (940) mentioned similar practices, claiming that bogomils were converting to Islam by seeing many common features of their religions. In addition, on bogomils tombstones, so-called – *stećkach*, we can see

---

aimed at reforming, in the name of an evangelical Christianity, the recently established Bulgarian Orthodox Church. The bogomils were so called after their founder, the priest Bogomil. The bogomils' central teaching, based on a dualistic cosmology, was that the visible, material world was created by the devil. Thus, they denied the doctrine of the incarnation and rejected the Christian conception of matter as a vehicle of grace. They rejected Baptism, the Eucharist, and the whole organization of the Orthodox Church. The moralteaching of the bogomils was as consistently dualistic. They condemned those functions of man that bring him into close contact with matter, especially marriage, the eating of meat, and the drinking of wine. In fact, the moral austerity of the bogomils invariably was acknowledged by their fiercest opponents". 14 Sep. 2018 https://www.britannica.com/topic/Bogomils.

5 Ivo Andrić, *The Development of Spiritual Life in Bosnia under the Influence of Turkish Rule*, (Duke University Press Durham and London, 1999).

6 Albert Doja, " A political history of Bektashism from Ottoman Anatolia to contemporary Turkey" , *Journal of Church and State*, Oxford, 2006.

subtitles such as Saracen or Saraćen [7], from the fourteenth and fifteenth centuries, which confirm the importance of the Bosnian Middle Ages of the Muslim factor. Genetically, the areas of the then Bosnia were religious and ethnic diversity, which also influenced the bogomils, and they instilled their traditions in the representatives of the dervish order. However, the peaceful coexistence between the bogomils and Muslims was interrupted by persecution of the followers of duality and subsequent expeditions of Mongolian warriors. The emptiness of the bogomils was filled with Islam, and for example, the descendant of Ban Kulina, the Hidajet feed, as the first of the Bosnian nobility, converted to Islam. Hidajet adopted Muslim faith in 1447, during the reign of Sultan Murat II (1421–1444, 1446–1451) [8].

The Bogomil religious community described above was absorbed by the dominant Islam in the Ottoman religious order. Nevertheless, this religion, next to the mainstream associated with Sunni (Shiites inhabited Persia – today's Iran), was subject to constant changes, leading to the creation of new trends. One of them was: Sufi brotherhood, founded in the thirteenth century in Anatolia by Bektash Wal from Niszapuru (who died in 1270). The cult gained its name (bektaszijja or bektashi – suficki tarikat) [9] and was particularly widespread in Turkey and the Balkans.

In the sixteenth century, Balim Sultan gave the final shape to beliefs and rituals in Balti Sultan by introducing a strong Shi'ite element to the doctrine (see the cult of Ali Ibn Abi Talib and 12 Imams)[10]. This element combines Bashkut's with the Alawites[11], creating a kind of religious conglomerate that also takes into account elements of Christianity and even the original pagan beliefs.

---

7 Hussam Timani, *"Saracens, in Muhammad in History, Thought, and Culture"*: An Encyclopedia of the Prophet of God (2 vol.), Edited by C. Fitzpatrick and A. Walker., Santa Barbara, ABC-CLIO, 2014, Vol. II, pp. 538–542.

8 Timani, *Saracens, in Muhammad in History, Thought, and Culture,* pp. 538–542. Imber Colin, *The Ottoman Empire.* (London: Palgrave/Macmillan, 2002).

9 H.T. Norris, *Popular Sufism in Eastern Europe: Sufi Brotherhoods and the Dialogue with Christianity and 'Heterodoxy' (Routledge Sufi),* Routledge Sufi series (20), Routledge, 2006, p. 79.

10 Robert Elsie, *Historical Dictionary of Albania, European historical dictionaries* (42), (Scarecrow Press, 2004), p. 40.

11 "Alevism i sa syncretic heterodox, and local traditions whose adherents follow the mystical (bāṭenī)[views on Ali and the Twelve Imams. The Bektashi sect follow the teachings of their descendant —the 13th century Alevi saint Haji Bektash Veli. Alevis are found primarily in Turkey among ethnic Turks and Kurds, and make up between 10–25 % of Turkey's population, the largest belief after Sunni Islam". Markus Dessler,

Bektashi – Mystical Balkan Islam

Bektashi had the following characteristic features:

a) Faith in the magic of letters,
b) Celibacy,
c) Developing and maintaining a Turkish literary language.

Bektaszijja is a religious syncretism that combines elements of shamanism, Zoroastrianism, Christianity, and esotericism. Its members did not keep sharia, jihad, and Ramadan. They also did not keep fasting and banning the consumption of alcohol and pork by the traditional confessions of Islam. In the sphere of obyczajową, the Bektashi ruled the equality of men and women. In addition, they practiced just like Christians: the ritual of confession, celibacy of the clergy, baptism, and remission of sins[12].

During the Ottoman Empire, Bectarism was a Janissary religion. They formed the troops of the Turkish infantry constituting the main component of the army from the fifteenth to the nineteenth century. Janczarski mirjades were created as a result of compulsory conscription to the army, and the candidates came from the conquered Christian population. Every family in Slovakia had to offer one Turkish son to the Turkish state, which fed the ranks of Janissaries. This octane habit was practiced until the first half of the nineteenth century. On the other hand, they were a great force, having a real influence on the politics of the empire. The association of Bekcatas and Janissaries was so strong that the brotherhood had an established position in the vicinity of the Turkish sultan. The slow fall of the empire also led to the liquidation of Sufi orders in Turkey. The center of Bektashi was in 1925–1967 in Albania. Nowadays, the brotherhood in Macedonia and Kosovo is particularly active in [13] the world of extremely radical Arab Islam, the Bektashi are considered infidels and spread heresy.

Until 1925, Turkey remained the world center of bektashija. However, after the takeover of power by the youngoturk, a secular model of the state began to apply in the Kemalist Turkey. This was connected directly with the introduction of a ban on the functioning of any religious institutions, including brotherhoods

---

Writing Religion: The Making of Turkish Alevi Islam, AAR Reflection and Theory in the Study of Religion, (Oxford University Press, 1 edition 2015).

12 Albert Doja, "A political history of Bektashism from Ottoman Anatolia to contemporary Turkey", *Journal of Church and State Oxford*, 2006.

13 Gloria Lotha, Encyclopedia Iranica - Bektāšīya. 14 Sep. 2018, https://www.britannica.com/topic/Bektashi.

and mystical groups. At that time, the world's center of Bytom's was transferred to Tirana, where Bectarism was considered one of the four largest confessions (along with Sunnis, Orthodox, and Catholics). Then in the 1950s, the Bektashi again began practicing in Turkey. Introduced in 1967 in Albania, a national ban on any religion meant taking over by the communist authorities all objects of religious worship (or teqe) and stopping the public activity of the community[14]. Reborn again in 1991 as a result of socioeconomic changes that took place after the collapse of the USSR and the breakdown of socialist Yugoslavia.

Dervish – An Esoteric Dancing Order

Another religious group operating in the Balkans, and taking into account the traditions of Sufism, was the Dervish Order. The first reports on the appearance of dervishes in Bosnia come from the thirteenth century. Sufi orders developed freely on the territory of the Balkans, mainly due to the practice of the principles of humanism and liberalism. This was a special value in the multiethnic and multiconfessional Bosnia. In this regard, the Sufi clergy allowed new followers to practice old, often pagan customs and religious rituals. Tarikaty such as Halvetije, Mewlewici, and Naxibendije spread the ideas of Salafism, gaining new followers in this crowd. Dervish presenting a liberal version of Islam, having a much freer character in comparison to Sunnis and Shiites, contributed to the acceptance of Islam by the Balkan population. Therefore, the Dervish ideology has left a lasting impression in the Balkan spiritual culture, mainly through the teachings of Sufi mystics, promoting religious tolerance, not only towards Muslims, but also towards the followers of Judaism and Christians.

The various Sufi orders have made an important component in the development of Islamic culture in the Balkans, including the principles of cosmopolitanism, as a distinctive feature of Bosnia in comparison with other state organisms functioning in the described period. This attitude was favored by the geographical location of Bosnia, where East and West met, mixing like in the proverbial crucible and melting pot[15].

---

14 Gloria Lotha, Encyclopedia Iranica - Bektāšīya. 14 Sep 2018, https://www.britannica.com/topic/Bektashi.

15 MELTING POT: a place where a variety of races, cultures, or individuals assimilate into a cohesive whole, the population of such a place, a process of blending that often results in invigoration or novelty. 14 Sep. 2018 https://www.merriam-webster.com/dictionary/melting%20pot.

Numerous scientific, religious and, above all, commercial contacts have also contributed to the adoption by the local population of a liberal variety of Muslim faith. The Islamization of the Bosnian population, supported by the Sufi mission of the friars, has built a solid framework for the peaceful coexistence of various denominations in Bosnia. She also had an ideological and intellectual character. Nevertheless, it is the trade of water and the numerous economic privileges granted by Ottoman rulers to the inhabitants of Bosnia, as well as cultural autonomy and the possibility of land succession mainly by Muslims (less often in the case of Slavs) who were an essential factor in building a multicultural and multiethnic Balkan community.

Sufi orders and dervishes existed outside official Islamic structures until the Ottoman state established madrasas[16] and jams (in Serbo-Croat – mosque, Arabic origin). Later, the dervishes from Bosnia created about 15,000 manuscripts in Arabic, Turkish, and Persian, as well as unique examples of calligraphy art. Many of these departments are located in museums in Istanbul, Vienna, or Cairo.

The brief history of the presence of Islam in the Balkans, presented above, shows unequivocally that this religion has become a permanent part of the religious and cultural image of this part of Europe. Currently, Slavic (Balkan) Muslims are quite a large ethnic group, mainly in the territory of Bosnia and Herzegovina, but also other parts of the former Yugoslavia (mainly Sandžak region (so-called sandzakini) – Serbian Rashka), Bulgaria (Pomacy), Kosovo, and Macedonia (Torbesze). Small Muslim communities also function in Croatia.

Considering the extensive structure of Balkan Muslims, and at the same time the limited framework of this chapter, only one of those groups professing Islam – the Balkan Goranians – will be considered in this study. Other communities, mainly Boszniacy, Pomacy, and Torbesze, require separate in-depth analyzes that would exceed the capacity of this text. The author decided to bring this community closer because in the European vocational literature it is not widely represented.

16 Arabic: school – Islamic theological seminary and law school attached to a mosque. The residential madrasah was a newer building form than the mosque, flourishing in most Muslim cities by the end of the twelfth century. A school for any kind of teaching, at any grade level. It may have courses in Islamic theology and religious law, but it is not a requirement. 14 Sep. 2018 https://www.seslisozluk.net/en/what-is-the-meaning-of-medresa/.

Gorani – Highlander Original Islam

Goranie is a specific ethnic group inhabiting the Kosovo–Albanian–Macedonian border region. Its representatives do not identify with any previously recognized nationality in the Balkans. Most of them maintain that they are neither Muslim Serbs nor Bulgarians nor Macedonians or Slavic Albanians. Their identity was created depending on the historical and political climate in this Balkan area. Such a pragmatic approach has allowed them to preserve their differences over the last century and to stay out of the way of ongoing Balkan conflicts.

The neutrality skill developed over the years has resulted in a lack of commitment to the last Albanian-Serb clash. Gora did not experience both NATO bombing and the effects of the Kosovo war during negotiations at Rambouillet[17].

The Goranians had their representative on the Serbian side and, therefore, they are perceived as traitors by the Kosovo Albanians. Nevertheless, in an independent Kosovo they were guaranteed one place in the parliament and an additional star on the official Kosovo flag. Most of them have dual citizenship, in addition to belonging to the Republic of Kosovo (the main part of the Goranic territory is now within the borders of the Republic of Kosovo) also have a Macedonian, Serbian or even Bulgarian passport. Generally, they do not associate them with the Kosovo Albanians, especially since the older generation practically does not know Albanian.

Despite the neutral attitude of the Goranieks to the last war, its indirect effect was a decline in the standard of living, rising unemployment, the emergence of organized crime, and the Szarina range became an important smuggling trail. The region is regularly patrolled by KFOR aircraft, because the chaos associated with recent warfare caused the activation of criminal organizations dealing with arms smuggling. In addition, near the border town of Brody, the Koscian Albanians built a large hotel in the middle of the forest. The local population is convinced that the facility serves as a laundry for dirty money, thus legalizing criminal activity. In addition, the Gorans have also distanced themselves from the activities of the Kosovo Liberation Army (there are serious assumptions that this organization was involved in criminal activities)[18] and therefore, monuments of the aforementioned UCK are not found on their territory.

17 Eric Herring, From Rambouillet to the Kosovo Accords: NATO's War against Serbia and Its Aftermath (PDF). The International Journal of Human Rights. 4 (3–4), 2000, pp. 224–245.

18 Marek Waldenberg, Yugoslavia (Yugoslavian mirror of international politics), Warsaw 2005, pp. 262–284.

In general, the inhabitants of Gora increasingly choose emigration and not only this short-lived earnings, but leave the homeland with whole families going to Italy, Turkey, Macedonia, or Croatia. They are forced to do so by both a harsh, mountainous climate and a constantly deteriorating socioeconomic situation, as well as Albanian demographic expansion. As shown by numerous examples from history, such nations in the majority of cases (in this case the Kosovo Albanians) are doomed to slow extinction, because as one of the Goranies rightly pointed out, that no one will notice their disappearances, just as no one notices their existence as a separate ethnic group, Goran is also a mirny (peaceful) nation, while the Albanians are living in conflict.[19]

Conclusion

Presented above considerations on the Balkan version of Islam fully confirm earlier staked main research hypothesis, which assumed that the main research hypothesis on this chapter is based on the submission that Balkan Islam is characterized by a large variety and synthesis of many cultural and religious traditions in the Balkans. This mainly applies to Islamic relations with Christianity and the creation of a special religious hybrid combining the ideas of Sufism with elements of Christianity. Also the research questions given at the beginning of the text were verified positively. The author of the text briefly exchanged and analyzed all Muslim nations and ethnic groups living in the Balkans (question number one), then described their sources (question number two), and posted their origin and characteristics described (question number three).

Generally, the brief description of Balkan Muslims presented above has a long and complicated history. As a result, the limited framework of this study does not exhaust this extensive research problem, and the potential reader only gets an introduction to this subject. It should be clearly stated that Balkan Muslims form quite a large group of Muslim followers, as confirmed by numerous historical, anthropological, linguistic, and cultural sources. The Balkan reception of Islam has, for several centuries, been extremely liberal and tolerant; she was full of deep spirituality and mysticism. In addition, it was the resultant of many religious traditions (mainly Christianity - Orthodoxy and Catholicism), which developed in parallel on the whole Balkans. This specific cultural and religious composition created a unique and multicolored picture of this part of Europe in

19 Marek Waldenberg, *Yugoslavia*, pp. 262–284, Victor A. Friedman, Determination and doubling in Balkan Borderlands, Harvard Ukrainian Studies, Volume 28, number 1–4, 2006, pp. 105–116.

which periods of peaceful religious coexistence were intertwined with bloody conflicts. The special exploration of Balkan religiosity is quoted by Bożidar Jezernik in his book entitled *Wild Europe of the Balkans in the Eyes of Western Travelers*. Jezernik states that "religion was the basis of divisions, ethnological language and theories played a secondary role here. The Bulgarian could have become Turk by converting to Islam, just as the Greek became Bulgarian, acknowledging the authority of the Exarchate." However, always Muslim threads appeared in every configuration.

Bibliography

1. Andrić, Ivo, *The Development of Spiritual Life in Bosnia under the Influence of Turkish Rule*, (Durham and London: Duke University Press, 1999).
2. Dessler, Markus, *Writing Religion: The Making of Turkish Alevi Islam*, AAR Reflection and Theory in the Study of Religion, (New York: Oxford University Press, 1 edition 2013).
3. Elsie, Robert, *Historical Dictionary of Albania, European Historical Dictionaries* (42), (Lanham, Maryland and Oxford: Scarecrow Press, 2004), p. 40.
4. Greenblatt, Miriam, *Süleyman the Magnificent and the Ottoman Empire* (New York: Benchmark Books Pinson, 2003),
5. Imber, Colin, *The Ottoman Empire*. (London: Palgrave/Macmillan, 2002).
6. Norris, H. T., *Islam in the Balkans: Religion and Society between the Arab World* (Columbia: University of South Carolina Carolina Press, 1993).
7. Pinson, Mark, *The Muslims of Bosnia-Herzegovina: Their Historic Development from the Middle Ages to the Dissolution of Yugoslavia* (Cambridge: Harvard University Press, 1994).
8. Van Antwerp Fine John, *The Early Medieval Balkans: Late Twelfth Century*, (Ann Arbor: University of Michigan Press, 1991), p. 171.
9. Waldenberg, Marek, Yugoslavia (Yugoslavian Mirror of International Politics), Warsaw: Scholar, 2005, pp. 262–284.
10. Doja, Albert, " A political history of Bektashism from Ottoman Anatolia to contemporary Turkey", *Journal of Church and State*, Oxford, 2006.
11. Friedman, Victor A., "Determination and doubling in Balkan Borderlanda", *Harvard Ukrainian Studies*, 28 (1–4), 2006, pp. 105–116.
12. Herring, Eric, "From Rambouillet to the Kosovo Accords: NATO's war against Serbia and its aftermath (PDF)", *The International Journal of Human Rights*, 4 (3–4), 2000, pp. 224–245.

13. Norris H.T., *Popular Sufism in Eastern Europe: Sufi Brotherhoods and the Dialogue with Christianity and 'Heterodoxy' (Routledge Sufi)*, Routledge Sufi series (20), London and New York: Routledge, 2006, p. 79.
14. Timani, Hussam, "*Saracens, in Muhammad in History, Thought, and Culture*": An Encyclopedia of the Prophet of God (2 vol.), Edited by C. Fitzpatrick and A. Walker., Santa Barbara: ABC-CLIO, 2014, Vol. II, pp. 538–542.

Internet Sources

1. Bogomils community, https://www.britannica.com/topic/Bogomils (14 Sep.2018).
2. Lotha Gloria, Encyclopedia Iranica – Bektāšīya, https://www.britannica.com/topic/Bektashi (14 Sep.2018).
3. Madrash definitione, https://www.seslisozluk.net/en/what-is-the-meaning-of-medresa/ (14 Sep. 2018).
4. Melting pot definitione, https://www.merriam-webster.com/dictionary/melting%20pot (14 Sep. 2018).

List of Figures

List of Tables

Note of Authors

1. **Ajili, Hadi** – Assistant Professor of international relations, Allameh Tabataba'i University, Tehran, Iran
2. **Doğan, Fazlı** – He has completed his doctorate at Selcuk University, Institute of Social Sciences International Relations Department with his PhD thesis titled "Power Transition Theory in International Relations: Britain, USA and China" in 2016. He has published several peer-reviewed articles in the field of international relations. He is currently working as an academician in the International Relations Department at Selcuk University. He maintains studies about International Relations Theories, American Foreign Policy, and Chinese foreign policy, etc.
3. **Fiedler, Radosław** – Professor at AMU, head of the Section for Non-European Political Studies in the Department of Political Science and Journalism. Author of numerous papers and monographs on the issues of the Middle East. His research interests are focused on the determinants of instability in the Middle East, the policy of the US and EU towards North Africa and the Middle East, the proliferation of nuclear weapons in the context of Iranian nuclear programme and EU polices in Central Asia. He has also been granted a research subsidy within: National Science Center, the EU Partnership and International Cooperation in Jordan, Eminence II in Georgia. Visiting professor in Columbia University. He coordinates the Erasmus+ programme and is vice-dean for international cooperation in his department. He is the President of the Fiedler's Foundation which fosters cross-cultural dialogue and the initiatives of local communities.
4. **Gardocki, Sylwester** – Assistant Professor at the Faculty of Political Science and International Studies, University of Warsaw
5. **Hlaváčková, Hana N.** – She holds a Ph.D. and works as an academic researcher at the Metropolitan University Prague at the Department of International Relations and European Studies. She is focused on security studies and EU. E-mail: hana.hlavackova@mup.cz. Her paper is the outcome of research project no. 57–02 " Territorial studies, economy and international relations" implemented by Metropolitan University Prague and funded by the Institutional Support for Long-term Strategic Development of Research Organisations in 2018

6. **Ickiewicz-Sawicka, Magdalena** – Ph.D., researcher and lecturer – Faculty of Management Engineering, Chair of Marketing and Entrepreneurship, Bialystok University of Technology, Poland; Scientific supervision: Department of Criminal Law and Criminology, Faculty of Law University of Bialystok, Poland; Scientific specialty: international criminology, public international law, international relations, international criminal law and philosophy of law; Research interests: the area of the Balkans with a particular focus on countries of the former Yugoslavia with a clear indication of Serbia, Kosovo and Republika Srpska in Bosnia and Herzegovina and legal aspects in the field of penal studies, political science, sociology and international relations as well as internationalized armed conflict, civil war, war crimes, genocide, social engineering, ethnic cleansing and conflict management (management of collective violence).; Contact: e-mail: m.ickiewicz@pb.edu.pl
7. **Kural, Muzaffer** – Candidate Dr. Ankara University, Institute for Turkish Revolution History, m.muzafferkural@gmail.com, Graduated from Ankara University's History Department. Holds master degree from the same university's department of contemporary history. During master studies, he was an exchange student at Adam Mickiewicz University, Poznan, Poland. (2012–2013). He is also a Guest Researcher at Prague Economic University's International Relations Department (15th May–15th August 2015) Prague, Czech Republic, and Researcher at Huelva University's Social Science Institute, (15th September 2015–15th February 2016) Huelva, Spain. Research area is Middle East
8. **Mieczkowska, Gabriela** – An economist, Islamic finance researcher and Consultant, based in London, UK. Author of publications in the area of alternative economies and ethical banking. Currently pursuing PhD in Economics with specialisation in Islamic finance solutions for conventional economies. Professional in field of data and business analytics. Personally, coffee connoisseur and home roaster
9. **Naxera, Vladimír** – Ph.D., Assistant Professor at the Department of Politics and International Relations, University of West Bohemia
10. **Nori, Javad** – Ph.D. student of International Relations at Islamic Azad University, Science and Research Branch, Tehran, Iran
11. **Oliaei, Mohammad** – Ph.D. student in Political science, Islamic Revolution Studies, Shahed University, Tehran, Iran
12. **Ożarowski, Rafał** – Professor in the Chair of Security at the Faculty of Law and Administration at the University of Business and Administration in Gdynia. He conducts his research on international security in the Middle East with a special focus on militarized non-state actors, international

terrorism, Lebanese and Iranian policy in the Middle East. Author of two monographs, co-editor of many books and author of many scientific articles. Visiting researcher in the Moshe Dayan Center in Tel-Aviv and the American University of Beirut and at the University of Calcutta and Allameh Tabataba'i University in Tehran. Professor Ożarowski is a member of Central East European International Studies Association (CEEISA), Polish International Studies Association (PISA) and the Polish Society of National Security (PSNS).

13. **Özlük, Erdem** – He holds a PhD in International Relations from Selcuk University, Turkey and currently works as an associate professor at the department of International Relations at Selcuk University. He has published several peer-reviewed articles in the field of international relations. His current research interests include theories of international relations as well as foreign policy analysis and US foreign policy. His recent book, *Emotional Approach to International Relations* (printed in Turkish, 2016), examines the role of emotions in international relations. He has also previously authored a book on the meaning and theories of the state in international relations (printed in Turkish, 2012)
14. **Ponížilová, Martina** – Ph.D., Assistant Professor at the Department of Politics and International Relations, University of West Bohemia, E-mail: mponizil@kap.zcu.cz
15. **Shah, Syed Subtain Hussain** – Ph.D. Research Scholar, Faculty of Political Science and Internatioanal Studies, University of Warsaw
16. **Skorokhod, Yuriy** – Professor in the Institute of International Relations at the Taras Shevchenko National University in Kyiv
17. **Sobol, Iwona** – She is a researcher and lecturer in the Department of International Financial Markets at the Faculty of Economics of the University of Gdańsk. She holds the PhD from the same university. Apart from giving regular courses at the University of Gdańsk, she also teaches at postgraduate studies, including the University of Gdańsk Executive MBA Studies. She has also given numerous lectures across universities in Europe within Erasmus Programme. Her scientific interests focus on Islamic economics and finance, international financial markets and international trade finance. She is a member of IESE Business School Alumni Association and Polish Economic Society
18. **Szymański, Adam** – He is Associate Professor at the Faculty of Political Science and International Studies, University of Warsaw; in 2012-2013 TÜBITAK research fellow at the Koç University in Istanbul. He has published widely on the EU enlargement, Turkish politics and democratization,

including articles in *European Foreign Affairs Review, PS: Political Science & Politics and Turkish Studies*

19. **Ulatowski, Rafał** – He is Assistant Professor at the Faculty of Political Science and International Studies, University of Warsaw. He earned his PhD from the University of Bonn/Germany in 2011, funded by the Konrad Adenauer Foundation Scholarship. He has delivered guest lectures at the University of Konstanz, Tsinghua University, amongst other institutions. Research fellowships at the Tsinghua University/ China (2013), University of Bonn (2013 and 2014-2015), Kyungpook National University/ Republic of Korea (2014), University of Strasbourg/ France (2015), Deutsches Polen-Instituts Darmstadt/ Germany (2015). His main research interest is in the international political economy, global energy market and German foreign policy.
20. **Zákravský, Jiří** – Assistant Professor at the Department of Political Science and International Relations at the University of West Bohemia in Pilsen, Czech Republic. His central area of research includes sports diplomacy and the use of sport as a political tool in general. Mainly, he is interested in the Basque nationalist movement and its relation to sport, for example football and cycling; however, as his paper about the State of Qatar and sports diplomacy proves, he does not refuse the opportunities to make "a research pilgrimage" outside this region

Studies in Politics, Security and Society

Edited by Stanisław Sulowski

Vol.	1	Robert Wiszniowski (ed.): Challenges to Representative Democracy. A European Perspective. 2015.
Vol.	2	Jarosław Szymanek: Theory of Political Representation. 2015.
Vol.	3	Alojzy Z. Nowak (ed.): Global Financial Turbulence in the Euro Area. Polish Perspective. 2015.
Vol.	4	Jolanta Itrich-Drabarek: The Civil Service in Poland. Theory and Experience. 2015.
Vol.	5	Agnieszka Rothert: Power of Imagination. Education, Innovations and Democracy. 2016.
Vol.	6	Zbysław Dobrowolski: Combating Corruption and Other Organizational Pathologies. 2017.
Vol.	7	Vito Breda: The Objectivity of Judicial Decisions. A Comparative Analysis of Nine Jurisdictions. 2017.
Vol.	8	Anna Sroka: Accountability and democracy in Poland and Spain. 2017.
Vol.	9	Anna Sroka / Fanny Castro-Rial Garrone / Rubén Darío Torres Kumbrián (eds.): Radicalism and Terrorism in the 21st Century. Implications for Security. 2017.
Vol.	10	Filip Pierzchalski: Political Leadership in Morphogenetic Perspective. 2017.
Vol.	11	Alina Petra Marinescu: The Discursive Dimension of Employee Engagement and Disengagement. Accounts of keeping and leaving jobs in present-day Bucharest organizations. 2017.
Vol.	12	Jacek Giedrojć: Competition, Coordination, Social Order. Responsible Business, Civil Society, and Government in an Open Society. 2017.
Vol.	13	Filip Ilkowski: Capitalist Imperialism in Contemporary Theoretical Frameworks. 2017.
Vol.	14	Leszek Leszczyński / Adam Szot (eds.): Discretionary Power of Public Administration. Its Scope and Control. 2017.
Vol.	15	Tadeusz Klementewicz: Understanding Politics. Theory, Procedures, Narratives. 2017.
Vol.	16	Tomasz Bichta: Political Systems of the Former Yugoslavia. 2018
Vol.	17	Miroslav Palárik / Alena Mikulášová / Martin Hetényi / Róbert Arpáš: The City and Region Against the Backdrop of Totalitarianism. 2018
Vol.	18	Jolanta Itrich-Drabarek / Stanisław Mazur / Justyna Wiśniewska-Grzelak (eds.): Understanding Politics. Theory, Procedures, Narratives. 2017.
Vol.	19	Jerzy Juchnowski / R. Jan Sielezin / Ewa Maj: The Image of "White" and "Red" Russia in the Polish Political Thought of the 19th and 20th Century. Analogies and Parallels. 2017.
Vol.	20	Roman Kuźniar: Europe in the International Order. 2018.
Vol.	21	Piotr Jaroszynski: Europe - the Clash of Civilisations. 2018.
Vol.	22	Stanisław Filipowicz: Truth and the Will to Illusion. 2018.

www.peterlang.com

www.ingramcontent.com/pod-product-compliance
Ingram Content Group UK Ltd.
Pitfield, Milton Keynes, MK11 3LW, UK
UKHW041824031026
15587UKWH00002B/542

9 783631 785669